Second Workshop on Trolling, Aggression and Cyberbullying (TRAC-2, 2020)

Marseille, France
11-16 May 2020

Editors:

Ritesh Kumar
Atul Kr. Ojha
Bornini Lahiri
Marcos Zampieri

Shervin Malmasi
Vanessa Murdock
Daniel Kadar

ISBN: 978-1-7138-1279-1

LREC 2020 Workshop
Language Resources and Evaluation Conference
11–16 May 2020

**Second Workshop on
Trolling, Aggression and Cyberbullying
(TRAC-2, 2020)**

PROCEEDINGS

Editors:
Ritesh Kumar, Atul Kr. Ojha, Bornini Lahiri, Marcos Zampieri,
Shervin Malmasi, Vanessa Murdock and Daniel Kadar

Proceedings of the LREC 2020 Second Workshop on Trolling, Aggression and Cyberbullying (TRAC-2, 2020)

Edited by:

Ritesh Kumar, Atul Kr. Ojha, Bornini Lahiri, Marcos Zampieri, Shervin Malmasi, Vanessa Murdock and Daniel Kadar

For more information:
European Language Resources Association (ELRA)
9 rue des Cordelières
75013, Paris
France
http://www.elra.info
Email: lrec@elda.org

Introduction

In the last few years, we have witnessed a gradual shift from largely static, read-only web to quickly expanding user-generated web. There has been an exponential growth in the availability and use of online platforms where users can post their own content. A major part of these platforms include social media websites and apps, blogs, Q&A forums and several similar platforms. All of these are almost exclusively user-generated websites. In all of these platforms and forums, humongous amount of data is created and circulated every minute. It has been estimated that there has been an increase of approximately 25% in the number of tweets per minutes and 22% increase in the number of Facebook posts per minute in the last 3 years. It is posited that approximately 500 million tweets are sent per day, 4.3 billion Facebook messages are posted and more than 200 million emails are sent each day, and approximately 2 million new blog posts are created daily over the web [1]. There is no such thing as a 'consolidated figure' of the number of comments and opinion generated on websites worldwide, but it can be safely assumed that such a figure would be staggering.

As the number of people and this interaction over the web has increased, incidents of aggression and related activities like trolling, cyberbullying, flaming, hate speech, etc. have also increased manifold across the globe. The reach and extent of Internet has given such incidents unprecedented power and influence to affect the lives of billions of people. It has been reported that such incidents of online abuse have not only created mental and psychological health issues for users, but they have impacted our lives in many other way, spanning from deactivating accounts to instances of self-harm and suicide. NLP and related methods have shown great promise in dealing with such abusive behaviour through early detection of inflammatory content.

This workshop focusses on the phenomena of online aggression, trolling, cyberbullying and other related phenomena, in both text (especially social media) and speech. The organisers aim to create a platform for academic discussions on this phenomena, based on previous joint work that they have done as part of a project funded by the British Council. We are particularly interested in promoting conversations dedicated to the automatic detection of aggression in both speech and text, that is, we hope that our workshop will not only be purely academic by nature but it will also generate real-life solutions to tackle the phenomena studied. As such the workshop also includes a shared task on 'Aggression Identification'. The task consisted of two sub-tasks - aggression identification (sub-task A) and gendered identification (sub-task B) - in three languages - Bangla, Hindi and English. For this task, the participants were provided with a dataset of approximately 5,000 instances from YouTube comments in each language. Additional data for testing was released at a later date.

Both the workshop and the shared task received a very encouraging response from the community. There were more than 70 registrations for the shared task. Out of these, 19 teams submitted their systems. The proceedings include 13 system description papers that were finally submitted by the authors. In addition to this, the workshop also includes 16 regular papers presented in the workshop.

We would like to thank all the authors for their submission and members of the Program Committee for their invaluable efforts in reviewing and providing feedback to all the papers. We would also like to thank all the members of the Organising Committee who have helped immensely in various aspects of the organisation of the workshop and the shared task.

---

[1] Source: https://www.gwava.com/blog/internet-data-created-daily/

Workshops Chairs

Ritesh Kumar, Dr. Bhimrao Ambedkar University, India
Atul Kr. Ojha, Charles University, Prague & Panlingua Language Processing LLP, India
Bornini Lahiri, Indian Institute of Technology-Kharagpur, India

Organising Committee

Ritesh Kumar, Dr. Bhimrao Ambedkar University, India
Atul Kr. Ojha, Charles University, Prague & Panlingua Language Processing LLP, India
Vanessa Murdock, Amazon Inc., USA
Marcos Zampieri, Rochester Institute of Technology, USA
Shervin Malmasi, Amazon Inc., USA
Bornini Lahiri, Indian Institute of Technology-Kharagpur, India
Daniel Kadar, Research Institute for Linguistics, Hungarian Academy of Sciences, Hungary

Shared Task Organising Committee

Ritesh Kumar, Dr. Bhimrao Ambedkar University, India
Atul Kr. Ojha, Charles University, Prague & Panlingua Language Processing LLP, India
Marcos Zampieri, Rochester Institute of Technology, USA
Shervin Malmasi, Harvard Medical School, USA

Editors

Ritesh Kumar, Dr. Bhimrao Ambedkar University, India
Atul Kr. Ojha, Charles University, Prague & Panlingua Language Processing LLP, India
Bornini Lahiri, Indian Institute of Technology-Kharagpur, India
Marcos Zampieri, Rochester Institute of Technology, USA
Shervin Malmasi, Amazon Inc., USA
Vanessa Murdock, Amazon Inc., USA
Daniel Kadar, Research Institute for Linguistics, Hungarian Academy of Sciences, Hungary

Programme Committee

A. Seza Doğruöz, Tilburg University, Netherlands
Adrián Pastor López Monroy, University of Houston, USA
Amitava Das, WIPRO Limited, India
Asif Ekbal, IIT-Patna, India
Atul Kr. Ojha, Charles University, Prague & Panlingua Language Processing LLP, India
Bornini Lahiri, Indian Institute of Technology-Kharagpur, India
Bruno Emanuel Martins, University of Lisbon, Portugal
Cheng-Te Li, National Cheng Kung University, Taiwan
Chuan-Jie Lin, National Taiwan Ocean University, Taiwan
Claudia Peersman, Lancaster University, UK
Cynthia van Hee, LT3, Ghent University, Belgium
Danilo Croce, University of Roma, Italy
Dennis Tenen, Columbia University, USA
Elizabeth Losh, William and Mary College, USA
Els Lefever, LT3, Ghent University, Belgium
Erik Velldal, University of Oslo, Norway
Eshwar Chandresekharan, Georgia Tech, USA
Fumito Masui, Kitami Institute of Technology, Japan
Girish Nath Jha, Jawaharlal Nehru University, India
Haris Papageorgiou, ATHENA Research and Innovation Center, Greece
Hugo Jair Escalante, INAOE, Mexico
Ingmar Weber, Qatar Computing Research Institute, Qatar
Jen Golbeck, University of Maryland, USA
Jacqueline Wernimont, Arizona State University, USA
Kalika Bali, MSRI Bangalore, India
Lee Gillam, University of Surrey, UK
Liang-Chih Yu, Yuan Ze University, Taiwan
Libby Hemphill, University of Michigan, USA
Lun-Wei Ku, Academia Sinica, Taiwan
Mainack Mondal, University of Chicago, USA
Manuel Montes-y-Gómez, INAOE, Mexico
Marco Guerini, Fondazione Bruno Kessler, Trento, Italy
Marcos Zampieri, Rochester Institute of Technology, USA
Matthew Fuller, University of London, UK
Michael Wiegand, Saarland University, Germany
Michael Paul, University of Colorado Boulder, USA
Min-Yuh Day, Tamkong University, Taiwan
Ming-Feng Tsai, National Chengchi University, Taiwan
Monojit Choudhury, MSRI Bangalore, India
Michal Ptaszynski, Kitami Institute of Technology, Japan
Nemanja Djuric, Uber ATC, USA
Pawan Goyal, IIT-Kharagpur, India
Pete Burnap, Cardiff University, UK
Preslav Nakov, Qatar Computing Research Institute, Qatar

Table of Contents

Conference Program

10:45–11:45   Paper Session II

10:45–11:05   *Aggression Identification in Social Media: a Transfer Learning Based Approach*
Faneva Ramiandrisoa and Josiane Mothe

11:05–11:25   *Multimodal Meme Dataset (MultiOFF) for Identifying Offensive Content in Image and Text*
Shardul Suryawanshi, Bharathi Raja Chakravarthi, Mihael Arcan and Paul Buitelaar

11:25–11:45   *A Comparative Study of Different State-of-the-Art Hate Speech Detection Methods in Hindi-English Code-Mixed Data*
Priya Rani, Shardul Suryawanshi, Koustava Goswami, Bharathi Raja Chakravarthi, Theodorus Fransen and John Philip McCrae

11:45–14:00   Poster Session

IRIT at TRAC 2020
Faneva Ramiandrisoa and Josiane Mothe

Bagging BERT Models for Robust Aggression Identification
Julian Risch and Ralf Krestel

Scmhl5 at TRAC-2 Shared Task on Aggression Identification: Bert Based Ensemble Learning Approach
Han Liu, Pete Burnap, Wafa Alorainy and Matthew Williams

The Role of Computational Stylometry in Identifying (Misogynistic) Aggression in English Social Media Texts
Antonio Pascucci, Raffaele Manna, Vincenzo Masucci and Johanna Monti

Aggression Identification in English, Hindi and Bangla Text using BERT, RoBERTa and SVM
Arup Baruah, Kaushik Das, Ferdous Barbhuiya and Kuntal Dey

LaSTUS/TALN at TRAC - 2020 Trolling, Aggression and Cyberbullying
Lütfiye Seda Mut Altın, Alex Bravo and Horacio Saggion

Spyder: Aggression Detection on Multilingual Tweets
Anisha Datta, Shukrity Si, Urbi Chakraborty and Sudip Kumar Naskar

Proceedings of the Second Workshop on Trolling, Aggression and Cyberbullying, pages 1–5
Language Resources and Evaluation Conference (LREC 2020), Marseille, 11–16 May 2020
© European Language Resources Association (ELRA), licensed under CC-BY-NC

Evaluating Aggression Identification in Social Media

Ritesh Kumar[1], Atul Kr. Ojha[2,3], Shervin Malmasi[4], Marcos Zampieri[5]
[1]Dr. Bhimrao Ambedkar University, Agra, [2]Charles University, Faculty of Mathematics and Physics Institute of
Formal and Applied Linguistics, Prague & [3]Panlingua Language Processing LLP, New Delhi, [4]Amazon Inc., USA,
[5]Rochester Institute of Technology, USA
ritesh78_llh@jnu.ac.in, shashwatup9k@gmail.com, shervin.malmasi@mq.edu.au, marcos.zampieri@rit.edu

Abstract

In this paper, we present the report and findings of the Shared Task on Aggression and Gendered Aggression Identification organised as part of the Second Workshop on Trolling, Aggression and Cyberbullying (TRAC - 2) at LREC 2020. The task consisted of two sub-tasks - aggression identification (sub-task A) and gendered aggression identification (sub-task B) - in three languages - Bengali, Hindi and English. For this task, the participants were provided with a dataset of approximately 5,000 instances from YouTube comments in each language. For testing, approximately 1,000 instances were provided in each language for each sub-task. A total of 70 teams registered to participate in the task and 19 teams submitted their test runs. The best system obtained a weighted F-score of approximately 0.80 in sub-task A for all the three languages. While approximately 0.87 in sub-task B for all the three languages.

Keywords: Aggression, Gendered Aggression, English, Hindi, Bengali, TRAC

1. Introduction

In recent years, there have been several studies exploring the computational modelling and automatic detection of abusive content in social media focusing on toxic comments[1], aggression (Kumar et al., 2018), cyberbullying (Xu et al., 2012; Dadvar et al., 2013), hate speech (Davidson et al., 2017), and offensive content (Zampieri et al., 2019a) to name a few. Prior studies have tackled abusive language identification in content from different platforms such as Twitter (Xu et al., 2012; Burnap and Williams, 2015; Davidson et al., 2017; Wiegand et al., 2018), Wikipedia comments[1], and Facebook (Kumar et al., 2018). A number of shared tasks been organized focusing on the automatic detection of offensive language (Struß et al., 2019; Zampieri et al., 2019b; Mandl et al., 2019), hate speech (Basile et al., 2019) and aggression (Kumar et al., 2018). These have motivated the creation of for various languages such as English, German, Hindi, Italian, Spanish, and others.

In this paper, we discuss the results of the second iteration of the TRAC shared task, organized as part of the Workshop on Trolling, Aggression and Cyberbullying at LREC 2020. The task consisted of two sub-tasks - aggression identification and gendered aggression identification on YouTube comments in three languages: Bengali, Hindi and English. To the best of our knowledge, TRAC-2 is the first shared task to include YouTube comments as training and testing data and the first shared task to include Bengali data. Both these novel aspects open new avenues for future research. The remainder of this paper is organized as follows. Section 2. discusses related studies and shared tasks to TRAC-2. Section 3. presents the setup and schedule of TRAC-2 and Section 4. presents the dataset used in the competition. Section 5. presents the approaches used by participants of the competition and Section 6. presents and analyzes the results they obtained. Finally, 7. concludes this paper and presents avenues for future work.

2. Related Work

Automatically identifying the various forms of abusive language online has been studied from different angles. Examples include trolling (Cambria et al., 2010; Kumar et al., 2014; Mojica, 2016; Mihaylov et al., 2015), flaming / insults (Sax, 2016; Nitin et al., 2012), radicalization (Agarwal and Sureka, 2015; Agarwal and Sureka, 2017), racism (Greevy and Smeaton, 2004; Greevy, 2004), misogyny ((Menczer et al., 2015; Frenda et al., 2019; Hewitt et al., 2016; Fersini et al., 2018; Anzovino et al., 2018; Sharifirad and Matwin, 2019)), online aggression (Kumar et al., 2018), cyberbullying (Xu et al., 2012; Dadvar et al., 2013), hate speech (Kwok and Wang, 2013; Djuric et al., 2015; Burnap and Williams, 2015; Davidson et al., 2017; Malmasi and Zampieri, 2017; Malmasi and Zampieri, 2018), and offensive language (Wiegand et al., 2018; Zampieri et al., 2019b). The terms used in the literature have overlapping properties as discussed in Waseem et al. (2017) and Zampieri et al. (2019a). The most important differences concern their target (e.g. hate speech is typically targeted at groups whereas cyberbulling targets individuals), which is represented in TRAC-2 Task B, and types (e.g. veiled or direct abuse), represented in TRAC-2 Task A.

Most related studies focus on English, but significant amount of work has been carried out for other languages too. This includes languages such as Arabic (Mubarak et al., 2020), German (Struß et al., 2019), Greek (Pitenis et al., 2020), Hindi (Mandl et al., 2019), and Spanish (Basile et al., 2019).

TRAC - 2 is the second iteration of the TRAC shared task on Aggression Identification (Kumar et al., 2018) hosted at the TRAC workshop at COLING 2018. The first edition of TRAC included English and Hindi data from Facebook and Twitter. It consisted of a three-way classification task with posts labelled as *overtly aggressive*, *covertly aggressive*, and *non-aggressive*. TRAC received 30 submissions and the results obtained by participants suggested that neural network-based systems and machine learning classifiers

---

[1]http://bit.ly/2FhLMVz

Language	Train Sub-task A				Train Sub-task B			Test Set				
	TOTAL	NAG	CAG	OAG	TOTAL	NGEN	GEN	NAG	CAG	OAG	NGEN	GEN
Bengali	**4,783**	2,600	1,116	1,067	**4,783**	3,880	903	789	169	242	1005	195
English	**5,329**	4,211	570	548	**5,329**	4,947	382	690	224	286	1023	177
Hindi	**4,981**	2,823	1,040	1,118	**4,981**	4,168	813	316	215	669	700	500

Table 1: Number of instances in each class in the TRAC-2 datasets.

(e.g. SVMs) achieved comparable performance.

Shared tasks similar to TRAC have been organized in recent years. One such example is OffensEval (SemEval-2019 Task 6) (Zampieri et al., 2019b) which focused on offensive language identification. OffensEval featured three sub-tasks: offensive language identification, offensive type identification, and offense target identification building on the annotation model introduced in the OLID dataset (Zampieri et al., 2019a) for English. This multiple sub-task model has been adopted by other shared tasks such as GermEval for German (Struß et al., 2019), HASOC (Mandl et al., 2019) for English, German, and Hindi, and HatEval (Basile et al., 2019) for English and Spanish.

3. Task Setup and Schedule

Participants enrolled to participate in any combination of tracks and languages. The registered participants were sent the links to the annotated datasets along with a description of the format of the dataset. The participants were allowed to use additional data for training the system, with the condition that the additional dataset should be either publicly available or make available immediately after submission. Use of non-public additional data for training was not allowed. The participants were given around 6 weeks to experiment and develop the system. After the 6 weeks of release of train and development sets, the test set was released and the participants had 7 days to test and upload their system. The complete timeline of the shared task is given in Table 2.

Date	Event
December 30, 2019	Announcement and registration
January 25, 2020	Train and dev set release
March 5, 2020	Test set release
March 12, 2020	System submission
March 11, 2020	Declaration of results
March 31, 2020	System description paper

Table 2: TRAC-2 timeline.

We made use of CodaLab [2] for the evaluation. Each team was allowed to submit up to 3 system runs for evaluation and their best run was included in the final ranking presented in this report.

4. Dataset

The participants of the shared task were provided with a dataset of approximately 5,000 randomly sampled YouTube comments for training and approximately 1,000 comments for development in each of Bnagla, Hindi and English.

For the sub-task on aggression identification, it annotated with 3 levels of aggression - Overtly Aggressive (OAG), Covertly Aggressive (CAG) and Non-Aggressive (NAG). For the second sub-task on gender identification, it was marked as gendered (GEN) or non-gendered (NGEN). For test, over 1,000 comments were provided [3]. The statistics of the complete dataset in each language is given in Table 1.

5. Participants and Approaches

A total of 70 participants registered for the shared task, with most of the teams registering to participate in both tracks and all the languages. Out of these, finally a total of 19 teams submitted their systems. All the teams who submitted their system were invited to submit the system description paper, describing the experiments conducted by them. Table 3, lists the participating teams and the language they took part in. Next we give a short description of the approach taken by each team for building their system. More details about the approaches could be found in the paper submitted by the respective teams.

- **abaruah** uses BERT, RoBERTa, DistilRoBERTa, and SVM-based classifiers for English. For Hindi and Bengali, multilingual BERT (M-BERT), XLM-RoBERTa and SVM classifiers were used.

- **AI_ML_NIT_Patna** uses Convolutional Neural Network and Long Short Term Memory with two different input text representations, FastText and One-hot embeddings. Their findings suggest that the LSTM model with FastText embedding performs better than other models for Hindi and Bengali datasets. On the other hand, the CNN model with FastText embedding gives better results for the English dataset.

- **FlorUniTo** uses word-embedding with an LSTM model.

- **Julian** uses multiple fine-tuned BERT models, based on bootstrap aggregating (bagging).

- **IRIT** uses the transformer-based language model BERT (Bidirectional Encoder Representation from Transformer) for two sub-tasks.

- **lastus** uses bidirectional Long Short Term Memory network (bi-LSTM) to build the purported model.

- **Ms8qQxMbnjJMgYcw** uses a single BERT-based system with two outputs for all tasks simultaneously.

---

[2] https://competitions.codalab.org/

[3] The complete dataset used for the shared task can be downloaded from the shared task website - https://sites.google.com/view/trac2/shared-task

Team	Bengali	English	Hindi	System Description Paper
Julian	✓	✓	✓	(Risch and Krestel, 2020)
abaruah	✓	✓	✓	(Baruah et al., 2020)
sdhanshu	✓	✓	✓	(Mishra et al., 2020)
Ms8qQxMbnjJMgYcw	✓	✓	✓	(Gordeev and Lykova, 2020)
FlorUniTo	✓	✓	✓	(Koufakou et al., 2020)
na14	✓	✓	✓	(Samghabadi et al., 2020)
AI_ML_NIT_Patna	✓	✓	✓	(Kumari and Singh, 2020)
asking28	✓	✓	✓	
Spyder	✓	✓	✓	(Datta et al., 2020)
zhixuan		✓		
lastus		✓		(Altın et al., 2020)
scmhl5		✓		(Liu et al., 2020)
IRIT		✓		(Ramiandrisoa and Mothe, 2020)
UniOr_ExpSys		✓		(Pascucci et al., 2020)
SAJA		✓		(Tawalbeh et al., 2020)
krishanthvs		✓		
bhanuprakash2708			✓	
saikesav564	✓			
debina			✓	
Total	**10**	**16**	**11**	**13**

Table 3: The teams that participated in the TRAC-2 shared task.

- **na14** uses an end-to-end neural model with attention on top of BERT that incorporates a multi-task learning paradigm addressing both sub-tasks simultaneously.

- **SAJA** uses transfer learning technique depending on universal sentence encoder (USE) embedding.

- **scmhl5** exploits the pre-trained Bert model to extract the text of each instance into a 768-dimensional vector of embeddings. Further it trains an ensemble of classifiers on the embedding features.

- **sdhansu** uses fine-tuning of various Transformer models on the different datasets. The utility of task label marginalization, joint label classification, and joint training on multilingual datasets as possible improvements to their models was also investigated. Their analysis suggests that the multilingual joint training approach is the best trade-off between computational efficiency and evaluation performance.

- **Spyder** uses three different models using Tf-Idf, sentiment polarity and machine learning-based classifiers.

- **UniOr_ExpSys** uses linguistic rules, stylistic features and a Sequential Minimal Optimization (SMO) algorithm in building their classifiers.

6.   Results

In this section, we present the results of the experiments carried out by different teams during the shared task. In the task, the participants were allowed to use other datasets, in addition to the one provided by the organizers. However, because of the lack of similar alternative datasets, all the groups used only the dataset provided for the task. As we mentioned earlier, for for the final testing of the system, 1000 instances were given to participants in each language for each sub-task.

The teams' result on Bengali, English and Hindi dataset is demonstrated in Table 4. In sub-task A , the best system obtained a weighted F-score of approximately 0.82 for Bengali, 0.80 for English and 0.81 for Hindi. In other words, the best system obtained approximately 0.80 F-score for all the three languages. In sub-task B, the best system obtained a weighted F-score of approximately 0.93 for Bengali, 0.87 for English and and 0.87 for Hindi.

7.   Conclusion

In this paper, we have presented the report of the Second Shared Task on Aggression Identification, organized with the TRAC-2 workshop at LREC-2020. The shared task feature two sub-tasks- aggression identification (sub-task A) in which systems were trained to discriminate between posts labeled as *overtly aggressive*, *covertly aggressive*, and *non-aggressive*, and gendered aggression identification (sub-task B) in which systems were trained to discriminate between *gendered* or *non-gendered* posts. Datasets in Bengali, Hindi and English were made available to participants. TRAC-2 received a very good response from the community which underlines the relevance of the task. More than 70 teams were registered and 19 teams submitted their systems. We found that most of the systems were developed using neural networks following the recent success of such approaches in recent related shared tasks (Zampieri et al., 2019b; Basile et al., 2019). The analysis of the performance of the best systems in the two sub-tasks shows that the three-way aggression identification task in sub-task A is still a challenging task for all languages in TRAC-2.

8.   Acknowledgements

The dataset used in the shared task is being develop under a project title 'Communal and Misogynistic Aggression' (The ComMA Project), funded by an Unrestricted Research Gift by Facebook Research.

Team	Bengali		English		Hindi	
	Task A	Task B	Task A	Task B	Task A	Task B
Julian	0.821	0.938	0.802	0.851	0.812	0.878
abaruah	0.808	0.925	0.728	0.870	0.794	0.868
sdhanshu	0.780	0.927	0.759	0.857	0.779	0.849
Ms8qQxMbnjJMgYcw	0.771	0.929	0.756	0.871	0.776	0.838
FlorUniTo	0.745	0.868	0.677	0.837	0.726	0.770
na14	0.736	0.920	0.714	0.857	0.718	0.800
AI_ML_NIT_Patna	0.717	0.879	0.660	0.822	0.654	0.736
asking28	0.685	0.815	0.714	0.710	0.700	0.733
Spyder	0.448	-	0.430	-	0.594	-
zhixuan	-	-	0.739	0.856	-	-
lastus	-	-	0.724	0.819	-	-
scmhl5	-	-	0.663	0.851	-	-
IRIT	-	-	0.635	0.820	-	-
UniOr_ExpSys	-	-	0.629	0.673	-	-
SAJA	-	-	0.607	0.856	-	-
krishanthvs	-	-	0.441	0.737	-	-
bhanuprakash2708	-	-	-	-	0.140	0.413
saikesav564	0.468	-	-	-	-	-
debina	-	-	-	-	-	0.412

Table 4: Performance of teams on Bengali, English & Hindi Dataset

9. Bibliographical References

Agarwal, S. and Sureka, A. (2015). Using knn and svm based one-class classifier for detecting online radicalization on twitter. In *International Conference on Distributed Computing and Internet Technology*.

Agarwal, S. and Sureka, A. (2017). Characterizing linguistic attributes for automatic classification of intent based racist/radicalized posts on tumblr micro-blogging website.

Altın, L. S. M., Bravo, A., and Saggion, H. (2020). Lastus/taln at trac - 2020 trolling, aggression and cyberbullying. In Ritesh Kumar, et al., editors, *Proceedings of the Second Workshop on Trolling, Aggression and Cyberbullying (TRAC-2020)*.

Anzovino, M., Fersini, E., and Rosso, P. (2018). Automatic identification and classification of misogynistic language on twitter. In Max Silberztein, et al., editors, *Natural Language Processing and Information Systems*.

Baruah, A., Das, K., Barbhuiya, F., and Dey, K. (2020). Aggression identification in english, hindi and bangla text using bert, roberta and svm. In Ritesh Kumar, et al., editors, *Proceedings of the Second Workshop on Trolling, Aggression and Cyberbullying (TRAC-2020)*.

Basile, V., Bosco, C., Fersini, E., Nozza, D., Patti, V., Rangel Pardo, F. M., Rosso, P., and Sanguinetti, M. (2019). SemEval-2019 task 5: Multilingual detection of hate speech against immigrants and women in twitter. In *Proceedings of SemEval*.

Burnap, P. and Williams, M. L. (2015). Cyber hate speech on twitter: An application of machine classification and statistical modeling for policy and decision making. *Policy & Internet*, 7(2).

Cambria, E., Chandra, P., Sharma, A., and Hussain, A. (2010). Do not feel the trolls. In *ISWC, Shanghai*.

Dadvar, M., Trieschnigg, D., Ordelman, R., and de Jong, F. (2013). Improving cyberbullying detection with user context. In *Advances in Information Retrieval*.

Datta, A., Si, S., Chakraborty, U., and Naskar, S. K. (2020). Spyder: Aggression detection on multilingual tweets. In Ritesh Kumar, et al., editors, *Proceedings of the Second Workshop on Trolling, Aggression and Cyberbullying (TRAC-2020)*.

Davidson, T., Warmsley, D., Macy, M., and Weber, I. (2017). Automated Hate Speech Detection and the Problem of Offensive Language. In *Proceedings of ICWSM*.

Djuric, N., Zhou, J., Morris, R., Grbovic, M., Radosavljevic, V., and Bhamidipati, N. (2015). Hate Speech Detection with Comment Embeddings. In *Proceedings of WWW*.

Fersini, E., Nozza, D., and Rosso, P. (2018). Overview of the evalita 2018 task on automatic misogyny identification (AMI). In Tommaso Caselli, et al., editors, *Proceedings of the Sixth Evaluation Campaign of Natural Language Processing and Speech Tools for Italian. (EVALITA 2018)*.

Frenda, S., Ghanem, B., Montes-y Gómez, M., and Rosso, P. (2019). Online hate speech against women: Automatic identification of misogyny and sexism on twitter. *Journal of Intelligent & Fuzzy Systems*, 36(5).

Gordeev, D. and Lykova, O. (2020). Bert of all trades, master of some. In Ritesh Kumar, et al., editors, *Proceedings of the Second Workshop on Trolling, Aggression and Cyberbullying (TRAC-2020)*.

Greevy, E. and Smeaton, A. F. (2004). Classifying racist texts using a support vector machine. In *Proceedings of the ACM SIGIR*.

Greevy, E. (2004). *Automatic text categorisation of racist webpages*. Ph.D. thesis, Dublin City University.

Hewitt, S., Tiropanis, T., and Bokhove, C. (2016). The problem of identifying misogynist language on twitter (and other online social spaces). In *Proceedings of the*

8th ACM Conference on Web Science, WebSci '16.

Koufakou, A., Basile, V., and Patti, V. (2020). Florunito@trac-2: Retrofitting word embeddings on an abusive lexicon for aggressive language detection. In Ritesh Kumar, et al., editors, *Proceedings of the Second Workshop on Trolling, Aggression and Cyberbullying (TRAC-2020)*.

Kumar, S., Spezzano, F., and Subrahmanian, V. (2014). Accurately detecting trolls in slashdot zoo via decluttering. In *Proceedings of ASONAM*.

Kumar, R., Ojha, A. K., Malmasi, S., and Zampieri, M. (2018). Benchmarking Aggression Identification in Social Media. In *Proceedings of TRAC*.

Kumari, K. and Singh, J. P. (2020). Ai_ml_nit_patna @ trac - 2: Deep learning approach for multi-lingual aggression identification. In Ritesh Kumar, et al., editors, *Proceedings of the Second Workshop on Trolling, Aggression and Cyberbullying (TRAC-2020)*.

Kwok, I. and Wang, Y. (2013). Locate the Hate: Detecting Tweets Against Blacks. In *Proceedings of AAAI*.

Liu, H., Burnap, P., Alorainy, W., and Williams, M. (2020). Scmhl5 at trac-2 shared task on aggression identification: Bert based ensemble learning approach. In Ritesh Kumar, et al., editors, *Proceedings of the Second Workshop on Trolling, Aggression and Cyberbullying (TRAC-2020)*.

Malmasi, S. and Zampieri, M. (2017). Detecting Hate Speech in Social Media. In *Proceedings of RANLP*.

Malmasi, S. and Zampieri, M. (2018). Challenges in discriminating profanity from hate speech. *Journal of Experimental & Theoretical Artificial Intelligence*, 30.

Mandl, T., Modha, S., Majumder, P., Patel, D., Dave, M., Mandlia, C., and Patel, A. (2019). Overview of the hasoc track at fire 2019: Hate speech and offensive content identification in indo-european languages. In *Proceedings of the 11th Forum for Information Retrieval Evaluation (FIRE)*.

Menczer, F., Fulper, R., Ciampaglia, G. L., Ferrara, E., Ahn, Y., Flammini, A., Lewis, B., and Rowe, K. (2015). Misogynistic Language on Twitter and Sexual Violence. In *Proceedings of the ACM Web Science Workshop on Computational Approaches to Social Modeling (ChASM)*.

Mihaylov, T., Georgiev, G. D., Ontotext, A., and Nakov, P. (2015). Finding opinion manipulation trolls in news community forums. In *Proceedings of CoNLL*.

Mishra, S., Prasad, S., and Mishra, S. (2020). Multilingual joint fine-tuning of transformer models for identifying trolling, aggression and cyberbullying at trac 2020. In Ritesh Kumar, et al., editors, *Proceedings of the Second Workshop on Trolling, Aggression and Cyberbullying (TRAC-2020)*.

Mojica, L. G. (2016). Modeling trolling in social media conversations.

Mubarak, H., Rashed, A., Darwish, K., Samih, Y., and Abdelali, A. (2020). Arabic Offensive Language on Twitter: Analysis and Experiments. *arXiv preprint arXiv:2004.02192*.

Nitin, Bansal, A., Sharma, S. M., Kumar, K., Aggarwal, A., Goyal, S., Choudhary, K., Chawla, K., Jain, K., and Bhasinar, M. (2012). Classification of flames in computer mediated communications.

Pascucci, A., Manna, R., Masucci, V., and Monti, J. (2020). The role of computational stylometry in identifying (misogynistic) aggression in english social media texts. In Ritesh Kumar, et al., editors, *Proceedings of the Second Workshop on Trolling, Aggression and Cyberbullying (TRAC-2020)*.

Pitenis, Z., Zampieri, M., and Ranasinghe, T. (2020). Offensive Language Identification in Greek. In *Proceedings of LREC*.

Ramiandrisoa, F. and Mothe, J. (2020). Irit at trac 2020. In Ritesh Kumar, et al., editors, *Proceedings of the Second Workshop on Trolling, Aggression and Cyberbullying (TRAC-2020)*.

Risch, J. and Krestel, R. (2020). Bagging bert models for robust aggression identification. In Ritesh Kumar, et al., editors, *Proceedings of the Second Workshop on Trolling, Aggression and Cyberbullying (TRAC-2020)*.

Samghabadi, N. S., Patwa, P., PYKL, S., Mukherjee, P., Das, A., and Solorio, T. (2020). Aggression and misogyny detection using bert: A multi-task approach. In Ritesh Kumar, et al., editors, *Proceedings of the Second Workshop on Trolling, Aggression and Cyberbullying (TRAC-2020)*.

Sax, S. (2016). Flame Wars: Automatic Insult Detection. Technical report, Stanford University.

Sharifirad, S. and Matwin, S. (2019). When a tweet is actually sexist. A more comprehensive classification of different online harassment categories and the challenges in NLP. *CoRR*, abs/1902.10584.

Struß, J. M., Siegel, M., Ruppenhofer, J., Wiegand, M., and Klenner, M. (2019). Overview of germeval task 2, 2019 shared task on the identification of offensive language. In *Proceedings KONVENS*.

Tawalbeh, S., Hammad, M., and AL-Smadi, M. (2020). Saja at trac 2020 shared task: Transfer learning for aggressive identification with xgboost. In Ritesh Kumar, et al., editors, *Proceedings of the Second Workshop on Trolling, Aggression and Cyberbullying (TRAC-2020)*.

Waseem, Z., Davidson, T., Warmsley, D., and Weber, I. (2017). Understanding Abuse: A Typology of Abusive Language Detection Subtasks. *Proceedings of ALW*.

Wiegand, M., Siegel, M., and Ruppenhofer, J. (2018). Overview of the GermEval 2018 Shared Task on the Identification of Offensive Language. In *Proceedings of GermEval*.

Xu, J.-M., Jun, K.-S., Zhu, X., and Bellmore, A. (2012). Learning from Bullying Traces in Social Media. In *Proceedings of NAACL*.

Zampieri, M., Malmasi, S., Nakov, P., Rosenthal, S., Farra, N., and Kumar, R. (2019a). Predicting the type and target of offensive posts in social media. In *Proceedings of NAACL*.

Zampieri, M., Malmasi, S., Nakov, P., Rosenthal, S., Farra, N., and Kumar, R. (2019b). SemEval-2019 task 6: Identifying and categorizing offensive language in social media (OffensEval). In *Proceedings of SemEval*.

Proceedings of the Second Workshop on Trolling, Aggression and Cyberbullying, pages 6–12
Language Resources and Evaluation Conference (LREC 2020), Marseille, 11–16 May 2020
© European Language Resources Association (ELRA), licensed under CC-BY-NC

TOCP: A Dataset for Chinese Profanity Processing

Hsu Yang and Chuan-Jie Lin
Department of Computer Science and Engineering
National Taiwan Ocean University
Keelung, Taiwan ROC

{10757013, cjlin}@ntou.edu.tw

Abstract
This paper introduced TOCP, a larger dataset of Chinese profanity. This dataset contains natural sentences collected from social media sites, the profane expressions appearing in the sentences, and their rephrasing suggestions which preserve their meanings in a less offensive way. We proposed several baseline systems using neural network models to test this benchmark. We trained embedding models on a profanity-related dataset and proposed several profanity-related features. Our baseline systems achieved an F1-score of 86.37% in profanity detection and an accuracy of 77.32% in profanity rephrasing.

Keywords: profanity detection, profanity rephrasing, Chinese profanity processing

1. Introduction

Abusive language is an important issue in the Internet. One of its major subclasses is profanity, which uses explicit profane words to express feelings or to insult other users (Ross *et al.*, 2016; Waseem, 2016; Wulczyn, *et al.*, 2017). Although profanity is not always abusive (Chen *et al.*, 2012; Clarke and Grieve, 2017; Davidson *et al.*, 2017) which can appear in positive expressions such as compliments ("This is fxxking awesome"), some readers might still feel uncomfortable thus it is not recommended.

Most of the available datasets nowadays are about abusive language. This issue is highly language-dependent, hence there have been many datasets built in different languages including English (Wassem and Hovy, 2016), German (Wiegand *et al.*, 2018; Davidson *et al.*, 2017), Dutch (Tulkens *et al.*, 2016), Greek (Pavlopoulos *et al.*, 2017), Arabic (Mubarak *et al.*, 2017), Slovene (Fišer *et al.*, 2016), and Indonesian (Alfina *et al.*, 2017). It is essential for us native speakers to build datasets in Chinese by ourselves.

In our previous work (Su *et al.*, 2017), we have built a small Chinese profanity dataset, which contains 2,044 sentences classified into 29 groups with profanity tagging and rephrasing information. As there are less than 100 sentences in each group, the amount of data is too few for machine learning or deep learning. This is the reason why we want to build a larger dataset.

Many proposed abusive detection systems were built by machine learning (Montani and Schüller, 2018; Tarasova, 2016) or deep learning (Park and Fung, 2017; Gambäck and Sikdar, 2017; Pavlopoulos et al., 2017; Badjatiya et al., 2017; Wiedemann et al., 2018). Besides word embeddings, two major types of features are often adopted.

The content-based features include keywords (Xiang *et al.*, 2012), words (Warner and Hirschberg, 2012), character n-grams (Mehdad and Tetreault, 2016), word n-grams (Yin *et al.*, 2009; Chen *et al.*, 2012), POS n-grams (Davidson *et al.*, 2017), and syntactic information (Burnap and Williams, 2014). We would like to see which features is useful for processing Chinese profanity, because Chinese text needs to be segmented but it is hard for a word segmentation system to recognized newly invented profane words.

Because Twitter is the most popular source for building abusive language datasets, another major class of features relates to user profiles or social media, such as gender (Waseem and Hovy, 2016), living place (Waseem and Hovy, 2016), user activities (Dadvar *et al.*, 2013; Balci and Salah, 2015), and neighboring posts (Yin *et al.*, 2009). We did not use these features because we could not have such information in the dataset or from the source websites.

According to our observations, we think that the main challenges of Chinese profanity processing are as follows:

(1) Insufficient training data: larger datasets are beneficial to machine learning and deep learning.
(2) High variety of Chinese profanity: nowadays the Internet users often invent new profane words with different characters with the same or similar soundings to bypass anti-harassment policy.
(3) Profane words in Taiwanese (a dialect commonly spoken in Taiwan): they do not have formal surface forms yet and are often transliterated in many different ways.
(4) Context-based rephrasing: a profane word may have more than one part-of-speech or meaning. Its rephrasing should take its contextual information into consideration.

The TOCP (**NTOU** **C**hinese **P**rofanity) dataset was built for developing Chinese profanity processing techniques. As stated in our previous work (Su *et al.*, 2017), detecting and rephrasing profanity not only reduce the abusive language in the Internet, but also make the text more comprehensible than the simple masking method. Moreover, the users will be educated and more aware of what kinds of expressions are offensive to the others. These reasons make this work important.

This paper is organized as follows. Section 2 describes the construction of TOCP dataset. Sections 3 and 4 propose several baseline systems for profanity detection and rephrasing. Section 5 delivers the evaluation results, and Section 6 concludes the paper.

2. Description of TOCP

We built the TOCP dataset in the similar way as our previous work (Su *et al.*, 2017) but in a larger scale from different websites. As a result, more types of profanity and rephrasing were discovered in this dataset. Details are given in the following subsections.

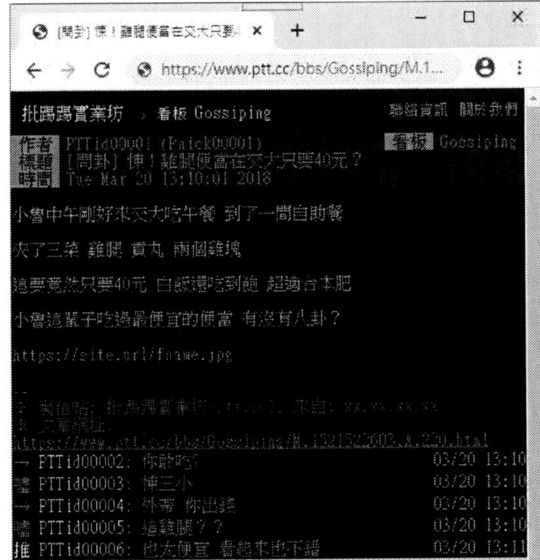

Figure 1. An Example of PTT Posts

2.1 Collecting Profanity Data

Most of the teams used crowdsourcing to prepare data annotation (Kolhatkar and Taboada, 2017; Wulczyn *et al.*, 2017). Unfortunately, our main sources of Chinese profanity were text written by Taiwanese users, and we cannot not find a popular crowdsourcing site where we could recruit enough annotators who were native speakers from Taiwan.

We considered PTT and Twitch as the source websites to collect profanity data. We recruited 10 undergraduate students to annotate profane expressions and provide rephrased expressions.

PTT Bulletin Board System
PTT[1] is a famous BBS site in Taiwan. According to its report[2] on Jan 2020, it has 251 boards related to diverse topics. A top-10 board can be visited by more than 1,000 or even 10,000 users at the same time.

Figure 1 shows an example of the webpage of a PTT post. The leading section shows some metadata about this post, followed by the content of the post, basically in text mode but with some styles of highlights or URLs linking to images in other websites. The title of the post in Figure 1 starts with "悚！" (*Terrifying*!) to express the author's surprise about the low price of a lunchbox in a university. But someone in the comment section replied "悚三小" (*Why the hxll is it terrifying*) which was quite offensive.

Below each post, other users can vote and give comments with a label '推' for like, '噓' for dislike, or '→' for a neutral opinion. Due to the restriction of the length of a line in the comment area, a long comment will be separated into several comment lines, but only the first line will show 'like' or 'dislike' while the other lines will be neutral. Note that a segmenting point is not necessary at the word boundary, which means the characters inside a Chinese word may be separated and appear in two different lines.

Figure 2. An Example of Twitch Live Streaming

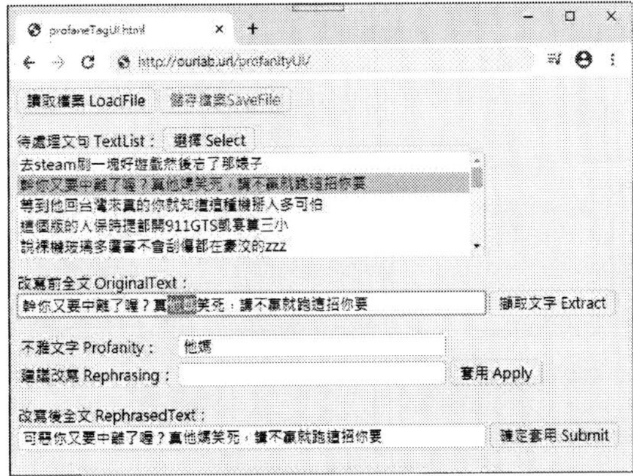

Figure 3. Profanity Annotation Tool

Moreover, if two or more users post comments at the same time, their lines may appear in an interleaving way.

Therefore, the comment lines should be preprocessed to restore the original sentences. Two comment lines were concatenated when (1) they were post by the same user and (2) the latter line was not labeled as 'like' or 'dislike'.

The same as our previous work, we used Google Search to retrieve PTT posts by submitting the profane keywords with the option "site:ptt.cc" for several weeks. We set the searching option for the newest posts in recent one week in order to avoid duplication. Finally, 7,250 posts with 1,043,231 sentences were collected. Only 39,937 of the sentences contain profane keywords.

Twitch Live Streaming
Twitch[3] is a live streaming platform mostly for video game playing. We considered the chatrooms of Twitch channels as a source of profanity, because haters often come to insult or harass the live streamers or the other users. Figure 2 shows an example of a Twitch live streaming channel. The main frame in the middle is the screen showing scenes of game playing, and the area in the right is the chatroom displaying real-time conversations among the viewers.

We monitored 17 streamers by a crawler for two weeks and collected 1,006,434 utterances in their chatrooms, where 14,950 of them contain profane keywords.

---

[1] https://www.ptt.cc/bbs/index.html

[2] https://www.ptt.cc/bbs/PttHistory/M.1581255677.A.F56.html

[3] https://www.twitch.tv/

```
[
  {
    "ID": "03166_63",
    "orginal_sentence": "幹你又要中離了喔？真他媽笑死，
        講不贏就跑這招你要",
    "source_website": "PTT",
    "profane_expression": [
      {
        "start": 0,
        "end": 1,
        "orginal_expression": "幹",
        "rephrased_expression": "可惡"
      },
      {
        "start": 10,
        "end": 12,
        "orginal_expression": "他媽",
        "rephrased_expression": ""
      }
    ]
  }, ...
]
```

Figure 4. An Example of TOCP data

2.2 Data Annotation

Now we have collected 2,049,665 sentences from social media and 54,887 of them contain profane keywords. It is time-consuming to annotate all the 54 thousand sentences, not to mention checking the other 1.5 million sentences to see if there is any new type of profanity being missed.

As an alternative, we clustered the 54,887 sentences into groups according to the profane keywords and randomly selected sentences to a certain amount in each group. Totally 16,450 sentences were selected

Ten undergraduate students were asked to annotate the real profane expressions in these sentences and provided one possible way to rephrase these expressions into less offensive ones. An annotation tool as shown in Figure 3 was developed for this purpose. If two annotators had different opinions, we would choose the more correct ones.

Finally, there were 17,578 profane expressions being identified in 14,285 sentences. As shown in Figure 4, each of the TOCP data contains an ID, an original sentence, its source web site, and a set of profane expressions appearing in this sentence. Each profane expression is represented by its starting and ending positions, the text of this profane expression, and a rephrasing suggestion.

Please note that the types of Chinese profanity targeted in this paper belong to the following categories.

(1) Terms related to "sexual intercourse"
(2) Terms related to sexual organs or substances
(3) Terms related to "bxtch"
(4) Terms related to "hxll"
(5) Terms in the pattern of "someone's relative's", a special pattern of profanity in Chinese

All 16,450 sentences are collected in the TOCP dataset provides, including those sentences not containing any profane expressions.

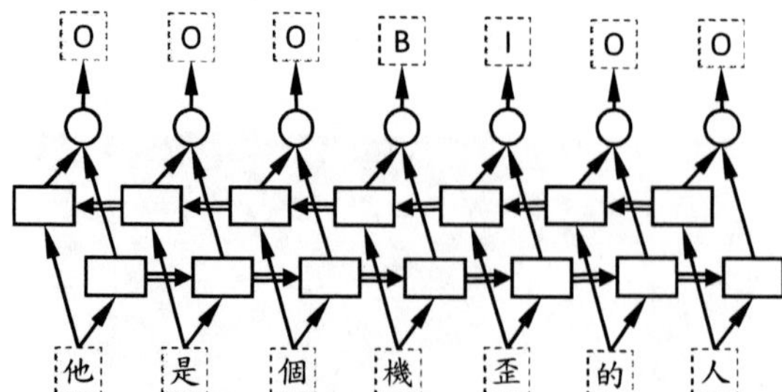

Figure 5. Sequetial-Labeling Profanity Detection

3. Profanity Detection

In this section, we proposed several baseline models to detect profane expressions with different embedding models and features.

3.1 Character-Based Sequence Labeling

The task of profanity detection is to identify profane expressions appearing in an input sentence. However, we think that word-based models may fail due to the limited ability of a Chinese word segmentation system to recognize profane words, especially when these words have many variants and a lot of them are out of vocabulary.

Therefore, we treated the profanity detection problem as a character-based sequence labeling task. Each Chinese character in an input sentence will be tagged with a label of BIO by the classifier to denote if this character is at the beginning (B), inside (I), or outside (O) of a profane expression. The final output of a profanity detection system are substrings in the input sentence tagged with consecutive BI labels.

Figure 5 shows an example of profanity detection by one layer of BiLSTM. The input "他是個機歪的人" (He is a bxtchy guy) is a Chinese sentence with 7 characters. Since the string "機歪" is a profane expression, the correct prediction should be a 'B' label for the character '機', an 'I' label for '歪', and 'O' labels for the other characters.

We tried 1 to 4 layers of BiLSTM, combining with 0 to 2 layers of ConvolutionalNN. Dropout rate was set at 0.5 to avoid overfitting. We also tried different sets of parameters.

3.2 Character Embedding

For embedding, one choice is to use pre-trained embedding models such as Google nnlm-zh-128 model[4] (Bengio *et al.*, 2003). It is a 128-dimension character embedding model trained on Chinese Google News 100B corpus.

However, these available Chinese character embeddings may not meet our needs. The main reason is that the training corpora for these models were general text which did not contain many profane expressions, not to mention those out-of-vocabulary profane words written in the same or similar sounding characters invented by Internet users to bypass anti-harassment policy.

For this reason, we proposed two methods to train profane-related embedding models. The first method was self-training which used one-hot encoding to learn embeddings

---

[4] https://tfhub.dev/google/nnlm-zh-dim128-with-normalization/2

8

from the training data directly. In order not to create high-dimensional vectors, we only took characters in the profane expressions and their context (up to 4 characters) into consideration, plus one dimension for "others".

Our second approach was to train an embedding model based on a profane-related corpus. We used PTT sentences which were not selected into the TOCP dataset to train the profane-related embedding model with a dimension of 100. Training tools were Word2Vec (Mikolov *et al.*, 2013) and fastText[5] (Bojanowski *et al.*, 2016) developed by Facebook AI Research Lab.

3.3 Character Features

Besides embeddings, text itself also provides important features for profanity detection. We designed several features as follows.

Profanity Keywords

The profanity detection rules introduced in Sec 5.1 consist of several sets of profanity keywords. For example, the rule "**YOU** + **RL** + 的" (your relative's) represents a special pattern of profanity in Chinese, where **YOU** is the set of the word "you" (你, 您,…) and **RL** is the set of terms for relatives or acquaintances such as 媽 (mother) or 老師 (teacher). We use two sets of Boolean features. One represents if a character belongs to any of the 45 profanity keyword sets. The other represents if a character belongs to a keyword set in the 24 profanity groups (cf. Sec 5.1).

Dictionary Common Terms

A Chinese character appearing in a profane word may also appear in a common word. For example, the character '幹' has many meanings other than "fxxk", such as "幹活" (working) or "樹幹" (tree stem). In order to avoid false alarm, we use a Boolean feature to denote if the substring containing the target character is a dictionary common term.

Pronunciation (Pinyin)

Because Internet users often write profane words in different characters with the same or similar soundings to bypass anti-harassment policy, the pronunciation features (*Pinyin* hereafter) were designed to identify these variants. We use two sets of Boolean features, 21 for consonants and 63 for vowels, to represent a character's pronunciation, and an additional integer feature for the tone of the target character (because Chinese is a tonal language).

These feature vectors would be concatenated with the word embedding vectors to form the input of a neural network.

4. Profanity Rephrasing

We treated the profanity rephrasing problem as a sequence-to-sequence problem. Figure 6 shows a common sequence-to-sequence model by using LSTM. The left part is an encoder which takes a sequence of characters as input, like "機歪" (bxtchy) in the figure. The right part is a decoder which generates a sequence of characters as output, like "機車" (a milder term for 'bxtchy') in the figure.

Commonly the input of a sequence-to-sequence model is the text to be rephrased. However, in our observation, contextual information is also important for rephrasing. For example, the character '屌' has many meanings (where the original meaning is "pxnis") as follows:

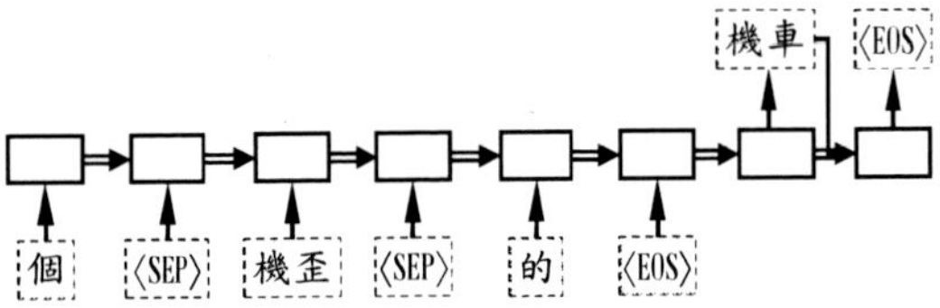

機車　⟨EOS⟩

個　⟨SEP⟩　機歪　⟨SEP⟩　的　⟨EOS⟩

Figure 6. Sequence-to-Sequence Profanity Rephrasing

Original:　金融 好 屌 阿 ～～～
Rephrased:　金融 好 屬害 阿 ～～～
(English:　Finance is so <u>cool</u>~~)

Original:　沒人 屌 你
Rephrased:　沒人 理 你
(English:　No one <u>cares about</u> you.)

So we put context into the input sequences in the format of PREC ⟨SEP⟩ PRFN ⟨SEP⟩ FOLW, where PREC is the preceding context, PRFN is the target profane expression, FOLW is the following context, and ⟨SEP⟩ is a separating symbol. We presume that word-based context is better than character-based, because the meaning can be correctly represented. Note that the output is only the rephrased text.

5. Experiments

All 16,450 sentences in the TOCP dataset were used to do the evaluation. The evaluation method was 10-fold cross-validation.

When evaluating profanity detection systems, the input was a whole sentence and the output was a set of strings recognized as profane expressions. The evaluation metrics were recall and precision based on the number of expressions. Note that an expression should be exactly the same as the human annotation to be counted as correct.

When evaluating profanity rephrasing systems, the input was a profane expression with its context (in its original text) in TOCP and the output was a rephrased string. The evaluation metric was the accuracy for profanity rephrasing, i.e. the ratio of expressions being correctly rephrased.

5.1 Rule-Based Systems

In our previous work (Su *et al.*, 2017), we have designed 29 rules to detect and rephrase profane expressions. Our first effort was to revised these rules according to the cases observed in TOCP. Finally, 41 detection and rephrasing rules (categorized into 24 groups) were formulated.

The performance of rule-based profanity detection is shown in Table 1. The first column shows the ID of profanity groups. Those groups having IDs with the same leading number are related to the same profane keywords. The second column shows the number of profane expressions tagged in TOCP belonging to each group. The overall F1-score is 79.58%.

Please note that there are 1,087 profane expressions which cannot be detected by our rules (denoted as "Other" in Table 1), because there are too many variations but too few examples to deduce general rules. If excluding these outliers, the F1-score becomes 82.08% (denoted as "Apply" in Table 1).

---

[5] https://fasttext.cc/

Group	#Sents	R	P	F1
1.0	854	51.99	58.12	54.88
1.1	2214	90.61	87.87	89.22
1.2	264	96.59	97.70	97.14
2.0	2760	84.75	59.07	69.61
3.0	1040	83.94	72.87	78.02
4.0	582	95.70	87.72	91.54
4.1	75	74.67	83.58	78.87
5.0	660	90.61	86.04	88.27
5.1	46	65.22	63.83	64.52
6.0	3716	87.65	95.77	91.53
7.0	337	92.28	92.01	92.15
8.0	37	97.30	46.75	63.16
9.0	24	100.00	58.54	73.85
10.0	21	100.00	100.00	100.00
11.0	139	100.00	97.20	98.58
11.1	227	60.35	44.19	51.02
12.0	685	95.62	91.35	93.44
12.1	2	100.00	25.00	40.00
13.0	268	99.25	97.79	98.52
14.0	36	36.11	19.40	25.24
15.0	1016	78.64	62.08	69.39
15.1	836	99.88	96.64	98.24
15.2	576	86.46	85.42	85.94
15.3	76	50.00	86.36	63.33
Other	1087	0.00	0.00	0.00
Total	17578	80.72	78.47	79.58
Apply	16491	86.04	78.47	82.08

Table 1. Performance of Rule-Based Profanity Detection

Group	Acc	Group	Acc
1.0	50.00	9.0	100.00
1.1	85.14	10.0	85.71
1.2	89.77	11.0	17.27
2.0	78.99	11.1	32.16
3.0	66.06	12.0	93.72
4.0	75.60	12.1	100.00
4.1	24.00	13.0	96.27
5.0	88.03	14.0	11.11
5.1	0.00	15.0	54.72
6.0	87.03	15.1	85.41
7.0	89.02	15.2	27.60
8.0	86.49	15.3	10.53
		Other	0.00
Total	71.13	Apply	88.12

Table 2. Performance of Rule-Based Profanity Rephrasing

The performance of rule-based profanity rephrasing is shown in Table 2. The overall accuracy was 71.13%, or 88.12% if the expressions were applicable with the new rules.

5.2 NN-Based Profanity Detection

Several neural network models have been tested, including 1 to 4 layers of bidirectional LSTM combining with 0 to 2 layers of Convolutional NN. The CNN layers were added in front of the BiLSTM layers. Dropout rate was set at 0.5 to avoid overfitting.

Table 3 shows the evaluation results of different NN-based profanity detection systems. We can see that the best systems were a 2-layer BiLSTM with or without a preceding CNN layer.

Model	R	P	F1
BiLSTM	84.77	80.92	82.80
BiLSTM*2	**85.54**	82.17	83.82
BiLSTM*3	85.05	81.00	82.97
BiLSTM*4	84.02	80.98	82.47
CNN + BiLSTM	79.36	78.04	78.69
CNN + BiLSTM*2	85.43	**82.31**	**83.84**
CNN*2 + BiLSTM	74.71	69.90	72.22

Table 3. Performance of NN-Based Profanity Detection

Model	R	P	F1
One-Hot (Char)	85.54	82.17	83.82
One-Hot (Word)	59.56	76.28	66.89
Google nnlm-zh-128	76.45	74.54	75.49
Pinyin	82.52	79.18	80.81
Word2Vec	86.44	84.41	85.41
fastText	85.67	83.70	84.67
Word2Vec + Pinyin	86.05	84.08	85.05
Word2Vec + KW	86.85	85.12	85.98
Word2Vec + KW + Dict	86.38	84.52	85.44
fastText + Pinyin	86.56	84.64	85.59
fastText + KW	**87.50**	**85.26**	**86.37**
fastText + KW + Dict	87.47	84.72	86.07
fastText + KW + Dict + Pinyin	**87.50**	84.53	85.99

Table 4. Comparison of Combinations of Embeddings and Features in Profanity Detection

We also tested different combinations of embedding models and features described in Sections 3.2 and 3.3. Embedding models include one-hot encoding (character-based, word-based, and pinyin-based), Google nnlm-zh-128 model, and our character embedding models trained on PTT sentences by Word2Vec (CBOW model) or fastText (Skip-gram model). Features include pinyin, profanity keywords (KW), and dictionary common terms (Dict).

The experimental results were shown in Table 4 where all systems were built with 2 layers of BiLSTM. The best system was achieved an F1-score of 86.37% by the character embedding trained by fastText combining with the keyword and dictionary-term features. The performance shown in these tables were measured after parameter tuning.

Some conclusions can be drawn from the results in Table 4: (1) The fastText-trained embedding achieved better performance than one-hot encoding, Google nnlm-zh-128, and Word2Vec-trained embedding; (2) The keyword and dictionary-term features improved the performance more than the pinyin feature; (3) The performance of the word-based one-hot encoding was poor, which supported our assumption that incorrect word segmentation would decrease the ability of profanity detection.

Moreover, all NN-based systems outperformed the rule-based detection system either in recall or precision. In the future, we would like to propose hybrid systems which can take advantages from these two kinds of approaches.

5.3 NN-Based Profanity Rephrasing

Our baseline systems for profanity rephrasing mainly differ in the contextual information. Besides using no context, we also took one character or one word preceding or following the target profane expression as context. All systems were built with LSTM models.

Word-Based			Char-Based		
Left	Right	Acc	Left	Right	Acc
0	0	74.83	0	0	73.15
0	1	76.11	0	1	74.12
1	0	**77.32**	1	0	74.43
1	1	76.47	1	1	74.42

Table 5. Performance of NN-Based Profanity Rephrasing

Batch	One-Hot	Word2Vec	fastText
32	76.92	75.71	77.28
64	77.00	75.48	77.06
128	77.32	75.21	76.61
256	76.71	--	--
512	64.21	--	--

Table 6. Comparison of Embeddings and Batch Sizes in Profanity Rephrasing

The choices of embeddings of the target profane expression and the context were the same as the ones in the detection experiments, only that the word-based models were trained on machine word-segmented data.

Table 5 shows the performance of NN-based profanity rephrasing. The systems not using contextual information were the worse systems. Word-based context was better than character-based context. The best system only considered one preceding word and achieved an accuracy of 77.32%, better than the rule-based rephrasing system.

In fact, we also tried to use the whole sentence as context, but the performance was too bad so we did not show the result here.

Table 6 shows the comparison of different embeddings and batch sizes for the best system in Table 5. Because one-hot encoding slightly outperformed the pre-trained word embedding models, it seems that the surface information is as useful as the semantics in profanity rephrasing.

6. Conclusion

This paper introduced TOCP, a larger dataset of Chinese profanity for detection and rephrasing. This dataset contains 16,450 sentences collected from social media websites, where 14,285 of them contains totally 17,578 profane expressions. Rephrasing suggestions to make these expressions less offensive are also provided. This dataset has been released in the Internet[6].

This paper also proposed several baseline systems for profanity detection and rephrasing to evaluate the dataset. Rule-based systems become worse because the rules cannot cover the great variety of profane expressions.

The best profanity detection system consists of two layers of BiLSTM preceded by CNN. Character embeddings were trained by fastText on the PTT sentences, a profanity-related dataset, and concatenated with the profanity keyword feature and dictionary common term feature. The F1-score of detection was 86.37%.

The best profanity rephrasing system took the profane expression and its preceding word as input, where word embeddings came from word-based one-hot encoding and the batch size was set to 128. The accuracy was 77.32%.

---

[6] http://nlp.cse.ntou.edu.tw/resources/TOCP/

We are now building another dataset for abusive language in Chinese. We will observe the similarity and difference between these two datasets.

7. Acknowledgements

This research was funded by the Taiwan Ministry of Science and Technology (grant: MOST 107-2221-E-019-038).

8. Bibliographical References

Alfina, I., Mulia, R., Fanany, M. I., and Ekanata, Y. (2017). Hate speech detection in the Indonesian language: a dataset and preliminary study. In *Proceedings of 2017 International Conference on Advanced Computer Science and Information Systems* (*ICACSIS*), pp. 233-238.

Badjatiya, P., Gupta, S., Gupta, M., and Varma, V. (2017). Deep learning for hate speech detection in Tweets. In *Proceedings of the 26th International Conference on World Wide Web Companion* (*WWW '17 Companion*), pp. 759-760.

Balci, K., and Salah, A. A. (2015). Automatic analysis and identification of verbal aggression and abusive behaviors for online social games. *Computers in Human Behavior*, 53:517-526.

Bengio, Y., Ducharme, R., Vincent, P., and Jauvin, C. (2003). A neural probabilistic language model. *Journal of Machine Learning Research*, 3:1137-1155.

Bojanowski, P., Grave, E., Joulin, A., and Mikolov, T. (2016). Enriching word vectors with subword information, arXiv:1607.04606.

Burnap, P., and Williams, M. L. (2014). Hate speech, machine classification and statistical modelling of information flows on Twitter: interpretation and communication for policy decision making. In *Proceedings of the Internet, Policy and Politics Conference*, pp. 1-18.

Chen, Y., Zhou, Y., Zhu, S., and Xu, H. (2012). Detecting offensive language in social media to protect adolescent online safety. In *Proceedings of the 2012 ASE/IEEE International Conference on Social Computing and 2012 ASE/IEEE International Conference on Privacy, Security, Risk and Trust,* (*SOCIALCOM-PASSAT '12*), pp. 71-80.

Clarke, I., and Grieve, J. (2017). Dimensions of abusive language on Twitter. In *Proceedings of the First Workshop on Abusive Language Online* (*ALW-*1), *the 55th Annual Meeting of the Association for Computational Linguistics* (*ACL 2017*), pp. 1-10.

Dadvar, M., Trieschnigg, D., and de Jong, F. (2013). Expert knowledge for automatic detection of bullies in social networks. In *Proceedings of the 25th Benelux Conference on Artificial Intelligence* (*BNAIC 2013*), pp. 57-64.

Davidson, T., Warmsley, D., Macy, M., and Weber, I. (2017). Automated hate speech detection and the problem of offensive language. In *Proceedings of the 11th International AAAI Conference on Web and Social Media* (*ICWSM17*), pp. 512-515.

Fišer, D., Erjavec, T., and Ljubešić, N. (2017). Legal framework, dataset and annotation schema for socially unacceptable on-line discourse practices in Slovene. In *Proceedings of the 1st Workshop on Abusive Language*

Online (*ALW1*), *the Annual Meeting of the Association of Computational Linguistics* (*ACL 2017*), pp. 46-51.

Gambäck, B., and Sikdar, U. K. (2017). Using convolutional neural networks to classify hate-speech. In *Proceedings of the 1st Workshop on Abusive Language Online* (*ALW1*), *the Annual Meeting of the Association of Computational Linguistics* (*ACL 2017*), pp. 71-75.

Kolhatkar, V., and Taboada, M. (2017). Constructive language in news comments. In *Proceedings of the First Workshop on Abusive Language Online* (*ALW*-1), *the 55th Annual Meeting of the Association for Computational Linguistics* (*ACL 2017*), pp. 11-17.

Mehdad, Y., and Tetreault, J. (2016). Do characters abuse more than words? In *Proceedings of the 17th Annual Meeting of the Special Interest Group on Discourse and Dialogue, Association for Computational Linguistics*, pp. 299-303.

Mikolov, T., Chen, K., Corrado, G., and Dean, J. (2013). Efficient estimation of word representation in vector space. In *the Workshop Track Proceedings of the 1st International Conference on Learning Representations*.

Montani, J. P., and Schüller, P. (2018). TUWienKBS at GermEval 2018: German abusive tweet detection. In *Proceedings of the GermEval 2018 Workshop, the 14th Conference on Natural Language Processing* (*KONVENS 2018*), pp. 45-50.

Mubarak, H., Darwish, K., and Magdy, W. (2017). Abusive language detection on Arabic social media. In *Proceedings of the 1st Workshop on Abusive Language Online* (*ALW1*), *the Annual Meeting of the Association of Computational Linguistics* (*ACL 2017*), pp. 52-56.

Park, J. H., and Fung, P. (2017). One-step and two-step classification for abusive language detection on Twitter," *Proceedings of the 1st Workshop on Abusive Language Online* (*ALW1*), *the Annual Meeting of the Association of Computational Linguistics* (*ACL 2017*), pp. 41-45.

Pavlopoulos, J., Malakasiotis, P., and Androutsopoulos, I. (2017). Deep learning for user comment moderation. In *Proceedings of the 1st Workshop on Abusive Language Online* (*ALW1*), *the Annual Meeting of the Association of Computational Linguistics* (*ACL 2017*), pp. 25-35.

Ross, B., Rist, M. Carbonell, G., Cabrera, B., Kurowsky, N., and Wojatzki, M. (2016). Measuring the reliability of hate speech annotations: The case of the European refugee crisis. In *Proceedings of NLP4CMC III: 3rd Workshop on Natural Language Processing for Computer-Mediated Communication. Bochumer Linguistische Arbeitsberichte*, 17:6-9.

Su, H.-P., Huang, Z.-J., Chang, H.-T., and Lin, C.-J. (2017). Rephrasing profanity in Chinese text. In *Proceedings of the First Workshop on Abusive Language Online* (*ALW*-1), *the 55th Annual Meeting of the Association for Computational Linguistics* (*ACL 2017*), pp. 18-24.

Tarasova, N. (2016). *Classification of Hate Tweets and Their Reasons using SVM*, master's thesis, Uppsala Universitet.

Tulkens, S., Hilte, L., Lodewyckx, E., Verhoeven, B., Daelemans, W. (2016). A dictionary-based approach to racism detection in Dutch social media. In *Proceedings of the Workshop Text Analytics for Cybersecurity and Online Safety* (*TA-COS*).

Warner, W., and Hirschberg, J. (2012). Detecting hate speech on the World Wide Web. In *Proceedings of the Workshop on Language and Social Media, The Association for Computational Linguistics*, pp. 19-26.

Waseem, Z. (2016). Are you a racist or am I seeing things? Annotator influence on hate speech detection on Twitter. In *Proceedings of the First Workshop on NLP and Computational Social Science. Association for Computational Linguistics*, pp. 138-142.

Waseem, Z. and Hovy, D. (2016). Hateful symbols or hateful people? Predictive features for hate speech detection on Twitter. In *Proceedings of the NAACL Student Research Workshop. Association for Computational Linguistics*, pp. 88-93.

Wiedemann, G., Ruppert, E., Jindal, R., and Biemann, C. (2018). Transfer learning from LDA to BiLSTM-CNN for offensive language detection in Twitter. In *Proceedings of the GermEval 2018 Workshop, the 14th Conference on Natural Language Processing* (*KONVENS 2018*), pp. 85-94.

Wiegand, M., Siegel, M., and Ruppenhofer, J. (2018). Overview of the GermEval 2018 Shared Task on the Identification of Offensive Language," *Proceedings of the GermEval 2018 Workshop, the 14th Conference on Natural Language Processing* (*KONVENS 2018*), pp. 1-10.

Wulczyn, E., Thain, N., and Dixon, L. (2017). Ex Machina: Personal attacks seen at scale. In *Proceedings of the 26th International Conference on World Wide Web* (*WWW 2017*), pp. 1391-1399.

Xiang, G., Fan, B., Wang, L., Hong, J., and Rose, C. (2012). Detecting offensive tweets via topical feature discovery over a large scale Twitter corpus. In *Proceedings of the 21st ACM International Conference on Information and Knowledge Management* (*ACM CIKM '12*), pp. 1980-1984.

Yin, D., Xue, Z., Hong, L., Davison, B. D., Kontostathis, A., and Edwards, L. (2009). Detection of harassment on Web 2.0. In *Proceedings of the Content Analysis in the WEB*, pp. 1-7.

Proceedings of the Second Workshop on Trolling, Aggression and Cyberbullying, pages 13–20
Language Resources and Evaluation Conference (LREC 2020), Marseille, 11–16 May 2020
© European Language Resources Association (ELRA), licensed under CC-BY-NC

A Multi-Dimensional View of Aggression when voicing Opinion

**Arjit Srivastava[1*], Avijit Vajpayee[2*], Syed Sarfaraz Akhtar[3*],
Naman Jain[2], Vinay Singh[1], Manish Shrivastava[1]**

[1]International Institute of Information Technology, Hyderabad, Telangana, India
[2]Department of Computer Science, Columbia University, New York, NY, USA
[3]Department of Linguistics, University of Washington, Seattle, WA, USA

arjit.srivastava@research.iiit.ac.in
{ssa2184, nj2387}@columbia.edu,
avijitv@uw.edu
vinay.singh@research.iiit.ac.in
m.shrivastava@iiit.ac.in

Abstract

The advent of social media has immensely proliferated the amount of opinions and arguments voiced on the internet. These virtual debates often present cases of aggression. While research has been focused largely on analyzing aggression and stance in isolation from each other, this work is the first attempt to gain an extensive and fine-grained understanding of patterns of aggression and figurative language use when voicing opinion. We present a Hindi-English code-mixed dataset of opinion on the politico-social issue of '2016 India banknote demonetisation' and annotate it across multiple dimensions such as aggression, hate speech, emotion arousal and figurative language usage (such as sarcasm/irony, metaphors/similes, puns/word-play).

Keywords: Social Media, Stance, Opinion, Aggression, Hate Speech, Figurative Language, Emotion

1. Introduction

There has been an explosion in terms of the amount of data generated by users online. Social media and online forums encourage users to share their thoughts with the world resulting in a vast resource of opinion-rich data. This has garnered a lot of attention from the research community as it allows for analyzing the interactions between users as well as their usage of informal language in depth.

Stance detection is the task of automatically determining the opinion of users with respect to a given issue. The author of the opinion may be in favour, against or neutral towards the issue. In this paper, we attempt to analyze with respect to stance, nuances of displayed aggression towards supporters / detractors of the opinion as well as the usage of various forms of figurative language such as metaphors, rhetorical questions, sarcasm, irony, puns and word-play. We additionally also look at the emotion arousal level and instances of hate speech. The target issue analyzed in this paper is '2016 Indian banknote demonetisation'. On 8 November 2016, the Government of India announced the demonetisation of all ₹500 and ₹1,000 banknotes of the Mahatma Gandhi Series. It also announced that new banknotes of ₹500 and ₹2,000 banknotes will be circulated in exchange for the demonetised banknotes. However, this decision received mixed reactions from the people of India with many people questioning its effectiveness.

Culpeper (2011) defined verbal aggression as *"any kind of linguistic behaviour which intends to damage the social identity of the target person and lower their status and*

prestige" (also cited by Kumar et al. (2018)). Baron and Richardson (2004) identified some characteristics of aggression as :

- Form of behaviour rather than an emotion, motive or attitude.

- Visible intention to hurt or harm (may not be physical).

- Must involve actions / intentions against living beings.

- Recipient is motivated to avoid such treatment.

People often express their opinion on socio-political issues on social media forums like Twitter by displaying aggression towards people that support a contradicting belief or towards particular group of stake-holders on the issue. Given below are some example tweets from our dataset on the target issue of demonetisation in India. The reader is warned on the strongly-worded and derogatory nature of these tweets.

1. **Tweet**: *'ye AAPtards aise behave kar rahe hain jaise Modi ji ne Notebandi nahi inki Nassbandi kara di ho'*

   Translation: *'These AAPtards are behaving as if its not demonetisation but castration for them.'*

   Gloss: *"AAP"*: Opposition political party, *"AAPtards"*: slang term for supporters of AAP (inspired by the English slang *"Libtards"*), *"Notebandi"*: demonetisation of higher currency notes, *"Nassbandi"*: castration

---

* These authors contributed equally to this work.

Tweet 1 is in favor of the decision and is overtly aggressive towards the people who are voicing their views against it. Due to its abusive language and suggestion of violence, it is also labeled as hate speech. Lastly, this tweet contains word-play as "Notebandi"(Demonetisation) rhymes with "Nass-bandi"(Castration).

2. **Tweet**: *'Aam admi se jyada politician ko dikate ho rhi h notebandi se aisa kyun?????'*

   Translation: *'Politicians seem to be more affected by demonetisation compared to the common man. Why is so ?'*

   In tweet 2, the author rhetorically questions why politicians seem to be more troubled about Demonetisation than the normal public, which is to imply that the general public supports the legislation and corrupt politicians are opposing it. This is an example of covert aggression towards the politicians while voicing favourable opinion on the decision.

3. **Tweet**: *'tera kejri mar jaye sala suar to modi ji vaise he ek din ke liye notebandi vapis le lege'*

   Translation: *'If your leader Kejri, a stupid pig, dies then Modi ji would take demonetisation back for a day.'*

   Gloss: *"Kejri"*: refering to Arvind Kejriwal (leader of opposition party AAP), *"Modi ji"*: Honorific refering to Narendra Modi (Prime Minister of India)

   Tweet 3 supports the decision of demonetisation and is overtly aggressive to both the members of AAP and their leader Arvind Kejriwal. Its author suggests that the opposition leader should die and proceeds to verbally abuse him.

4. **Tweet**: *'what if .. Modi Ji says Mitron ,,, kal raat ko zyada ho gayi thi ,,. Kuch nahi badla he.. #NoteBandi'*

   Translation: *'What if Modi says that he had too much to drink last night and nothing has really changed. #Demonetisation.'*

   Tweet 4 makes a sarcastic joke about how Prime Minister Modi might have been joking and hung over while making this sudden announcement. Despite its humorous take, this tweet is non-aggressive and neutral in stance.

The main contributions of this paper is a unified dataset of 1001 Hindi-English code-mixed tweets annotated for multiple dimensions namely -

- Stance (favourable, against, neutral)

- Aggression (covert, overt, non-aggressive)

- Hate Speech (true, false)

- Figurative language use

  - Sarcasm / Irony / Rhetorical Questions (true, false)

  - Puns / Word-play (true, false)

  - Metaphors / Similes (true, false)

- Emotion arousal (1 to 5 rating)

This is the first attempt at analysing social media opinion on a political issue across varied modalities. More in depth datasets like the one we present here are required for -

- Analyzing the not so apparent forms of verbal aggression displayed on social media.

- Better understanding linguistic patterns when voicing opinion and displaying aggression.

- Analyzing social dynamics of opinion.

- Facilitate classification models that leverage corpora annotated for auxiliary tasks through transfer learning, joint modelling as well as semi-supervised label propagation methods.

The structure of this paper is as follows. In section 2, we review related work in the fields of stance detection, aggression detection, hate speech detection, figurative language constructions, emotion analysis and code-mixed data analysis. In section 3, we explain the annotation guidelines used to for creation of this dataset. Section 4 we present statistics and analysis on the corpus. Finally, section 5 we present our conclusions as well as lay out scope of extending this work.

2. Related Work

User generated data from social media forums like Twitter has attracted a lot of attention from the research community. Mohammad et al. (2017) and Krejzl et al. (2017) analyzed stance in tweets and online discussion forums respectively. The task of stance detection on tweets at SemEval 2016 (Mohammad et al., 2016) led to targeted interest in the area with contributions from Augenstein et al. (2016), Liu et al. (2016) etc. Aggression and offensive language was the focus of a SemEval 2019 task (Zampieri et al., 2019b) and some of the works on aggression identification are Kumar et al. (2018), Zampieri et al. (2019a). Closely related is detecting hate speech in social media which has been explored by Malmasi and Zampieri (2017), Schmidt and Wiegand (2017), Davidson et al. (2017), Badjatiya et al. (2017) among others.

Domains of verbal aggression, abuse, hate have till now been studied in isolation from stance and opinion mining. Additionally, usage of figurative language expressions such as sarcasm, metaphor, rhetorical questions, puns etc.,

---

** The dataset is publically available at : https://github.com/arjitsrivastava/MultidimensionalViewOpinionMining

when voicing opinion or displaying aggression, has not been explored in depth. As most of the datasets available are annotated with a singular task at hand, it precludes understanding the correlations along multiple dimensions. The next frontier is analyzing in depth these patterns and correlations. To do this, we undertook a data annotation effort on a singular set of tweets for multiple tasks previously studied separately. We hope that this dataset makes way for joint modelling / multi-task learning systems as well provide insights on underlying latent factors.

For this work, we wished to analyze multiple dimensions of opinion on a single target issue. The choice of demonetisation of higher currency notes in India 2017 as our target issue was motivated by the familiarity of the authors and annotators with its nuances as well as the highly polarizing nature of opinions on the topic. Gafaranga (2007) describes code-mixing as use of linguistic units from different languages in a single utterance or sentence and code-switching as the co-occurrence of speech extracts belonging to two different grammatical systems. Majority of user generated data on social media is code-mixed and consequently, so is our dataset. Code mixed datasets for Hindi-English tweets have been previously created for humor (Khandelwal et al., 2018), sarcasm (Swami et al., 2018a), aggression (Kumar et al., 2018), hate speech (Bohra et al., 2018) and emotion (Vijay et al., 2018).

3. Annotation

Swami et al. (2018b) had collected 3500 code-mixed Hindi-English tweets using the Twitter Scraper API filtering by the keywords *"notebandi"* and *"demonetisation"* over a period of 6 months after Demonetisation was implemented and annotated them for stance (favourable, against and neutral). We randomly sampled 1001 tweets from this dataset and annotated these sampled tweets for the dimensions (3 domain expert annotators for each dimension) :

- Aggression : Overt vs. Covert vs. Neutral

- Hate Speech : True vs. False

- Sarcasm / Irony / Rhetorical Question : True vs. False

- Metaphor / Simile : True vs. False

- Pun / Word-play : True vs. False

- Emotion Arousal : 5 point ordinal scale

The final label on each binary classification dimension was taken as the majority label from choices of 3 annotators. For aggression classification, which was a multi-class classification, adjudication was provided by us for cases where no simple majority could be reached. For emotion arousal levels, scores from individual annotators were averaged for the final emotion arousal level score.

We also re-annotated the original dataset for stance for it had favourable or against tags only on tweets that displayed outright support or disapproval respectively. We found

that majority of opinion was displayed through attacking / supporting other opinions on the issue i.e. examples of indirect or implied support / disapproval. For example look at the tweet below -

5. **Tweet**: *'Notebandi k khilaf kyu ho...? Kaale dhan m share holder ho kya @ArvindKejriwal'*

   Translation: *'Why are you against demonetisation ? Are you are shareholder in black money @ArvindKejriwal'*

   Gloss: *"kale dhan"*: black money, *"Arvind Kejriwal"*: Leader of opposition political party AAP, *"Notebandi"*: demonetisation

Tweet 5 was originally classified as a neutral stance. We feel that cases like above can be confidently annotated as favourable to the issue (i.e. favourable to demonetisation). The author rhetorically and sarcastically questions the opinion, intentions and reasons of those against the issue (in this case leader of opposition party). This tweet is also an example of what we consider covert aggression.

For aggression annotation, we follow the guidelines by Kumar et al. (2018) who had presented a detailed typology of aggression on Hindi-English code-mixed data. We only annotate for aggression level and they had additional layers based on discursive role (attack, defend, abet) and discursive effect (physical threat, sexual aggression, gendered aggression, racial aggression, communal aggression, casteist aggression, political aggression, geographical aggression, general non-threatening aggression, curse). The definitions for 3 aggression levels along with examples from our dataset are :

Covertly-Aggressive (C) Contains text which is an indirect attack and is often packaged as (insincere) polite expressions (through the use of conventionalized polite structures) such as satire, rhetorical questions, etc.

   6. **Tweet**: *'Notebandi ka niyam : khata nahi hai to khulwao. Aam aadmi : khulwa to lun. Par bhai bank main ghusun Kasey ?'*

      Translation: *'Rule of Demonetisation: If you don't have an account then open one. Common man: I'll open but let me know how to enter the bank first?'*

      Disapproval of demonetisation through sarcastic reference to long queues in front of banks due to high demand for exchange of demonetised currency.

Overtly-Aggressive (O) Contains texts in which aggression is overtly expressed either through the use of specific kind of lexical items, syntactic structures or lexical features.

7. **Tweet**: *'Ye Notebandi Atankbaadiyo aur Bharashtachaariyo ki NAKEBANDI hai. Sare Rashtrabhakta is nakebandi ke sath aur samarthan me aye.'*

   Translation: *'Demonetisation is a barricading of terrorists and corrupt. All the nationalists should support this barricading.'*

Non-Aggressive (NAG) Refers to texts which are not lying in the above two categories.

8. **Tweet**: *'kya Aam aadmi ke liye NoteBandi ka Faisla Shi hai?'*

   Translation: *'Is the decision of demonetisation in the favour of common man?'*

Prior works regarding sarcasm and irony detection on social media data like Reddit (Wallace et al., 2014) and Twitter (Bamman and Smith, 2015) have shown that context is essential in understanding sarcasm. Therefore, most social media datasets of sarcasm are self-annotated i.e. hashtag specific twitter scraping like #sarcasm and #notsarcasm. As we are re-annotating a previously scraped dataset which was not self-annotated through specific hashtags, we rely on the domain knowledge of context expert annotators on the Indian socio-political scenario and focus issue of demonetisation. This however is not a drawback because in a dataset like ours , rich with strongly opinionated tweets, annotating sarcasm is fairly easy. In the current scope of the research, rhetorical questions are thought of as functioning similar to sarcasm and irony. We understand that fine grained linguistic differences between sarcasm, irony and rhetorical questions exist, for our purpose we have clubbed them into a single category of figurative language. Similarly, puns and word-play are merged into a single category of figurative language as well and the annotation guidelines were based on the SemEval 2017 task of detecting english puns (Miller et al., 2017). Rhyming usage of 'Notebandi' (demonetisation) with 'Nasbandi' (castration) as shown in the earlier examples, was the most common word-play seen. A third figurative language category of metaphors (and occasionally similes) can also be clearly observed in our corpus. Metaphor identification has been typically treated as a token level or phrase level tagging task (Shutova and Teufel, 2010). To be consistent we other figurative language categories used in this work, we annotated metaphors at the tweet level which was also the annotation level for SemEval 2015 task on figurative language in Twitter data (Ghosh et al., 2015). The following tweet is an example of metaphor usage -

9. **Tweet**: *'kabhi kabhi sher ka shikar karne ke liye bhed (aam janta) ko chara banana padta hai. notebandi'*

   Translation: *'Sometimes sheep need to be sacrificed in order to to hunt lions Demonetisation.'*

In tweet 9, 'sheep' is a metaphor for some members of common public and 'lions' is a metaphor for large scale corruption.

Burnap and Williams (2015) defined hate speech as responses that include written expressions of hateful and antagonistic sentiment toward a particular race, ethnicity, or religion. They used a binary classification scheme of hate speech vs. non hate speech, which was also followed by Bohra et al. (2018) for their dataset on Hindi-English code-mixed tweets. Malmasi and Zampieri (2017) used a 3 way classification scheme between hate speech vs. offensive language but not hate speech vs. no offensive language. As aggression levels are highly predictive of offensive language but not of hate speech category, we used a binary classification speech. However annotators faced difficulty in differentiating over a personal attack full of hatred than a community being targeted. An example :

10. **Tweet**: *'ab itni taklif hai to atmadaah kyo nahi kar lete notebandi k khilf. Delhi walo ko bhi mukti milegi tumse'*

   Translation: *'If you have such a huge issue with it, why don't you perform a self-immolation? The people of Delhi would also get freedom from you'*

In tweet 10, the author is referring to Arvind Kejriwal who is the leader of opposition party AAP and also the Chief Minister of Delhi (capital of India). The author suggests Kejriwal should kill himself to free the residents of Delhi. In the process of supporting the decision of Demonetisation, the author of the tweet is making extreme and graphic suggestions towards one of the main opponents of target issue.

Emotion classification in text is widely understood as lying across two orthogonal dimensions - valence (polarity of emotion) and arousal (intensity of emotion) (Russell and Barrett, 1999). Despite that, many works on emotion classification in text have generally used directly annotated 6 emotion categories (happy, sad, anger, fear, disgust, surprise) instead of first annotating arousal and valence separately before mapping them into emotion categories. We restricted the scope for this project to analyze only for emotion arousal level as emotion valence level is analogous to sentiment. For emotion arousal level, Bradley and Lang (1999) averaged annotations on a 9 point scale and Mohammad (2018) used a Best-Worst scale to obtain fine-grained scores. Similar to the SemEval 2017 task (Rosenthal et al., 2019) for sentiment analysis on Twitter, we use a 5-point ordinal scale (Very Low, Low, Neutral, High, Very High) for emotion arousal level.

4. Data Statistics and Analysis

Table 1 presents the tweet level average statistics on the corpus. The dataset tweets contain majorly Hindi language tokens (written in Roman script instead of Devnagri). A total of 119 tweets had discernible code-mixing (3 or more english words). As our tweets were sampled from the dataset by Swami et al. (2018b) who had referred to their dataset as code-mixed, we continue to refer it that way. Subsequent model building on this corpus would benefit from special handling for token-level spelling differences that come with Devnagri to Latin script switching for Hindi.

Table 2 has the corpus wide statistics across various phenomena annotated. There is a significant skew towards favourable stance in the corpus. To accommodate for this imbalance, subsequent analysis of phenomena with respect to stance contain marginal class percentage statistics, for example percentage of sarcastic tweets in favour of the issue with respect to total number of tweets favourable to the issue. Another point to note is the very low number of hate speech instances. This could be attributed to the stringent guideline that only directed abusive attacks on specific groups/communities are to be regarded as hate speech. Annotations with looser guidelines, where personal offensive language against individuals are also considered hate speech, would correlate highly with overt aggression category. Since we annotated on tweets regarding a polarizing legislation, it was expected that a fair amount would display aggression (either covert or overt). The same observation is evident from the statistics.

Avg. # tokens	21.1
Avg. # tokens (EN)	1.0
Avg. # tokens (HI)	16.9
Avg. # tokens (Rest)	3.2

Table 1: Tweet Level Statistics

4.1. Annotation Agreement

We used Fleiss's kappa to measure inter-annotator agreement on categorical annotation tasks and the results are given in table 3. Due to the clear polarizing nature of issue at hand, annotations for stance were of very high

Task	Category	# Tweets
Stance	Favour	583
	Against	180
	Neutral	238
Aggression	Overt	140
	Covert	264
	None	597
Hate Speech	True	29
Figurative Language	Sarcasm / Irony / Rhetorical Ques.	163
	Word-play / Pun	140
	Metaphor / Simile	189

Table 2: Distribution of annotations across corpus

Task	Fleiss's kappa
Stance	0.84
Aggression	0.62
Hate Speech	0.47
Sarcasm / Irony / Rhetorical Questions	0.61
Puns / Word-play	0.72
Metaphors / Similes	0.65

Table 3: Fleiss's kappa score on multiple annotations across dimensions

Spearman's Rank Correlation Emotion Arousal		
Annotator	2	3
1	0.655	0.652
2		0.64

Table 4: Spearman correlation on emotion arousal annotations across annotator pairs

correlation. Hate speech annotations had the worst kappa score and can be attributed to what constitutes a personal abusive attack. For figurative language use, the annotations for puns and word-play were of higher correlation as can be expected due to the apparentness in surface forms. Annotations for sarcasm / irony / rhetorical questions while still being of high agreement had lower agreement rate than both metaphors / similes as well as word-play. This can be attributed to the general greater subjective nature of sarcasm as well as it being a more context-dependent phenomenon than metaphor or word-play.

Table 4 gives the Spearman's rank correlation coefficient across 3 annotators for emotional arousal which has been rated on an ordinal scale of 1 to 5. Although annotating for emotion is a fairly difficult task and annotating for only the arousal dimension even more so. However, we achieve a decent average correlation of 0.65 which can be attributed to the fact that these tweets were sampled for a polarizing issue which had clearly apparent emotional states (high arousal emotions like anger as well as low arousal emotions like sadness). For each pair of annotators, the results of emotional arousal agreement were statistically significant with p-values $<<< 0.005$.

4.2. Stance specific analysis

Table 5 presents the statistics of hate speech across stance classes. An anomalous observation is the higher marginal percentage of hate speech evidence for *neutral* stance. This could be attributed to the poorer understanding of what constitutes hate speech. Additionally, upon investigating we found tweets similar to the one given below. Though the tweet does not take a definitive stance on the issue at hand (demonetisation), it is an abusive personal attack at an individual as well as a group.

11. **Tweet:** *'MR. RAVISH VYAPARI IMAANDAR HAI.KANOON KA SANMAAN KARTSHAI. PAR*

MEDIA NEWS AUR TV SAB SAALE CHOR AUE HARAMKHOR HAI. NOTEBANDI'

Translation: *'Mr. Ravish, businessmen are honest and respect the law. But media, news and TV (personalities) are thieves and bastards.'*

Glosses: *"Ravish"*: Refering to news anchor Ravish Kumar

Tweet 11, defends integrity of businessmen while attacking and name calling news personalities.

Stance	Marginal Class % of Hate Speech
Favour	2.92%
Against	2.2%
Neutral	3.36%

Table 5: Distribution of hate speech across stance

Table 6 gives the distribution of aggression categories (*covert / overt / non*) across stance. It is interesting to note the comparisons for overt vs. covert aggression when in favour (majority population stance in this sample) as opposed to against (minority population in this sample) on the issue. Although covert aggression evidence is always more than overt aggression evidence across stance categories, the difference is much lesser for *favourable* stance samples. It is not difficult to hypothesise that holding a majority stance on issues will lead to open bullying in a lot of cases. Users in minority tend to be more covert to possibly avoid being bullied by the majority group. Though validating this social hypothesis based on analysis of multiple issues is beyond our current scope.

Table 7 presents the distributions of figurative language use across stance classes. It is evident from the data of *against* issue category, the usage of all types of figurative language is consistently high. It should also be noted that evidence for sarcasm is especially higher in *against* issue opinion (minority stance in this dataset). Keeping in mind the observations on covert aggression when voicing minority stance, it can be noted that covert aggression is expressed through figurative language like sarcasm and puns. Metaphors are not as disguised as sarcasm and

Stance	Aggression	Marginal Class % Aggression
	Overt	8.3%
Against	Covert	40%
	None	**51.7%**
	Overt	17.8%
Favour	Covert	23.8%
	None	**58.3%**
	Overt	8.8%
Neutral	Covert	22.3%
	None	**68.9%**

Table 6: Distribution of aggression across stance

puns and we see that it does not follow the same pattern with respect to stance. The scope of this work is limited to a single issue and it would be interesting to note if these trends are observed across datasets. A dataset of annotations of multiple issues would allow for hypothesis testing to validate these trends.

Finally in table 8, statistics for emotion arousal are presented across stance classes. Opposed to prior analyzed phenomena (hate speech, aggression and figurative language use), the data for emotion arousal is ordinal on a 1 to 5 scale. The average emotion arousal for *favourable* stance (majority class) is much more than that in *against* stance (minority class). Similarly, looking at the very high arousal state bucket of *5* emotion arousal (when all three annotators gave a 5 rating), the percentage for majority stance (favourable) is three times than that for minority stance (against). These findings are in line with the observations for other phenomena like overt aggression and figurative language use in the majority stance. The higher percentage of lowest arousal state tweets when against the issue must also be noted. These lowest arousal tweets correspond to emotions like depression and sadness.

5.   Conclusion and Future Work

This research was motivated by the need to provide a ground-work for analysis of the nuances of opinion on social media with respect to aggression and figurative language use. The observed correlations are encouraging and call for a deeper analysis of these social dynamics. Testing for statistical significance along with corpus-linguistic analysis of informative words for each category was beyond our current scope. The first aim would be to create similar corpora on wide variety of issues (not limited to political debate) to evaluate the consistency of these trends and determine significance of our findings.

Though the scope of this project was limited to corpus creation and analysis of interactions across phenomena, the larger goal is to allow for better classification systems on social media data. An immediate goal is to build baseline models and analyze their performance on the different phenomena annotated in this corpus. It would be interesting to compare performance of models that directly model a single dimension with those models that have cascaded or joint modeling on multiple dimensions. Another avenue we would like to explore is semi-supervised label propagation utilizing both larger corpora on a single dimension such as sarcasm as well as this corpus containing multi-dimensional annotations. Having a single corpus of annotations across dimensions has allowed the possibility to explore transfer learning strategies in classification.

For the sake of keeping this breadth-wise annotation effort manageable, we annotated for a 1001 tweets. We plan to extend this dataset to all 3500 tweets from the original dataset created by Swami et al. (2018b). We further plan to annotate these tweets for named entities as well as 6 emotion classes similar to Vijay et al. (2018).

Stance	Sarcasm / Irony / Rhetorical Question		Pun / Word-play		Metaphor / Simile	
	Raw Count	Marginal Class %	Raw Count	Marginal Class %	Raw Count	Marginal Class %
Against	45	**25%**	30	**16.7%**	35	19.4%
Favour	76	13%	84	14.4%	123	**21.1%**
Neutral	42	17.6%	26	10.9%	31	13%

Table 7: Distribution of figurative language across stance

Stance	Marginal Class %					Emotional Arousal Class Avg.
	1-2	2-3	3-4	4-5	5	
Favour	3.6%	23.67%	49.91%	18.01%	4.8%	3.26
Against	13.3%	26.67%	47.78%	10.56%	1.67%	2.91
Neutral	10.9%	36.97%	44.12%	6.72%	1.3%	2.83

Table 8: Marginal distribution of emotional arousal across stance

6. Bibliographical References

Augenstein, I., Rocktäschel, T., Vlachos, A., and Bontcheva, K. (2016). Stance detection with bidirectional conditional encoding. *arXiv preprint arXiv:1606.05464*.

Badjatiya, P., Gupta, S., Gupta, M., and Varma, V. (2017). Deep learning for hate speech detection in tweets. In *Proceedings of the 26th International Conference on World Wide Web Companion*, pages 759–760.

Bamman, D. and Smith, N. A. (2015). Contextualized sarcasm detection on twitter. In *Ninth International AAAI Conference on Web and Social Media*.

Baron, R. A. and Richardson, D. R. (2004). *Human aggression*. Springer Science & Business Media.

Bohra, A., Vijay, D., Singh, V., Akhtar, S. S., and Shrivastava, M. (2018). A dataset of hindi-english code-mixed social media text for hate speech detection. In *Proceedings of the second workshop on computational modeling of peopleâs opinions, personality, and emotions in social media*, pages 36–41.

Bradley, M. M. and Lang, P. J. (1999). Affective norms for english words (anew): Instruction manual and affective ratings. Technical report, Technical report C-1, the center for research in psychophysiology â.

Burnap, P. and Williams, M. L. (2015). Cyber hate speech on twitter: An application of machine classification and statistical modeling for policy and decision making. *Policy & Internet*, 7(2):223–242.

Culpeper, J. (2011). Impoliteness: Using language to cause offence. *Impoliteness: Using Language to Cause Offence*, pages 1–292, 01.

Davidson, T., Warmsley, D., Macy, M., and Weber, I. (2017). Automated hate speech detection and the problem of offensive language. In *Eleventh international aaai conference on web and social media*.

Gafaranga, J. (2007). 11. code-switching as a conversational strategy. *Handbook of multilingualism and multilingual communication*, 5(279):17.

Ghosh, A., Li, G., Veale, T., Rosso, P., Shutova, E., Barnden, J., and Reyes, A. (2015). Semeval-2015 task 11: Sentiment analysis of figurative language in twitter. In *Proceedings of the 9th International Workshop on Semantic Evaluation (SemEval 2015)*, pages 470–478.

Khandelwal, A., Swami, S., Akhtar, S. S., and Shrivastava, M. (2018). Humor detection in english-hindi code-mixed social media content: Corpus and baseline system. *arXiv preprint arXiv:1806.05513*.

Krejzl, P., Hourová, B., and Steinberger, J. (2017). Stance detection in online discussions. *CoRR*, abs/1701.00504.

Kumar, R., Reganti, A. N., Bhatia, A., and Maheshwari, T. (2018). Aggression-annotated corpus of hindi-english code-mixed data. In *Proceedings of the Eleventh International Conference on Language Resources and Evaluation (LREC 2018)*.

Liu, C., Li, W., Demarest, B., Chen, Y., Couture, S., Dakota, D., Haduong, N., Kaufman, N., Lamont, A., Pancholi, M., et al. (2016). Iucl at semeval-2016 task 6: An ensemble model for stance detection in twitter. In *Proceedings of the 10th International Workshop on Semantic Evaluation (SemEval-2016)*, pages 394–400.

Malmasi, S. and Zampieri, M. (2017). Detecting hate speech in social media. *arXiv preprint arXiv:1712.06427*.

Miller, T., Hempelmann, C., and Gurevych, I. (2017). SemEval-2017 task 7: Detection and interpretation of English puns. In *Proceedings of the 11th International Workshop on Semantic Evaluation (SemEval-2017)*, pages 58–68, Vancouver, Canada, August. Association for Computational Linguistics.

Mohammad, S., Kiritchenko, S., Sobhani, P., Zhu, X., and Cherry, C. (2016). Semeval-2016 task 6: Detecting stance in tweets. In *Proceedings of the 10th International Workshop on Semantic Evaluation (SemEval-2016)*, pages 31–41.

Mohammad, S. M., Sobhani, P., and Kiritchenko, S. (2017). Stance and sentiment in tweets. *ACM Trans. Internet Technol.*, 17(3), June.

Mohammad, S. (2018). Obtaining reliable human ratings of valence, arousal, and dominance for 20,000 english words. In *Proceedings of the 56th Annual Meeting of the Association for Computational Linguistics (Volume 1: Long Papers)*, pages 174–184.

Rosenthal, S., Farra, N., and Nakov, P. (2019). Semeval-

2017 task 4: Sentiment analysis in twitter. *arXiv preprint arXiv:1912.00741*.

Russell, J. A. and Barrett, L. F. (1999). Core affect, proto-typical emotional episodes, and other things called emotion: dissecting the elephant. *Journal of personality and social psychology*, 76(5):805.

Schmidt, A. and Wiegand, M. (2017). A survey on hate speech detection using natural language processing. In *Proceedings of the Fifth International Workshop on Natural Language Processing for Social Media*, pages 1–10.

Shutova, E. and Teufel, S. (2010). Metaphor corpus annotated for source-target domain mappings. In *LREC*, volume 2, pages 2–2.

Swami, S., Khandelwal, A., Singh, V., Akhtar, S. S., and Shrivastava, M. (2018a). A corpus of english-hindi code-mixed tweets for sarcasm detection. *CoRR*, abs/1805.11869.

Swami, S., Khandelwal, A., Singh, V., Akhtar, S. S., and Shrivastava, M. (2018b). An english-hindi code-mixed corpus: Stance annotation and baseline system. *CoRR*, abs/1805.11868.

Vijay, D., Bohra, A., Singh, V., Akhtar, S. S., and Shrivastava, M. (2018). Corpus creation and emotion prediction for hindi-english code-mixed social media text. In *Proceedings of the 2018 Conference of the North American Chapter of the Association for Computational Linguistics: Student Research Workshop*, pages 128–135.

Wallace, B. C., Kertz, L., Charniak, E., et al. (2014). Humans require context to infer ironic intent (so computers probably do, too). In *Proceedings of the 52nd Annual Meeting of the Association for Computational Linguistics (Volume 2: Short Papers)*, pages 512–516.

Zampieri, M., Malmasi, S., Nakov, P., Rosenthal, S., Farra, N., and Kumar, R. (2019a). Predicting the type and target of offensive posts in social media. *arXiv preprint arXiv:1902.09666*.

Zampieri, M., Malmasi, S., Nakov, P., Rosenthal, S., Farra, N., and Kumar, R. (2019b). Semeval-2019 task 6: Identifying and categorizing offensive language in social media (offenseval). In *Proceedings of the 13th International Workshop on Semantic Evaluation*, pages 75–86.

Towards Non-Toxic Landscapes: Automatic Toxic Comment Detection Using DNN

Ashwin Geet D'Sa, Irina Illina, Dominique Fohr

Université de Lorraine, CNRS, Inria, LORIA

F-54000 Nancy, France

Abstract

The spectacular expansion of the Internet has led to the development of a new research problem in the field of natural language processing: automatic toxic comment detection, since many countries prohibit hate speech in public media. There is no clear and formal definition of hate, offensive, toxic and abusive speeches. In this article, we put all these terms under the umbrella of "toxic speech". The contribution of this paper is the design of binary classification and regression-based approaches aiming to predict whether a comment is toxic or not. We compare different unsupervised word representations and different DNN based classifiers. Moreover, we study the robustness of the proposed approaches to adversarial attacks by adding one (healthy or toxic) word. We evaluate the proposed methodology on the English Wikipedia Detox corpus. Our experiments show that using BERT fine-tuning outperforms feature-based BERT, Mikolov's and fastText representations with different DNN classifiers.

Keywords: hate speech detection, word embeddings, deep neural networks

1. Introduction

The past few years have seen a tremendous rise in the usage of Internet and social networks. Unfortunately, the dark side of this growth is an increase in toxic speech. Toxic speech is a type of offensive communication mechanism. Toxic speech can target different societal characteristics such as gender, religion, race, disability, etc. (Delgado and Stefancic, 2014) and reflects a certain "state of society". There is no uniform definition of toxic speech in the scientific literature and there is no clear distinction between *hate, offensive, toxic and abusive speech* (Gröndahl *et al.*, 2018; Waseem *et al.*, 2017; Davidson *et al.*, 2017). We refer to these collectively with the generic term of *toxic* speech.

Manually monitoring and moderating the Internet and social media content to identify and remove toxic speech is extremely expensive. This article aims at designing methods for automatic toxic speech detection on the Internet. Despite the studies already published on this subject, the results show that the task remains very difficult (Nobata *et al.*, 2016; Saleem *et al.*, 2017). In this paper, we use semantic content analysis methodologies from *Natural Language Processing* (NLP) and methodologies based on *Deep Neural Networks* (DNN).

Very recently, DNNs have become the state-of-the-art method for toxic speech detection. Badjatiya *et al.* (2017) investigated the application of DNNs for hate speech detection and compared it with various classical features like character n-grams, Term Frequency-Inverse Document Frequency (TF-IDF) values, Bag of Word Vectors (BoWV), and Global Vectors for Word Representation (GloVe) (Pennington *et al.*, 2014). They found DNN methods to significantly outperform the existing shallow methods. Zhang *et al.* (2018) combined Convolutional neural network (CNN) and Recurrent neural network (RNN) by giving the output of CNN to RNN with Gated Recurrent Unit (GRU). Van Aken *et al.* (2018) proposed a combination of shallow models and DNN methods that outperforms all the individual models. Several evaluations of a range of NLP features was performed by Nobata *et al.* (2016). Stammbach *et al.* (2018) reported different pre-processing techniques and their impact on the final classification. Wulczyn *et al.* (2017) went beyond the simple classification task and developed a method that combines crowdsourcing and machine learning to analyse personal attacks.

Currently, one of the most powerful semantic context representations are those obtained from BERT (*Bidirectional Encoder Representations from Transformers*) (Devlin *et al.*, 2019; Young *et al.*, 2018). Compared to Mikolov's embedding (Mikolov *et al.*, 2013), BERT model takes into account large left and right semantic contexts of words and can generate different semantic representations for the same word based on its context. Furthermore, pre-trained BERT model can be *fine-tuned* to a specific NLP task (Peters *et al.*, 2019). The BERT model has resulted into new state-of-the-art for several NLP tasks.

In this article, we investigate several approaches based on different state-of-the-art DNN models and word representations for the task of automatic toxic comment detection. Among the classifiers, we used top performing DNNs in the field of NLP: CNN and RNN. CNN allows the extraction of local features in text, e.g. pertinent sequences of words. RNN is able to extract long-term dependencies that are definitely useful for toxic comment detection (Del Vigna *et al.*, 2017). To take into account the semantic context of the document, we propose to use different representations: Mikolov's, fastText and BERT embeddings. We compare these against transformers based BERT fine-tuning. The designed systems are evaluated on publicly available corpus of toxic comments from Wikipedia. The work of Bodapati *et al.* (2019) compares CNN based and fastText classifiers with various character and word based input representations to BERT fine-tuning. As compared to Bodapati *et al.* (2019), we go beyond binary classification and propose a regression-based method. Furthermore, we analyse the robustness of these approaches with adversarial attacks by adding a toxic or healthy word to the comment. Additionally, we have compared CNN based architecture against RNN based Bi-LSTM and Bi-GRU classifiers. It should be noted that our results of binary classification are not directly comparable to Bodapati *et al.* (2019) due to differences in training and pre-processing setup.

The rest of the paper is organized as follows: Section 2 describes the approaches. The experiment protocol and the data are described in section 3. The classification results are discussed in section 4.

2. Proposed methodology

Figure 1 presents a schema of our proposed methodology along with the different word representations. We first describe the different word representations and then discuss the DNN classifiers that we evaluate. In all our approaches, the DNN outputs represent the toxicity of a comment.

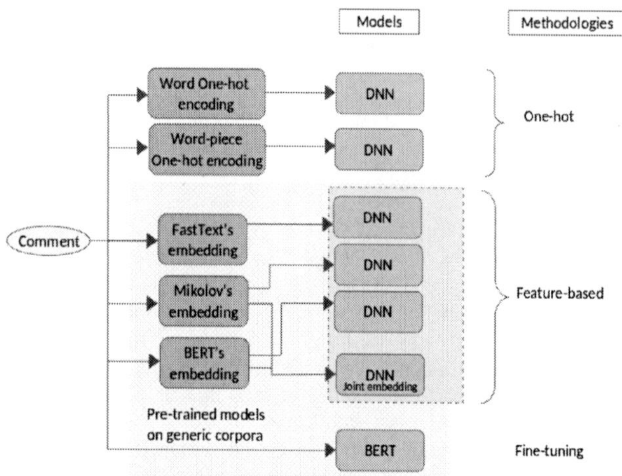

Figure 1: Proposed system architecture for toxic comment detection.

2.1 Comment representations

2.1.1 Baseline approach: one-hot representation

Our baseline is the classical one-hot input representation, wherein each input word is represented by a one-hot vector. Only the N most frequent words of training corpus are selected. The other words are represented as UNK. One-hot vectors are used as input to DNN classifier. The DNN will classify these sequences of one-hot vectors as toxic or non-toxic. The first hidden layer of the DNN computes the word embeddings. The weights of this embedding layer are trained together with the weights of the other layers of the network. The particularity here is that we do not exploit any pre-trained word embeddings and the entire training is performed using only the task specific corpus.

2.1.2 Feature-based approaches

Embedding models entail vector-based word representations which are usually pre-trained on large datasets. In this work, pre-trained word representations are used as features in task-specific DNN architectures. The DNN network classifies these sequences of word embeddings as toxic or non-toxic. We study and compare three state-of-the-art unsupervised word embedding models:

- **Mikolov's word embedding**, which represent each word by taking into account a relatively small window of left and right context words (Mikolov *et al.*, 2013).
- **fastText subword embedding.** It is an extension of Mikolov's embedding, which takes into account subword information and allows us to include rare and out-of-vocabulary words (Bojanowski *et al.*, 2016; Mikolov *et al.*, 2018).
- **BERT WordPiece model (Devlin *et al.*, 2019).** This model takes into account long left and right contexts of words. Thanks to this model, for each comment, embedding of each word-piece can be computed and

used as input for DNN classifier. In the case of BERT model, the same word-piece can have different embeddings depending on the context.

It is important to note that these representations are pre-trained on corpora not specific to our task of toxic comment detection. Hence, will not be efficient to model the specificity of toxic speech (slang, affronts, abuse, etc.).

2.1.3 BERT fine-tuning approach

The principle of fine-tuning consists in starting from a pre-trained model and updating the model parameters on the task specific corpus. As our task of hate speech detection is an NLP task where context plays a critical role, the architecture of BERT will be very appropriate. We take the same BERT pre-trained model as in Section 2.1.2 and we fine-tune this model using our training data. For fine-tuning, the hyper-parameters: batch size, learning rate, and the number of the training epochs are varied.

2.2 DNN classifiers

The task of toxic comment detection can be viewed from two perspectives:

- **A binary classification task:** The neural network is directly trained to decide if a comment is toxic or non-toxic.
- **A regression task:** For each comment we compute a score between 0 and 1 as a normalized average of labels from different annotators. The neural network is trained for predicting these scores (regression task). A threshold on the predicted score can be used to decide if the comment is toxic or not. The threshold is adjusted on the development set to maximize the F1-score.

We investigate three state-of-the-art DNN architectures for our tasks:

- CNN to identify local patterns in the comments;
- bi-directional Long Short-Term Memory (bi-LSTM) to capture long range dependencies in the comments;
- bi-directional Gated Recurrent Unit (bi-GRU), to capture long range dependencies with lesser model parameters;

3. Experimental setup

3.1 Data description

3.1.1 Wikipedia Detox corpus

We used the data collected in the framework of *Wikipedia Detox* project (Wulczyn *et al.*, 2017), including user's talks. In our work we exploited only the **toxicity** part of the corpus. This part contains 160k comments from English Wikipedia talk pages, each labelled by approximately 10 annotators via crowd-sourcing, on a spectrum of how toxic/healthy the comment is with regard to the conversation.

The following toxicity rates are used by annotators: *very toxic, toxic, neither, healthy, very healthy*. According to this label definition, toxic speech corresponds to *very toxic* and *toxic* labels.

For many comments in the Wikipedia Detox corpus, there is a disagreement between annotators. Sometimes, it is difficult to define a dominant label for a comment. To perform the **binary classification** (toxic or not toxic), for each comment, we decided to use the following majority vote labelling:

if   [(# of very toxic and toxic annotations) >
(# of healthy and very healthy annotations)]
and   [(# of very toxic and toxic annotations) > 2]
comment is *toxic*
otherwise comment is *non-toxic*

Some examples of the toxic comments are: *"You are a big fat idiot, stop spamming my userspace", "What the fuck is your problem?", "God damn it fuckers, i am using the god damn sand box"*.

3.1.2   Train, development and test corpus

We used the train/development/test partition provided with the Detox corpus (respectively 96k, 32k, 32k). Training data is used to train our classifiers and to fine-tune the BERT model. Development corpus is used to tune the hyper-parameters. Test corpus is used to evaluate the performance of the system. We compared the classifier predictions in terms of **F1-score.**

3.2   Data pre-processing

For many NLP tasks, training data pre-processing has an important impact on the performance of the system. Moreover, DNN approaches are data-driven. These two factors give a very high importance to the pre-processing.

Detox corpus	Training	Development	Test
# comments	88.9K	32.1K	31.8K
# toxic comments	16.0K	5.6K	5.5K
# non-toxic comments	72.9k	26.5K	26.3K
Corpus size (word count)	4.3M	1.9M	1.9M
# unique words	106K	64K	64K

Table 1: Statistics on *Wikipedia Detox* data after pre-processing. 'K' denotes thousand, 'M' denotes million.

We decided to set the maximum length of a comment to 200 words for reducing the computation time and for avoiding the out-of-memory problems for BERT (because it is a very large model). For this, we keep the first 200 words of each comment of the training, development and test sets. We removed the toxic comments with more than 200 words per comment from the training set because it is possible that the toxic part of the comment is located after the 200th word. We performed this removal only for training. This pre-processing removed about 5% of toxic comments from the training set. Table 1 shows that toxic comments represent only about 17% of all comments. So, our corpus has an unbalanced class distribution.

We converted all words to lowercase and used uncased BERT, fastText and Mikolov's pre-trained models. We removed the punctuations for the Mikolov's, fastText and one-hot approach. We kept the punctuation for the BERT model.

3.3   Embedding models

As Detox corpus is limited in size, we used pre-trained models:

Mikolov's word embedding: provided by *Google*[1] and pre-trained on a wide corpus of 100G words from Google news corpus. Embedding dimension is 300 for 3M words.
fastText subword embedding: provided by *Facebook*[2] and pre-trained on Wikipedia 2017, UMBC webbase and statmt.org news datasets with total 16B tokens. Embedding dimension is 300, the vocabulary is 1M words.
BERT-base WordPiece model: English (uncased) model provided by *Google*, pre-trained on *BookCorpus* and *Wikipedia*, with 12 transformer layers and 12 self-attention heads. The embedding size is 768, the number of WordPieces is 30k (including the punctuations). The total number of parameters is 110 million.
WordPiece BERT model and fastText models succeed to represent all words in our corpus. Mikolov's embedding is a word based model. Some words from our corpus are not included in its vocabulary i.e, *Out-Of-Vocabulary* (OOV) words. Our training set has 86.5k occurrences of OOVs (2%), development set has 45.8k OOV occurrences (2.4%) and the test set has 45.3k (2.4%). To obtain an embedding for these OOV, we compute an average of the embeddings of all the words in the vocabulary.

3.4   DNN model configurations

The evaluated configurations are presented in the following: for one-hot approach we keep the 75K or 100K most frequent words. For CNN based model we explored one or two convolutional layers (filter size between 3 and 5), followed by two dense layers (with 64-256, 16-64 dense units), with or without dropout. For bi-LSTM and bi-GRU, we explored one or two layers (with 50, 128 units), followed by one or two dense layers (with 64-256, 16-64 dense units), with or without dropout. We use L2 regularization and *adam* optimizer. For fine-tuning BERT we used maximum sequence length of 256, batch size of 32, learning rate of $2 \cdot 10^{-5}$ and 2 epochs.

4.   Results and Discussion

4.1   Binary classification

Table 2, part A, shows the results for baseline methods for one-hot approach: using words or using the same word-pieces as in BERT. Part B focuses on pre-trained embeddings for feature-based approaches. Moreover, we concatenate Mikolov's and BERT embeddings together and use it as input features to DNN (indicated as *'Mikolov's+BERT word embedding'* in Table 2). In this model, words split into word-pieces by BERT tokenizer are averaged and concatenated with corresponding Mikolov's word embedding. The embeddings obtained by averaging the word-piece tokens are indicated as *'BERT word embedding'*. For *'Mikolov's+BERT fine-tun. word emb.'* configuration we concatenate Mikolov's and BERT fine-tuned embeddings. The results of Part C are obtained by BERT fine-tuning. For the two parts (A, B), we have experimented with three different classifiers: CNN, bi-LSTM and bi-GRU.

As shown in the table, our proposed methods in part B and C show better performance than the baseline methods in part A. Among the classifiers, bi-LSTM and bi-GRU performs slightly better than the CNN. Mikolov's embedding of part B performs worse than one-hot approach. This can be due to the presence of OOV words: the one-hot approach models N most frequent words of training corpus, while Mikolov's embeddings is trained on non-toxic corpus

---

and it is possible that some important toxic words (slang) of our corpus are missing in the Mikolov's pre-trained model. BERT with words (*BERT word embedding*) slightly underperforms compared to BERT word-piece embeddings. This can be due to some loss of information while averaging the embeddings. BERT embedding performed better than one-hot approach. Joint embedding (*Mikolov's+BERT*) give slightly better performance than BERT embedding alone. The best method is BERT fine-tuning which achieves 78.2% F1-score. Joint embedding *Mikolov's+BERT fine-tuned word embedding* achieves the performance close to BERT fine-tuning. Table 2 exhibits that BERT is effective for both the fine-tuning and feature-based approaches. It is worth noting that the evaluated models have a different numbers of learned parameters: DNN based classifier models have about 1M parameters, whereas BERT fine-tuned model has 110M parameters. BERT embedding is a good trade-off between performance and number of model parameters.

	CNN	bi-LSTM	bi-GRU
A. One-hot approaches			
Word-based	72.9	74.2	73.9
Word-piece based	73.1	74.1	74.4
B. Feature-based approaches			
Mikolov's embedding	70.6	72.7	72.0
fastText embedding	73.3	74.1	74.8
BERT embedding	75.0	75.6	75.7
BERT word embedding	74.2	75.4	75.5
Mikolov's+BERT word emb.	75.9	76.1	76.3
Mikolov's+BERT fine-tun. word emb.	78.0	78.0	78.0
C. BERT fine-tuning			
BERT fine-tuning		**78.2**	

Table 2: Binary classification F1-score for different classifiers and different input representations.

A preliminary error analysis shows that sometimes non-toxic speech can be misclassified as toxic speech in the presence of words like *bullies, anti-semitism*. For example, the comment *"You're a nice guy Irishpunktom. It takes guts to speak against bullies."* is misclassified as toxic. Likewise, toxic speech is misclassified as non-toxic speech due to sarcasm, irony, rhetoric question, etc. For example, *"Thats fine. Thank your extreme rudeness. That front page looks so unwelcoming."* is misclassified as non-toxic.

4.2 Classification using regression model

These experiments compare the performances based on the regression model. A threshold is applied to the regression score to decide if the comment is toxic or not. We use bi-LSTM classifier as it gives the best performance according to Table 2.

We observe that BERT model is more powerful than other models. As for binary classification, BERT fine-tuning gives the best results. Mikolov's+BERT word embedding shows the results close to BERT fine-tuning. We obtained the following results in terms of RMSE (*Root Mean Square Error*) and MAE (*Mean Absolute Error*):

Word-based one-hot	0.065	and	0.050;
Word-piece based one-hot	0.065	and	0.050;
Mikolov's	0.066	and	0.049;
fastText	0.062	and	0.047;
BERT	0.062	and	0.047;
Mikolov's+BERT word emb.	0.06	and	0.047;
BERT fine-tuning	0.06	and	0.047.

These measures further confirm our conclusions.

4.3 Robustness evaluation

In order to evaluate the robustness of our classification systems, we added a toxic word ('*fuck*') to each comment of the test set and a healthy word ('*love*') to each comment of the test set. Table 4 shows the percentage of correctly classified comments that change from predicted *non-toxic* to *toxic* comments when a toxic word is appended, and from *toxic* to *non-toxic* when a healthy word is appended. In these experiments, we use bi-LSTM (the best DNN according to Table 2) and the threshold of 0.6 with the regression model. We perform the tests only on feature-based models.

A. *One-hot approaches*	
Word-based	72.9
Word-piece based	74.1
B. *Feature-based approaches*	
Mikolov's embedding	74.1
fastText embedding	75.7
BERT embedding	76.2
Mikolov's+BERT fine-tun. word emb.	77.7
C. *BERT fine-tuning*	
BERT fine-tuning	**78.0**

Table 3: F1-score for Bi-LSTM classifier and different input representations using a threshold on regression model.

	Binary classification			Regression model		
	Mikolov	*fast Text*	*BERT*	*Mikolov*	*fast Text*	*BERT*
non-toxic to toxic	88.0	78.1	37.5	71.9	78.0	**34.1**
toxic to non-toxic	6.5	4.8	**4.1**	10.9	10.0	7.6

Table 4: Percentage of correctly classified comments, a new word is appended. Bi-LSTM and different models.

We observe that all models are susceptible to the word appending attacks, as also observed in (Gröndahl *et al.*, 2018). Classifiers using Mikolov's and fastText embeddings are more sensitive to appending of a single word. Classifier using BERT embedding is more robust.

5. Conclusion

In this article, we have investigated several approaches for toxic comment classification using DNNs. We explored feature-based unsupervised comment representations using Mikolov's, fastText and BERT pre-trained models. These representations are used as input for DNN networks. These approaches are compared to the BERT fine-tuning. We designed binary classification and regression-based approaches. On Wikipedia Detox corpus, our analysis has shown that BERT fine-tuning is the most efficient at this task. Moreover, BERT embedding is the most robust to word attacks. Among DNN based classifiers, bi-LSTM performs better than CNN and bi-GRU at classifying toxic speech.

In the future, we would like to study the impact of data bias on toxic speech detection (Wiegand *et al.*, 2019) and to perform depth study of the multi-class classification (Vaswani *et al.*, 2017). A detailed error analysis to evaluate the linguistic phenomena will also be performed. Moreover, models like XLNet pre-trained model (Yang *et al.*, 2019) or ULMFiT pre-trained language model (Howard and Ruder, 2018) can be studied.

6. Acknowledgements

This work was funded by the M-PHASIS project supported by the French National Research Agency (ANR) and German National Research Agency (DFG) under contract ANR-18-FRAL-0005.

7. References

Aken van, B., Risch, J., Krestel, R., and Löser, A. (2018). Challenges for Toxic Comment Classification: An In-Depth Error Analysis. *In Proceedings of the 2nd Workshop on Abusive Language Online (ALW2)*, pp. 33-42.

Badjatiya, P., Gupta, S., Gupta, M., and Varma, V. (2017). Deep Learning for Hate Speech Detection in Tweets. *In Proceedings of the 26th International Conference on World Wide Web Companion*, pp. 759-760.

Bodapati, S., Gella, S., Bhattacharjee, K., and Al-Onaizan, Y. (2019). Neural Word Decomposition Models for Abusive Language Detection. *In Proceedings of the Third Workshop on Abusive Language Online*, pp. 135-145.

Bojanowski, P., Grave, É., Joulin, A., and Mikolov, T. (2017). Enriching Word Vectors with Subword Information. *Transactions of the Association for Computational Linguistics*, 5, 135-146.

Davidson, T., Warmsley, D., Macy, M., and Weber, I. (2017). Automated Hate Speech Detection and the Problem of Offensive Language. *In Proceedings of the Eleventh International AAAI Conference on Web and Social Media.*

Del Vigna, F., Cimino, A., Dell'Orletta, F., Petrocchi, M., and Tesconi, M. (2017). Hate me, Hate me not: Hate Speech Detection on Facebook. *In Proceedings of the First Italian Conference on Cybersecurity (ITASEC17)*, pp. 86-95.

Delgado, R., and Stefancic, J. (2014). Hate Speech in Cyberspace. *Wake Forest L. Rev.*, 49, 319.

Devlin, J., Chang, M. W., Lee, K., and Toutanova, K. (2019). BERT: Pre-training of Deep Bidirectional Transformers for Language Understanding. *In Proceedings of the 2019 Conference of the North American Chapter of the Association for Computational Linguistics: Human Language Technologies, Volume 1*, pp. 4171-4186.

Gröndahl, T., Pajola, L., Juuti, M., Conti, M., and Asokan, N. (2018). All You Need is" Love" Evading Hate Speech Detection. *In Proceedings of the 11th ACM Workshop on Artificial Intelligence and Security*, pp. 2-12.

Howard, J., and Ruder, S. (2018). Universal Language Model Fine-tuning for Text Classification. *In Proceedings of the 56th Annual Meeting of the Association for Computational Linguistics, Volume 1: Long Papers*, pp. 328-339.

Liu, X., He, P., Chen, W., and Gao, J. (2019). Multi-Task Deep Neural Networks for Natural Language Understanding. *In Proceedings of the 57th Annual Meeting of the Association for Computational Linguistics*, pp. 4487-4496.

Mikolov, T., Grave, É., Bojanowski, P., Puhrsch, C., and Joulin, A. (2018). Advances in Pre-Training Distributed Word Representations. *In Proceedings of the Eleventh International Conference on Language Resources and Evaluation* (LREC 2018).

Mikolov, T., Sutskever, I., Chen, K., Corrado, G. S., and Dean, J. (2013). Distributed Representations of Words and Phrases and their Compositionality. *In Proceedings of the Advances in Neural Information Processing Systems*, pp. 3111-3119.

Nobata, C., Tetreault, J., Thomas, A., Mehdad, Y., and Chang, Y. (2016). Abusive Language Detection in Online User Content. *In Proceedings of the 25th International Conference on World Wide Web*, pp. 145-153.

Pennington, J., Socher, R., and Manning, C. D. (2014). Glove: Global Vectors for Word Representation. *In Proceedings of the 2014 Conference on Empirical Methods in Natural Language Processing (EMNLP)*, pp. 1532-1543.

Peters, M. E., Ruder, S., and Smith, N. A. (2019). To Tune or Not to Tune? Adapting Pretrained Representations to Diverse Tasks. *In Proceedings of the 4th Workshop on Representation Learning for NLP (RepL4NLP-2019)*, pp. 7-14.

Saleem, H. M., Dillon, K. P., Benesch, S., and Ruths, D. (2017). A Web of Hate: Tackling Hateful Speech in Online Social Spaces. *arXiv preprint arXiv:1709.10159.*

Stammbach, D., Zahraei, A., Stadnikova, P., and Klakow, D. (2018). Offensive Language Detection with Neural Networks for Germeval Task 2018. *In Proceedings of the 14th Conference on Natural Language Processing, 2018,* p. 58.

Vaswani, A., Shazeer, N., Parmar, N., Uszkoreit, J., Jones, L., Gomez, A. N., and Polosukhin, I. (2017). Attention is all you need. *In Proceedings of the Advances in Neural Information Proc. Systems.*

Waseem, Z., Davidson, T., Warmsley, D., & Weber, I. (2017). Understanding Abuse: A Typology of Abusive Language Detection Subtasks. *In Proceedings of the First Workshop on Abusive Language Online*, pp. 78-84.

Wiegand, M., Ruppenhofer, J., and Kleinbauer, T. (2019). Detection of Abusive Language: the Problem of Biased Datasets. *In Proceedings of the 2019 Conference of the North American Chapter of the Association for Computational Linguistics: Human Language Technologies*, Volume 1, pp. 602-608.

Wulczyn, E., Thain, N., and Dixon, L. (2017). Ex machina: Personal attacks seen at scale. *In Proceedings of the 26th International Conference on World Wide Web*, pp. 1391-1399.

Yang, Z., Dai, Z., Yang, Y., Carbonell, J., Salakhutdinov, R., and Le, Q. (2019). XLNET: Generalized Autoregressive Pretraining for Language Understanding. *In Proceedings of the Advances in Neural Information Processing Systems*, pp. 5754-5764.

Young, T., Hazarika, D., Poria, S., and Cambria, E. (2018). Recent Trends in Deep Learning based Natural Language Processing. IEEE *Computational Intelligence Magazine*, 13(3), pp. 55-75.

Zhang, Z., Robinson, D., and Tepper, J. (2018, June). Detecting Hate Speech on Twitter using a Convolution-GRU based Deep Neural Network. *In Proceedings of the European Semantic Web Conf.*, pp.745-760. Springer, Cham.

Proceedings of the Second Workshop on Trolling, Aggression and Cyberbullying, pages 26–31
Language Resources and Evaluation Conference (LREC 2020), Marseille, 11–16 May 2020
© European Language Resources Association (ELRA), licensed under CC-BY-NC

Aggression Identification in Social Media: a Transfer Learning Based Approach

Faneva Ramiandrisoa[1,2]**, Josiane Mothe**[1]
[1]IRIT, Université de Toulouse, France
[2] Université d'Antananarivo
{faneva.ramiandrisoa, josiane.mothe}@irit.fr

Abstract

The way people communicate have changed in many ways with the outbreak of social media. One of the aspects of social media is the ability for their information producers to hide, fully or partially, their identity during a discussion; leading to cyber-aggression and interpersonal aggression. Automatically monitoring user-generated content in order to help moderating it is thus a very hot topic. In this paper, we propose to use the transformer based language model BERT (*Bidirectional Encoder Representation from Transformer*) (Devlin et al., 2019) to identify aggressive content. Our model is also used to predict the level of aggressiveness. The evaluation part of this paper is based on the dataset provided by the TRAC shared task (Kumar et al., 2018a). When compared to the other participants of this shared task, our model achieved the third best performance according to the weighted F1 measure on both Facebook and Twitter collections.

Keywords: Information systems, Information retrieval, Social media, Cyber-agression, TRAC Trolling, Aggression and Cyber-bulling

1.   Introduction

Over the years, social media has become one of the key ways people communicate and share opinions (Pelicon et al., 2019). These platforms such as Twitter or WhatsApp, have changed the way people communicate (Décieux et al., 2019). Indeed, the ability to fully or partially hide their identity leads people to publish things that they probably would never say to someone face to face (Pelicon et al., 2019). Several studies have observed the proliferation of abusive language and increase of aggressive and potentially harmful contents on social media (Zhu et al., 2019). Although most of the forms of abusive language are not criminal, they can lead to a deterioration of public discourse and opinions, which can in turn generate a more radicalized society (Pelicon et al., 2019).

Some studies focus on the automatic detection of abusive language as a first step. Different types of abusive content detection have been defined and studied such as hate speech (Warner and Hirschberg, 2012), cyberbulling (Dadvar et al., 2013), aggression (Kumar et al., 2018a).

In parallel, different evaluation forums propose shared tasks to foster the development of systems to help abusive language detection. Among them, we can cite: TRAC (Kumar et al., 2018a), GermEval (Struß et al., 2019) and SemEval-2019 Task 6 (Zampieri et al., 2019).

The objective of SemEval-2019 Task 6 and GermEval is to detect offensive language in tweets, respectively in English and German. To solve these shared tasks, participants heavily rely on deep learning approaches as well as transfer learning using the transformer based language model BERT (Devlin et al., 2019); with good success (Struß et al., 2019; Zampieri et al., 2019).

As for the TRAC shared task, the objective is to detect aggression in Facebook and Twitter posts and comments. Deep learning approaches are also widely used in this shared task and achieved the best performance (Kumar et al., 2018a). However, no participant used transfer learn-ing based on BERT model while this model achieved good performance on offensive language detection and on a wide range of Natural Language Processing (NLP) tasks. Indeed, BERT model broke several records for how well models can handle language-based tasks. Moreover, to the best of our knowledge, the BERT model has never been used on the TRAC dataset in the literature. This statement motivated us to conduce this work and evaluate a BERT model approach on the TRAC task.

In this paper, we proposed a model that uses transfer learn-ing technique based on the on BERT model to address the problem of aggression identification on Facebook and Twit-ter content (more details in Section 3.). We evaluate the model on the dataset provided by the TRAC shared task. We also compare our model with the ones of the partic-ipants to the shared task. For this, we adopted the same rules as during the shared task (Kumar et al., 2018a).

The rest of this paper is organized as follows: Section 2. presents related work in the area of offensive detection and different existing shared tasks in this domain; Section 3. describes the methodology we propose for aggression de-tection; Section 4. describes in detail the TRAC dataset and evaluation measures we use for evaluation; Section 5. presents the results and discusses them; finally, Section 6. concludes this paper and presents some future work.

2.   Related Work

Recent overviews of related work on the detection of abu-sive language are presented in (Schmidt and Wiegand, 2017) and (Mishra et al., 2019). (Schmidt and Wiegand, 2017) presents a survey on hate speech detection using Nat-ural Language Processing (NLP). The authors report that supervised learning approaches are predominantly used for this later task. Support vector machines (SVM) and recur-rent neural networks are the most widespread. The authors also report that features are widely used for hate speech detection, such as simple surface features (e.g. bag of words, n-grams, etc.), word generalization (e.g. word embedding, etc.), knowledge-based features (e.g. ontology, etc.), ... (Mishra et al., 2019) report a survey of automated abuse detection methods as well as a detailed overview of datasets that are annotated for abuse. The authors notice that many researchers have exclusively relied on text based features for abuse detection while the recent state of the art approaches rely on word-level Convolutional Neural Networks (CNN) and Recurrent Neural Networks (RNN).

Within shared tasks on abusive language detection, participants heavily use deep learning techniques that achieved good performances. This is the case for GermEval (Struß et al., 2019), SemEval-2019 Task 6 (Zampieri et al., 2019) and TRAC (Kumar et al., 2018a).

GermEval (Struß et al., 2019) is a shared task that focuses on the detection of offensive language on German tweets. During this shared task, the best performing system on the various sub-tasks of the challenge uses the transformer based language model BERT (Devlin et al., 2019), which convinced us to consider BERT in our work as well.

SemEval-2019 Task 6 (Zampieri et al., 2019) is a shared task that focused on identification and classification of offensive language in social media, more precisely on English tweets. During the SemEval-2019 Task 6, the transformer based language model BERT (Devlin et al., 2019) was also widely used and achieved top performances, and even in the case it did not achieve the best performance, overall it performed well.

Finally, TRAC (Kumar et al., 2018a) is a shared task that focuses on aggression identification considering both English and Hindi languages. The objective is to classify texts into three classes: **Non-Aggressive (NAG)**, **Covertly Aggressive (CAG)**, and **Overtly Aggressive (OAG)**. Facebook posts and comments are provided for training and validation, while, for testing, two different sets, one from Facebook and one from Twitter, were provided. The best performance during the shared task was achieved with deep learning approaches whether on Facebook test set or Twitter test set (Kumar et al., 2018a). During this shared task, apart from deep learning approaches, such as CNN + LSTM architecture (Ramiandrisoa, 2020), participants considered classical machine learning methods (e.g. Random Forests) based on features as in (Ramiandrisoa and Mothe, 2018; Arroyo-Fernández et al., 2018; Risch and Krestel, 2018). However, no team used BERT model for aggression detection and according to our knowledge, it was also never used on the TRAC dataset. In this paper, we propose to use this transformer based language model for aggression detection on TRAC dataset since it achieved good results on other shared tasks, specifically on abusive language detection and it has also advanced the state of the art for eleven Natural Language Processing (NLP) tasks (Devlin et al., 2019).

In the next Section, we describe the methodology we adopted as well as the TRAC dataset we used.

3. Methodology

According to related work where the transformer-based language model BERT (Devlin et al., 2019) achieves the top performance on offensive language and hate speech detection, we decided to adopt it for the aggression detection

problem. For best understanding of our model, in this section, we provide first a short description of BERT model before describing our model.

3.1. BERT details

BERT or Bidirectional Encoder Representations from Transformers is a new method of pre-training language representations which obtains state-of-the-art results on a wide range of NLP tasks. Using BERT has two stages : pre-training and fine-tuning.

During pre-training, a deep bidirectional representation is trained on unlabeled data by jointly conditioning on both left and right context in all layers. Pre-training is fairly expensive but fortunately a number of pre-trained models were trained at Google on the same corpus data composed of BooksCorpus (800M words) (Zhu et al., 2015) and English Wikipedia (2,500M words). These pre-trained BERT models are publicly available on github[1], so most of NLP researchers do not need to pre-train their own model from scratch. Two model sizes of pre-trained BERT model are released which are $BERT_{Base}$ and $BERT_{Large}$. The $BERT_{Base}$ model contains 12 layers of size 768, 12 self-attention heads and 110M parameters, while the $BERT_{Large}$ model contains 24 layers of size 1024, 16 self-attention heads and 340M parameters.

Compared to pre-training, fine-tuning is relatively inexpensive. Fine-tuning BERT model consists of consists of adding one additional output layer to the pre-trained model, then train it on labeled data from the downstream task to create a new model. With this method, there is no need of task-specific architecture modifications. In other words, the fine-tuning is a transfer learning of pre-trained BERT model. More details on BERT can be found in (Devlin et al., 2019).

3.2. Model details

In this work, we fine-tuned the $BERT_{Large}$ model since it gives better performance than the $BERT_{Base}$ model in a variety of tasks (Devlin et al., 2019).

As BERT is a pre-trained model, it requires a specific format for the input data. As input, it requires three sequences (of the same length): sequence of token IDs, sequence of mask IDs and sequence of segment IDs. In others words, we should convert all texts in our corpus into triplets of sequences.

In the following, we detail how to transform a given text into a triplet of sequences as illustrated in Figure 1:

1) Break text into sequence of tokens by using the BERT tokenizer. A maximum sequence length is fixed in order to have the same length for all sequences in the corpus. So longer sequences are truncated to the size of maximum sequence length minus two and shorter sequences are padded. In this paper, we set the maximum sequence length to 40 tokens because the maximum length of our preprocessed text is equal to 32 in the training set and 31 in the validation set. In other words, we do not cut any texts during training.

---

2) Add the token "[CLS]" at the beginning of the sequence of tokens and the token "[SEP]" at the end.

3) Convert each token in the sequence of tokens into ID by using also the BERT tokenizer. The result of the conversion is the sequence of token IDs.

4) Pad with 0 the sequence of token IDs with length less than the maximum sequence length fixed in step 1).

5) Build the sequence of mask IDs which is used to indicate which elements in the sequence of token IDs are real tokens and which are padding elements. The mask has 1 for real tokens and 0 for padding tokens. Figure 1 illustrates this process on an example.

6) Build the sequence of segment IDs which contains only 0 as elements because we classify a text. See Figure 1 for an illustrative example.

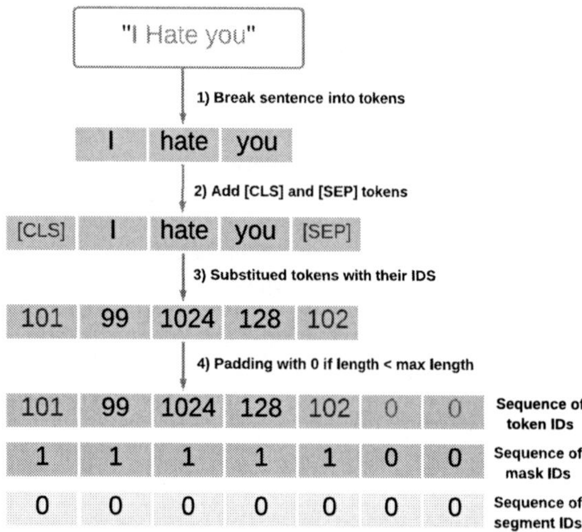

Figure 1: The sequence of token IDs, sequence of mask IDs and sequence of segment IDs from a text. In that illustrative example, the maximum sequence length is fixed to 7.

With regard to the output, a linear layer composed of three nodes is added. This is because there are three classes in the TRAC shared task dataset.

During training, more precisely fine-tuning, we used a batch size of 8, the Adam optimizer with a learning rate of 2e-5 and a number of epochs of 3 as parameters. For the implementation, we used the library pytorch-pretrained-bert[2]. Training was carried out on a Nvidia Geforce GTX 1080TI GPU and took about 39 minutes in total.

In the next sections, we report the evaluation framework and then the results of our fine-tuned BERT model.

---

[2]https://github.com/shehzaadzd/ pytorch-pretrained-BERT, accessed on February, 04th 2020

4.   Evaluation framework

In this section, we detail the dataset we used in this paper to evaluate our model as well as how we preprocessed it for text cleaning; we also present the evaluation measure.

4.1.   Data

4.1.1.   Data Description

The dataset used in this work is the dataset provided for the TRAC shared task (Kumar et al., 2018a) which is a subset of dataset describes in (Kumar et al., 2018b). It consists in English and Hindi randomly sampled Facebook and Twitter comments. In this study, we focused on the English part only, which is detailed in Table 1.

In the dataset, comments are annotated with 3 levels of aggression:

- Non-Aggressive (NAG) : this label is used for data that is generally not intended to be aggressive and mostly used while wishing or supporting individuals or groups.

- Covertly Aggressive (CAG) : this label is used for data that contains hidden aggression and sarcastic negative emotions such as using metaphorical words to attack an individual or a group.

- Overtly Aggressive (OAG) : this label is used for data that contains open and direct aggression such as a direct verbal attack pointed towards any group or individual.

The dataset in the shared task was divided in three sets: training, validation and test. The training and validation sets are used to build models and are only composed of comments from Facebook. Considering English only, the training set is composed of 11,999 comments while the validation set is composed of 3,001 comments.

For the test set, two collections were given: the first is composed of 916 comments crawled from Facebook and the second is composed of 1,257 comments crawled from Twitter. The collection built from Twitter is what the organizers named the *surprise collection* and the idea behind this collection is to test the power of generalization of the developed model. Indeed, the model is trained on Facebook content but tested on both Facebook and Twitter contents.

Number of	Train	Validation	Test	
			Facebook	Twitter
texts	11,999	3,001	916	1,257
OAG	2,708	711	144	361
CAG	4,240	1,057	142	413
NAG	5,051	1,233	630	483

Table 1: Distribution of training, validation and testing data on English TRAC 2018 data collection.

4.1.2.   Preprocessing

In this section, we describe the preprocessing steps we applied on Facebook and Twitter comments in order to clean them before using it to learn the model when training and to evaluate it when testing.

Emoticon substitution : we used the online emoji project on github `https://github.com/carpedm20/emoji` [3] to map the emoticon unicode to substituted phrase. Then we treat the substituted phrase into regular English phrase.

HashTag segmentation : HashTags are commonly used in social media like Twitter, Instagram, Facebook,... In order to detect whether an HashTag contains abusive or offensive words, we used an open source word segmentation available on github `https://github.com/grantjenks/python-wordsegment` [4]. One example would be "#asshole" segmented as "asshole" which is offensive in this case.

Misc. : we converted all texts into lowercase. Also all "URL" is substituted by "http". And Finally, we removed all digit, punctuation, email and non UTF-8 word.

4.2. Evaluation measure

The evaluation metric used in this paper is the same measure as used in the TRAC shared task which is the weighted F1. The weighted F1 is equal to the average of the F1 (given by equation 1) of each class label; it is an weighted average, weighted by the number of instances for each class label.

$$F1 = 2\frac{R * P}{R + P} \tag{1}$$

where $P = \frac{TP}{TP+FP}$ is the precision, $R = \frac{TP}{TP+FN}$ is the recall, TP denotes the true positives, FP the false positives, and FN the false negatives.

5. Results

Table 2 (resp. Table 3) summarizes our results on Facebook (resp. on Twitter) test set. In each table, we can see the three best results from participants in the TRAC workshop and our model which is the fine-tuned of the large pre-trained BERT model.

On Facebook test set, the fine-tuned BERT model (our model) achieves a weighted F1 of 0.627, clearly exceeding the baseline and ranks our model 3rd when compared to the participants of the TRAC shared task.

Systems	Weighted F1
Saroyehun (Aroyehun and Gelbukh, 2018)	**0.642**
EBSI-LIA-UNAM (Arroyo-Fernández et al., 2018)	0.632
BERT-based model (ours)	0.627
DA-LD-Hildesheim (Modha et al., 2018)	0.618

Table 2: Results for the English task on Facebook test set. Bold value is the best performance.

On Twitter test set, the fine-tuned BERT model (our model) achieves a weighted F1 of 0.595, clearly exceeding the baseline and ranks also our model 3rd when compared to TRAC shared task participants.

Systems	Weighted F1
vista.ue (Raiyani et al., 2018)	**0.601**
Julian (Risch and Krestel, 2018)	0.599
BERT-based model (ours)	0.595
saroyehun (Aroyehun and Gelbukh, 2018)	0.592

Table 3: Results for the English task on Twitter test set. Bold value is the best performance.

In view of these results, our model can easily generalize from one social media platform to another one. Indeed, our model is trained on Facebook comments and achieved good performance, the same 3rd rank, when tested on both Facebook and Twitter comments. It is worth noticing that the systems that outperforms ours are not the same on the two collections, showing that there are less stable than ours. The next step is to test our model on other social media content.

5.1. Discussion

Figures 2 and 3 present the confusion matrices of our model on Facebook and Twitter test sets respectively. When analysing the results of our model according to weighted F1 on both test sets, we can see that our model mislabelled several NAG instances with CAG class. In general, our model shows better performance on classes with many training instances compared with classes with less training instances except with CAG class. Our model has some difficulty to identify the CAG class. Indeed, even though the OAG class has the smaller number of instances, the performance on the OAG class is better than on the CAG class which has more instances.

On the Facebook test set, CAG is the class where our model is less performing, with an F1 score of 0.36, followed by OAG class with an F1 score of 0.55 and NAG with 0.71. From the figure 2, we can see that it is hard for our model to distinguish CAG from NAG as it predicts 181 NAG instances as CAG. We can see this also holds between OAG and NAG where our model predicts 74 NAG instances as OAG. This second case may be due to the number of instances in the data set (used to train the model) because we have about 2 times more NAG cases than OAG cases.

On the Twitter test set, the most problematic class to identify was also CAG where our model got an F1 score of 0.38, followed by OAG with an F1 score of 0.66 and NAG with 0.73. Figure 3 shows that not only our model has some difficulty to distinguish CAG from NAG but also has some difficulty to distinguish CAG from OAG.

6. Conclusion and Future Work

This paper details the model we propose to solve aggression detection. It also reports the results we obtained on the TRAC English dataset (Facebook and Twitter based) (Kumar et al., 2018a). For this, we trained a neural network based classifier by fine-tuning the pre-trained BERT$Large$ model.

The evaluation shows that our model is able to detect aggression in social media content and achieves the 3rd best

---

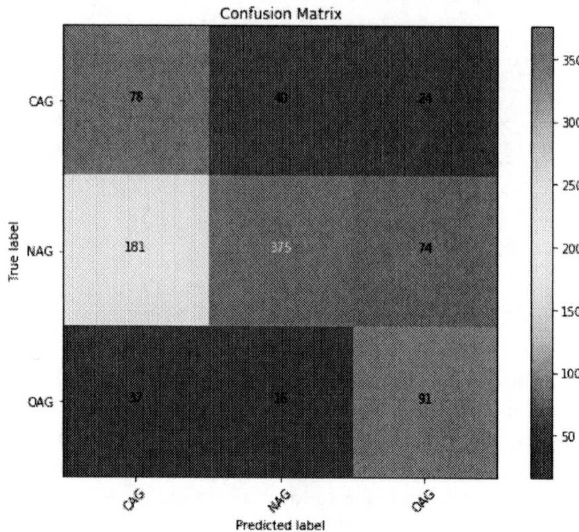

Figure 2: Heatmap of the confusion matrix of our model on Facebook test set.

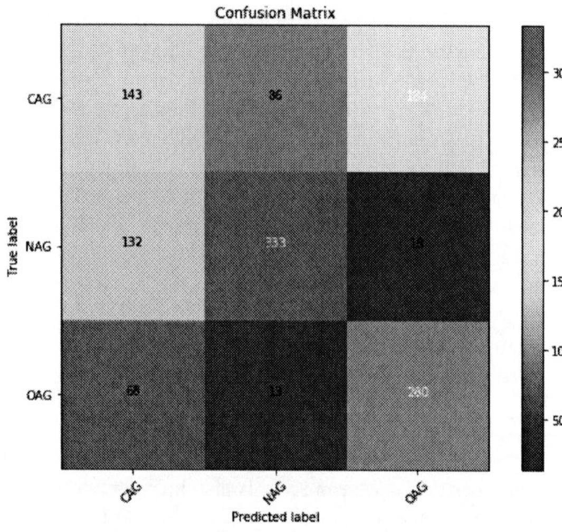

Figure 3: Heatmap of the confusion matrix of our model on Twitter test set.

result both on Facebook and Twitter test sets and this, even if the model is trained on Facebook comments only.

For Future work, we plan to apply our model to the second edition of the TRAC shared task[5]. Also we plan to improve our preporcessing step by enlarging the training set with data augmentation techniques or using external datasets because it has been shown to be effective in (Aroyehun and Gelbukh, 2018). As for information representation, the Information Nutritional Label could be worth investigating as well since it has been shown to be interesting to represent information for various IR tasks (Fuhr et al., 2018; Lespag-

____

[5] https://sites.google.com/view/trac2/home, accessed on February, 04th 2020

nol et al., 2019), possibly combined with a key-phrase representation which is semantically richer than word representation (Mothe et al., 2018). We also plan to test our model on related collections, tasks, and sub-tasks in order to evaluate its robustness.

Ethical issue. While TRAC challenge has its proper ethical policies, detecting aggressive content from user's posts raises ethical issues that are beyond the scope of the paper.

7. Bibliographical References

Aroyehun, S. T. and Gelbukh, A. F. (2018). Aggression detection in social media: Using deep neural networks, data augmentation, and pseudo labeling. In *Proceedings of the First Workshop on Trolling, Aggression and Cyberbullying, TRAC@COLING 2018, Santa Fe, New Mexico, USA, August 25, 2018*, pages 90–97.

Arroyo-Fernández, I., Forest, D., Torres-Moreno, J., Carrasco-Ruiz, M., Legeleux, T., and Joannette, K. (2018). Cyberbullying detection task: the EBSI-LIA-UNAM system (ELU) at coling'18 TRAC-1. In *Proceedings of the First Workshop on Trolling, Aggression and Cyberbullying, TRAC@COLING 2018, Santa Fe, New Mexico, USA, August 25, 2018*, pages 140–149.

Dadvar, M., Trieschnigg, D., Ordelman, R., and de Jong, F. (2013). Improving cyberbullying detection with user context. In *Advances in Information Retrieval - 35th European Conference on IR Research, ECIR 2013, Moscow, Russia, March 24-27, 2013. Proceedings*, pages 693–696.

Décieux, J. P., Heinen, A., and Willems, H. (2019). Social media and its role in friendship-driven interactions among young people: A mixed methods study. *YOUNG*, 27(1):18–31.

Devlin, J., Chang, M., Lee, K., and Toutanova, K. (2019). BERT: pre-training of deep bidirectional transformers for language understanding. In *Proceedings of the 2019 Conference of the North American Chapter of the Association for Computational Linguistics: Human Language Technologies, NAACL-HLT 2019, Minneapolis, MN, USA, June 2-7, 2019, Volume 1 (Long and Short Papers)*, pages 4171–4186.

Fuhr, N., Giachanou, A., Grefenstette, G., Gurevych, I., Hanselowski, A., Jarvelin, K., Jones, R., Liu, Y., Mothe, J., Nejdl, W., et al. (2018). An information nutritional label for online documents. In *ACM SIGIR Forum*, volume 51, pages 46–66. ACM New York, NY, USA.

Kumar, R., Ojha, A. K., Malmasi, S., and Zampieri, M. (2018a). Benchmarking aggression identification in social media. In *Proceedings of the First Workshop on Trolling, Aggression and Cyberbullying, TRAC@COLING 2018, Santa Fe, New Mexico, USA, August 25, 2018*, pages 1–11.

Kumar, R., Reganti, A. N., Bhatia, A., and Maheshwari, T. (2018b). Aggression-annotated corpus of hindi-english code-mixed data. In *Proceedings of the Eleventh International Conference on Language Resources and Evaluation, LREC 2018, Miyazaki, Japan, May 7-12, 2018*.

Lespagnol, C., Mothe, J., and Ullah, M. Z. (2019). Information nutritional label and word embedding to estimate information check-worthiness. In *ACM SIGIR conference on research and development in information retrieval*, pages 941–944.

Mishra, P., Yannakoudakis, H., and Shutova, E. (2019). Tackling online abuse: A survey of automated abuse detection methods. *CoRR*, abs/1908.06024.

Modha, S., Majumder, P., and Mandl, T. (2018). Filtering aggression from the multilingual social media feed. In *Proceedings of the First Workshop on Trolling, Aggression and Cyberbullying, TRAC@COLING 2018, Santa Fe, New Mexico, USA, August 25, 2018*, pages 199–207.

Mothe, J., Ramiandrisoa, F., and Rasolomanana, M. (2018). Automatic keyphrase extraction using graph-based methods. In *Proceedings of the 33rd Annual ACM Symposium on Applied Computing*, pages 728–730.

Pelicon, A., Martinc, M., and Novak, P. K. (2019). Embeddia at semeval-2019 task 6: Detecting hate with neural network and transfer learning approaches. In *Proceedings of the 13th International Workshop on Semantic Evaluation, SemEval@NAACL-HLT 2019, Minneapolis, MN, USA, June 6-7, 2019*, pages 604–610.

Raiyani, K., Gonçalves, T., Quaresma, P., and Nogueira, V. B. (2018). Fully connected neural network with advance preprocessor to identify aggression over facebook and twitter. In *Proceedings of the First Workshop on Trolling, Aggression and Cyberbullying, TRAC@COLING 2018, Santa Fe, New Mexico, USA, August 25, 2018*, pages 28–41.

Ramiandrisoa, F. and Mothe, J. (2018). IRIT at TRAC 2018. In *Workshop on Trolling, Aggression and Cyberbullying, in International Conference of Computational Linguistics (TRAC@COLING 2018), Santa Fe, New Mexico, USA, 25/08/2018*, pages 19–27, http://www.aclweb.org. Association for Computational Linguistics (ACL).

Ramiandrisoa, F. (2020). Aggression Identification in Posts - two machine learning approaches. In *Workshop on Machine Learning for Trend and Weak Signal Detection in Social Networks and Social Media*.

Risch, J. and Krestel, R. (2018). Aggression identification using deep learning and data augmentation. In *Proceedings of the First Workshop on Trolling, Aggression and Cyberbullying, TRAC@COLING 2018, Santa Fe, New Mexico, USA, August 25, 2018*, pages 150–158.

Schmidt, A. and Wiegand, M. (2017). A survey on hate speech detection using natural language processing. In *Proceedings of the Fifth International Workshop on Natural Language Processing for Social Media, SocialNLP@EACL 2017, Valencia, Spain, April 3, 2017*, pages 1–10.

Struß, J. M., Siegel, M., Ruppenhofer, J., Wiegand, M., and Klenner, M. (2019). Overview of germeval task 2, 2019 shared task on the identification of offensive language. In *Proceedings of the 15th Conference on Natural Language Processing, KONVENS 2019, Erlangen, Germany, October 9-11, 2019*.

Warner, W. and Hirschberg, J. (2012). Detecting hate speech on the world wide web. In *Proceedings of the Second Workshop on Language in Social Media*, pages 19–26, Montréal, Canada, June. Association for Computational Linguistics.

Zampieri, M., Malmasi, S., Nakov, P., Rosenthal, S., Farra, N., and Kumar, R. (2019). Semeval-2019 task 6: Identifying and categorizing offensive language in social media (offenseval). In *Proceedings of the 13th International Workshop on Semantic Evaluation, SemEval@NAACL-HLT 2019, Minneapolis, MN, USA, June 6-7, 2019*, pages 75–86.

Zhu, Y., Kiros, R., Zemel, R. S., Salakhutdinov, R., Urtasun, R., Torralba, A., and Fidler, S. (2015). Aligning books and movies: Towards story-like visual explanations by watching movies and reading books. In *2015 IEEE International Conference on Computer Vision, ICCV 2015, Santiago, Chile, December 7-13, 2015*, pages 19–27.

Zhu, J., Tian, Z., and Kübler, S. (2019). UM-IU@LING at SemEval-2019 task 6: Identifying offensive tweets using BERT and SVMs. In *Proceedings of the 13th International Workshop on Semantic Evaluation*, pages 788–795, Minneapolis, Minnesota, USA, June. Association for Computational Linguistics.

Proceedings of the Second Workshop on Trolling, Aggression and Cyberbullying, pages 32–41
Language Resources and Evaluation Conference (LREC 2020), Marseille, 11–16 May 2020
© European Language Resources Association (ELRA), licensed under CC-BY-NC

Multimodal Meme Dataset (MultiOFF) for Identifying Offensive Content in Image and Text

Shardul Suryawanshi, Bharathi Raja Chakravarthi,
Mihael Arcan, Paul Buitelaar
Insight SFI Research Centre for Data Analytics
Data Science Institute, National University of Ireland Galway
{shardul.suryawanshi, bharathi.raja, mihael.arcan, paul.buitelaar}@insight-centre.org

Abstract

A meme is a form of media that spreads an idea or emotion across the internet. As posting meme has become a new form of communication of the web, due to the multimodal nature of memes, postings of hateful memes or related events like trolling, cyberbullying are increasing day by day. Hate speech, offensive content and aggression content detection have been extensively explored in a single modality such as text or image. However, combining two modalities to detect offensive content is still a developing area. Memes make it even more challenging since they express humour and sarcasm in an implicit way, because of which the meme may not be offensive if we only consider the text or the image. Therefore, it is necessary to combine both modalities to identify whether a given meme is offensive or not. Since there was no publicly available dataset for multimodal offensive meme content detection, we leveraged the memes related to the 2016 U.S. presidential election and created the MultiOFF multimodal meme dataset for offensive content detection dataset. We subsequently developed a classifier for this task using the MultiOFF dataset. We use an early fusion technique to combine the image and text modality and compare it with a text- and an image-only baseline to investigate its effectiveness. Our results show improvements in terms of Precision, Recall, and F-Score. The code and dataset for this paper is published in *https://github.com/bharathichezhiyan/ Multimodal-Meme-Classification-Identifying-Offensive-Content-in-Image-and-Text*

Keywords: multimodal data, classification, memes, offensive content, opinion mining

1. Introduction

A meme is "an element of a culture or system of behavior passed from one individual to another by imitation or other non-genetic behaviors"[1]. Memes come in a wide range of types and formats including, but not limited to images, videos, or twitter posts which has an increasing impact on social media communication (French, 2017; Suryawanshi et al., 2020). The most popular form of content corresponds to memes as images containing text in them. Due to the multimodal nature of the meme, it is often difficult to understand the content from a single modality (He et al., 2016). Therefore, it is important to consider both modalities to understand the meaning or intention of the meme. Unfortunately, memes are responsible for spreading hatred in society, because of which there is a requirement to automatically identify memes with offensive content. But due to its multimodal nature, memes which often are the combination of text and image are difficult to regulate by automatic filtering.

Offensive or abusive content on social media can be explicit or implicit (Waseem et al., 2017; Watanabe et al., 2018; Rani et al., 2020) and could be classified as explicitly offensive or abusive if it is unambiguously identified as such. As an example, it might contain racial, homophobic, or other offending slurs. In the case of implicit offensive or abusive content, the actual meaning is often obscured by the use of ambiguous terms, sarcasm, lack of profanity, hateful terms, or other means. As they fall under this criterion, memes can be categorized as implicit offensive content. Hence it is difficult to classify them as offensive for human annotators

as well as for machine learning approaches.

To address the issues with identifying offensive meme, we created the MultiOFF dataset by extending an existing memes dataset on the 2016 U.S. Presidential Election. Details about the data annotation process are explained in Section 4.. We address the classification task through an early fusion deep learning technique that combines the text and image modalities of a meme.

Our contributions are as follows:

I We created the MultiOFF dataset for offensive content detection, consisting of 743 memes which are annotated with an offensive or not-offensive label.

II We used this dataset to implement a multimodal offensive content classifier for memes.

III We addressed issues associated with multimodal classification and data collection for memes.

2. Offensive Content

Offensive content intends to upset or embarrasses people by being rude or insulting (Drakett et al., 2018). Past work on offensive content detection focused on hate speech detection (Schmidt and Wiegand, 2017; Ranjan et al., 2016; Jose et al., 2020), aggression detection (Aroyehun and Gelbukh, 2018), trolling (Mojica de la Vega and Ng, 2018), and cyberbullying (Arroyo-Fernández et al., 2018). In the case of images, offensive content has been studied to detect nudity (Arentz and Olstad, 2004; Kakumanu et al., 2007; Tian et al., 2018), sexually explicit content, objects used to promote violence, and racially inappropriate content (Connie et al., 2018; Gandhi et al., 2019).

---

[1]https://www.lexico.com/en/definition/meme

(a) Example 1

(b) Example 2

Figure 1: Examples of offensive memes from MultiOff dataset.

Due to the multitude of terms and definitions used in literature for offensive content, the SemEval 2019 task categorized offensive text as targeted, untargeted offensive text, if targeted then targeted to a group or an individual Zampieri et al. (2019). Inspired by this, we define an offensive meme as a medium that spreads an idea or emotion which intends to damage the social identity of the target person, community, or lower their prestige.

A meme can be considered as implicitly abusive since it uses a non-offensive sentence in combination with a provoking image or the other way around. The use of an unrelated text often obscures the actual meaning of a derogatory image or the other way around. The obscure nature of the meme resulted in the differences in opinion amongst the annotators, hence we provided multiple examples of offensive memes and non-offensive memes. The examples are shown in Appendix A. In the first example from Figure 1, the meme is attacking a minority as it tries to paint religion in a bad manner. This is noticeable from the visual cues from the image, i.e., attire of the characters in the image. The second example 1 is attacking Hillary (Democratic candidate in 2016 U.S. presidential election) supporters by shaming them. This meme follows similar behavior as the first example as the idea behind the meme is unknown due to obscure text. Nevertheless, the image associated with the text clears this doubt and conveys the idea. To build an automatic offensive detection system, we therefore have to have a good understanding of the textual and visual features of the meme.

3. Related work

The related section covers the work done in identifying offensive content in text and image. It also describes the research done in the area of meme analysis as well as multi-modality.

3.1. Offensive Content in Text

Warner and Hirschberg (2012) model offensive language by developing a Support Vector Machine (SVM) classifier, which takes in features manually derived from the text and classifies if the given text is abusive or not. Djuric et al. (2015) have used n-gram features to classify if the speech is abusive or not. There are many text-based datasets available for aggression identification (Watanabe et al., 2018), hate speech identification (Davidson et al., 2017) and Offensive language detection (Wiegand et al., 2018; Zampieri et al., 2019). Amongst the work mentioned, Watanabe et al. (2018) relies on unigrams and pattern of the text for detecting hate speech. These patterns are carefully crafted manually and then provided to machine learning models for further classification. Wiegand et al. (2018; Zampieri et al. (2019) deals with the classification of hateful tweets in the German language and addresses some of the issues in identifying offensive content. All this research puts more weight on features of single modality i.e. text and manual feature extraction. We work on memes which have more than one modality, i.e. image and text and feature extraction is automatically done with deep learning techniques.

3.2. Offensive Content in Image

Identifying offensive content in an image based on skin detection techniques have been proposed for nudity detection (Arentz and Olstad, 2004; Kakumanu et al., 2007; Tian et al., 2018). Several works proposed convolutional neural networks (CNNs) to identify appropriate or in-appropriate images for children (Connie et al., 2018). The research done by Gandhi et al. (2019) deals with offensive images and non-compliant logos. They developed an offensive and non-compliant image detection algorithm that identifies the offensive content in the image. They have categorized images as offensive if it has nudity, sexually explicit content, objects used to promote violence or racially inappropriate content. The dataset that has been used by authors is being created by finding similar images by comparing the embeddings of the images. The classifier takes advantage of a pre-trained object detector to identify the type of an object in the image. This research heavily relies on object detection. In our research, we are relying on automatically derived features through a pre-trained CNN, which is capable of classifying memes with relatively fewer resources. Hu et al. (2007) proposed a novel framework for classifying pornographic web pages by using both image and text. The authors used a decision tree to divide Web pages into continuous text, the discrete text, and the image. According to content representations, the algorithm fuses the result from the image classifier and the text classifier to detect inappropriate content. They showed that their fusion algorithm outperforms those by individual classifiers. While this work is identifying pornographic content on the web page, it relies on skin detection. Unlike our research, the content that they are trying to identify is less obscure and rather explicit.

3.3. Offensive Content in Memes

He et al. (2016) proposed a meme extraction algorithm that automatically extracts textual features from data posted during events such as the anti-vaccination movement[2]. The process of extraction is done by identifying independent phrases and by clustering the mutation variant of each phrase associated with the meme. This work studies the convergence and peak times of memes. Drakett et al. (2018), in their research, address online harassment of marginalized groups by abusing memes, using thematic analysis of 240 sample memes. This research studies memes from a psycho-linguistic perspective.

3.4. Multimodal Datasets

TUMBLR dataset by (Hu and Flaxman, 2018) is a multi-modal sentiment analysis dataset collected from Tumblr (a microblogging site). This dataset has been loosely labelled on the tags attached to the posts available on Tumblr. Their dataset relies on the tag attached to the social media posts as a label while the MultiOFF dataset used in by us is anno-tated manually. They emphasize more on emotion analysis, unlike our research which gives importance to the detection of offensive content. Duong et al. (2017) proposes differ-ent types of architectural designs that can be used to clas-sify multimodal content. While their research delves into emotion classification based on multimodal data, it does not match with the objective of this research, i.e. binary classi-fication of memes into offensive and non-offensive. Smitha et al. (2018) suggests manual extraction of features from the given meme which can be used to classify them in pos-itive, negative and neutral classes. On one hand, sentences related which belong emotions such as sadness, anger, dis-gust would be classified as negative. On the other hand, the sentences which hint happiness and surprise would be cat-egorized in positive classes and the rest of the memes are treated as neutral. Their dataset is not publicly available. While our work is the first to create a dataset for the memes to detect offensive content using voluntary annotators.

3.5. Summary

Most of the studies mentioned above focus on meme clas-sification on a single modality. The ones that have been dealing with multimodal content rely on machine learning approaches that require handcrafted features derived from the data to classify the observations. Internet memes are in the form of images with text, this adds visual elements to the message. As multimodal approaches that are capable of classification rely on manual feature extraction, the system with automatic feature extraction can be used to provide a generic and robust solution to these difficulties. Deep neural network has the capability of deriving such features with minimal manual intervention, however, an annotated dataset for memes was not publicly available. Recently, a shared task on emotions in memes (Memotion Analysis)

was published in Semeval 2020 (Sharma et al., 2020) while we were creating our dataset. The details of the data collec-tion are not explained in the shared task. However, we are the first one to collect a multimodal offensive meme dataset using voluntary annotators.

4. MultiOFF Dataset

An event such as the 2016 U.S. Presidential Election can be used as a reference to identify offensive content on social media. The initial dataset has been accessed from Kaggle.[3] This dataset has image URLs and the text embedded in the images. The memes have been collected from social media sites, such as Reddit, Facebook, Twitter and Instagram.

4.1. Data Pre-processing

The dataset from Kaggle has many images and may unre-lated features such as a timestamp (date published), link (post URL), author, network, likes or upvotes. Those that did not serve the objective of the research were removed, i.e., only the URL link and text (caption) were used from the existing dataset. The captions contained a lot of un-wanted symbols such as //n or @. As this was hinder-ing the readability of the text, all such symbols were re-moved from the text during the initial data pre-processing step. Furthermore, the observations in the form of long text posts were removed from the dataset and only the one with less than or equal to 20 sentences of text were kept. Each of the image URLs has been verified for its availability and the image has been obtained locally for training the classifiers for offensive content.

4.2. Data Collection and Annotation

We constructed the MultiOFF dataset by manually anno-tating the data into either the offensive or non-offensive category. The annotators, which used Google Forms (Chakravarthi et al., 2019; Chakravarthi et al., 2020b; Chakravarthi et al., 2020a), were given instructions to la-bel if a given meme is offensive or non-offensive based on the image and text associated with it. The guidelines about the annotation task are as follows:

I The reviewer must review the meme as shown in Figure 6a in two categories either offensive or Non-offensive.

II Memes can be deemed offensive if it intends the fol-lowing:

   (a) Personal Attack (Figure 6b)

   (b) Homophobic abuse (Figure 6c)

   (c) Racial abuse (Figure 5a)

   (d) Attack on Minority (Figure 5b)

   (e) Or Non-offensive otherwise (Figure 5c)

III Most of the memes come with an image and caption.

IV The reviewer must understand that images here are acting as context and play an important role in con-veying the intention behind it. So indeed, images or text alone sometimes may not be meaningful.

[2]https://www.msdmanuals.com/professional/pediatrics/childhood-vaccination/anti-vaccination-movement

[3]https://www.kaggle.com/SIZZLE/2016electionmemes

V In case of doubt that if the meme is sarcastic, the benefit of the doubt should be given and it should be labelled as offensive.

VI While annotating the data, annotators should consider the population exposed to the content in the meme overall.

Once pre-processing and annotation guidelines were made, only six male annotators volunteered for the task. To avoid gender bias, efforts were made to balance the gender ration of the annotation task. Finally, eight annotators (six male; two female) agreed to participate in the annotation campaign.

The annotation process has been done in two steps. In the first step, a set of 50 memes has been given to each of the eight annotators. As there was no ground truth defined, the majority of the vote has been considered as the gold standard and the Fleiss' kappa (Fleiss and Cohen, 1973) has been calculated for this majority vote. Initially, the maximum and minimum value of kappa lied in the interval between 0.2 and 0.3, which showed a "fair agreement" between the annotators. After the initial run, we asked the annotators for their feedback on the task. The issues that annotators faced while labelling the data were as follows:

I Annotators had a different interpretation of sarcastic memes. The majority of sarcastic memes had a conflict of opinion between the annotators. Example number two from Figure 1 is one such meme.

II As the annotators were unfamiliar with US politics, they were labelling the memes as offensive simply if their sentiments were hurt.

In an attempt to resolve these issues and concerns raised by the annotators, we updated the annotation guidelines and added **V** and **VI** in the given annotation guideline.

After improving the annotation guidelines, a set of 50 new memes were identified and distributed to each annotator. Similar to the first set of annotations, kappa was calculated, resulting in a "moderate agreement" between the annotators (0.4 and 0.5).

After achieving moderate agreement, we sent all the memes to the annotators. In this phase, each meme was annotated by only one annotator. The response provided by the annotators has been taken as the final ground truth. According to psychology (Gilbert, 2006), gold standards for measuring sentiments can be a reported reaction of the audience on the content and this response can be taken as ground truth. Data annotation in itself is a challenging and emotionally draining task for the annotators as the memes in the dataset do hurt the sentiment and opinions of the annotators. Defining annotation guidelines, analyzing the annotation and overcoming the disagreement is an achievement in itself.

4.3. Dataset Statistics

After the initial data pre-processing 4.1. and data collection 4.2., the newly created dataset has 743 annotated memes. Table 1 shows a summary of the dataset used for training, validating and evaluating our work.

Data	avg#w	avg#s	off	n-off	Total
Train	41	2	187	258	445
Test	47	2	59	90	149
Val	45	2	59	90	149

Table 1: Summary statistics for the meme dataset based on the 2016 U.S. Presidential Election (avg#w: average number of words, avg#s: average number of sentences, off: offensive, and n-off: non-offensive).

Since the number of non-offensive memes is higher than that of offensive ones, we balanced this by using different class weights while training our classifier.

5. Methodology

In this section, we give insights on baselines and multimodal approaches for meme classification on our Multi-OFF dataset. The subsection regarding data transformation gives insights on text and image vectorization. Baselines for text and image elaborates on the baseline models used on each modality. Finally, the multimodal approach summarises the multimodal experiments performed on the MultiOFF dataset.

5.1. Data Transformation

The text in each observation contained stopwords, non-alphanumeric symbols, words with both upper and lower cases were removed and the rest of the text has been lowercased. As a next step, the processed text has been transformed into vector sequences. Text transformation is different for each baseline. For text baseline models (Logistic Regression, Naive Bayes, Deep Neural Network), the text has been transformed into vectors according to the index and count of the word in the local vocabulary. The rest of the classifiers are using GloVe (Pennington et al., 2014) as word embeddings. Images that were locally obtained during the initial data pre-processing were converted into trainable vectors using automatic feature extraction in Convolutional Neural Network (CNN) trained on the ImageNet dataset (Deng et al., 2009).

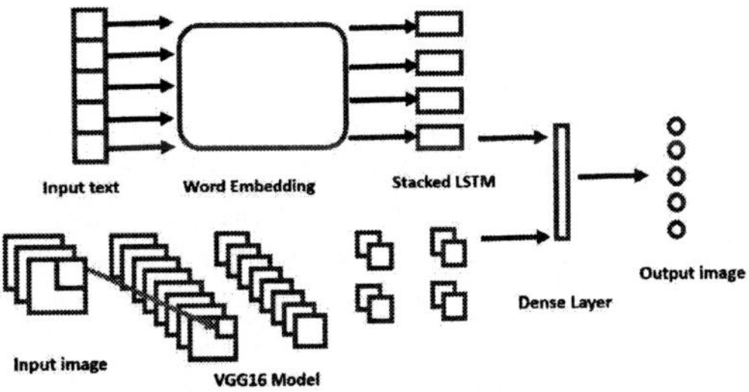

Figure 2: Early fusion model for combining visual and textual data associated with the meme.

5.2. Baseline Models for Textual Data

Logistic regression (LR) and *Naive Bayes* (NB), have been used to classify memes based on the provided textual information for a single modality experiment. The standard bag-of-word approach has been followed. Apart from these machine learning algorithms, a neural network with four layers, a stacked Long Short Term Memory (LSTM) network (Gers, 1999), a Bidirectional LSTM and a CNN have been compared for meme classification based on text.

Logistic regression (LR) used for classification is helpful if the targeted classes in the data are linearly separable (Hosmer Jr et al., 2013). This bag of word approach has been used for creating a text vector x_i. LR works with the basic assumption that the class of the observation and features are in a linear relationship with each other. The probability of the class p is being predicted for the text data which has been classified either *offensive* (p) or *non-offensive* ($1 - p$).

$$\ell = \log_b \frac{p}{1 - p} = \beta_i x_i$$

Where, ℓ is the log-odds, b is the base of the logarithm, and β_i are parameters of the model. If this probability is beyond the threshold then the observation has been set as *offensive*, *non-offensive* otherwise.

Naive Bayes (NB) builds the hypothesis with the assumption that each feature is independent of each other features (McCallum et al., 1998). Eventually, NB calculates the probability of the classes given the text vector. In NB, probabilities of class *offensive* and *non-offensive* class given the text vector have been calculated. Training examples have been labeled as per the conditional probability of the class.

$$p(C_k \mid \mathbf{x}) = \frac{p(C_k)\, p(\mathbf{x} \mid C_k)}{p(\mathbf{x})}$$

Where, C_k is class label, x is a feature vector, $p(C_k)$ is prior probability, $p(x|C_k)$ is likelihood, $p(x)$ is probability of feature or evidence.

A Deep Neural Network (DNN) has been used as the third baseline. A neural network with four layers has been designed to classify the meme based on text. The embedding layer that has been used in this baseline is made from the training vocabulary. The neural network has been trained solely on the training data from scratch and no transfer learning approaches have been used in this baseline. A text vector representation is a count of the word sequence from the vocabulary which is using a local word embedding to represent each word. The embedding layer takes in the input of 100 dimensions and provides embeddings of 50 dimensions. A flatten layer precedes a fully connected layer to ensure that all the embeddings get flatten before sent to fully connected layers. The output of this neural network is "sigmoid" to calculate the probability of the class. Binary cross-entropy loss function and gradient descent are used to tune all the hyperparameters associated with the hidden layer.

Stacked LSTM A bag of word approach of treating each word as a separate unit does not preserve the context of the word. LSTM is a neural network that preserves the context of the term by treating text data as a time sequence. LSTM has been used to extract the text feature. It saves the relevant information from the text which could be used later without facing the issue of vanishing gradient descent. In this approach, two LSTMs are stacked together. A stacked LSTM has the capability of building a higher representation of the data. As the output of an LSTM layer has been fed as input into the other. In the architecture for this baseline, stacked LSTMs are used as feature extractors before the data is being sent to the classification layer. Word embeddings are created using a pre-trained GloVe dataset. The use of pre-trained word embedding leverages the contextual meaning of the word globally.

Bidirectional LSTM (BiLSTM) uses GloVe for word embeddings. Unlike LSTM, BiLSTM saves the past as well as future data sequences to preserve the context of the targeted word. In this architecture, only one BiLSTM has been used. The output of this layer has been connected to the classification layer with a sigmoid activation function which gives out the probability of the offensive class.

CNN approaches are suitable for text as it can be represented in a learnable vector form. As text can be represented in such form, CNN can be relied upon to classify the text data as well. In this baseline, two basic building blocks of CNN are used. The convolutional layer and maxpooling layer with the output of previously connected to the input of the later has been used. Three such convolutional blocks have been used before the classification layer. The flattening layer before the classification layer converts the vector in one dimension for the fully connected dense layer. Finally, the output of this layer has been cascaded to the final layer with sigmoid as a primary choice for activation function.

5.3. Baseline Model for Images

A CNN architecture developed by the Visual Geometry Group (VGG) at the University of Oxford has been used to classify the targeted image data (Simonyan and Zisserman, 2014). This specific architecture has 16 layers and is known as VGG16. The model is pre-trained on the ImageNet dataset and has been used as the baseline in our experiments. Images were loaded into an array and changed into a fixed shape as per VGG16 specifications. All the values in the matrix were in the range between 0 and 255. VGG architecture has two convolution layers both with Relu as an activation function. The output of the activation function has been fed to the max-pooling layer which later has been followed by a fully connected layer which also uses "Relu" (Wang, 2017) as an activation function. Instead of a fully connected layer, a Global Average Pooling layer has been used which later is connected to a Dense layer with the *Sigmoid* activation function to predict class probability.

In **Network Surgery**, all the 16 layers in VGG16 have been frozen by converting all the parameters in the layers as untrainable. This has been done to prevent the pre-trained network again on new data. The top layer in the model i.e. 1000 classes of ImageNet is not required and hence removed.

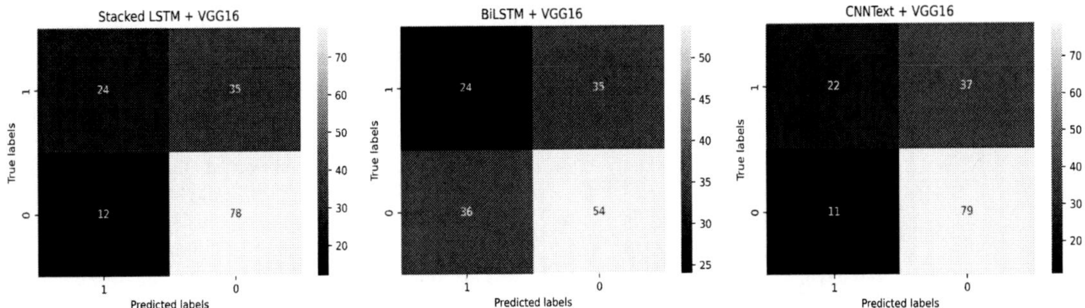

Figure 3: Confusion matrix for Multimodal classifier with Stacked LSTM, BiLSTM and CNN.

Meme			
Text on meme	Donald Trump and his squad look like The Purge 3	So you're against immigration? Splendid! When do you leave?	Hillary Clinton's policies for black Americans summed up in one picture
True Label	Non-offensive	Non-offensive	Offensive
Text Classifier	Non-offensive	offensive	Non-offensive
Image Classifier	Offensive	Non-offensive	Offensive
Stacked LSTM + VGG16	Offensive	Non-offensive	Offensive
BiLSTM + VGG16	Non-offensive	offensive	Non-offensive
CNNText + VGG16	Non-offensive	offensive	Offensive

Figure 4: Predictions from the Stacked LSTM + VGG16 classifier.

5.4. Multimodal Approach

To support our research hypothesis, the text and image classifiers are evaluated individually. Additionally, we combined the modalities (text and image), which is known as the "Early Fusion Approach" (Duong et al., 2017).

As shown in Figure 2 (Hu and Flaxman, 2018), the text and image modalities in their vector form have been fed into the classifier. In this architecture, both modalities are required to classify the offensive content. A new vector has been formed by the concatenation of both modalities which represents a meme as a whole and hence can be used for classification.

The setup for each of the experiment remains the same in the case of training. As the amount of data is insufficient to train a DNN, we take advantage of pre-trained embed-dings. On the one hand, pre-trained VGG16 on the ImageNet dataset has been used for images, while GloVe has been used to represent word embeddings.

Stacked LSTM + VGG16: VGG16 has been used to extract image features. It is a CNN model, pre-trained on the ImageNet dataset. The same Stacked LSTM approach used in the text baseline has been used in the multimodal experiment.

BiLSTM + VGG16: In this experiment, Bi-directional LSTM has been used to vectorise the text, which was combined with the image features. This combination gives rich information about the training example and stands a better chance of getting classified in the correct category.

CNNText + VGG16: In this experimental setting, image features have been carried out by a pre-trained VGG16 net-

Type	Classifier	P	R	F
Text	LR	0.58	0.40	0.48
	NB	0.52	0.45	0.49
	DNN	0.47	0.54	0.50
	Stacked LSTM	0.39	0.42	0.40
	BiLSTM	0.42	0.23	0.30
	CNN	0.39	0.84	0.54
Image	VGG16	0.41	0.16	0.24
Multi	Stacked LSTM + VGG16	0.40	0.66	0.50
	BiLSTM + VGG16	0.40	0.44	0.41
	CNNText + VGG16	0.38	0.67	0.48

Table 2: Precision, recall and F1-score for the baseline and multimodal classifiers.

work on the ImageNet dataset and textual features have been extracted by using a CNN model. These features are concatenated and fed as input to a stacked LSTM model. The output of the LSTM model is connected to the dense layer which then is combined with the image features to represent the meme. The CNNText+ VGG16 approach leverages the CNN architecture text as used in the baselines above.

6.   Results and Discussion

The set of 743 memes has been randomly split into train, validation and test dataset. Table 1 shows the data statistics. All approaches mentioned in the previous section are applied to the text, extracted from the memes, whereby *early fusion approaches* have been used to implement a DNN to combine the two targeted modalities. The Table 2 shows the results of the meme classification experiments. Later on, these baselines, except LR, NB, and DNN, have been extended to build the multimodal classifier that can classify the meme based on textual and visual features of the meme. From Table 2, it is evident that **Logistic regression** performs best in predicting the offensive meme category based on the text. Classification of offensive language with the **CNN on text** provides the highest recall, which highlights its capability of retrieving the offensive meme. On the other hand, the precision of 0.39 shows that many memes are being mislabeled as offensive. **VGG16** generates the lowest recall, which shows that only 0.16 of memes were retrieved from the total pool of offensive memes. According to the same table, DNN on text has a 0.5 F1-score, but it showed an inferior recall value of 0.55 when compared to the recall of Stacked LSTM + VGG16 (0.66). As mentioned earlier, DNN is the only model with local embeddings. Hence it is showing better precision, recall, F1-score than other models. It is showing better results for memes related to this domain but may as well fail in generalising.

It can be seen from the Table 2 that the text classifier based on the Stacked LSTM, BiLSTM and CNN text show improvements in terms of recall when text and image features are considered. The last three entries in Table 2 report the evaluation results for the multimodal classifier. On average, the precision of 0.40 is achieved for all three multimodal approaches. This has been achieved without suffering from a poor recall, as recall for all of them is in a range between 0.44 and 0.67. As a result, a balanced F1-score has been achieved which maintains the inclination of getting more precision without reducing recall. Figure 3 shows an interesting fact about the multimodal classifiers. All the classifiers end up identifying the same number of offensive memes, while the recall of each distinguishes them from each other. An ensemble model could be built by leveraging the strength of multiple classifier to identify the offensive content. Figure 4 shows the predictions of stacked LSTM text classifier, VGG16 image classifier, and their combined multimodal classifiers. In the first example, the true label for the meme is non-offensive, whereby the text classifier predicts it correctly. Differently, the image classifier predicts the same meme as offensive, while the BiLSTM + VGG16 and CNNText + VGG16 classifier correctly labels it as Non-offensive. In the third meme, we can see an offensive content in terms of a child holding a gun to his head. This image in itself can be deemed as offensive but the text associated with it is vaguely Non-offensive if considered alone. The text classifier fails to identify the true label. On the other hand, the image classifier identifies the right label followed by the multimodal classifier.

7.   Conclusions and Future Work

In this work, we implementer an approach on offensive content classification in memes based on images and text associated with it. For this purpose we enriched an existing memes dataset with offensive or non-offensive labels with the help of voluntary annotators. This MultiOFF dataset was the used to train and evaluate a multimodal classification system for detecting offensive memes. Results demonstrate the improvement in retaining offensive content (recall) when both text and image modality associated with the meme was considered.

Although results in Table 2 show that the ability to retain most of the offensive content will be increased by a multimodal classifier, it is still debatable if the accuracy of such a multimodal approach is reliable. As a remedy, manual evaluation by an administrator should be imcluded before blocking offensive content. The result shown by the text classifier shows accuracy close to the multimodal classifier and sometimes better. While the image classifier has a lesser chance of identifying and retaining offensive memes on its own, the multimodal classifier shows improvements in retaining offensive memes. This suggests that there are more chances of improving accuracy by increasing the weight of textual features while combining it with visual elements of the meme. The future direction of this research focuses on the usage of tags associated with social media posts which are treated as the label of the post while collecting the data. This will help us to gather more training data. For this work, we used the 2016 Presidential Election Memes dataset, but to avoid the biases caused due to use of the specific domain, a variety of memes can be included from different domains. The approach of combining modalities can be extended for other multimedia content such as audio and video. Concatenating the image and text embeddings for representing memes could be improved upon by fusing embeddings. As it is hard to explain the abstract features that are responsible for identifying offensive content, the inclusion of more training data will help us to understand it. For automatic evaluation of a meme, we need text as the different modality. This text is often embedded on the meme. Hence to capture the embedded text, we can use OCR techniques.

Acknowledgements

This publication has emanated from research supported in part by a research grant from Science Foundation Ireland (SFI) under Grant Number SFI/12/RC/2289_P2, co-funded by the European Regional Development Fund, as well as by the H2020 project Prêt-à-LLOD under Grant Agreement number 825182.

References

Arentz, W. A. and Olstad, B. (2004). Classifying offensive sites based on image content. *Comput. Vis. Image Underst.*, 94(1-3):295–310, April.

Aroyehun, S. T. and Gelbukh, A. (2018). Aggression detection in social media: Using deep neural networks, data augmentation, and pseudo labeling. In *Proceedings of the First Workshop on Trolling, Aggression and Cyberbullying (TRAC-2018)*, pages 90–97, Santa Fe, New Mexico, USA, August. Association for Computational Linguistics.

Arroyo-Fernández, I., Forest, D., Torres-Moreno, J.-M., Carrasco-Ruiz, M., Legeleux, T., and Joannette, K. (2018). Cyberbullying detection task: the ebsi-lia-unam system (elu) at coling'18 trac-1. In *Proceedings of the First Workshop on Trolling, Aggression and Cyberbullying (TRAC-2018)*, pages 140–149, Santa Fe, New Mexico, USA, August. Association for Computational Linguistics.

Chakravarthi, B. R., Priyadharshini, R., Stearns, B., Jayapal, A., S, S., Arcan, M., Zarrouk, M., and McCrae, J. P. (2019). Multilingual multimodal machine translation for Dravidian languages utilizing phonetic transcription. In *Proceedings of the 2nd Workshop on Technologies for MT of Low Resource Languages*, pages 56–63, Dublin, Ireland, August. European Association for Machine Translation.

Chakravarthi, B. R., Jose, N., Suryawanshi, S., Sherly, E., and McCrae, J. P. (2020a). A sentiment analysis dataset for code-mixed Malayalam-English. In *Proceedings of the 1st Joint Workshop of SLTU (Spoken Language Technologies for Under-resourced languages) and CCURL (Collaboration and Computing for Under-Resourced Languages) (SLTU-CCURL 2020)*, Marseille, France, May. European Language Resources Association (ELRA).

Chakravarthi, B. R., Muralidaran, V., Priyadharshini, R., and McCrae, J. P. (2020b). Corpus creation for sentiment analysis in code-mixed Tamil-English text. In *Proceedings of the 1st Joint Workshop of SLTU (Spoken Language Technologies for Under-resourced languages) and CCURL (Collaboration and Computing for Under-Resourced Languages) (SLTU-CCURL 2020)*, Marseille, France, May. European Language Resources Association (ELRA).

Connie, T., Al-Shabi, M., and Goh, M. (2018). Smart content recognition from images using a mixture of convolutional neural networks. In Kuinam J. Kim, et al., editors, *IT Convergence and Security 2017*, pages 11–18, Singapore. Springer Singapore.

Davidson, T., Warmsley, D., Macy, M., and Weber, I. (2017). Automated hate speech detection and the problem of offensive language. In *Proceedings of the 11th International AAAI Conference on Web and Social Media*, ICWSM '17, pages 512–515.

Deng, J., Dong, W., Socher, R., Li, L.-J., Li, K., and Fei-Fei, L. (2009). Imagenet: A large-scale hierarchical image database. In *2009 IEEE conference on computer vision and pattern recognition*, pages 248–255, Miami, Florida, USA. Ieee.

Djuric, N., Zhou, J., Morris, R., Grbovic, M., Radosavljevic, V., and Bhamidipati, N. (2015). Hate speech detection with comment embeddings. In *Proceedings of the 24th international conference on world wide web*, pages 29–30, New York, NY, USA. ACM.

Drakett, J., Rickett, B., Day, K., and Milnes, K. (2018). Old jokes, new media–online sexism and constructions of gender in internet memes. *Feminism & Psychology*, 28(1):109–127.

Duong, C. T., Lebret, R., and Aberer, K. (2017). Multimodal classification for analysing social media. *ArXiv*, abs/1708.02099.

Fleiss, J. L. and Cohen, J. (1973). The equivalence of weighted kappa and the intraclass correlation coefficient as measures of reliability. *Educational and Psychological Measurement*, 33:613–619, 10.

French, J. H. (2017). Image-based memes as sentiment predictors. In *2017 International Conference on Information Society (i-Society)*, pages 80–85, Dublin, Ireland. IEEE.

Gandhi, S., Kokkula, S., Chaudhuri, A., Magnani, A., Stanley, T., Ahmadi, B., Kandaswamy, V., Ovenc, O., and Mannor, S. (2019). Image matters: Detecting offensive and non-compliant content/logo in product images. *arXiv preprint arXiv:1905.02234*.

Gers, F. (1999). Learning to forget: continual prediction with lstm. *9th International Conference on Artificial Neural Networks: ICANN '99 (Edinburgh, UK)*.

Gilbert, D. T. (2006). *Stumbling on Happiness*. Alfred A. Knopf, New York, New York, United States.

He, S., Zheng, X., Wang, J., Chang, Z., Luo, Y., and Zeng, D. (2016). Meme extraction and tracing in crisis events. In *2016 IEEE Conference on Intelligence and Security Informatics (ISI)*, pages 61–66, Tucson, AZ, USA. IEEE.

Hosmer Jr, D. W., Lemeshow, S., and Sturdivant, R. X. (2013). *Applied logistic regression*, volume 398. John Wiley & Sons.

Hu, A. and Flaxman, S. (2018). Multimodal sentiment analysis to explore the structure of emotions. In *Proceedings of the 24th ACM SIGKDD International Conference on Knowledge Discovery & Data Mining*, pages 350–358, London, UK. ACM.

Hu, W., Wu, O., Chen, Z., Fu, Z., and Maybank, S. (2007). Recognition of pornographic web pages by classifying texts and images. *IEEE Transactions on Pattern Analysis and Machine Intelligence*, 29(6):1019–1034, June.

Jose, N., Chakravarthi, B. R., Suryawanshi, S., Sherly, E., and McCrae, J. P. (2020). A survey of current datasets for code-switching research. In *2020 6th International Conference on Advanced Computing & Communication Systems (ICACCS)*.

Kakumanu, P., Makrogiannis, S., and Bourbakis, N. (2007). A survey of skin-color modeling and detection methods. *Pattern recognition*, 40(3):1106–1122.

McCallum, A., Nigam, K., et al. (1998). A comparison of event models for naive bayes text classification. In *AAAI-98 workshop on learning for text categorization*, volume 752, pages 41–48. Citeseer.

Mojica de la Vega, L. G. and Ng, V. (2018). Modeling trolling in social media conversations. In *Proceedings of the Eleventh International Conference on Language Resources and Evaluation (LREC 2018)*, Miyazaki, Japan, May. European Language Resources Association (ELRA).

Pennington, J., Socher, R., and Manning, C. (2014). Glove: Global vectors for word representation. In *Proceedings of the 2014 conference on empirical methods in natural language processing (EMNLP)*, pages 1532–1543, Doha, Qatar.

Rani, P., Suryawanshi, S., Goswami, K., Chakravarthi, B. R., Fransen, T., and McCrae, J. P. (2020). A comparative study of different state-of-the-art hate speech detection methods for Hindi-English code-mixed data. In *Proceedings of the Second Workshop on Trolling, Aggression and Cyberbullying*, Marseille, France, May. European Language Resources Association (ELRA).

Ranjan, P., Raja, B., Priyadharshini, R., and Balabantaray, R. C. (2016). A comparative study on code-mixed data of Indian social media vs formal text. In *2016 2nd International Conference on Contemporary Computing and Informatics (IC3I)*, pages 608–611, Dec.

Schmidt, A. and Wiegand, M. (2017). A survey on hate speech detection using natural language processing. In *Proceedings of the Fifth International Workshop on Natural Language Processing for Social Media*, pages 1–10, Valencia, Spain, April. Association for Computational Linguistics.

Sharma, C., Paka, Scott, W., Bhageria, D., Das, A., Poria, S., Chakraborty, T., and Gambäck, B. (2020). Task Report: Memotion Analysis 1.0 @SemEval 2020: The Visuo-Lingual Metaphor! In *Proceedings of the 14th International Workshop on Semantic Evaluation (SemEval-2020)*, Barcelona, Spain, Sep. Association for Computational Linguistics.

Simonyan, K. and Zisserman, A. (2014). Very deep convolutional networks for large-scale image recognition. *arXiv preprint arXiv:1409.1556*.

Smitha, E., Sendhilkumar, S., and Mahalaksmi, G. (2018). Meme classification using textual and visual features. In *Computational Vision and Bio Inspired Computing*, pages 1015–1031. Springer.

Suryawanshi, S., Chakravarthi, B. R., Verma, P., Arcan, M., McCrae, J. P., and Buitelaar, P. (2020). A dataset for troll classification of Tamil memes. In *Proceedings of the 5th Workshop on Indian Language Data Resource and Evaluation (WILDRE-5)*, Marseille, France, May. European Language Resources Association (ELRA).

Tian, C., Zhang, X., Wei, W., and Gao, X. (2018). Color pornographic image detection based on color-saliency preserved mixture deformable part model. *Multimedia Tools and Applications*, 77(6):6629–6645, Mar.

Wang, Z. (2017). Temporal-related convolutional-restricted-boltzmann-machine capable of learning relational order via reinforcement learning procedure. *International Journal of Machine Learning and Computing*, 7:1–8, 02.

Warner, W. and Hirschberg, J. (2012). Detecting hate speech on the world wide web. In *Proceedings of the second workshop on language in social media*, pages 19–26, Stroudsburg, PA, USA. Association for Computational Linguistics.

Waseem, Z., Davidson, T., Warmsley, D., and Weber, I. (2017). Understanding abuse: A typology of abusive language detection subtasks. *arXiv preprint arXiv:1705.09899*.

Watanabe, H., Bouazizi, M., and Ohtsuki, T. (2018). Hate speech on twitter: A pragmatic approach to collect hateful and offensive expressions and perform hate speech detection. *IEEE Access*, 6:13825–13835.

Wiegand, M., Siegel, M., and Ruppenhofer, J. (2018). Overview of the germeval 2018 shared task on the identification of offensive language. Proceedings of GermEval 2018, 14th Conference on Natural Language Processing (KONVENS 2018), Vienna, Austria – September 21, 2018, pages 1 – 10. Austrian Academy of Sciences, Vienna, Austria.

Zampieri, M., Malmasi, S., Nakov, P., Rosenthal, S., Farra, N., and Kumar, R. (2019). SemEval-2019 task 6: Identifying and categorizing offensive language in social media (OffensEval). In *Proceedings of the 13th International Workshop on Semantic Evaluation*, pages 75–86, Minneapolis, Minnesota, USA, June. Association for Computational Linguistics.

A Appendix: Examples from Annotation Guidelines

(a) Example of meme intended for Racial abuse

(b) Example of meme intended for attacking minorities

(c) Example of non-offensive meme

Figure 5: Example images

(a) Example of google form

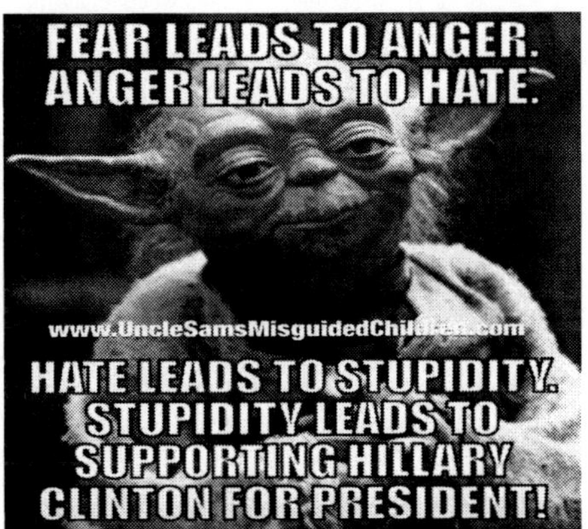

(b) Example of meme intended for personal attack.

(c) Example of meme intended for Homophobic abuse

Figure 6: Example images

Proceedings of the Second Workshop on Trolling, Aggression and Cyberbullying, pages 42–48
Language Resources and Evaluation Conference (LREC 2020), Marseille, 11–16 May 2020
© European Language Resources Association (ELRA), licensed under CC-BY-NC

A Comparative Study of Different State-of-the-Art Hate Speech Detection Methods for Hindi-English Code-Mixed Data

Priya Rani, Shardul Suryawanshi, Koustava Goswami,
Bharathi Raja Chakravarthi, Theodorus Fransen, and John P. McCrae
Insight SFI Research Centre for Data Analytics, Data Science Institute, National University of Ireland Galway
{priya.rani, shardul.suryawanshi, koustava.goswami, bharathi.raja, theodorus.fransen, john.mccrae}@insight-centre.org

Abstract

Hate speech detection in social media communication has become one of the primary concerns to avoid conflicts and curb undesired activities. In an environment where multilingual speakers switch among multiple languages, hate speech detection becomes a challenging task using methods that are designed for monolingual corpora. In our work, we attempt to analyze, detect and provide a comparative study of hate speech in a code-mixed social media text. We also provide a Hindi-English code-mixed data set consisting of Facebook and Twitter posts and comments. Our experiments show that deep learning models trained on this code-mixed corpus perform better.

Keywords: Hate Speech, Code mixing, Convolutional Neural Networks

1. Introduction

Hate speech is a direct or indirect statement targeted towards a person or group of people intended to demean and brutalize another or use derogatory language on the basis of ethnicity, religion, disability, gender or sexual orientation (Schmidt and Wiegand, 2017). Due to the massive rise in user-generated content from social media, hate speech has also steadily increased. Hate speech, targeting a particular individual or group of people, can cause personal trauma, cyberbullying, panic in the society, and discrimination. In response to the growth in the hate content from social media, there has been a large number of works on automatic hate speech detection to alleviate online harassment (Warner and Hirschberg, 2012; Zimmerman et al., 2018; MacAvaney et al., 2019; Ibrohim and Budi, 2019; Nobata et al., 2016).

Code mixing is a phenomenon which occurs when the speaker uses two languages together in the course of a single utterance (Wardhaugh, 1986; Chakravarthi et al., 2018; Chakravarthi et al., 2019). The speaker makes use of the grammar or lexicon from more than one language. It is considered as a natural and common phenomenon in multilingual societies and is reflected in user-generated content on social media (Ranjan et al., 2016; Jose et al., 2020; Priyadharshini et al., 2020; Chakravarthi et al., 2020b; Chakravarthi et al., 2020a). The task of identifying hate speech becomes even more challenging when the content is code-mixed since lexical items, phrases and sentences from different languages may co-exist within a sequence, and computational models are required to recognize and process these simultaneously. Hate Speech is common on social media, and content generated by Indian-language speakers is no exception (Suryawanshi et al., 2020a; Suryawanshi et al., 2020b). It assumes an additional significance due to high internet infiltration and rich linguistic diversity. In addition to this, the use of the Roman script for Indian languages mixed with native scripts is widespread among social networking sites due to difficulty in typing tools and familiarity with English, which adds to the overall complexity of the problem.

While there is some relevant and independent work on code-mixed social media content, few efforts have been made to detect hate speech in Hindi-English code-mixed data. In the light of the gap in this research area, our contributions described in this paper are the following:

- An annotated Hindi-English code-mixed data set containing hate speech. To the best of our knowledge, this is the first Hindi-English code-mixed data set which contains posts/tweets written in both the Roman and the native Devanagari script.

- A comparative study of performance of five different classifiers including machine learning and deep learning on the three different Hindi-English code-mixed data sets.

- An extensive discussion of the micro F1 score of all the trained models for each data set, not provided in the experiments reported on by Bohra et al. (2018).

We have also evaluated the performance of the classifiers and deep learning model on the same data set used by Bohra et al. (2018). The rest of the paper is organized as follows. We explain related works in Section 2. Section 3. presents the details of the data set. Section 4. reports on approaches we used to classify the hate speech content. In Section 5., we present our results accompanied by a detailed error analysis. Section 6. concludes the paper.

2. Related Work

In the digital era of the global world, various areas of research have studied computer-mediated communication from different perspectives. Language usage on social media websites, in emails and in chat rooms has been studied concerning phenomena such as speech acts, code-switching, gender, communalism, politeness and impoliteness. Lots of research has been done on gender and sexuality in hate speech detection, and there has been significant progress over time.

Important early work on hate speech detection was carried out by Spertus (1997), who built a prototype system *Smokey* using a C4.5 decision tree generator to determine feature-based rules that could categorize abusive messages. Since then, hate speech detection has achieved milestones, and several models have been trained to detect hate speech. Yin et al. (2009) were the first to use a supervised learning approach to detect harassment on web 2.0. They classified social media posts using a support-vector machine (SVM) based on local contextual and sentiment features. Malmasi and Zampieri (2017) examined character n-grams, word n-grams and skip-grams to detect hate speech in social media. They trained their classifier on an English data set with three labels and achieved an accuracy of 78%. A Hindi-English code-mixed data set was created to study the problem of hate speech detection in such data. They classified the tweets using character n-grams, word n-grams, punctuation, lexicon and negations features with an SVM and random forest. The best result was obtained by SVM with an accuracy of 71.7% when all the features were used together to detect hate speech (Bohra et al., 2018). A convolution neural network model was proposed by Mathur et al. (2018) to detect offensive tweets in Hindi-English code switched language. Bohra et al. (2018) created a Hindi-English code-mixed data set to study the problem of hate speech detection in such data. The data set contains Twitter data in the Roman script only. They classified the tweets using character n-grams, word n-grams, punctuation, lexicon and negations features with an SVM and random forest. They reported results on the linear classifying approach that uses hand-engineered features. The best result was obtained by SVM with an accuracy of 71.7% when all the features were used together to detect hate speech.

3. Corpus Creation and Annotation

Taking into account the aim of the present study, we chose to use social media data, as this data is best known for code-mixing. The corpus used for the study comes from two of the biggest social networking sites: Facebook and Twitter.

3.1. Corpus collection

Three different data sets have been used for the current study.

- The first data set was collected from Github [1]. Data set-1 consist of 4575 Hindi-English code-mixed annotated tweets in the Roman script only. Tweets were extracted from twitter using the Twitter API. In order to remove the noise from the data set, rigorous pre-processing was carried out, which resulted in the removal of URLs and punctuation, replacing user names and emoticons (Bohra et al., 2018).

- Data set-2 was taken from a Shared Task called HASOC, which was organised at FIRE 2019. It consists of 4665 annotated posts partially collected from Twitter and Facebook. The collection was done with the help of the Twitter API using specific hashtags and keywords which helped in crawling an unbiased data set (Mandl et al., 2019).

- In addition to Data set-1 and Data set-2 set we created a third data set (Data set-3) which has also been used for an aggression detection task (Kumar et al., 2018). This unannotated data set contains 3367 posts and tweets which were annotated by us. The data for the current corpus was crawled from Facebook and Twitter. The data was collected using some of the popular hashtags around such contentious themes as a beef ban, India vs Pakistan cricket matches, election results, opinions on movies, etc., i.e., topics that are typically discussed among Indians and may give rise to hate speech.

Detailed statistics of the three data sets are provided in Table 1.

Data Set	Hate	Not-Hate	Total
DATA SET-1 (Bohra et al., 2018)	2290	2289	4579
DATA SET-2 (HASOC data set)	2419	2246	4665
DATA SET-3 (ours)	478	2889	3367

Table 1: Statistics of the three data sets. Data set-1 contains Posts/Tweets in the Roman script only, Data set-2 has the Posts/Tweets in Devanagari script only and Data set-3 (our data) has Posts/Tweets in both the Roman and the Devanagari script.

3.2. Annotation Guidelines

Annotation is an integral part in the development of any automatic recognition system. Annotated data provides useful quantitative information about the occurrence of certain contextual features. As the first two data sets were already annotated, we carried out annotation only for our data set. The annotation was carried out using a flat tag set described in the annotation guideline[2]. It is used for training and testing the system for automatic hate speech recognition. A simple binary classification method in which we distinguish between hate speech and non-hate speech posts was applied. The two labels use for this categorization are *Hate* and *Not Hate*.

- A post has been marked as hate if the post contains any linguistic behaviour which is intended to target an individual or community and shows dissent using offensive and abusive content. This includes both direct and indirect offensive language as well as threats. Indirect offensive posts are expressed through sarcasm, satire or apparently polite language. Hate speech content also includes offensive reference to one's sexuality and sexual orientation as well as race and religion, i.e., posts targeting a specific community to demean them. Any post in a thread endorsing previously expressed hate speech was also marked as hate (HATE).

[1] https://github.com/deepanshu1995/
HateSpeech-Hindi-English-Code-Mixed-Social-Media-Texts

[2] https://www.dropbox.com/s/
lydv9tt7kh4k01b/Hate%20speech%20annotation%
20guideline%20line.pdf?dl=0

Label	Examples
Hate	Tweets: "rssabvp vhp bajarangdal have no balls whenever bjp came at center laffada bjpvhp rssabvp start voilence in streets colleges hotels pubs as if they have no balls" Translation : RSS ABVP VHP Bajarangda has no balls. Whenever Bjp came to power, there is chaos everywhere. BJP VHP RSS ABVP starts violence in streets, colleges, hotels, and pubs. Tweets : " मर्द की कीमती चीज़ उसकी ज़ुबान होती है सीना तो बहुत से हीजड़ो का भी 56 इंच होता है .. #BHU_लाठीचार्ज #bhu_molestation #BHUProtests" Translation: The most precious thing about a man is his words, not the length of the chest as even a spado has 56" chest.
Not Hate	Tweets: "Lathi Charge in BHU. छात्राओं पर बरसी लाठी.#bhu_molestation #UnsafeBHU #BHULathiCharge #BHUUproar #BHURow " Translation: Lathi Charge in BHU. Female students were beaten by sticks Tweets: "@gurmeetramrahim एक तेरा सहारा मिल जाए रबा दुनिया दी परवाह नहीं करना ।। blessing chahiye bht sari msg dikhani h #blockbustermsg " Translation: If I get your support @gurmeetramrahim than I won't care for anything else, I need your blessing to show the messages.

Figure 1: Examples of the posts/tweets with their labels

- Posts which do not contain any offence or profanity, either covert or overt, and do not target any individual, community or group were marked as non-hate (NOT HATE).

A list of relevant examples illustrating this binary classification is shown in Figure 1.

3.3. Inter-annotator agreement

In order to test the validity of the annotation, an inter-annotator agreement was calculated using Kripendorff's α using Krippendorf 0.32 based on the Thomas Grill implementation[3]. The annotation was completed by six annotators: three male and three female in three different phases. In order to make the annotation process more accessible and user-friendly, 33 Google forms were made which contained the necessary annotator information, annotation scheme and 100 posts in each Google form. In the very first phase, 500 posts were annotated by all the six annotators. An inter-annotator agreement was calculated before the completion of the first annotation phase, after which changes in the annotation guidelines [4] were made since the inter-annotator agreement score was below par for hate speech detection. The second phase of the annotation was conducted with another set of 500 posts/tweets.

While calculating the inter-annotator agreement after the second round of annotation, we found that one of the annotators had difficulty understanding social media language while another annotator was unable to finish the annotation task; consequently, the inter-annotator agreement was very poor. Therefore we eliminated both annotators, which resulted in a much higher agreement score compared to the previous score. After completion of the second round of annotation, a preliminary experiment was done to train the system, followed by a third phase of annotation, conducted on the rest of the tweets. The final inter-annotator agreement was calculated on 4 sets x 3367 posts each. Krippendorff α score turned out to be 0.47, which is quite reliable.

In those cases where annotators did not agree, there was generally not enough context to infer the true meaning and intent of a post. Examples of such posts are given in the next subsection.

3.4. Complicated cases

The results of the inter-annotator experiment after the completion of the first phase of annotation gave very poor agreement among the annotators. One of the main reasons for the poor agreement among the annotators was the annotation guidelines. The initial annotation guidelines were not adequate enough to pinpoint important distinctions between hate speech and non-hate speech and the interpretation of the tags as well as hashtags. Therefore, specific changes were made in the annotation guidelines to continue the second phase of annotation. Secondly, several posts were not very explicit from a pragmatical point of view; hence, each annotator made their own subjective inference about the post. A few instances are being discussed here.

Example 1 and 2 show a strong criticism of the BJP government by the users on specific events that happened recently. Rather than marking these examples as non-hate, one of the annotators felt that these posts are more than mere criticisms; these were perceived as an insult to the current government, i.e., as hate speech, where users are targeting and demeaning a particular political organisation.

(1) *The protest against #bhu_molestation and the way govt is dealing again shows how scared the BJP is of independent movements #BHU*

(2) *Sirf banaras ghumiye mat yaha ke bare me sooche bhi #bhu_molestation*
Translation - Do not think about Banaras just come and take a tour.

Another set of tweets which were difficult to annotate were the ones which consist of one single phrase and hashtags as given in examples 3 and 4. Whether the words in these tweets reflect mere criticism or contain demeaning content

---

[3] https://pypi.org/project/krippendorff/
[4] https://github.com/sharduls007/Hate_speech_detection_Hindi_English_codemixed

Models trained	Data set-1	Data set-2	Data set-3	Combined
SVM	0.62	0.52	0.87	0.64
MNB	0.63	0.66	0.87	0.65
KNN	0.63	0.60	0.87	0.50
DT	0.57	0.65	0.85	0.66
Character-lavel CNN	0.71	0.74	0.82	0.86

Table 2: Accuracy of linear classifiers and character level CNN model trained individually and combined on the three data sets

Models	Data set-1	Data set-2	Data set-3	Combined
SVM	0.38	0.34	0.47	0.39
MNB	0.42	0.64	0.47	0.46
KNN	0.53	0.54	0.53	0.47
DT	0.55	0.61	0.61	0.65
Character-label-CNN	0.67	0.74	0.71	0.74

Table 3: Micro F1 score of the trained linear classifiers and character level CNN model trained individually and combined on the three data sets

and explicitly target some individual or group is not very clear and hence quite subjective.

(3) *landacquisitionbill #landacquisitionordinance !!!*

(4) *abki_bar_ beti_par_war #bhu_molestation*
Translation - Violence against daughters

In order to tackle the difficulty in annotating these cases we redefined the definition of hate speech for our data set. We marked the tweets/posts as hate speech only if they directly or indirectly target an individual, a group or an organisation based on race, religion, caste or gender. Posts which merely criticize such entities are not considered hate speech. We also marked posts/tweets which led to any kind of violence towards any individual, group or organisation as hate speech.

4. Classification Performance

All three data sets were used for the hate/non-hate detection task with traditional machine learning and deep learning algorithms. We conducted the experiments with four different machine learning classifiers, namely a support-vector machine (SVM), K-Nearest Neighbours (KNN), multinomial naïve Bayes (MNB) and a decision tree (DT). Term frequency (TF) weighting was employed as feature.

For the Deep Learning model, we experimented with a character-based Convolution Neural Network (CNN) (Zhang et al., 2015). The idea behind adopting the state-of-the-art model is that Twitter data contains sentences with lots of different characters (e.g., hashtags, emoticons) which are an inherent part of the message being communicated. A character-based CNN model takes all these character sequences into account, pre-empting the need for pre-processing and reducing the need for feature engineering. It was hypothesised that it should give a better understanding of the sentences compared to the linear classifiers in terms of defining classes. Therefore, no feature engineering or pre-processing was carried out. The CNN model is capable of taking all the characters into account to build a character

embedding space. As these posts are short sentences, we have adjusted the number of filters to 128 compare to main paper where 256 filters are used and have kept the filter size as it is which 7*7 with convolution layers, two dense layers which used 1024 neuron and 50% dropout to adjust the overfitting issue keeping in mind that the texts are short text.

Out of the total data in each data set, 20% was set aside as test set and 10% as validation set. The remaining 70% of the data was used to train the models. More extensive experimentation and research were performed using our data set to show problems of the code-mixed text. One of the main challenges while building the model was the class distribution imbalance in data set-3, wherein it contains less hate-speech than non-hate-speech, which was forcing the model for imbalance training. To overcome the issue, we have taken the help of weighted classes where we have calculated the distribution of two classes 'hate-speech' and 'non-hate-speech' over the data. Based on the calculation, a weight of ratio 1:6 was given to the classes, which means the class 'not hate-speech' has six times higher weights of class 'hate speech' while computing the loss function. In this case the loss function will not be only based on the main class distribution data but the loss becomes a weighted average when the weight of each sample is specified by class weights and its corresponding class. Thus weighting the data helped the model to be trained more accurately.

4.1. Results

Overall we see varying performance across the classifier, with some performing much better out-of-sample than others. Every experiment was carried out with each data set once and also on the combined data set. Table 2 describes the accuracy for each data set using SVM, KNN, MNB and DT. The accuracy for Data set 1, 2 and 3 and the Combined data set using the CNN model is 0.71, 0.74, 0.82 and 0.86, respectively. Table 3 shows the micro F1 score of the models trained with the data sets. The F1 scores using the CNN model for Data set 1-3 and the Combined data set are 0.67, 0.74 0.71 and 0.74, respectively. It was found that the character-level CNN model gives a better performance than the other classifiers in all cases. Looking at the micro F1 score of the models, we can observe that the character-level CNN model is quite good with "real" social media data as contained in our data set. When we say "real" data, we mean natural, raw data, not subjected to pre-processing, containing a high level of code-mixing. It was fed into the model with all the stop words, punctuation, emoticons, URLs and hashtags. SVM and MNB perform worst with an identical F1 score of 0.47. KNN performs slightly better with 0.53, while DT is better again with 0.61. The reason behind the poor performance of the classifiers is that these need cleaned data.

Model	Accuracy
(Bohra et al., 2018) (SVM)	0.71
(Bohra et al., 2018) (Random Forest)	0.66
Character-level CNN	0.71

Table 4: A comparison of the accuracy of the Linear approaches in the baseline paper with our Deep learning model for Data set-1.

As mentioned in the previous section, one of the data sets was developed by Bohra et al. (2018). We compared the results of their experiment (which we treat as the baseline) with our CNN model. Table 4 compares the results based on the accuracy obtained by the baseline paper and our CNN model. It is interesting to note that the baseline experiment with the SVM using Character N-Grams, Word N-Grams, Punctuation, Lexicon and Negations as the features obtains the same accuracy as the CNN model which is 0.71, while random forest obtains an accuracy of 0.66. It would have been much easier to compare the performance of the two systems if Bohra et al. (2018) had reported the F1 score of their experiments.

5. Manual Evaluation

To understand the shortcomings of the models and to get a deeper understanding of the problems associated with code-mixed data classification, a manual inspection has been performed on a set of wrongly classified sentences.

(5) *Bhai tu khud **rape** karega to bhi kuch nahi bolenge. Khush?*
Translation - Brother even if you do the rape, we will not say anything. Happy?

(6) *bjp Wale rajyo me **murder** ya rape nahi hote kya...*
Translation - No rape has been done in BJP ruled states.

A possible reason for the fact that example (5) and example (6) were wrongly marked as hate speech is the presence of lexical "rape" and "murder", shown in bold letters; the model might have taken these as a key for a hate-speech utterance.

(7) *Once a chutiya always a chutiya...*
Translation - Once a fucker always a fucker

(8) *Yup and this is a most disturbing part of this. Yaani yaar nobody is going to ask the girl even **rape** ho jaey k aagy uski life kysi guzray gi.*
Translation - Yup and this is a most disturbing part of this. It means even if a girl has been raped; no one is going to ask her how her life will be in future.

The linear classifiers could not classify most of the tweets correctly if the sentence structure is complicated, as shown in example number 7 and 8 where Hindi words are incorporated into the English word order. The case becomes even more complicated when one part of the tweet is represented with English word order and the other with Hindi. The fact that example 7 and 8 were correctly classified by the character-level CNN model shows that the deep learning method performed much better than the linear classifiers. It is likely that since the CNN model classifies the tweets on character basis, the context as well as the linguistic structure is more appropriately captured than in the case of the other classifiers.

(9) *lagta hai ki kiran bedi ki jamanat bi japt ho gayi! #delhidecides*
Translation - It seems that Kiran Bedi's bail was also confiscated

The tweets which were sarcastic, such as the one in example (9), also played an important role as these were mis-classified. The tweets target one of the individuals from a leading political organisation, and as the presence of a targeted entity in an utterance is obligatory in our definition of hate speech, this tweet should have been marked as hate. However, the system marked it as not hate. Other kinds of "indirect hate tweets" were not correctly classified by either the linear classifiers or the CNN model.

(10) *#FallofBJPStarts #bhu_molestation #BHUunsafe @ KPadmaRani1 @ neo_pac @ pankhuripathak @ polysmind*

Moreover, the tweets (see example number 10) which contain only hashtags were classified randomly by linear classifiers. On the other hand, the CNN model marked all theses tweets as not-hate. This is the most interesting and debatable case; even the annotators faced difficulty in annotating tweets of this type due to the lack of the written context, which is necessary to infer the real intention of the users, and agreeing on one tag.

6. Conclusion and Future Work

In this paper, we presented an annotated corpus of Hindi-English code-mixed text, consisting of tweets and the corresponding annotations. We have discussed the development of a hate speech annotated data set of 3.5k tweets and Facebook comments in English-Hindi code-mixed language. We have discussed the annotation scheme that was used to annotate the data set. We believe that the annotation of hate speech or any other cyberbullying task depends on how we define it and is necessary to state our definition clearly to the annotators. This data set could prove to be an invaluable resource for understanding as well as automatically identifying hate speech and other related phenomena like trolling over the web, mainly on social media platforms.

We have also given a description of the supervised systems built using linear classifiers and a character-level CNN model for Hate Speech detection on three different data sets. In contrast to linear methods, the deep learning model was able to capture the syntax and semantics of the hate speech more accurately even in the case of unbalanced and unprocessed data set. Thus, we could observe the fundamental difference in the way linear classifiers like SVM and CNN models learn.

In the future, we plan to apply and experiment with techniques that could successfully cover/identify larger linguistic patterns that our shallow parses currently cannot detect. We also plan to model a system which could be useful for detecting hate speech in closely-related and minority language code-mixed data.

7. Acknowledgment

This publication has emanated from research supported in part by a research grant from Science Foundation Ireland (SFI) under Grant Number SFI/12/RC/2289 (Insight), SFI/12/RC/2289_P2 (Insight_2), & SFI/18/CRT/6223 (CRT-Centre for Research Training in Artficial Intelligence) co-funded by the European Regional Development Fund as well as by the EU H2020 programme under grant agreements 731015 (ELEXIS-European Lexical Infrastructure), 825182 (Prêt-à-LLOD), and Irish Research Council grant IRCLA/2017/129 (CARDAMOM-Comparative Deep Models of Language for Minority and Historical Languages). The authors are grateful to Ajay Bohra and his team for sharing their data set and for their support. We would also like to thank our annotators for their contribution and lending us their precious time.

8. References

Bohra, A., Vijay, D., Singh, V., Akhtar, S. S., and Shrivastava, M. (2018). A dataset of hindi-english code-mixed social media text for hate speech detection. In *Proceedings of the second workshop on computational modeling of people's opinions, personality, and emotions in social media*, pages 36–41.

Chakravarthi, B. R., Arcan, M., and McCrae, J. P. (2018). Improving wordnets for under-resourced languages using machine translation. In *Proceedings of the 9th Global WordNet Conference (GWC 2018)*, page 78.

Chakravarthi, B. R., Priyadharshini, R., Stearns, B., Jayapal, A., S, S., Arcan, M., Zarrouk, M., and McCrae, J. P. (2019). Multilingual multimodal machine translation for Dravidian languages utilizing phonetic transcription. In *Proceedings of the 2nd Workshop on Technologies for MT of Low Resource Languages*, pages 56–63, Dublin, Ireland, August. European Association for Machine Translation.

Chakravarthi, B. R., Jose, N., Suryawanshi, S., Sherly, E., and McCrae, J. P. (2020a). A sentiment analysis dataset for code-mixed Malayalam-English. In *Proceedings of the 1st Joint Workshop of SLTU (Spoken Language Technologies for Under-resourced languages) and CCURL (Collaboration and Computing for Under-Resourced Languages) (SLTU-CCURL 2020)*, Marseille, France, May.

Chakravarthi, B. R., Muralidaran, V., Priyadharshini, R., and McCrae, J. P. (2020b). Corpus creation for sentiment analysis in code-mixed Tamil-English text. In *Proceedings of the 1st Joint Workshop of SLTU (Spoken Language Technologies for Under-resourced languages) and CCURL (Collaboration and Computing for Under-Resourced Languages) (SLTU-CCURL 2020)*, Marseille, France, May. European Language Resources Association (ELRA).

Ibrohim, M. O. and Budi, I. (2019). Multi-label hate speech and abusive language detection in Indonesian twitter. In *Proceedings of the Third Workshop on Abusive Language Online*, pages 46–57, Florence, Italy, August. Association for Computational Linguistics.

Jose, N., Chakravarthi, B. R., Suryawanshi, S., Sherly, E., and McCrae, J. P. (2020). A survey of current datasets for code-switching research. In *2020 6th International Conference on Advanced Computing and Communication Systems (ICACCS)*.

Kumar, R., Reganti, A. N., Bhatia, A., and Maheshwari, T. (2018). Aggression-annotated corpus of hindi-english code-mixed data. *In the Proceedings of the Eleventh International Conference on Language Resources and Evaluation*.

MacAvaney, S., Yao, H.-R., Yang, E., Russell, K., Goharian, N., and Frieder, O. (2019). Hate speech detection: Challenges and solutions. *PLOS ONE*, 14(8):1–16, 08.

Malmasi, S. and Zampieri, M. (2017). Detecting hate speech in social media. In *Proceedings of the International Conference Recent Advances in Natural Language Processing, RANLP 2017*, pages 467–472, Varna, Bulgaria, September. INCOMA Ltd.

Mandl, T., Modha, S., Majumder, P., Patel, D., Dave, M., Mandlia, C., and Patel, A. (2019). Overview of the hasoc track at fire 2019: Hate speech and offensive content identification in indo-european languages. In *Proceedings of the 11th Forum for Information Retrieval Evaluation*, pages 14–17.

Mathur, P., Shah, R., Sawhney, R., and Mahata, D. (2018). Detecting offensive tweets in hindi-english code-switched language. In *Proceedings of the Sixth International Workshop on Natural Language Processing for Social Media*, pages 18–26.

Nobata, C., Tetreault, J., Thomas, A., Mehdad, Y., and Chang, Y. (2016). Abusive language detection in online user content. In *Proceedings of the 25th International Conference on World Wide Web*, WWW '16, pages 145–153, Republic and Canton of Geneva, Switzerland. International World Wide Web Conferences Steering Committee.

Priyadharshini, R., Chakravarthi, B. R., Vegupatti, M., and McCrae, J. P. (2020). Named entity recognition for code-mixed Indian corpus using meta embedding. In *2020 6th International Conference on Advanced Computing and Communication Systems (ICACCS)*.

Ranjan, P., Raja, B., Priyadharshini, R., and Balabantaray, R. C. (2016). A comparative study on code-mixed data of indian social media vs formal text. In *2016 2nd International Conference on Contemporary Computing and Informatics (IC3I)*, pages 608–611, Dec.

Schmidt, A. and Wiegand, M. (2017). A survey on hate speech detection using natural language processing. In *Proceedings of the Fifth International Workshop on Natural Language Processing for Social Media*, pages 1–10, Valencia, Spain, April. Association for Computational Linguistics.

Spertus, E. (1997). Smokey: Automatic recognition of hostile messages. In *Proceedings of the Ninth Conference on Innovative Applications of Artificial Intelligence*, pages 1058–1065.

Suryawanshi, S., Chakravarthi, B. R., Arcan, M., and Buitelaar, P. (2020a). Multimodal meme dataset (Multi-OFF) for identifying offensive content in image and text. In *Proceedings of the Second Workshop on Trolling, Aggression and Cyberbullying*, Marseille, France, May. European Language Resources Association (ELRA).

Suryawanshi, S., Chakravarthi, B. R., Verma, P., Arcan, M., McCrae, J. P., and Buitelaar, P. (2020b). A dataset for troll classification of Tamil memes. In *Proceedings of the 5th Workshop on Indian Language Data Resource and Evaluation (WILDRE-5)*, Marseille, France, May. European Language Resources Association (ELRA).

Wardhaugh, R. (1986). An introduction to socinguistic.

Warner, W. and Hirschberg, J. (2012). Detecting hate speech on the world wide web. In *Proceedings of the Second Workshop on Language in Social Media*, pages 19–26, Montréal, Canada, June. Association for Computational Linguistics.

Yin, D., Xue, Z., Hong, L., Davison, B. D., Kontostathis, A., and Edwards, L. (2009). Detection of harassment on web 2.0. *Proceedings of the Content Analysis in the WEB*, 2:1–7.

Zhang, X., Zhao, J., and LeCun, Y. (2015). Character-level convolutional networks for text classification. In *Proceedings of the 28th International Conference on Neural Information Processing Systems - Volume 1*, NIPS'15, page 649–657, Cambridge, MA, USA. MIT Press.

Zimmerman, S., Kruschwitz, U., and Fox, C. (2018). Improving hate speech detection with deep learning ensembles. In *Proceedings of the Eleventh International Conference on Language Resources and Evaluation (LREC 2018)*, Miyazaki, Japan, May. European Language Resources Association (ELRA).

Proceedings of the Second Workshop on Trolling, Aggression and Cyberbullying, pages 49–54
Language Resources and Evaluation Conference (LREC 2020), Marseille, 11–16 May 2020
© European Language Resources Association (ELRA), licensed under CC-BY-NC

IRIT at TRAC 2020

Faneva Ramiandrisoa[1,2]**, Josiane Mothe**[1,3]
[1]IRIT, UMR 5505 CNRS Université de Toulouse, France
[2] Université d'Antananarivo
[3] ESPE, UT2J
{faneva.ramiandrisoa, josiane.mothe}@irit.fr

Abstract

This paper describes the participation of the IRIT team in the TRAC *(Trolling, Aggression and Cyberbullying)* 2020 shared task (Bhattacharya et al., 2020) on Aggression Identification and more precisely to the shared task in English language. The shared task was further divided into two sub-tasks: (a) aggression identification and (b) misogynistic aggression identification. We proposed to use the transformer based language model BERT *(Bidirectional Encoder Representation from Transformer)* for the two sub-tasks. Our team was qualified as twelfth out of sixteen participants on sub-task (a) and eleventh out of fifteen participants on sub-task (b).

Keywords: Information systems, Information retrieval, Social media, Cyber-agression, TRAC Trolling, Aggression and cyber-bullying, BERT

1. Introduction

Social media has become one of the key ways people communicate and share opinions (Pelicon et al., 2019). These platforms, such as Twitter or WhatsApp, allow people to fully or partially hide their identity and this leads to the proliferation of abusive language and an increase of aggressive and potential harmful content on social media (Zhu et al., 2019). Automatically monitoring user-generated content in order to help moderate social media content is thus an important topic and has attracted significant attention in recent years as evidenced in recent publications (Mishra et al., 2019; Struß et al., 2019; Zampieri et al., 2019). Several studies focus on the automatic detection of abusive language such as hate speech (Warner and Hirschberg, 2012), cyberbullying (Dadvar et al., 2013), aggression (Kumar et al., 2018). Different evaluation forums have also been proposed in order to foster the development of systems to help abusive language detection. Among them, we can mention TRAC (Kumar et al., 2018), GermEval (Struß et al., 2019), and SemEval-2019 Task 6 (Zampieri et al., 2019).

In this work, we report the work we carried out on aggression identification and our participation in the second edition of TRAC *(Trolling, Aggression and Cyberbullying)*. The objective of TRAC shared task is to automatically detect aggression in text. During the first edition, the objective was to develop a classifier that could make a 3-way classification between "Overtly Aggressive", "Covertly Aggressive" and "Non-aggressive" text data. Deep learning approaches were widely used during the shared task and achieved the best performance (Kumar et al., 2018).

For the second edition of TRAC (Bhattacharya et al., 2020), the organizers proposed two sub-tasks: (a) aggression identification and (b) misogynistic aggression identification. The objective of sub-task (a) is the same as in the first edition of TRAC which is to classify the text according to 3 classes. The objective of sub-task (b) is to develop a binary classifier for classifying the text as "gendered" or "non-gendered".

For our participation in this second edition of TRAC, we proposed variants of a model that use transfer learning based on the BERT model (more details in Section 4.) to tackle the problem of the two sub-tasks.

The rest of this paper is organized as follows: Section 2. presents related work in the area of abusive language detection; Section 3. describes the TRAC data set as well as the pre-processing we developed; Section 4. describes the methodology we propose to answer the TRAC challenge as well as the submitted runs; Section 5. presents the results and discusses them; finally, Section 6. concludes this paper and presents some future work.

2. Related Work

Automatically detecting abusive language from textual analysis has gained momentum (Maitra and Sarkhel, 2018). Schmidt and Wiegand (2017) present a survey on hate speech detection using Natural Language Processing (NLP). The authors report that supervised learning approaches, such as support vector machines (SVM) and recurrent neural networks, are predominantly used to solve the the problem. They also report that features such as simple surface features (eg. bag of words, n-grams, etc.), word generalization (eg. word embedding, etc.), knowledge-based features (eg. ontology, etc.), are widely used for hate speech detection. On the other hand, Mishra et al. (2019) report an overview of abuse detection methods as well as a detailed overview of data sets that are annotated for abusive language detection. The authors noticed that many researchers have relied on text-based features for abuse detection while the recent state of the art approaches rely on deep learning approaches such as Convolutional Neural Networks (CNN) and Recurrent Neural Networks (RNN). Several European projects and workshops are tackling this challenge (Laurent, 2020; Hoang et al., 2020) and a number of evaluation forums that deal with offensive content, hate speech and aggression have been organized recently. These initiatives confirm the increasing interest in this field (Pelicon et al., 2019). To solve this challenge, participants heavily use deep learning techniques and achieve the best effectiveness. This is the case in GermEval (Struß et al., 2019), SemEval-2019 Task 6 (Zampieri et al., 2019) and the first edition of TRAC (Kumar et al., 2018).

The first edition of TRAC (Kumar et al., 2018), denoted as TRAC 2018 in the remainder of this paper, focused on aggression identification considering both English and Hindi languages. The objective was to classify texts into three classes: **Non-Aggressive (NAG)**, **Covertly Aggressive (CAG)**, and **Overtly Aggressive (OAG)**. Facebook posts and comments were provided for training and validation, while, for testing, two different sets, one from Facebook and one from Twitter, were provided. The best performance during the shared task in English language was achieved with deep learning approaches both on Facebook and Twitter test sets (Kumar et al., 2018). During this shared task, apart from deep learning approaches, participants considered classical machine learning methods (eg. Random Forests) based on features as in (Ramiandrisoa and Mothe, 2018; Arroyo-Fernández et al., 2018; Risch and Krestel, 2018). In Hindi language, Logistic regression over lexical features gave the best performance on Facebook set and second best performance on Twitter sets (Samghabadi et al., 2018).

In the next section, we will describe the second edition of TRAC, denoted as TRAC 2020 in the remainder of this paper, in which we participated as well as the methodology we adopted.

3. Data and preprocessing

In this section, we detail the data set used during the second edition of TRAC as well as how we preprocessed it for text cleaning and added external data to increase the training data set.

3.1. Data set

The second edition of the TRAC shared task (Bhattacharya et al., 2020) (TRAC 2020) was divided into two sub-tasks, namely aggression identification (sub-task (a)) and misogynistic aggression identification (sub-task (b)). The organizers provided a new data set, different from the ones made available during TRAC 2018. The training and validation sets are composed of 5,000 aggression-annotated data from social media each in Bangla (in both Roman and Bangla script), Hindi (in both Roman and Devanagari script) and English. The test set is composed of 1,200 data from social media each in Bangla, Hindi and English. During this edition, we used the English parts only.

For sub-task (a), each text data is labeled as Non-Aggressive (NAG), Covertly Aggressive (CAG), or Overtly Aggressive (OAG). The label NAG is used for text that is generally not intended to be aggressive, CAG is used for text that contains hidden or indirect aggression and finally OAG is used for text that contains open and direct aggression.

For sub-task (b), each text data is labeled as gendered (GEN) or non-gendered (NGEN). The text instances used in both sub-tasks are the same, just labels are different. Table 1 details the English data set used in this work.

3.2. Preprocessing

In this section, we describe the preprocessing steps we applied to the data instances in order to clean them. We also

Number of	Train	Validation	Test
texts	4,263	1,066	1,200
OAG	435	113	286
CAG	453	117	224
NAG	3,375	836	690
GEN	309	73	175
NGEN	3,954	993	1,025

Table 1: Distribution of training, validation and test data on English TRAC 2020 data collection.

describe the two methods we used we used to enlarge the data set in order to get a balanced data set because as we can see in table 1, classes are imbalanced. In various applications balanced data sets have been shown to perform better than imbalanced ones (Chawla et al., 2002; Khan et al., 2017), and various methods have been developed to overcome data imbalance (Prati et al., 2015).

Data Preprocessing : we converted all texts into lowercase and all "URL" are substituted by "http". We also substituted emoticon into their text equivalents by using the online emoji project on github[1]. We treated the substituted phrase as regular English phrase. Finally, we removed non UTF-8 words.

Enlarging the data sets : we added more data in order to increase the number of items in low populated classes. We enlarged the data set for sub-task (a) only because, in that case, we have the data set of TRAC 2018 (the first edition) at our disposal which is annotated with the same class labels as used for sub-task (a).

We proposed two methods to complement the data set for the sub-task (a):

(i) for the first method, we used all the data set provided during the first edition, i.e. we used the training, validation and the two test sets. For this, we took all the text data labeled as CAG or OAG from the TRAC 2018 sets and added them to the training data of TRAC 2020. The resulting data set is called first enlarged data set and is composed of 14,039 texts where there is 6,305 CAG, 4,359 OAG and 3,375 NAG.

(ii) for the second method , we used only the training set of TRAC 2018. More precisely we took some of the text data labeled as CAG or OAG, respectively 2,922 and 2,940, and added them to the training data of TRAC 2020 in order to have the same number of instances per classes to train the model. The resulting data set is called second enlarged data set and is composed of 10,125 of text data where the number of items in each class is 3,375.

In the next section, we describe the models associated to the runs we submitted to TRAC 2020 shared task.

4. Methodology

We submitted five runs during the TRAC 2020 shared task, three for sub-task (a) and two for sub-task (b). These five

---

[1] https://github.com/carpedm20/emoji, accessed on February, 04th 2020

runs are based on a system that uses BERT model (Devlin et al., 2019). More precisely, we used the BERT model combined in parallel with a low-dimensional multi-head attention layer (Projected Attention Layers or PALs) which was proposed by (Stickland and Murray, 2019) and denoted as BERT_Pals in the remainder of this paper. BERT_Pals was designed for multi-task learning but it can be used for a single task learning. We used BERT_Pals because it gave better result than just BERT on the validation set during the model training.

To understand the BERT_Pals model, let us first explain the original BERT model architecture. The original BERT model is simply a stack of BERT layers. In the literature, two types of BERT architecture are widely used: BERT-large (composed of 24 BERT layers) and BERT-base (composed of 12 BERT layers).

BERT takes in a sequence of tokens[2] and outputs a vector representation of that sequence. Each token in the sequence has its own hidden vector and these hidden vectors are transformed with the first BERT layer to get the first hidden states. The first hidden states are transformed through successive BERT layers and get at the end the final hidden states[3].

A BERT layer follows a transformer architecture based on a multi-head attention layer (Vaswani et al., 2017). The multi-head layer consists of n different dot-product attention mechanisms

The BERT_Pals model modify the original BERT by adding a task-specific function in parallel with each BERT layer. Figure 1 provides an illustration of the architecture of the BERT_Pals model with only two layers for simplicity.

For a more detailed explanation of the BERT_Pals model, we refer readers to (Stickland and Murray, 2019). The code of (Stickland and Murray, 2019) is also open-source and is available in github[4].

In their work, Stickland and Murray (2019) used the same configuration of BERT-base architecture as in (Devlin et al., 2019). However, in our work, we changed it to the configuration of BERT-large architecture because Devlin et al. (2019) stated that BERT-large achieved better performances than BERT-base. For the other configurations, which are specific to BERT_Pals, we used the same as in (Stickland and Murray, 2019)' work, except the task sampling that is useless in the case of a single task. Indeed, in our work, we train the model on one task only so we do not need to use the tasks sampling method which is essential for multi-task learning.

4.1. Runs submitted to TRAC 2020

Sub-task (a): For this sub-task, we submitted three runs obtained from BERT_Pals models that were trained with a mini-batch size of 32, a maximum sequence length of 40 tokens, Adam optimizer with learning rate of 2e-5, number of epochs of 3 and learning rate warm-up over the first 10

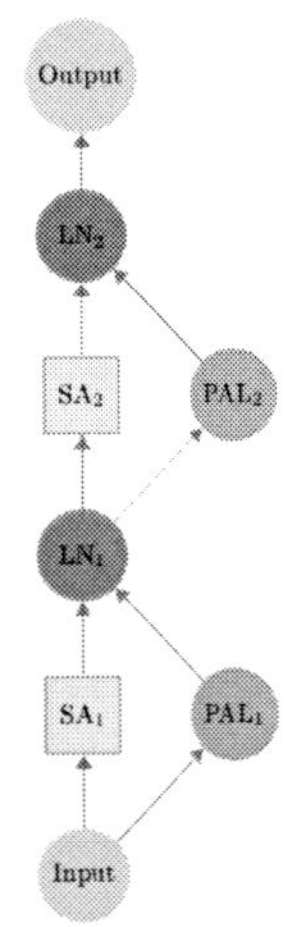

Figure 1: Schematic diagram (Stickland and Murray, 2019) of adding Projected Attention Layers or PALs in parallel with self-attention (SA) layers in a BERT model, with only two layers for simplicity. LN refers to layer-norm.

% of the steps. The difference between these three models is the training data on which they were trained. The first model (model_A_1) was trained on the training data of TRAC 2020 only, while the second model (model_A_2) was trained on the first enlarged data and finally the last model (model_A_3) was trained on the second enlarged data.

Sub-task (b): For this sub-task, we submitted two systems also obtained from BERT_Pals models trained with a mini-batch size of 32, a maximum sequence length of 40 tokens, adam optimizer with learning rate of 2e-5, number of epochs of 3 and learning rate warm-up over the first 10% of steps. The difference between the models was also the data on which they were trained. The first model (model_B_1) was trained on the training data of TRAC 2020 only while the second model (model_B_2) was trained on both the training and validation data of TRAC 2020.

The training was carried out on an Nvidia Geforce GTX 1080TI GPU and took between 3 to 6 minutes in total.

In the next sections, we report the results we obtained during the TRAC 2020 shared task.

5. Results

This section reports the results our team obtained on the English data sets when participating to TRAC 2020. More details on other participants' systems are presented in (Kumar et al., 2020).

Table 2 presents the results we obtained for sub-task (a) and table 3 the ones for sub-task (b).

For sub-task (a), we can see that the model (model_A_3) trained on the balanced data set gives the best performance (weighted F1 of 0.6352). Nonetheless, this model achieved just the twelfth rank over sixteen participants runs during the TRAC 2020 challenge, where the best team achieved a weighted F1 of 0.8029.

For sub-task (b), we can see that the model (model_B_1) trained on the training data of TRAC 2020 only gives the

---

_[2] A special classification embedding ([CLS]) is always inserted as the first token of every sequence.

_[3] Only the final hidden state of [CLS] is used as the aggregate sequence representation for classification or regression tasks.

_[4] `https://github.com/AsaCooperStickland/Bert-n-Pals`

System	F1 (weighted)	Accuracy
model_A_1	0.6179	0.6958
model_A_2	0.5894	0.645
model_A_3	**0.6352**	**0.6967**

Table 2: Results of our three models for sub-task (a) on English test set. Bold font highlights the best performance.

best performance according to weighted F1 (0.8202) while the model (model_B_2) trained on both training and validation sets of TRAC 2020 gives the best result when considering accuracy score. Nonetheless the model_B_1 achieved just eleventh rank over fifteen participants runs during the TRAC 2020 challenge where the best team achieved a weighted F1 of 0.8716. We should mention that the performance of our models are closer to the best in this sub-task (b) than in sub-task (a).

System	F1 (weighted)	Accuracy
model_B_1	**0.8202**	0.8433
model_B_2	0.7870	**0.8542**

Table 3: Results of our two models for sub-task (b) on English test set. Bold font highlights the best performance.

5.1. Discussion

When analyzing the results of our models according to confusion matrix on sub-task (a), we can see that they hardly identify CAG. From the confusion matrix presented in figure 2, we can see that our best model confuses NAG and CAG, and the same holds for CAG and OAG. It confirms our hypothesis, when reading some texts from the training set, that it is easier to distinguish texts labelled as NAG from texts labelled as OAG than from texts labelled as CAG. This difficulty to detect CAG is the main weakness of our model, this is why our ranking is so poor during the competition. With BERT_Pals, we are able to detect the six CAG while using normal/original BERT, we do not even predict CAG at all.

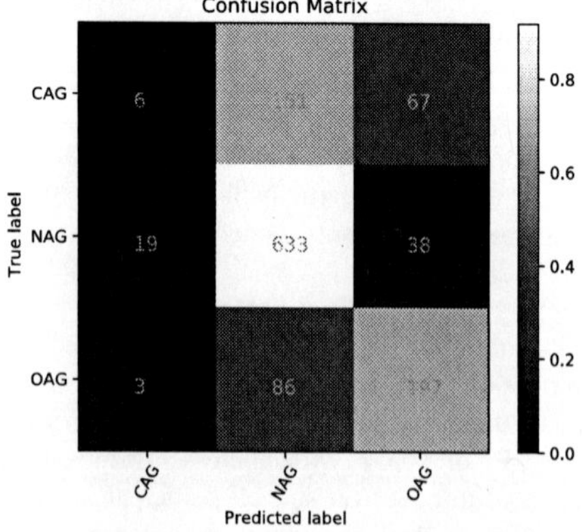

Figure 2: Heatmap of the confusion matrix for our best model (model_A_3) on sub-task (a)

For the sub-task (b), our model performs better than for sub-task (a) but hardly predict GEN cases as we can see in Figure 3 for our best model; the same holds for the other model which does not even predict GEN cases at all. This is likely to be due to the imbalanced nature of the data set as there are about thirteen times more NGEN cases than GEN cases. This finding confirms what (Pelicon et al., 2019) said in their work that transfer learning with BERT does not perform well on imbalanced data sets.

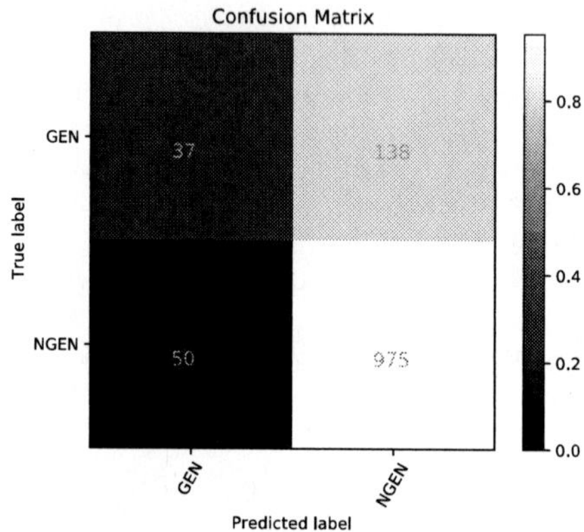

Figure 3: Heatmap of the confusion matrix for our best model (model_B_1) on sub-task (b)

6. Conclusion and Future Work

In this paper, we presented our participation in the second edition of TRAC shared task in English language for both sub-tasks: (a) aggression identification and (b) misogynistic aggression identification. We used BERT model to tackle the problem of the two sub-tasks. On the first sub-task, our best model achieved a weighted F1 of 0.6352 which ranked our team on the twelfth place over sixteen participants runs. On the second sub-task, our best model achieved a weighted F1 of 0.8202 which placed our team to the eleventh rank over fifteen participants runs. However, in this second task, the performance of our models are closer to the best.

We noticed that the class imbalances in the data set had a significant impact on the performance of our models. Adding instances from an external data set to the minority classes on sub-task (a) proved to be the most consistent technique to improve the performance of our models. Nevertheless on this sub-task, our models met another problem which is to differentiate *covertly* aggressive cases and non-aggressive cases.

Our aim for the short term future work is to balance the data set for sub-task (b) in order to see if it improves the results. We also plan to test different techniques to tackle the problem of imbalanced data sets. For long term future work, we aim to make our proposed models more robust to imbalanced data set. We also plan to investigate why it is hard for our models to detect covertly aggressive by analyzing the text in the training data set with keywords extraction technique such as the one we developed in (Mothe et al., 2018). We may also investigate more on keywords by using them instead of long text as input to our models.

Ethical issue. While TRAC challenge has its proper ethical policies, detecting aggressive content from user's posts raises ethical issues that are beyond the scope of the paper.

7. Bibliographical References

Arroyo-Fernández, I., Forest, D., Torres-Moreno, J., Carrasco-Ruiz, M., Legeleux, T., and Joannette, K. (2018). Cyberbullying detection task: the EBSI-LIA-UNAM system (ELU) at coling'18 TRAC-1. In *Proceedings of the 1st Workshop on Trolling, Aggression and Cyberbullying, TRAC@COLING 2018*, pages 140–149.

Bhattacharya, S., Singh, S., Kumar, R., Bansal, A., Bhagat, A., Dawer, Y., Lahiri, B., and Ojha, A. K. (2020). Developing a multilingual annotated corpus of misogyny and aggression.

Chawla, N. V., Bowyer, K. W., Hall, L. O., and Kegelmeyer, W. P. (2002). Smote: synthetic minority over-sampling technique. *Journal of artificial intelligence research*, 16:321–357.

Dadvar, M., Trieschnigg, D., Ordelman, R., and de Jong, F. (2013). Improving cyberbullying detection with user context. In *Advances in Information Retrieval - 35th European Conference on IR Research, ECIR 2013, Moscow, Russia, March 24-27, 2013. Proceedings*, pages 693–696.

Devlin, J., Chang, M., Lee, K., and Toutanova, K. (2019). BERT: pre-training of deep bidirectional transformers for language understanding. In *Proceedings of the 2019 Conference of the North American Chapter of the Association for Computational Linguistics: Human Language Technologies, NAACL-HLT 2019, Minneapolis, MN, USA, June 2-7, 2019, Volume 1 (Long and Short Papers)*, pages 4171–4186.

Hoang, T. B. N., Marchand, P., Milard, B., and Mothe, J. (2020). *Workshop on Machine Learning for Trend and Weak Signal Detection in Social Networks and Social Media, Toulouse, France, Feb. 27-28, 2020, Proceedings. -*.

Khan, S. H., Hayat, M., Bennamoun, M., Sohel, F. A., and Togneri, R. (2017). Cost-sensitive learning of deep feature representations from imbalanced data. *IEEE transactions on neural networks and learning systems*.

Kumar, R., Ojha, A. K., Malmasi, S., and Zampieri, M. (2018). Benchmarking aggression identification in social media. In *Proceedings of the First Workshop on Trolling, Aggression and Cyberbullying, TRAC@COLING 2018, Santa Fe, New Mexico, USA, August 25, 2018*, pages 1–11.

Kumar, R., Ojha, A. K., Malmasi, S., and Zampieri, M. (2020). Evaluating aggression identification in social media. In Ritesh Kumar, et al., editors, *Proceedings of the Second Workshop on Trolling, Aggression and Cyberbullying (TRAC-2020)*, Paris, France, may. European Language Resources Association (ELRA).

Laurent, M. (2020). Hatemeter Project: Analysis of hate speech on twitter at the crossroads of computer science,

humanities and social sciences. In *Workshop on Machine Learning for Trend and Weak Signal Detection in Social Networks and Social Media*, 2.

Maitra, P. and Sarkhel, R. (2018). A k-competitive autoencoder for aggression detection in social media text. In *Proceedings of the First Workshop on Trolling, Aggression and Cyberbullying, TRAC@COLING 2018, Santa Fe, New Mexico, USA, August 25, 2018*, pages 80–89.

Mishra, P., Yannakoudakis, H., and Shutova, E. (2019). Tackling online abuse: A survey of automated abuse detection methods. *CoRR*, abs/1908.06024.

Mothe, J., Ramiandrisoa, F., and Rasolomanana, M. (2018). Automatic keyphrase extraction using graph-based methods. In *Proceedings of the 33rd Annual ACM Symposium on Applied Computing, SAC 2018, Pau, France, April 09-13, 2018*, pages 728–730.

Pelicon, A., Martinc, M., and Novak, P. K. (2019). Embeddia at semeval-2019 task 6: Detecting hate with neural network and transfer learning approaches. In *Proceedings of the 13th International Workshop on Semantic Evaluation, SemEval@NAACL-HLT 2019*, pages 604–610.

Prati, R. C., Batista, G. E., and Silva, D. F. (2015). Class imbalance revisited: a new experimental setup to assess the performance of treatment methods. *Knowledge and Information Systems*, 45(1):247–270.

Ramiandrisoa, F. and Mothe, J. (2018). IRIT at TRAC 2018. In *Workshop on Trolling, Aggression and Cyberbullying, in International Conference of Computational Linguistics (TRAC@COLING 2018)*, pages 19–27, http://www.aclweb.org. Association for Computational Linguistics (ACL).

Risch, J. and Krestel, R. (2018). Aggression identification using deep learning and data augmentation. In *Proceedings of the First Workshop on Trolling, Aggression and Cyberbullying, TRAC@COLING 2018, Santa Fe, New Mexico, USA, August 25, 2018*, pages 150–158.

Samghabadi, N. S., Mave, D., Kar, S., and Solorio, T. (2018). Ritual-uh at TRAC 2018 shared task: Aggression identification. In *Proceedings of the First Workshop on Trolling, Aggression and Cyberbullying, TRAC@COLING 2018, Santa Fe, New Mexico, USA, August 25, 2018*, pages 12–18.

Schmidt, A. and Wiegand, M. (2017). A survey on hate speech detection using natural language processing. In *Proceedings of the Fifth International Workshop on Natural Language Processing for Social Media, SocialNLP@EACL 2017, Valencia, Spain, April 3, 2017*, pages 1–10.

Stickland, A. C. and Murray, I. (2019). BERT and pals: Projected attention layers for efficient adaptation in multi-task learning. In *Proceedings of the 36th International Conference on Machine Learning, ICML 2019, 9-15 June 2019, Long Beach, California, USA*, pages 5986–5995.

Struß, J. M., Siegel, M., Ruppenhofer, J., Wiegand, M., and Klenner, M. (2019). Overview of germeval task 2, 2019 shared task on the identification of offensive language. In *Proceedings of the 15th Conference on Natural Lan-*

guage Processing, KONVENS 2019, Erlangen, Germany, October 9-11, 2019.

Vaswani, A., Shazeer, N., Parmar, N., Uszkoreit, J., Jones, L., Gomez, A. N., Kaiser, L., and Polosukhin, I. (2017). Attention is all you need. In *Advances in Neural Information Processing Systems 30: Annual Conference on Neural Information Processing Systems 2017, 4-9 December 2017, Long Beach, CA, USA*, pages 5998–6008.

Warner, W. and Hirschberg, J. (2012). Detecting hate speech on the world wide web. In *Proceedings of the Second Workshop on Language in Social Media*, pages 19–26, Montréal, Canada, June. Association for Computational Linguistics.

Zampieri, M., Malmasi, S., Nakov, P., Rosenthal, S., Farra, N., and Kumar, R. (2019). Semeval-2019 task 6: Identifying and categorizing offensive language in social media (offenseval). In *Proceedings of the 13th International Workshop on Semantic Evaluation, SemEval@NAACL-HLT 2019*, pages 75–86.

Zhu, J., Tian, Z., and Kübler, S. (2019). UM-IU@LING at SemEval-2019 task 6: Identifying offensive tweets using BERT and SVMs. In *Proceedings of the 13th International Workshop on Semantic Evaluation*, pages 788–795, Minneapolis, Minnesota, USA, June. Association for Computational Linguistics.

Proceedings of the Second Workshop on Trolling, Aggression and Cyberbullying, pages 55–61
Language Resources and Evaluation Conference (LREC 2020), Marseille, 11–16 May 2020
© European Language Resources Association (ELRA), licensed under CC-BY-NC

Bagging BERT Models for
Robust Aggression Identification

Julian Risch and Ralf Krestel
Hasso Plattner Institute, University of Potsdam
Prof.-Dr.-Helmert-Str. 2-3, 14482 Potsdam, Germany
julian.risch@hpi.de, ralf.krestel@hpi.de

Abstract

Modern transformer-based models with hundreds of millions of parameters, such as BERT, achieve impressive results at text classification tasks. This also holds for aggression identification and offensive language detection, where deep learning approaches consistently outperform less complex models, such as decision trees. While the complex models fit training data well (low bias), they also come with an unwanted high variance. Especially when fine-tuning them on small datasets, the classification performance varies significantly for slightly different training data. To overcome the high variance and provide more robust predictions, we propose an ensemble of multiple fine-tuned BERT models based on bootstrap aggregating (bagging). In this paper, we describe such an ensemble system and present our submission to the shared tasks on aggression identification 2020 (team name: Julian). Our submission is the best-performing system for five out of six subtasks. For example, we achieve a weighted F1-score of 80.3% for task A on the test dataset of English social media posts. In our experiments, we compare different model configurations and vary the number of models used in the ensemble. We find that the F1-score drastically increases when ensembling up to 15 models, but the returns diminish for more models.

Keywords: neural networks, offensive language, aggression, hate speech, ensemble learning, transformer model, BERT

1. Robust Aggression Identification

Aggression in social media posts, such as tweets or Facebook posts, has become omnipresent. Ignoring it is inappropriate because it can inflict real damage in real-world life (Hsueh et al., 2015; Rösner et al., 2016). Text classification approaches can detect such malicious behavior, and more fine-grained classifications can identify subclasses of aggression, for example, different severity levels or target groups (Zampieri et al., 2019a). These classifiers alone cannot solve the problem of online aggression because they do not reach its root cause — the attackers behind aggressive posts. However, they still play an essential role in combating aggression by supporting content moderators, who remove these posts from online platforms or criminal prosecutors, who hold attackers accountable.

The current trend for research on natural language processing with deep neural networks is to develop more and more complex models. The complexity is expressed in the number of parameters, which is in the hundreds of millions for transformer-based language models, such as Bidirectional Encoder Representations from Transformers (BERT) (Devlin et al., 2018). More precisely, *large* BERT models span 24 layers and 340 million parameters, and even *base* BERT models span 12 layers and 110 million parameters. Typically, these models are pre-trained on large corpora, for example, on collections of web pages with billions of tokens. For down-stream tasks, e.g., text classification, they are fine-tuned on smaller datasets. While the pre-training is unsupervised, the fine-tuning for down-stream tasks is typically supervised learning.

The fine-tuning fits the model well to the labeled training data, and the model's bias is typically low. It does not suffer from underfitting. The strong classification performance reported on training, validation, and test datasets proves this. In fact, overfitting can be more of an issue, especially for smaller datasets. The number of parameters is much larger than the typical number of samples in hand-labeled datasets. Standard regularization techniques, such as dropout and limiting the number of training steps with early stopping, can be used to cope with overfitting problems.

However, the model's variance is high. Even slight variations in the input data or a slight change of the random seed, which affects, for example, the randomly initialized weights of the final prediction layer (prediction head) result in large changes in classification performance. In our initial experiments, we find that the performance varies in a range of up to five percentage points in F1-score.

Contributions. We address the issue of high variance of fine-tuned BERT models on small datasets with an ensembling approach. To this end, we propose to combine the predictions of multiple BERT models that are trained with bootstrap aggregating on slightly differing training datasets and with varying weight initialization in the final prediction layer. Our experiments show that an ensemble achieves a two percentage points higher F1-score than single models. Further, we optimize the number of ensembled models and find that the performance increases for up to 15 models and stays the same for larger ensembles.

Outline. The rest of this paper is structured as follows: In Section 2, we give an overview of related shared tasks and transformer-based neural networks. We then briefly introduce the dataset and point out the imbalanced class distribution in Section 3. Further, the training procedure for the BERT models and the ensembling technique is described in the same section. Our experiments in Section 4 evaluate the F1-score on the validation and test datasets, and we describe the model configurations that achieved the best results. An additional experiment studies how the number of ensembled models affects the classification performance. In Section 5, we discuss the results and analyze misclassifications based on confusion matrices before we conclude with directions for future work in Section 6.

2. Related Work

The last three years came with a variety of shared tasks in the broad field of aggression identification. We give an overview of these tasks in the following. Afterward, we summarize related work on transformer neural networks and ensembles for aggression identification since we combine both techniques in our approach.

Shared Tasks. The by far largest shared task concerning the number of participants and the dataset size is the Kaggle challenge on toxic comment classification.[1] The dataset comprises English user comments from Wikipedia discussion pages. Thanks to a large number of shared tasks in conference workshops, labeled datasets cover a diverse set of languages besides English. For example, there is Spanish (Fersini et al., 2018), Italian (Bosco et al., 2018), Hindi (Kumar et al., 2018a; Bhattacharya et al., 2020), Bangla (Bhattacharya et al., 2020), German (Wiegand et al., 2018; Struß et al., 2019), and Arabic, Danish, Greek, and Turkish (Zampieri et al., 2020).

The shared tasks differ not only in language but also in the precise task and respective class labels. For example, HatEval deals with hate speech against immigrants and women (Basile et al., 2019), HaSpeeDe with hate speech detection in general (Bosco et al., 2018), IberEval has a task on automatic misogyny identification (Fersini et al., 2018), OffensEval covers offensive language (Zampieri et al., 2019b), and TRAC focuses on aggression (Kumar et al., 2018a; Bhattacharya et al., 2020). To the best of our knowledge, there is no common definition for the task of identifying aggressive or otherwise offensive social media posts. Instead, the different shared tasks use varying terminology: hate speech, toxic comments, offensive language, abusive language, aggression, and misogyny identification. Waseem et al. (2017) provide an overview of abusive language detection subtasks.

Transformer Models. Our approach builds on Bidirectional Encoder Representations from Transformers (BERT) (Devlin et al., 2018). BERT is a task-agnostic language representation model, which consists of multiple layers of bidirectional transformers by Vaswani et al. (2017). After being pre-trained on a large corpus, it can not only be fine-tuned for text classification but also for many other tasks, such as named entity recognition, question answering, and text summarization. The training objective of the model uses a masking technique. Given a sentence, 15% of the input tokens are masked, and the task is to predict these tokens. This technique overcomes the limitation of unidirectional processing and is also superior to language models that combine right-to-left and left-to-right processing (Peters et al., 2018). Our implementation uses the Python-based framework for adapting representation models (FARM) by *deepset*.[2]

BERT has been used in other shared tasks on hate speech or offensive language detection (Mozafari et al., 2019; Nikolov and Radivchev, 2019). We first published the idea of ensembling multiple BERT models in the context of a shared task on offensive language detection for German tweets (Risch et al., 2019). However, our experiments in this previous publication only show that ensembles of five or ten BERT models outperform a single model. It does not answer what the optimal number of models in such an ensemble is.

Our submission to the last edition of the aggression identification shared task in 2018 uses another ensembling technique: stacking (Risch and Krestel, 2018). The predictions of bidirectional recurrent neural networks and logistic regression classifiers are weighted for each social media post individually. Depending on features extracted from the post, such as its text length or the number of out-of-vocabulary words, one or the other classifier's predictions are emphasized. Thereby, we account for the fact that individual classifiers are specialized to make predictions for longer or shorter posts, for example. The difference to the bootstrap aggregating approach is that the goal was not to reduce variance but to combine classifiers that were trained on different features (word embeddings, character n-grams). On the English dataset, the best single model achieves an F1-score of 58% and the ensemble 61% for English. The results on the Hindi dataset are similar (best single model: 61% and ensemble: 63%).

3. Bootstrap Aggregating BERT Models

This section presents our approach for the shared task. It begins with a brief description of the task dataset and further describes the classification model, the training procedure, and the ensembling strategy. The Python code for our submission is publicly available online.[3]

3.1. Dataset

The shared task[4] is based on three datasets: an English, a Hindi, and a Bangla dataset of about 6000 social media posts each (Kumar et al., 2020). It comprises two independent tasks. The first task, task A: aggression identification, is a 3-way classification into non-aggressive (NAG), covertly aggressive (CAG), and overtly aggressive (OAG) posts. Covertly aggressive posts include indirect attacks that use, e.g., satire or rhetorical questions, while overtly aggressive posts contain lexical features that are considered aggressive (Kumar et al., 2018b). Table 1 gives an overview of the dataset sizes for this task. The second task, task B: misogynistic aggression identification, is a binary classification task with two labels: gendered (GEN) and non-gendered (NGEN). Gendered aggression is defined as attacks based on gender (roles), and includes homophobic and transgender attacks (Kumar et al., 2018b). Table 2 gives an overview of the dataset sizes for this task. Figure 1 and Figure 2 list one English-language example post per class label.

---

[1] https://www.kaggle.com/c/
jigsaw-toxic-comment-classification-challenge
[2] https://github.com/deepset-ai/FARM
[3] https://hpi.de/naumann/projects/
repeatability/text-mining.html
[4] https://sites.google.com/view/trac2/
shared-task

Table 1: Training, validation, and test dataset sizes for task A per language.

	Training			Validation			Test			Total		
	NAG	CAG	OAG	NAG	CAG	OAG	NAG	CAG	OAG	NAG	CAG	OAG
English	3375	453	435	836	117	113	690	224	286	4901	794	834
Hindi	2245	910	829	578	211	208	325	191	684	3148	1312	1721
Bangla	2078	898	850	522	218	217	712	225	251	3312	1341	1318

Table 2: Training, validation, and test dataset sizes for task B per language.

	Training		Validation		Test		Total	
	NGEN	GEN	NGEN	GEN	NGEN	GEN	NGEN	GEN
English	3954	309	993	73	1025	175	5972	557
Hindi	3323	661	845	152	633	567	4801	1380
Bangla	3114	712	766	191	986	202	4866	1105

text: Great video👏👏👏
tokens: Great, video, [UNK], [UNK], [UNK]
label: non-aggressive (NAG)

RSS agenda is to demolished opposite options
tokens: RS, ##S, agenda, is, to, demolished, opposite, options
label: covertly aggressive (CAG)

You are soo fucked up that you can't understand someone else's perspective…
tokens: You, are, so, ##o, fucked, up, that, you, can, ', t, understand, someone, else, ', s, perspective, ., ., .
label: overtly aggressive (OAG)

Figure 1: Training samples for task A (aggression identification).

text: I think feminists are lesbians,OAG,GEN
tokens: I, think, feminist, ##s, are, lesbian, ##s
label: gendered (GEN)

text: kill all those womens who file faje rape and dowry cases,CAG,NGEN
tokens: kill, all, those, women, ##s, who, file, f, ##aj, ##e, rape, and, do, ##wry, cases
label: non-gendered (NGEN)

Figure 2: Training samples for task B (misogynistic aggression identification).

3.2. Classification Model

The tokenizer for BERT uses word pieces so that the model learns an embedding for each token. The vocabulary consists of 30,000 tokens. Custom tokens can be added to extend this vocabulary, but then there is no pre-trained representation for the added tokens. A larger dataset than the one provided for this task is needed to make proper use of custom tokens.

We refrain from any complex data pre-processing and use only three small steps. First, all characters are converted to lowercase. Second, we insert whitespaces before and after every emoji so that they can be tokenized as separate tokens. Third, we limit the sequence length to 200 tokens. The sequence length defines how many tokens are cut off from overly long sequences. Only a few posts are affected by this choice. With a maximum sequence length of 200 tokens, 0.9% of all training samples are affected. A maximum sequence length of 220 or 230 tokens reduces this number to 0.5%.

The tokenizer is the same as used for pre-training the BERT model. For this reason, emojis and non-Latin characters are unknown tokens, which are replaced with a common [UNK] symbol. Without inserting whitespace around emojis, the example post "Great video👏👏👏" would be tokenized as "Great, [UNK]". With our pre-processing, it is tokenized as "Great, video, [UNK], [UNK], [UNK]". On the word embedding level, we use a dropout of 10%, which means that every tenth word is randomly removed from the input to regularize the model.

We use the BERT *base* model, which has 768 hidden units.[5] Therefore, the final prediction layer is a dense layer with softmax activation that maps the 768-dimensional vectors to three outputs for the multi-class classification and to two outputs for the binary classification.

3.3. Training Procedure

We train each model for up to ten training epochs and halt the training if no learning progress is made for two subsequent evaluation periods. This early stopping mechanism monitors the weighted F1-score on a 10% validation set. An evaluation on this set runs every 40 batches. With a batch size of 48, there are approximately two evaluations per epoch.

Each training process starts with a different random seed. Thereby, not only does the random initialization of the weights of the final prediction layer vary among the models, but also the random data split for the early stopping is chosen differently. As the loss function, we use cross-

---

[5] https://huggingface.co/bert-base-uncased

entropy loss weighted by the class distribution. The learning rate is set to $5 \cdot 10^{-5}$ but uses a warmup phase as it is standard for fine-tuning BERT models. We use a linear learning rate warmup for the first 30% of the training up to the rate of $5 \cdot 10^{-5}$. Afterward, the rate linearly decays until the end of the training (ten epochs max). Deviations from this general configuration for different runs of our approach are described in Section 4.

3.4. Ensembling Strategy

The motivation for our ensembling approach is the instability of the classification performance across different fine-tuning runs of the same model. For example, Devlin et al. report[6] that the accuracy on small datasets, such as the Microsoft Research Paraphrase Corpus (MRPC) with 3,600 samples varies between 84% and 88%. This variance occurs when fine-tuning even the exact same pre-trained model. The recommended approach is to restart the fine-tuning multiple times. When fine-tuning BERT models on the shared task dataset, we are confronted with the same varying classification performance. Slight changes to the training data and model hyperparameters, such as the random seed, cause the fine-tuned models to achieve very different results on the hold-out test dataset. These models only differ in the model weights in the final dense layer (the prediction head) when the training starts. In summary, the BERT models that are fine-tuned on the small shared task dataset are unstable and have a high variance.

Our ensembling strategy is a variance reduction technique: bootstrap aggregation (bagging). We train up to 25 BERT models of the same kind on slightly different subsets of the data. A soft majority voting combines the predictions of these models:

$$\hat{y} = \operatorname*{argmax}_{j} \sum_{i=1}^{n} p_{i,j}$$

where $p_{i,j}$ is the probability for class label j predicted by the i-th classifier (out of n classifiers). It sums up the probability mass assigned per class label and chooses the label with the highest probability as the ensemble's prediction. In other words, it chooses the class label that is most likely predicted. In contrast to that, a hard majority voting would choose the label that is most often predicted.

4. Evaluation

We evaluate our approach for both shared tasks on the test dataset and report the best model configurations. Two additional experiments study how the ensembling affects classification performance. The first experiment shows how many models should be ensembled to achieve the best performance. The second experiment is an ablation study to find out whether the random data splits or the random weight initialization cause the ensemble's superior performance compared to single models.

4.1. Shared Task Performance

The shared task uses the weighted F1-score for the evaluation. As a consequence, the score for the majority class is

more important than for the other classes. Table 3 lists the performance that our approach achieved on the test dataset. In five out of six tasks, our approach outperforms all other shared task participants (15 teams). The only exception is the English-language version of task B. We believe the inferior results of our model for this task are caused by using a case-sensitive BERT model. For all other tasks, we used case-agnostic BERT models, which outperform the case-sensitive ones.

The largest gap to the second-best submission is at the English-language version of task A. Our approach achieves a 4.4 percentage points better F1-Score than the second-best approach.

Table 4 lists the model configurations that achieved the best results on the test dataset. Note that the number of submissions for the test dataset was limited to three per task and language. Therefore, we can evaluate only a small set of different configurations. This limitation is also the reason why we can only assume that a case-agnostic BERT model would achieve a higher F1-score for the English version of task B than the case-sensitive model that we used for our submission. We did not submit the predictions of such a case-sensitive model due to the limited number of allowed submissions.

4.2. Optimizing the Number of BERT Models

With the following experiment, we study how many models should be included in the ensemble to achieve the highest weighted F1-score at the shared task. To this end, we fine-tune 100 BERT models that only differ in the initial random seed. All these models have the same architecture and the same hyperparameters, such as batch size or learning rate. However, the varying seed determines the randomly initialized weights for the final dense layer of the model (the prediction head), the order in which the training samples are processed, their distribution among the training batches, and finally, the 90% training and 10% percent validation split.

For each number from 1 to 50, which we call ensemble size, we select subsets of the 50 fine-tuned models of that size. For example, to build an ensemble of 50 models out of 100 trained models, there are $\binom{100}{50} \approx 10^{29}$ possible combinations. As we cannot evaluate that many combinations, we randomly sample 1 000 combinations per ensemble size. The ensemble's predictions are generated with soft majority voting. Each ensemble is then evaluated on the exact same hold-out test dataset.

The top line in Figure 3 (random dataset split, random weight initialization) shows the weighted F1-scores that are achieved on average across the 1 000 combinations per ensemble size. The score increases for ensembles of up to 10 to 15 models, after which the advantage of adding even more models diminishes. The performance of a single model is, on average, about four percentage points worse than the best ensemble. We could not use the official test dataset for our experiment. Therefore, we use the official validation dataset for the evaluation and 90% of the official training dataset for training. 10% of the training dataset are used for the early stopping mechanism. The model seems to underfit because this mechanism halts the training too

---

[6]`https://github.com/google-research/bert/blob/master/README.md`

Table 3: Weighted F1-score (in percent) on the test dataset. Our approach outperforms the best submission by other teams in five out of six subtasks.

	English		Hindi		Bangla	
	Task A	Task B	Task A	Task B	Task A	Task B
Our Submission	**80.29**	85.14	**81.28**	**87.81**	**82.19**	**93.85**
Best Other Submission	75.92	**87.16**	79.44	86.89	80.83	92.97

Table 4: Configurations of our best-performing submissions on the test dataset.

	English		Hindi		Bangla	
	Task A	Task B	Task A	Task B	Task A	Task B
Language of models	English	English	multilingual	multilingual	multilingual	multilingual
Number of models	20	25	15	15	15	25
Letter casing	uncased	cased	uncased	uncased	uncased	uncased
Sequence length	220	220	200	200	200	230
Cross entropy loss	weighted	weighted	non-weighted	weighted	weighted	weighted
Hold-out data	10%	10%	20%	10%	20%	10%
Patience	2	2	1	2	1	2

early on the smaller dataset.

This experiment — in particular the fine-tuning of 100 BERT models and combining and evaluating the predictions of thousands of subsets of these models — is computationally expensive. It took approximately seven hours on two Nvidia GeForce GTX 1080 Ti GPUs with 11GB memory to complete the experiment. Training time and inference time increase linearly with the ensemble size.

4.3. Ablation Study

This experiment studies whether training on slightly different subsets of data or differently initializing weights in the final prediction layer (prediction head) causes the ensemble's strong performance. Our hypothesis is that the reason is the weight initialization. To test this hypothesis, we compare four different variations of our approach. Figure 3 shows the weighted F1-scores for all four variations per ensemble size.

First, we vary not only the random seeds for the weight initialization but also the training and validation split. As a consequence, the training data of the models differ slightly. Second, we vary the random seeds for the weight initialization while using the exact same training and validation split. For this variation, all models are trained on the exact same training data. Third, we use the same weight initialization for all models but vary the random splits of training and validation data. Fourth, we keep both the weight initialization and data splits fixed across all models. In the fourth variation, all trained models are identical, and thus, ensembling does not improve the performance. The test set is the exact same in all four variations.

The plot in Figure 3 confirms our hypothesis. The strong performance of our ensembles is mainly caused by using varying weight initializations for the individual models. The varying training and validation dataset splits have a smaller effect.

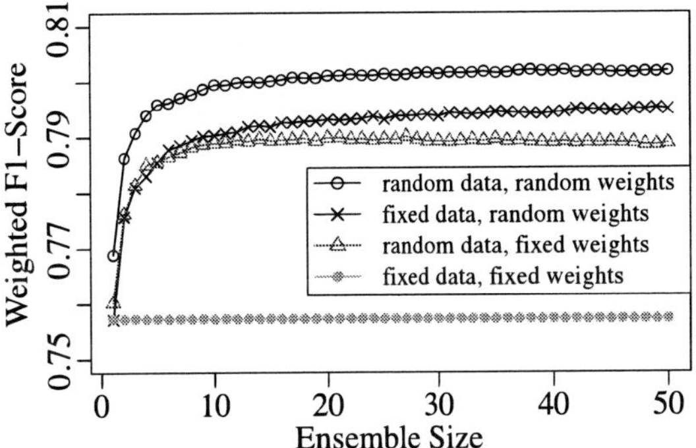

Figure 3: The increased performance of an ensemble of BERT models is mainly due to random weight initialization rather than random splits of training and validation data.

5. Discussion

Figure 4, Figure 5, and Figure 6 show normalized confusion matrices for task A on the test datasets. For task A on the English test dataset, the most frequent (with regard to relative numbers) misclassification is predicting *CAG* instead of *OAG* (28% of all posts labeled as *OAG*). On the Hindi dataset, *NAG* is more frequently misclassified as *CAG* (23% of all posts labeled as *NAG*). On the Bangla dataset, *CAG* is most often misclassified as *NAG* (31% of all posts labeled as *CAG*). For all three languages, *NAG* and *CAG* are often mixed up, and the same holds for *CAG* and *OAG*. This result is not to our surprise as *NAG* is more similar to *CAG* than to *OAG* and *OAG* is more similar to *CAG* than to *NAG*. A non-aggressive post is easier to distinguish from an overtly aggressive post than from a covertly aggressive one.

A weakness of our approach is the vocabulary of the BERT models. First, the meaning of emojis is ignored, and they are tokenized as unknown symbols, although they frequently occur in the dataset. For example, 😂 is the most frequent emoji in the English training dataset (488 occur-

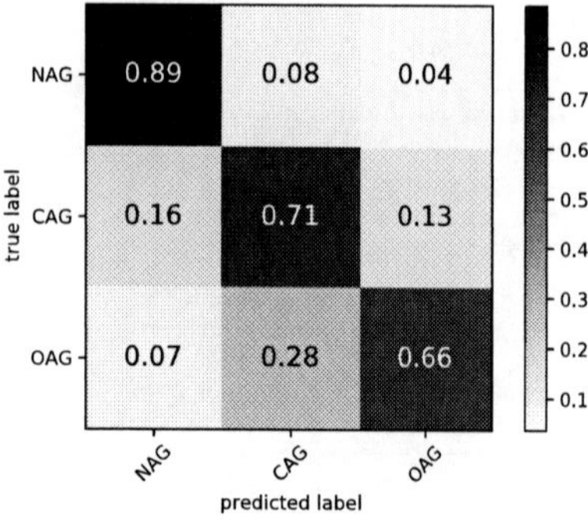

Figure 4: Confusion matrix for task A on the English test dataset.

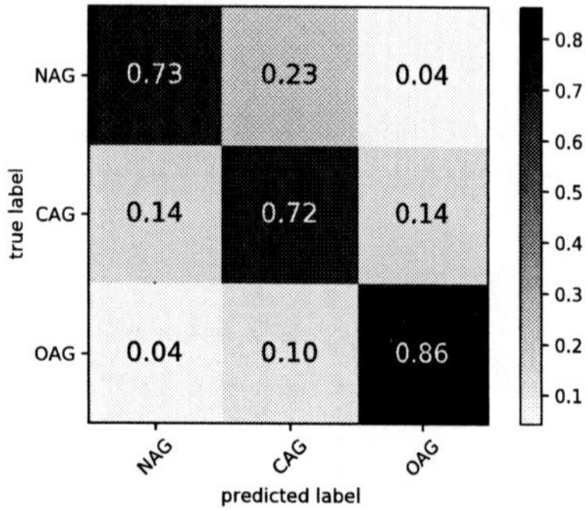

Figure 5: Confusion matrix for task A on the Hindi test dataset.

rences) followed by 👍 (239 occurrences). We assume that the model's performance could be improved by replacing each emoji with its text representation from the Unicode standard, such as *face with tears of joy* or *thumbs up*.

Moreover, the Hindi and Bangla datasets contain non-Latin characters. The pre-trained multilingual BERT that we use for our submission discards all these characters. However, there is another BERT model that overcomes this issue. It is called *multilingual cased* and is trained on non-normalized text (no lower casing, accent stripping, or Unicode normalization). This model is tailored to datasets with non-Latin characters, and we assume it would perform better than our current approach for the Hindi and Bangla datasets.

Last but not least, note that the class distribution of the Hindi test dataset for both tasks is much different compared to the training and validation datasets. Presumably, the reason for that is that the test dataset was sampled from a different social media platform than the training and validation datasets. More details can be found in the dataset description paper (Bhattacharya et al., 2020).

6. Conclusions and Future Work

When fine-tuning complex neural networks, such as BERT, one issue on small datasets is the instability of the classification performance. From one random weight initialization to the next or with slight changes to the training data, the performance can vary significantly, and training needs to be restarted many times to select a well-performing model. To overcome the issue of instability, we use bootstrap aggregating (bagging) as a variance reduction technique and combine the predictions of multiple BERT models in an ensemble. Our approach outperforms all other participating teams at five out of six tasks. In our experiments, we further show that the classification performance of an ensemble increases for up to 15 BERT models. Adding more models does not improve the ensemble. The ensembling approach outperforms a single BERT model by approximately two percentage points on average. One direction for future work is to evaluate ensembles of BERT and its successors, such as generalized autoregressive pre-training for language understanding (XLnet) (Yang et al., 2019).

7. Bibliographical References

Basile, V., Bosco, C., Fersini, E., Nozza, D., Patti, V., Pardo, F. M. R., Rosso, P., and Sanguinetti, M. (2019). Semeval-2019 task 5: Multilingual detection of hate speech against immigrants and women in twitter. In *Proceedings of the International Workshop on Semantic Evaluation (SemEval@NAACL)*, pages 54–63. Association for Computational Linguistics.

Bhattacharya, S., Singh, S., Kumar, R., Bansal, A., Bhagat, A., Dawer, Y., Lahiri, B., and Ojha, A. K. (2020). Developing a multilingual annotated corpus of misogyny and aggression. *arXiv preprint arXiv:2003.07428*.

Bosco, C., Felice, D., Poletto, F., Sanguinetti, M., and Maurizio, T. (2018). Overview of the EVALITS 2018 hate speech detection task. In *Proceedings of the Evaluation Campaign of Natural Language Processing and Speech Tools for Italian (EVALITA)*, volume 2263, pages 1–9. CEUR.

Devlin, J., Chang, M.-W., Lee, K., and Toutanova, K. (2018). Bert: Pre-training of deep bidirectional transformers for language understanding. *arXiv preprint arXiv:1810.04805*.

Fersini, E., Rosso, P., and Anzovino, M. (2018). Overview of the task on automatic misogyny identification at IberEval 2018. In *Proceedings of the Workshop on Evaluation of Human Language Technologies for Iberian Languages (IberEval@SEPLN)*, pages 214–228. CEUR.

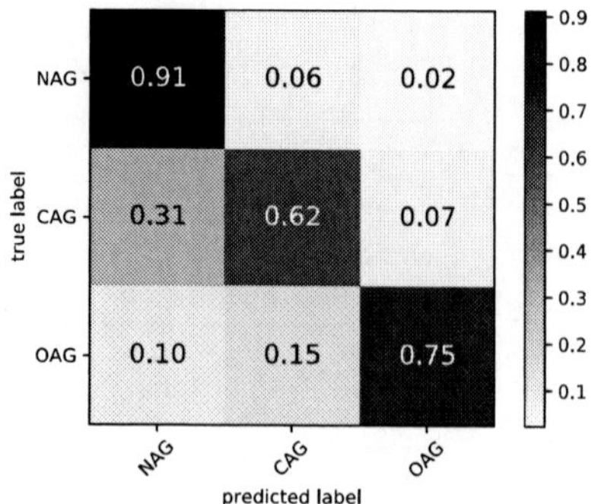

Figure 6: Confusion matrix for task A on the Bangla test dataset.

Hsueh, M., Yogeeswaran, K., and Malinen, S. (2015). "leave your comment below": Can biased online comments influence our own prejudicial attitudes and behaviors? *Human Communication Research*, 41(4):557–576.

Kumar, R., Ojha, A. K., Malmasi, S., and Zampieri, M. (2018a). Benchmarking aggression identification in social media. In *Proceedings of the Workshop on Trolling, Aggression and Cyberbullying (TRAC@COLING)*, pages 1–11. Association for Computational Linguistics.

Kumar, R., Reganti, A. N., Bhatia, A., and Maheshwari, T. (2018b). Aggression-annotated Corpus of Hindi-English Code-mixed Data. In *Proceedings of the International Conference on Language Resources and Evaluation (LREC)*. European Language Resources Association.

Kumar, R., Ojha, A. K., Malmasi, S., and Zampieri, M. (2020). Evaluating aggression identification in social media. In *Proceedings of the Workshop on Trolling, Aggression and Cyberbullying (TRAC@LREC)*. European Language Resources Association.

Mozafari, M., Farahbakhsh, R., and Crespi, N. (2019). A bert-based transfer learning approach for hate speech detection in online social media. In *Proceedings of the International Conference on Complex Networks and Their Applications (COMPLEX NETWORKS)*, pages 928–940. Springer.

Nikolov, A. and Radivchev, V. (2019). Nikolov-radivchev at semeval-2019 task 6: Offensive tweet classification with bert and ensembles. In *Proceedings of the International Workshop on Semantic Evaluation (SemEval@NAACL)*, pages 691–695. Association for Computational Linguistics.

Peters, M., Neumann, M., Iyyer, M., Gardner, M., Clark, C., Lee, K., and Zettlemoyer, L. (2018). Deep contextualized word representations. In *Proceedings of the Conference of the North American Chapter of the Association for Computational Linguistics (NAACL)*, pages 2227–2237. Association for Computational Linguistics.

Risch, J. and Krestel, R. (2018). Aggression identification using deep learning and data augmentation. In *Proceedings of the Workshop on Trolling, Aggression and Cyberbullying (TRAC@COLING)*, pages 150–158. Association for Computational Linguistics.

Risch, J., Stoll, A., Ziegele, M., and Krestel, R. (2019). hpidedis at germeval 2019: Offensive language identification using a german bert model. In *Proceedings of the Conference on Natural Language Processing (KONVENS)*, pages 403–408. German Society for Computational Linguistics & Language Technology.

Rösner, L., Winter, S., and Krämer, N. C. (2016). Dangerous minds? effects of uncivil online comments on aggressive cognitions, emotions, and behavior. *Computers in Human Behavior*, 58:461–470.

Struß, J. M., Siegel, M., Ruppenhofer, J., Wiegand, M., and Klenner, M. (2019). Overview of germeval task 2, 2019 shared task on the identification of offensive language. In *Proceedings of the Conference on Natural Language Processing (KONVENS)*, pages 352–363. German Soci-

ety for Computational Linguistics & Language Technology.

Vaswani, A., Shazeer, N., Parmar, N., Uszkoreit, J., Jones, L., Gomez, A. N., Kaiser, Ł., and Polosukhin, I. (2017). Attention is all you need. In *Advances in Neural Information Processing Systems (NeurIPS)*, pages 5998–6008. Curran Associates, Inc.

Waseem, Z., Davidson, T., Warmsley, D., and Weber, I. (2017). Understanding abuse: A typology of abusive language detection subtasks. In *Proceedings of the Workshop on Abusive Language Online (ALW@ACL)*, pages 78–84. Association for Computational Linguistics.

Wiegand, M., Siegel, M., and Ruppenhofer, J. (2018). Overview of the germeval 2018 shared task on the identification of offensive language. In *Proceedings of the Conference on Natural Language Processing (KONVENS)*, pages 1–10. Austrian Academy of Sciences.

Yang, Z., Dai, Z., Yang, Y., Carbonell, J., Salakhutdinov, R. R., and Le, Q. V. (2019). Xlnet: Generalized autoregressive pretraining for language understanding. In H. Wallach, et al., editors, *Advances in Neural Information Processing Systems (NeurIPS)*, pages 5753–5763. Curran Associates, Inc.

Zampieri, M., Malmasi, S., Nakov, P., Rosenthal, S., Farra, N., and Kumar, R. (2019a). Predicting the type and target of offensive posts in social media. In *Proceedings of the Conference of the North American Chapter of the Association for Computational Linguistics (NAACL)*, pages 1415–1420. Association for Computational Linguistics.

Zampieri, M., Malmasi, S., Nakov, P., Rosenthal, S., Farra, N., and Kumar, R. (2019b). Semeval-2019 task 6: Identifying and categorizing offensive language in social media (OffensEval). In *Proceedings of the International Workshop on Semantic Evaluation (SemEval@NAACL)*, pages 75–86. Association for Computational Linguistics.

Zampieri, M., Nakov, P., Rosenthal, S., Atanasova, P., Karadzhov, G., Mubarak, H., Derczynski, L., Pitenis, Z., and Çöltekin, c. (2020). SemEval-2020 Task 12: Multilingual Offensive Language Identification in Social Media (OffensEval 2020). In *Proceedings of the International Workshop on Semantic Evaluation (SemEval@COLING)*. Association for Computational Linguistics.

Proceedings of the Second Workshop on Trolling, Aggression and Cyberbullying, pages 62–68
Language Resources and Evaluation Conference (LREC 2020), Marseille, 11–16 May 2020
© European Language Resources Association (ELRA), licensed under CC-BY-NC

Scmhl5 at TRAC-2 Shared Task on Aggression Identification: Bert Based Ensemble Learning Approach

Han Liu, Pete Burnap, Wafa Alorainy, Matthew L. Williams
Cardiff University, Cardiff, United Kingdom
{liuh48, burnapp, alorainyws, williamsm7}@cardiff.ac.uk

Abstract

This paper presents a system developed during our participation (team name: scmhl5) in the TRAC-2 Shared Task on aggression identification. In particular, we participated in English Sub-task A on three-class classification ('Overtly Aggressive', 'Covertly Aggressive' and 'Non-aggressive') and English Sub-task B on binary classification for Misogynistic Aggression ('gendered' or 'non-gendered'). For both sub-tasks, our method involves using the pre-trained Bert model for extracting the text of each instance into a 768-dimensional vector of embeddings, and then training an ensemble of classifiers on the embedding features. Our method obtained accuracy of 0.703 and weighted F-measure of 0.664 for Sub-task A, whereas for Sub-task B the accuracy was 0.869 and weighted F-measure was 0.851. In terms of the rankings, the weighted F-measure obtained using our method for Sub-task A is ranked in the 10th out of 16 teams, whereas for Sub-task B the weighted F-measure is ranked in the 8th out of 15 teams.

Keywords: Bert, Ensemble Learning, Aggression Identification, Word Embedding

1. Introduction

In the era of social networks, we have witnessed an increase in people misusing the platforms for propagating messages that are offensive and/or aggressive. Therefore, it has been a priority research topic for people to develop tools for automatic detection of offensive language (Burnap and Williams, 2015; Burnap and Williams, 2016).

Due to the rapid growth of data relating to online social interactions, machine learning approaches have been increasingly popular for natural language processing in social media analysis, such as word embedding through neural network based learning approaches. In this paper, we describe a system based on Bert embedding and ensemble learning, for participating in a shared task on aggression identification (Kumar et al., 2020) in the Second Workshop on Trolling, Aggression and Cyberbullying. In particular, we entered two sub-tasks (A and B) of the above-mentioned shared task, where one is about a three-class classification task for identifying that a text message is 'Overtly Aggressive' (OAG), 'Covertly Aggressive' (CAG) or 'Non-aggressive' (NAG), whereas the other one is about a binary classification task for identifying that a message is 'gendered' (GEN) or 'non-gendered' (NEGN). We obtained accuracy of 0.703 and weighted F-measure of 0.664 for Sub-task A, whereas for Sub-task B the accuracy and weighted F-measure were 0.869 and 0.851, respectively. Moreover, the weighted F-measure obtained using our method for Sub-task A is ranked in the 10th out of 16 teams, where the weighted F-measure ranked in the first place is 0.803. For Sub-task B, the weighted F-measure obtained using our method is ranked in the 8th out of 15 teams, where the weighted F-measure ranked in the first place 0.872.

The rest of this paper is organized as follows: Section 2 provides a review of recently published works on identification of aggressive languages. In Section 3, we describe the shared task dataset in detail and present the method that we adopted for developing our system for aggression identification. In Section 4, we report the results obtained on both the validation data and the test data. In Section 5, the conclusion of this paper is drawn and some further directions are suggested towards advancing the effectiveness of aggression identification.

2. Related Work

Since the spread of online offensive and/or aggressive language could lead to disruptive anti-social outcomes, it has become critical in many countries to consider the posting of such language as a legal issue (Banks, 2010) and to take actions against the propagation of aggression, cyberbullying and hate speech (Banks, 2011).

In the context of machine learning based identification of offensive and/or aggressive language, traditional approaches of feature extraction from text include Bag-of-Words (BOW) (Kwok and Wang, 2013; Liu et al., 2019a), N-grams (NG) in word level (Perez and Luque, 2019; Liu and Forss, 2014; Watanabe et al., 2018), NG in character level (Gambäck and Sikdar, 2017; Perez and Luque, 2019), typed dependencies (Burnap and Williams, 2016), part-of-speech tags (Davidson et al., 2017), dictionary based approaches (Tulkens et al., 2016) and othering lexicons (Burnap and Williams, 2016; Alorainy et al., 2019). Some traditional learning approaches used for training classifiers include Support Vector Machine (SVM) (Burnap and Williams, 2016; Indurthi et al., 2019; Perez and Luque, 2019; Orasan, 2018), Naive Bayes (NB) (Kwok and Wang, 2013; Liu et al., 2019a), Decision Trees (DT) (Watanabe et al., 2018; Liu et al., 2019a), Logistic Regression (LR) (Xiang et al., 2012; Waseem and Hovy, 2016), decision tree ensembles such as Random Forest (RF) (Burnap and Williams, 2015; Orasan, 2018) and Gradient Boosted Trees (Badjatiya et al., 2017), ensembles based on SVM (Malmasi and Zampieri, 2018) and fuzzy approaches (Liu et al., 2019a; Liu et al., 2019b). Moreover, some challenges in terms of discriminating hate speech from profanity have been highlighted in (Malmasi and Zampieri, 2018) for justifying the necessity of extracting deeper features instead of superficial ones (e.g., BOW and NG). From this perspective, embedding learning approaches have recently become the state of the art for automatic extraction of semantic features, e.g. Word2Vec (Nobata et al., 2016), Glove (Zhang et al., 2018; Badjatiya et al., 2017; Kshirsagar et al., 2018; Orasan, 2018), FastText (Pratiwi et al., 2018; Herwanto et al., 2019; Galery et al., 2018). There are also some end-to-end learning approaches of Deep Neural Networks (DNN) (Nina-Alcocer, 2019; Yuan et al., 2016; Ribeiro and Silva, 2019), e.g. Convolutional Neural Networks (CNN) (Gambäck and Sikdar, 2017; Park and Fung, 2017; Roy et al., 2018; Huang et al., 2018), Long-Short Term Memory (LSTM) (Badjatiya et al., 2017; Pitsilis et al., 2018; Nikhil et al., 2018; Kumar et al., 2018) and Gated Recurrent Unit (GRU) (Zhang et al., 2018; Galery et al., 2018) or combination of different DNN architectures in an ensemble setting (Madisetty and Desarkar, 2018), which are adopted for enhancement of feature representation and classification, based on word embeddings produced by Word2Vec, Glove or FastText. However, embedding approaches such as Word2Vec can not achieve contextualized representation of words, i.e. the same word used in different contexts is represented in the same numeric vector using the above-mentioned approaches, which could affect the classification performance due to the lack of contextual information from the features. In order to achieve effectively contextualized representation of features, some more advanced embedding approaches including ELMo (Bojkovsky and Pikuliak, 2019) and Bert (Mozafari et al., 2019; Nikolov and Radivchev, 2019) have recently been developed showing the state of the art performance for offensive and/or aggressive language identification and other similar tasks of natural language processing. There are also applications of Bert in the setting of ensemble learning, e.g. an ensemble of Bert models has been applied to an offensive language identification shared task (Risch et al., 2019).

3. Methodology and Data

In this section, we will provide details of the data set provided for the shared task and present the procedure of our method in detail.

3.1. Dataset

The dataset (Bhattacharya et al., 2020) provided for the shared task contains 6529 text instances in total, which involves a training set of 4263 instances, a validation set of 1066 instances and a test set of 1200 instances. The characteristics of the data set are shown in Table 1.

Table 1: Class Frequency on Training, Validation and Test Sets

Task	Class	Training Set	Validation Set	Test set
Sub-task EN-A	NAG	3375	836	690
	CAG	453	117	224
	OAG	435	113	286
Sub-task EN-B	NGEN	3954	993	1025
	GEN	309	73	175

For Sub-task A, the frequency distribution among the three classes 'NAG', 'CAG' and 'OAG' in the training set is 3375:453:435, whereas the distributions in the validation

and test sets are 836:117:113 and 690:224:286, respectively. The above details indicate that the training set has a class frequency distribution very similar to the one in the validation set but the validation set and the test set show considerably different distributions, which may lead to the case that the performance obtained on the validation set is different from the one obtained on the test set.

For Sub-task B, the frequency distribution between the two classes 'NGEN' and 'GEN' is 3954:309, whereas the distributions in the validation and test sets are 993:73 and 1025:175, respectively. Similar to the characteristic found for Sub-task A, the above details for Sub-task B indicate again a considerable difference on the class frequency distribution between the validation set and the test set, while the training set and the validation set show very similar distributions. The above characteristic may also result in the case that the performance obtained on the validation set is different from the one obtained on the test set.

3.2. Method

The method used for Sub-task A on aggression identification involves two main steps, namely, extraction of embedding features and ensemble learning for classification. Before the two main steps, the text for each instance is preprocessed by removing hashtags, mentions and URLs, converting all words to their lower cases and transforming all emojis to their text descriptions.

In the feature extraction step, each text instance is transformed into a 768-dimensional feature vector by using the pre-trained Bert embedding model (Devlin et al., 2018). In particular, we used the base uncased model of Bert, which consists of 12 layers alongside 768 units per layer. In this setting, each token (word) is transformed into a 768-dimensional vector, so an instance that involves m tokens would be represented in the form of a $m \times 768$ matrix (m vectors). On this basis, the 768-dimensional feature vector of each instance is obtained by averaging the above-mentioned m word vectors.

In the classification step, the classifier is trained in the setting of ensemble learning. In particular, the creation of an ensemble through our designed approach involves four levels, namely, feature sub-sampling, class imbalance handling, multi-class handling and training of base classifiers. The whole framework of ensemble setting is illustrated in Fig. 1.

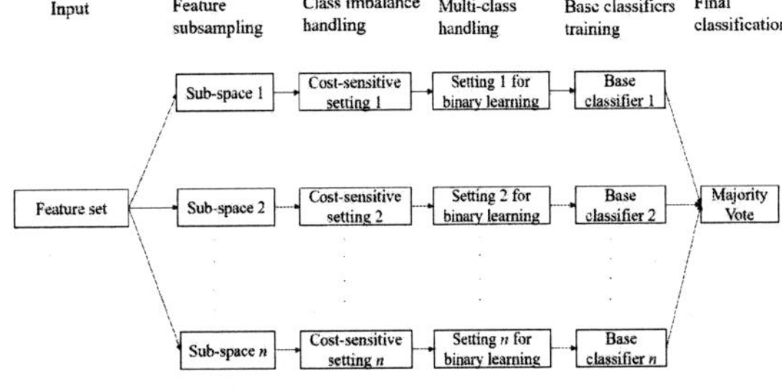

Figure 1: Framework of Ensemble Setting

In the top level for feature sub-sampling, the aim is to encourage the creation of diversity among base classifiers, which is achieved by adopting the random subspace (RS) method (Ho, 1998) to draw n subsets of the original feature set, such that n different classifiers are trained on the n feature subsets.

In the second level for class imbalance handling, a cost-sensitive learning method is adopted to enable the classifier trained on each feature subset (drawn in the top level) to be cost-sensitive, no matter which one of the supervised learning algorithms is adopted for training classifiers.

In the third level for multi-class handling, the aim is to transform the 3-class classification problem for suiting a 2-class learning algorithm, i.e. some algorithms cannot directly perform multi-class learning, so a specific strategy of multi-class handling needs to be involved to enable that 2-class learning algorithms can work. Some popular strategies include 'one-against-all', 'one-against-one', 'random error correction code' and 'exhaustive error correction code'.

In the fourth level for training of base classifiers, a supervised learning algorithm needs to be adopted, where the Stochastic Gradient Descent algorithm is chosen in our setting for training n linear classifiers on the n feature subsets produced by the RS method. The final classification is made by fusing the outputs of n linear classifiers through majority voting.

The method used for Sub-task B on identification of misogynistic aggression is almost the same as the one adopted for Sub-task A, but the only difference is that the third level for multi-class handling is dropped, due to the fact that Sub-task B involves a binary classification problem. Therefore, the method used for Sub-task B involves three levels, namely, feature sub-sampling, class imbalance handling and training of base classifiers.

4. Results

In this section, we describe the experimental setup and discuss the results obtained in the development and testing stages.

4.1. Development Stage

In the development stage, we conducted experiments by using the pre-trained Bert embedding model and various learning algorithms, namely, Support vector machine (SVM), Naive Bayes (NB), Stochastic Gradient Descent (SGD) and a fuzzy rule learning approach (Fuzzy) (Huehn and Huellermeier, 2009), due to their relatively low computational complexity and the suitability of this kind of traditional learning algorithms for processing small data (Liu et al., 2019a). In particular, the results shown in Tables 2 and 3 were obtained by using the validation set for evaluating the performance of classifiers produced by various algorithms and determining which algorithm is used to train the base classifiers in the setting of random subspace based ensemble learning.

Before feature extraction, all the instances were pre-processed by removing hashtags, mentions and URLs and converting all words to their lower cases. Also, all the emojis were transformed into their text descriptions by using the emoji-java library[1].

In the feature extraction stage, each text instance was transformed into a 768-dimensional feature vector using the pre-trained base uncased model of Bert, which is based on the Java library of easy-bert[2]. The above decision is based on the considerations that a base Bert model requires less memory than a large Bert model and all words in the text for each instance have been converted to lower cases in the pre-processing stage leading to the unnecessity of using a cased Bert model.

In the classification stage, we used the implementations of various algorithms from the Weka library (Hall et al., 2009). In terms of hyper-parameter settings, SVM was set to normalize the training data and train a non-linear classifier using the polynomial kernel and the sequential minimal optimization algorithm (SMO) (Platt, 1998), where the complexity parameter C is set to 1.0 and the batch size is set to 100. The fuzzy rule learning approach was set to involve 2 runs of rule optimization and using 1/3 of the training data for rule pruning, where the product T-norm was used to compute the degree to which an instance is covered by a fuzzy rule and the rule stretching method (Huehn and Huellermeier, 2009) is adopted to classify any instances that are not covered by any fuzzy rules. SGD was set to train a linear classifier using the Hinge loss with the learning rate (lr) of 0.01 through 500 epochs, where the batch size was set to 100 and the regularization constant is set to 0.0001. Moreover, all of the algorithms (SVM, NB, Fuzzy and SGD) were adopted for training classifiers in a cost sensitive setting, i.e. the trained classifiers are made cost-sensitive by assigning higher cost to the case of misclassifying instances of the minority class. In addition, due to the case that SGD is essentially a two-class learning algorithm, the three-class classification problem was transformed to suit classifiers trained by SGD through using the 'random error correction code' method.

Table 2: Results on Validation Data for Sub-task EN-A

Method	F1(NAG)	F1(CAG)	F1(OAG)	F1(Weighted)	Accuracy
SVM	0.890	0.016	0.337	0.735	**0.796**
NB	0.557	**0.261**	0.084	0.475	0.414
Fuzzy	0.868	0.126	0.228	0.719	0.757
SGD	0.886	0.017	**0.367**	0.736	**0.796**
RS	**0.891**	0.101	0.269	**0.738**	0.794

For Sub-task A, the results obtained on the validation set are shown in Table 2, which indicates that SGD and SVM perform considerably better than NB and the fuzzy approach. Although SVM and SGD show almost the same performance in terms of weighted F-measure, SGD outperforms SVM for the minority class 'OAG'. Moreover, SGD is capable of training updateable classifiers in the setting of incremental learning, i.e., previously trained classifiers can be updated by learning incrementally from instances newly added into the training set. This is an essential advantage of SGD in comparison with SVM (based on SMO) that cannot effectively achieve incremental learning. Therefore, we chose to adopt the SGD algorithm for training and optimizing base classifiers in the setting of ensemble learning, in order to achieve a more effective way of advancing the per-

---

[1]https://github.com/vdurmont/emoji-java

[2]https://github.com/robrua/easy-bert

formance further using a new/updated data set without the need to retrain each base classifier.

The ensemble is created following the procedure shown in Fig. 1. In particular, the RS method is adopted to draw 10 feature subsets, where the size of each subspace is set to 0.5, so there are totally 10 base classifiers trained on the 10 feature subsets. The hyper-parameter settings of SGD are exactly the same as the ones described above about training a single classifier. The results shown in Table 2 indicate that the creation of an ensemble in the above settings leads to a marginal improvement of the performance in comparison with the production of a single classifier by SGD.

For Sub-task B, we followed the same procedure for text pre-processing, feature extraction and classification. For training of the classifiers, we adopted the same set of algorithms (with the same settings of hyper-parameters) for evaluating performance on the validation set. The results shown in Table 3 indicate again the phenomenon that SGD and SVM perform considerably better than NB and the fuzzy approach. Although SGD performs marginally worse than SVM in terms of weighted F-measure, SGD outperforms SVM for the minority class 'GEN'. As mentioned earlier in this section, SGD is capable of updating previously trained classifiers by learning incrementally from instances newly added into the training set, so we chose to adopt the SGD algorithm again for training and optimizing base classifiers in the setting of ensemble learning.

Table 3: Results on Validation Data for Sub-task EN-B

Method	F1(NGEN)	F1(GEN)	F1(Weighted)	Accuracy
SVM	0.967	0.171	0.912	0.936
NB	0.566	0.152	0.538	0.426
Fuzzy	0.96	0.146	0.904	0.923
SGD	0.959	0.265	0.911	0.922
RS	0.965	0.417	**0.928**	0.934

Following the same ensemble settings adopted for Sub-task A, an ensemble of SGD classifiers is built with a cost-sensitive setting for Sub-task B, but the step for multi-class handling is dropped, given that Sub-task B is a binary classification task. The results shown in Table 3 indicate that the creation of an ensemble leads to an improvement of the performance on weighted F-measure and the score for the minority class, in comparison with the production of a single classifier by using any one of the standard learning algorithms.

4.2. Testing Stage

Based on the results shown in Tables 2 and 3 for the two sub-tasks, we merged the training and validation sets for augmenting the sample size for creating an ensemble of classifiers in the above-described setting (based on Bert, RS and SGD). The results obtained on the test set for the two sub-tasks are shown in Table 4.

It can be seen from Table 4 that the performance obtained on the test set gets considerably lower (by about 7%) in comparison with the one obtained on the validation set for both Sub-tasks A and B, which is likely due to the difference on the data distribution between the two sets of instances, i.e. the weight of the majority class gets lower on

Table 4: Performance on Test Data

Task	Class	F1(Class)	F1(Weighted)	Accuracy
Sub-task EN-A	NAG	0.8152	0.6637	0.7025
	CAG	0.3106		
	OAG	0.5746		
Sub-task EN-B	NGEN	0.9264	0.8514	0.8692
	GEN	0.4120		

the test set, in comparison with the weight on the validation set, for both Sub-tasks.

For Sub-task A, comparing the results shown in Table 2 and Table 4, we can see that the weighted F1-score gets lower on the test set, which seems to be due mainly to the case that the F1-score for the majority class 'NAG' gets lower. Moreover, the F1-scores for the other two classes 'CAG' and 'OAG' get much higher on the test set. Given that the class frequency distribution among the three classes 'NAG', 'CAG' and 'OAG' is 836:117:113 on the validation set and is 690:224:286 on the test set, it seems that the performance difference is likely to result from the difference on the data distribution.

For Sub-task B, comparing the results shown in Table 3 and Table 4, we can see again that the weighted F1-score gets lower on the test set, which seems to be due mainly to the case that the F1-score for the majority class 'NGEN' gets lower. Moreover, for the minority class 'GEN', the F1-score obtained on the test set is almost the same as the score obtained on the validation set. Given that the frequency distribution between the two classes 'NGEN' and 'GEN' is 993:73 on the validation set and is 1025:175 on the test set, it seems that the change in the data distribution does not really impact on the performance for the minority class 'GEN" but shows a considerable impact on the performance for the majority class 'NGEN'.

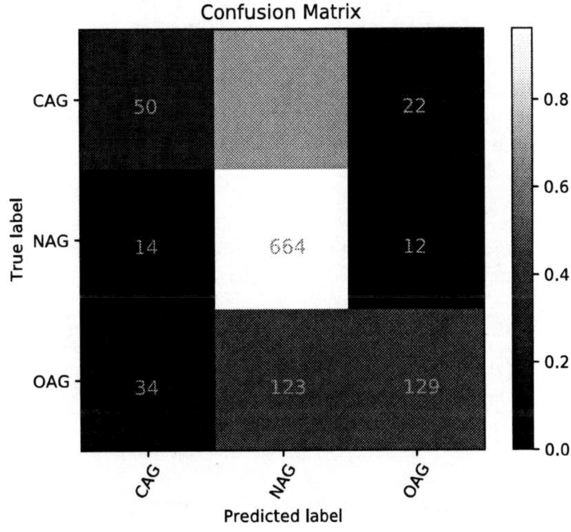

Figure 2: Sub-task EN-A, scmhl5 CodaLab 571565 (An ensemble of SGD classifiers trained on embedding features prepared by Bert and RS)

More detailed results obtained on the test set for the two sub-tasks are shown in Figs. 2 and 3 in the form of con-

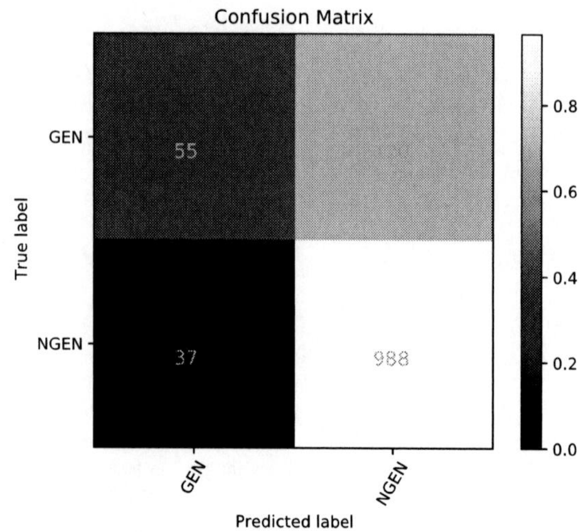

Figure 3: Sub-task EN-B, scmhl5 CodaLab 571564 (An ensemble of SGD classifiers trained on embedding features prepared by Bert and RS)

fusion matrixes, which indicate that the cases of incorrect classifications mainly result from false negatives for the minority class, i.e. some instances of aggressive language were not successfully detected due to the insufficient ability to generalize thoroughly on test instances.

Based on the results shown in Table 4 and Figs. 2 and 3, we tried to reduce the learning rate (lr) from 0.01 to 0.005 towards achieving better optimization of the parameters of the SGD classifiers, i.e. reducing the learning rate can generally help better avoid the case of local optimization. The results obtained by using the lower value of 'lr' are shown in Tables 5 and 6, which indicate that the performance gets slightly lower after reducing the learning rate for both sub-tasks A and B. The results suggest that the reduction of the learning rate may increase the chance of overfitting on a small data set and thus lower the generalization performance on test data.

Table 5: Results for Sub-task EN-A (obtained by deploying an ensemble of SGD classifiers trained on embedding features prepared by Bert and RS).

System	F1 (weighted)	Accuracy
Bert+RS+SGD(lr=0.01)	**0.6637**	0.7025
Bert+RS+SGD(lr=0.005)	0.6300	0.6842

Table 6: Results for Sub-task EN-B (obtained by deploying an ensemble of SGD classifiers trained on embedding features prepared by Bert and RS).

System	F1 (weighted)	Accuracy
Bert+RS+SGD(lr=0.01)	**0.8514**	0.8692
Bert+RS+SGD(lr=0.005)	0.8428	0.87

5. Conclusion

We participated in the shared task on aggression identification in the 2nd Workshop on Trolling, Aggression and Cyberbullying. In particular, we entered two English sub-tasks (A and B) for identifying the intensity of aggression (i.e. 'Overtly Aggressive', 'Covertly Aggressive' or 'Non-aggressive') and detecting misogynistic aggression (i.e. 'gendered' or 'non-gendered'). We built two systems for the above-mentioned sub-tasks, and both systems were built in the setting of ensemble learning based on the embedding features extracted using the pre-trained Bert model. We obtained a weighted F1-score of 0.664 for Sub-task A and a score of 0.851 for Sub-task B.

In future, we will explore the effectiveness of extracting multiple types of embedding features using various embedding models (e.g. Bert and ELMo), towards achieving more advanced settings of ensemble learning through both early fusion (in the feature level) and late fusion (in the classification level). It is also worth exploring the use of a larger volume of external data for updating the SGD classifiers in the setting of incremental learning, towards advancing the generalization performance further. In addition, we will add a further experiment by selecting a subset of the test set that has the same class frequency distribution as the validation set, in order to investigate whether the performance obtained on the test subset can be more similar to the one obtained on the validation set after making the class frequency distribution consistent between the two data sets.

Bibliographical References

Alorainy, W., Burnap, P., Liu, H., and Williams, M. (2019). The enemy among us: Detecting cyber hate speech with threats-based othering language embeddings. *ACM Transactions on the Web*, 13(3):1–26.

Badjatiya, P., Gupta, S., Gupta, M., and Varma, V. (2017). Deep learning for hate speech detection in tweets. In *Proceedings of the 26th International Conference on World Wide Web Companion*, pages 759–760, Perth, Australia, 3-7 April.

Banks, J. (2010). Regulating hate speech online. *International Review of Law, Computers and Technology*, 24(3):233–239.

Banks, J. (2011). European regulation of cross-border hate speech in cyberspace: The limits of legislation. *European Journal of Crime, Criminal Law and Criminal Justice*, 19(1):1–13.

Bhattacharya, S., Singh, S., Kumar, R., Bansal, A., Bhagat, A., Dawer, Y., Lahiri, B., and Ojha, A. K. (2020). Developing a multilingual annotated corpus of misogyny and aggression.

Bojkovsky, M. and Pikuliak, M. (2019). STUFIIT at SemEval-2019 Task 5: Multilingual hate speech detection on twitter with MUSE and ELMo embeddings. In *Proceedings of the 13th International Workshop on Semantic Evaluation*, pages 464–468, Minneapolis, Minnesota, USA, 6-7 June.

Burnap, P. and Williams, M. L. (2015). Cyber hate speech on twitter: An application of machine classification and statistical modeling for policy and decision making. *Policy & Internet*, 7(2):223–242.

Burnap, P. and Williams, M. (2016). Us and them: identifying cyber hate on twitter across multiple protected characteristics. *EPJ Data Science*, 5(11).

Davidson, T., Warmsley, D., Macy, M., and Weber, I. (2017). Automated Hate Speech Detection and the Problem of Offensive Language. In *Proceedings of ICWSM*.

Devlin, J., Chang, M.-W., Lee, K., and Toutanova, K. (2018). BERT: Pre-training of deep bidirectional transformers for language understanding. In Marilyn Walker, et al., editors, *Proceedings of Annual Conference of the North American Chapter of the Association for Computational Linguistics*, New Orleans, Louisiana. Association for Computational Linguistics.

Galery, T., Charitos, E., and Tian, Y. (2018). Aggression identification and multi lingual word embeddings. In Ritesh Kumar, et al., editors, *Proceedings of the First Workshop on Trolling, Aggression and Cyberbullying (TRAC-2018)*, Santa Fe, New Mexico, USA. Association for Computational Linguistics.

Gambäck, B. and Sikdar, U. K. (2017). Using Convolutional Neural Networks to Classify Hate-speech. In *Proceedings of the First Workshop on Abusive Language Online*, pages 85–90.

Hall, M., Frank, E., Holmes, G., Pfahringer, B., Reutemann, P., and Witten, I. H. (2009). The WEKA data mining software: an update. *SIGKDD Explorations*, 11(1):10–18.

Herwanto, G. B., Ningtyas, A. M., Nugraha, K. E., and Trisna, I. N. P. (2019). Hate speech and abusive language classification using fastText. In *2019 International Seminar on Research of Information Technology and Intelligent Systems (ISRITI)*, Yogyakarta, Indonesia, 5-6 December.

Ho, T. K. (1998). The random subspace method for constructing decision forests. *IEEE Transactions on Pattern Analysis and Machine Intelligence*, 20(8):832–844.

Huang, Q., Inkpen, D., Zhang, J., and Bruwaene, D. V. (2018). Cyberbullying intervention based on convolutional neural networks. In Ritesh Kumar, et al., editors, *Proceedings of the First Workshop on Trolling, Aggression and Cyberbullying (TRAC-2018)*, Santa Fe, New Mexico, USA. Association for Computational Linguistics.

Huehn, J. C. and Huellermeier, E. (2009). FURIA: An algorithm for unordered fuzzy rule induction. *Data Mining and Knowledge Discovery*, 19:293–319.

Indurthi, V., Syed, B., Shrivastava, M., Chakravartula, N., Gupta, M., and Varma, V. (2019). Fermi at SemEval-2019 Task 5: Using sentence embeddings to identify hate speech against immigrants and women on twitter. In *Proceedings of the 13th International Workshop on Semantic Evaluation*, pages 70–74, Minneapolis, Minnesota, USA, 6-7 June.

Kshirsagar, R., Cukuvac, T., McKeown, K., and McGregor, S. (2018). Predictive embeddings for hate speech detection on twitter. In *Proceedings of the Second Workshop on Abusive Language Online (ALW2)*, pages 26–32, Brussels, Belgium, 31 October.

Kumar, R., Bhanodai, G., Pamula, R., and Chennuru, M. R. (2018). TRAC-1 shared task on aggression identification: IIT(ISM)@COLING'18. In Ritesh Kumar, et al., editors, *Proceedings of the First Workshop on Trolling, Aggression and Cyberbullying (TRAC-2018)*, Santa Fe, New Mexico, USA. Association for Computational Linguistics.

Kumar, R., Ojha, A. K., Malmasi, S., and Zampieri, M. (2020). Evaluating aggression identification in social media. In Ritesh Kumar, et al., editors, *Proceedings of the Second Workshop on Trolling, Aggression and Cyberbullying (TRAC-2020)*, Paris, France, May. European Language Resources Association (ELRA).

Kwok, I. and Wang, Y. (2013). Locate the hate: Detecting Tweets Against Blacks. In *Twenty-Seventh AAAI Conference on Artificial Intelligence*.

Liu, S. and Forss, T. (2014). Combining N-gram based similarity analysis with sentiment analysis in web content classification. In *Proceedings of the International Joint Conference on Knowledge Discovery, Knowledge Engineering and Knowledge Management*, pages 530–537, Rome, Italy, 21-24 October.

Liu, H., Burnap, P., Alorainy, W., and Williams, M. L. (2019a). A fuzzy approach to text classification with two stage training for ambiguous instances. *IEEE Transactions on Computational Social Systems*, 6(2):227–240.

Liu, H., Burnap, P., Alorainy, W., and Williams, M. L. (2019b). Fuzzy multi-task learing for hate speech type identification. In *WWW '19 The World Wide Web Conference*, pages 3006–3012, San Francisco, CA, USA, 13-17 May.

Madisetty, S. and Desarkar, M. S. (2018). Aggression detection in social media using deep neural networks. In Ritesh Kumar, et al., editors, *Proceedings of the First Workshop on Trolling, Aggression and Cyberbullying (TRAC-2018)*, Santa Fe, New Mexico, USA. Association for Computational Linguistics.

Malmasi, S. and Zampieri, M. (2018). Challenges in Discriminating Profanity from Hate Speech. *Journal of Experimental & Theoretical Artificial Intelligence*, 30:1–16.

Mozafari, M., Farahbakhsh, R., and Crespi, N. (2019). A BERT-based transfer learning approach for hate speech detection in online social media. In *International Conference on Complex Networks and Their Applications*, pages 928–940, Lisbon, Portugal, 10-12 December.

Nikhil, N., Pahwa, R., Nirala, M. K., and Khilnani, R. (2018). LSTMs with attention for aggression detection. In Ritesh Kumar, et al., editors, *Proceedings of the First Workshop on Trolling, Aggression and Cyberbullying (TRAC-2018)*, Santa Fe, New Mexico, USA. Association for Computational Linguistics.

Nikolov, A. and Radivchev, V. (2019). Nikolov-Radivchev at SemEval-2019 Task 6: Offensive tweet classification with BERT and ensembles. In *Proceedings of the 13th International Workshop on Semantic Evaluation*, pages 691–695, Minneapolis, Minnesota, USA, 6-7 June.

Nina-Alcocer, V. (2019). HATERecognizer at SemEval-2019 Task 5: Using features and neural networks to face hate recognition. In *Proceedings of the 13th Interna-*

tional Workshop on Semantic Evaluation, pages 409–415, Minneapolis, Minnesota, USA, 6-7 June.

Nobata, C., Tetreault, J., Thomas, A., Mehdad, Y., and Chang, Y. (2016). Abusive Language Detection in Online User Content. In *Proceedings of the 25th International Conference on World Wide Web*, pages 145–153. International World Wide Web Conferences Steering Committee.

Orasan, C. (2018). Aggressive language identification using word embeddings and sentiment features. In Ritesh Kumar, et al., editors, *Proceedings of the First Workshop on Trolling, Aggression and Cyberbullying (TRAC-2018)*, Santa Fe, New Mexico, USA. Association for Computational Linguistics.

Park, J. H. and Fung, P. (2017). One-step and two-step classification for abusive language detection on twitter. In *1st Workshop on Abusive Language Online*, pages 41–45, Vancouver, Canada, 4 August.

Perez, J. M. and Luque, F. M. (2019). Atalaya at SemEval 2019 Task 5: Robust embeddings for tweet classification. In *Proceedings of the 13th International Workshop on Semantic Evaluation*, pages 64–69, Minneapolis, Minnesota, USA, 6-7 June.

Pitsilis, G. K., Ramampiaro, H., and Langseth, H. (2018). Effective hate-speech detection in twitter data using recurrent neural networks. *Applied Intelligence*, 48(12):4730–4742.

Platt, J. (1998). Fast training of support vector machines using sequential minimal optimization. In Bernhard Scholkopf, et al., editors, *Advances in Kernel Methods - Support Vector Learning*, Cambridge, MA, USA. MIT Press.

Pratiwi, N. I., Budi, I., and Alfina, I. (2018). Hate speech detection on indonesian instagram comments using FastText approach. In *International Conference on Advanced Computer Science and Information Systems (ICACSIS)*, Yogyakarta, Indonesia, 27-28 October.

Ribeiro, A. and Silva, N. (2019). INF-HatEval at SemEval-2019 Task 5: Convolutional neural networks for hate speech detection against women and immigrants on twitter. In *Proceedings of the 13th International Workshop on Semantic Evaluation*, pages 420–425, Minneapolis, Minnesota, USA, 6-7 June.

Risch, J., Stoll, A., Ziegele, M., and Krestel, R. (2019). hpiDEDIS at GermEval 2019: Offensive language identification using a German BERT model. In *Proceedings of the 15th Conference on Natural Language Processing (KONVENS)*, pages 403–408, Erlangen, Germany, 8-11 October. German Society for Computational Linguistics & Language Technology.

Roy, A., Kapil, P., Basak, K., and Ekbal, A. (2018). An ensemble approach for aggression identification in English and Hindi text. In Ritesh Kumar, et al., editors, *Proceedings of the First Workshop on Trolling, Aggression and Cyberbullying (TRAC-2018)*, Santa Fe, New Mexico, USA. Association for Computational Linguistics.

Tulkens, S., Hilte, L., Lodewyckx, E., Verhoeven, B., and Daelemans, W. (2016). A Dictionary-based Approach to Racism Detection in Dutch Social Media. In *Proceed-ings of the Workshop Text Analytics for Cybersecurity and Online Safety (TA-COS)*, Portoroz, Slovenia.

Waseem, Z. and Hovy, D. (2016). Hateful symbols or hateful people? predictive features for hate speech detection on twitter. In *Proceedings of NAACL-HLT 2016*, pages 88–93, San Diego, California, USA, 12-17 June.

Watanabe, H., Bouazizi, M., and Ohtsuki, T. (2018). Hate speech on twitter: A pragmatic approach to collect hateful and offensive expressions and perform hate speech detection. *IEEE Access*, PP(99):1–11.

Xiang, G., Fan, B., Wang, L., Hong, J., and Rose, C. (2012). Detecting offensive tweets via topical feature discovery over a large scale twitter corpus. In *Proceedings of the 21st ACM international conference on Information and knowledge management*, pages 1980–1984, Maui, Hawaii, USA, 29 October-2 November.

Yuan, S., Wu, X., and Xiang, Y. (2016). A two phase deep learning model for identifying discrimination from tweets. In *19th International Conference on Extending Database Technology*, pages 696–697, Bordeaux, France, 15-18 March.

Zhang, Z., Robinson, D., and Tepper, J. (2018). Detecting Hate Speech on Twitter Using a Convolution-GRU Based Deep Neural Network. In *Lecture Notes in Computer Science*. Springer Verlag.

Proceedings of the Second Workshop on Trolling, Aggression and Cyberbullying, pages 69–75
Language Resources and Evaluation Conference (LREC 2020), Marseille, 11–16 May 2020
ⓒ European Language Resources Association (ELRA), licensed under CC-BY-NC

The Role of Computational Stylometry in Identifying (Misogynistic) Aggression in English Social Media Texts

Antonio Pascucci[1]**, Raffaele Manna**[1]**, Vincenzo Masucci**[2]**, Johanna Monti**[1]
"L'Orientale" University of Naples - UNIOR NLP Research Group[1], Expert System Corp.[2]
Via Duomo 219 Naples (Italy)[1], Via Nuova Poggioreale 60 Naples (Italy)[2]
{apascucci,rmanna,jmonti}@unior.it, vmasucci@expertsystem.com

Abstract

In this paper, we describe UniOr_ExpSys team participation in TRAC-2 (Trolling, Aggression and Cyberbullying) shared task, a workshop organized as part of LREC 2020. TRAC-2 shared task is organized in two sub-tasks: *Aggression Identification* (a 3-way classification between "Overtly Aggressive", "Covertly Aggressive" and "Non-aggressive" text data) and *Misogynistic Aggression Identification* (a binary classifier for classifying the texts as "gendered" or "non-gendered"). Our approach is based on linguistic rules, stylistic features extraction through stylometric analysis and Sequential Minimal Optimization algorithm in building the two classifiers.

Keywords: Computational Stylometry, Aggression Identification, Social Media

1. Introduction

The spread of offensive and hate speech on social media is one of the issues that mostly concerns the scientific community. The number of hate and offensive posts and comments on social media is growing day by day and the measures adopted by social media managers are often not enough. Most of the time, haters'accounts are simply temporarily blocked, and no other effective measures to combat the phenomenon are taken. In this paper, we describe our participation in TRAC-2 (Ritesh Kumar and Zampieri, 2020) workshop shared task and the results we achieved. TRAC-2 workshop shared task (now in its second edition), focuses on trolling, aggression and cyberbullying detection in a given corpus built ad hoc by the task organizers and is organized in two sub-tasks: *Aggression Identification* task and *Misogynistic Aggression Identification* task. TRAC-2 workshop shared task includes texts in three different languages: Bangla, Hindi and English for both sub-tasks. The participants are allowed to compete for the tasks and the languages they prefer. Considering the importance of linguistic knowledge in our approach, we decided to participate only in the two English sub-tasks (since we don't have linguistic knowledge in Bangla and Hindi). The method we use for text data classification, indeed, is based on a hybrid approach of Computational Stylometry, Machine Learning and Linguistic Rules. This research has been carried out in the context of two innovative industrial PhD projects in cooperation between the "L'Orientale" University of Naples and Expert System Corp. (a semantic intelligence company that creates artificial intelligence, cognitive computing and semantic technology software). That's the reason why we chose the name "UniOr_ExpSys" for our team. The paper is organized as follows: in Section 2 we show Related work in Hate and Offensive speech detection. Section 3 focuses on methodology and data. Results are in Section 4 and Conclusions are in Section 5.

2. Related work

Over the last few years, hate speech (HS) and offensive speech (OS) detection, has generated interest in scholars

(for a survey, see (Schmidt and Wiegand, 2017) and (Fortuna and Nunes, 2018)). The advent of social media represents the main cause of the HS and OS spread. Social networks are an extremely efficient means of communication, but, unfortunately, not everyone makes proper use of them. Increasing vulgarity in online conversations has emerged as a relevant issue in society as well as in science (Ramakrishnan et al., 2019). The difference between HS and OS is subtle but significant and can be summarized as: HS is deemed to be harmful on the basis of defined *protected attributes* such as race, disability, sexuality and so on. In other words, HS is the intention to denigrate "a person or persons on the basis of (alleged) membership in a social group identified by attributes such as race, ethnicity, gender, sexual orientation, religion, age, physical or mental disability, and others" (Britannica, 2015); instead, OS can be described as a speech that "Causes someone to feel hurt, angry, or upset : rude or insulting"[1].

Research on detecting HS presence in social media has been carried out by (Malmasi and Zampieri, 2017). The scholars investigated the dataset built by (Davidson et al., 2017), composed of 14,509 English tweets annotated by three annotators into one of the following three classes: HATE (tweets containing HS), OFFENSIVE (tweets containing OS) and OK (non-offensive tweets). (Malmasi and Zampieri, 2017) used a linear Support Vector Machine to perform multi-class classification and achieved the best performance of 0.78 of text correctly classified with character 4-grams feature. A very ambitious project is *Contro l'odio* (literally *Against hate*), a web platform for monitoring and contrasting discrimination and HS against immigrants in Italy (Capozzi et al., 2019). The classifier they built is trained with the *Italian Hate Speech Corpus* (IHSC) (Sanguinetti et al., 2018), a collection of about 6,000 HS tweets. *Contro l'odio* project extends the research outcomes that emerged from the *Italian Hate Map* project (Musto et al., 2016), combining computational linguistics methods that

---

[1] `https://www.merriam-webster.com/`
`dictionary/offend`

allow users to access a huge amount of information through interactive maps. (De Smedt et al., 2018) proposed a report on multilingual cross-domain (Extremism, Jidahism, Sexism and Racism) perspectives on online HS detection to identify common features of HS across domains. The scholars exploited different techniques (sentiment analysis, text classification, keyword extraction, and collocation extraction) and argued that it is hard to come up with a linguistic definition of HS, because there is no standardized "list of bad words", and if there is, then perpetrators are very creative in coining new offensive terminology.

Cyberbullying is also part of HS and OS, especially if we consider that social media represent real breeding grounds in which new and increasingly sophisticated forms of cyberbullying are being developed. The detection and classification of textual cyberbullying on social media has been well investigated in (Dinakar et al., 2011), (Xu et al., 2012), (Dadvar et al., 2013), and (Burnap and Williams, 2015). With the aim of monitoring the presence of cyberbullying in online texts, CREEP's project (Menini et al., 2019) main goal is to support supervising persons (e.g., educators) at identifying potential cases of cyberbullying. Stylistic features extraction in cyberbullying texts has been also investigated in (Pascucci et al., 2019) with a focus on features that belong to ten different cyberbullying categories characterized by text. Interesting research has been carried out by (Sprugnoli et al., 2018), who built a corpus of WhatsApp chats through a role-play by three classes of students aged 12 and 13 made of 14,600 tokens. In their corpus, the scholars distinguish four cyberbullying roles (Harasser, Victim, Bystander-defender, Bystander-assistant) and different classes of insults or discrimination, such as Body Shame, Sexism, Racism and Sexual Harassment. Their data have been annotated by two annotators and 1,203 cyberbullying expressions have been identified, corresponding to almost 6,000 tokens (41.1% of the whole corpus). Italian scientific community pays a great deal of attention to HS and OS detection shared task, and a few linguistic resources (Sanguinetti et al., 2018), (Poletto et al., 2017), and (Del Vigna et al., 2017) have been developed regarding HS Facebook and Twitter comments in Italian.

The following is a short and certainly not exhaustive list that includes HS and OS shared tasks organized in the last few years:

- *HaSpeeDe* (Bosco et al., 2018), a shared task on HS detection, based on two datasets from two different online social platforms differently featured from the linguistic and communicative point of view. The shared task has been organized in the context of EVALITA 2018 (a periodic evaluation campaign of natural language processing and speech tools for the Italian language);

- *Germeval* (Wiegand et al., 2018), classification of German tweets from Twitter. It included a coarse-grained binary classification task and a fine-grained multiclass classification task;

- *AMI* (Fersini et al., 2018), a shared task on automatic misogyny identification divided in two subtasks: Subtask A on misogyny identification and Subtask B about misogynistic behaviour categorization and target classification. *AMI* shared task has been organized in the context of EVALITA 2018;

- *Hateval* (Basile et al., 2019), a shared task on multilingual detection of HS against immigrants and women in twitter organized as part of SemEval 2019. The shared task involved a total of 74 participants to detect HS in the dataset and to distinguish if the incitement was against an individual rather than a group;

- *Offenseval* (Zampieri et al., 2019b), also organized in the context of SemEval 2019, focuses on identifying and categorizing OS in social media. The task was based on a dataset (OLID - Offensive Language Identification Dataset) (Zampieri et al., 2019a) built ad hoc for this occasion. *Offenseval* was organized in three sub-tasks: in sub-task A, the goal was to discriminate between offensive and non-offensive posts. In subtask B, the focus was on the type of offensive content in the post, and in sub-task C, systems had to detect the target of the offensive posts. The 2020 *Offenseval* edition will be held as part of COLING 2020.

- *TRAC-1* (Kumar et al., 2018a), the first workshop on trolling, aggression and cyberbullying. TRAC-1 shared task (Kumar et al., 2018b) has been organized as part of COLING 2018 conference. TRAC-1 included a shared task on Aggression Identification (Kumar et al., 2018a). The task was to develop a classifier that could make a 3-way classification between Overtly Aggressive (OAG), Covertly Aggressive (CAG), or Non-Aggressive (NAG) text data in Hindi and English. It involved 130 teams, but only 30 of these submitted their systems. Besides, only 20 teams decided to submit their system description paper. TRAC-1 shared task organizers provided two test sets for Hindi and English: the first one was composed of 916 English Facebook comments and 970 Hindi Facebook comments. Additionally, 1,257 English tweets and 1,194 Hindi tweets have been provided as the surprise test set. The three best performing teams in English language in TRAC-1 shared task are: *vista.ue* (Raiyani et al., 2018), *Julian* (Risch and Krestel, 2018), and *saroyehun* (Aroyehun and Gelbukh, 2018). In Table 1 the three systems performances are reported in terms of F1-weighted.

	saroyehun	Julian	vista.ue
Facebook Test set	0.642	0.601	0.581
Surprise Test set	0.592	0.599	0.600

Table 1: Performances achieved by the three TRAC-1 best teams on the TRAC-1 Facebook test set and the Surprise test set for English language

TRAC-2 takes its cue from TRAC-1 workshop.

3. Methodology and Data

In this section, we describe our approach to text classification and TRAC-2 shared task data.

3.1. Methodology

Our approach to text analysis and features extraction is a hybrid approach of Computational Stylometry (CS), Machine Learning (ML) and Linguistic Rules (LR).

CS can be described as a set of techniques that allow scholars to find out information about the authors of texts through an automatic linguistic analysis of texts. One of the main assumptions in CS is that each author operates choices which are influenced by sociological (age, gender and education level) and psychological (personality, mental health and being a native speaker or not) factors (Daelemans, 2013) which determine a unique writing style. With this in mind, it is natural that stylistic features play a fundamental role in detecting author's traits. Considering that stylistic features detected over the years by the scholars are at least one hundred, we summarize in a short list some main stylistic features studied in literature: sentence length (Argamon et al., 2003), vocabulary richness (De Vel et al., 2001), word length distributions (Zheng et al., 2006), punctuation (Baayen et al., 1996), use of a specific class of verbs or adjectives, use of first/third person, n-grams, readability index (Lucisano and Piemontese, 1988), use of metaphors. Concerning ML, it is known that there are so many definitions, but the most exhaustive and concise is: ML is the computer ability to learn from data and consists in making predictions on unknown data on the basis of parameters identified during the training process.

Lastly, the LR writing process is carried out thanks to COGITO©, Expert System's semantic intelligence software, by which it is possible to write rules to process the texts and extract all the characteristics. An important aspect of the software is that it allows to perform word-sense disambiguation, that is crucial in text analysis, exploiting the power of its semantic network. Our standard approach to text analysis consists of the following steps:

- *Linguistic Definition of Stylometric Features*: since each author operates grammatical choices when writing a text, we organize all the grammatical characteristics of the texts under study in a taxonomy to detect the authorial fingerprint based on the grammatical choices done. This first step is carried out thanks to COGITO©, that allows us to write LR;

- *Semantic Engine Development*: we train the semantic engine to extract the features from the analyzed texts. The semantic engine is implemented thanks to COGITO©'s semantic network (*Sensigrafo*) - that can operate word-sense disambiguation - with the addition of the rules we built;

- *Training Set Analysis*: the training set is analysed and all features (based on the grammatical choices done by the writer) are extracted;

- *ML*: In the last step, we exploit the features extracted to train the model to detect these features in the dataset. ML process is carried out exploiting WEKA platform (Hall et al., 2009) (a software with machine learning tools and algorithms for data analysis) thanks to which it is possible to build a classifier with the support of one of the algorithms available.

3.2. Task description and Data

TRAC-2 workshop shared task (now in its second edition), focuses on trolling, aggression and cyberbullying detection in a given corpus build ad hoc by the task organizers and is organized in two sub-tasks:

- Sub-task-A: *Aggression Identification* task, for which participant have to build a 3-way classifier to detect if the texts are (OAG), (CAG), or (NAG);

- Sub-task-B: *Misogynistic Aggression Identification* task, for which participants have to build a binary classifier for classifying texts as Gendered (GEN) or Non-Gendered (NGEN).

As we reported, TRAC-2 shared task included also a second SubTask (*Misogynistic Aggression Identification*), as opposed to TRAC-1, which included only the *Aggression Identification* SubTask. TRAC-2 shared task includes texts in three different languages: Bangla, Hindi and English (as opposed to TRAC-1, which didn't include Bangla) for both sub-tasks (Bhattacharya et al., 2020). The participants are allowed to compete for the tasks and the languages they prefer. As we mentioned in Section 3.1, building ad hoc LR and exploiting our semantic network plays a crucial role in our approach, so considering that we have no linguistic knowledge in Bangla and Hindi, we decided to take part only in the two English sub-tasks.

3.2.1. Evaluation Metric

The systems submitted to TRAC-2 shared task have been evaluated on the basis of weighted macro-averaged F-scores. It means that the individual F-score of each class has been weighted by the proportion of the concerned class in the test set. The final F-score represents the average of these individual F-scores of each class.

3.2.2. Preprocessing

As usual in social media text data analysing, we cleaned the texts before analysying them. We removed @ symbol (it means that we also removed all mentions), we also removed hashtags (#), URLs, and emojis.

3.2.3. Training set and Dev set analysis

TRAC-2 English shared task training set is composed of 4,217 text data labelled both for SubTask A and for SubTask B. Besides this, a Dev set composed of 1,064 text data even those labelled for both SubTasks was also delivered. In order to detect the best performing algorithm between Random Forest (RF) (Liaw et al., 2002), Simple Logistic (SL) (Peng et al., 2002), and Sequential Minimal Optimization (SMO) (Platt, 1998), we built three different classifiers. Firstly, we train the three different model with the Training set for both SubTasks and we tested it on the Dev set. The results are shown in Table 2 (SubTask A) and Table 3 (SubTask B).

3.2.4. Cross-validation

Cross-validation is a method used to test the performance of a model. The 10-folds cross-validation phase also confirmed that SMO classifier performances were better than those of the classifiers trained with the other two algorithms

Classifier	Precision	Recall	F-Measure
RF	0.537	0.495	0.498
SL	0.472	0.449	0.454
SMO	0.546	0.528	**0.530**

Table 2: Evaluation on SubTask A Dev set using SubTask A Training set as training, where all performances reported should be read as weighted

Classifier	Precision	Recall	F-Measure
RF	0.659	0.618	0.616
SL	0.630	0.595	0.594
SMO	0.663	0.630	**0.630**

Table 3: Evaluation on SubTask B Dev set using SubTask A Training set as training, where all performances reported should be read as weighted

(RF and SL). The results of the 10-folds cross-validation test on both SubTasks Training sets are shown in Table 4 (SubTask A) and Table 5 (SubTask B).

Classifier	Precision	Recall	F-Measure
RF	0.510	0.508	0.501
SL	0.503	0.505	0.496
SMO	0.569	0.523	**0.527**

Table 4: 10-folds Cross-validation on SubTask A Training set, where all performances reported should be read as weighted

Classifier	Precision	Recall	F-Measure
RF	0.595	0.592	0.589
SL	0.645	0.644	**0.642**
SMO	0.642	0.642	**0.642**

Table 5: 10-folds Cross-validation on SubTask B Training set, where all performances reported should be read as weighted

Considering the performances achieved in both Dev set evaluation tests and in the two 10-folds cross-validation tests, we decided to analyze the Test set with the classifier we built with the support of the SMO algorithm.

3.2.5. TRAC-2 Test set

The Test set developed by Trac-2 shared task organizers is composed of 1,200 text data to be labelled in both Sub-Tasks. As we mentioned above, in SubTask A it is possible to label text data as: OAG, CAG, or NAG. In SubTask B texts can be labelled as GEN or NGEN. Despite each team was allowed to submit up to three systems for evaluation, we decided to submit just one for both SubTasks. The decision originated from the fact that the SMO algorithm was the best performing algorithm since the analysis TRAC-2 training and dev set. As shown above, other classifiers trained with other algorithms achieved worse performances.

4. Results

In this section, we show the results achieved by UniOr_ExpSys in both SubTasks. In the following few lines, we describe our hybrid approach of CS, ML and LR. Thanks to COGITO©we are able to build ad hoc linguistic rules to recognize stylistic features in texts. After this process, we train a semantic engine to extract the aforementioned features. The semantic engine is implemented thanks to the semantic network with the addition of the rules we built. Then, the training set is analysed and all features are extracted. In the last step, we exploit the features extracted to train the model to detect these features in the dataset. For the ML process, we exploit the WEKA platform and we built a classifier with the support of the SMO Algorithm. Please note that our system is trained with TRAC- 2 training set and TRAC - 1 dataset with regard to SubTask A and only with TRAC-2 training set with regard to SubTask B. The results achieved in TRAC-2 SubTask A (*Aggression Identification task*) and TRAC-2 SubTask B (*Misogynistic Aggression Identification task*) are shown in Table 6 and Table 7 respectively.

System	F1 (weighted)	Accuracy
CS-LR-SMO	**0.6291**	0.62

Table 6: Results for Sub-task EN-A.

System	F1 (weighted)	Accuracy
CS-LR-SMO	**0.6733**	0.6183

Table 7: Results for Sub-task EN-B.

4.1. Error analysis

It is important to highlight that our approach pays close attention to linguistic and stylistic aspects. Each feature is extracted thanks to the linguistic analysis of texts. In several instances, it has not been possible to extract stylistic features characterizing that specific category of texts (especially because texts were too short). Another fundamental aspect required by our approach is represented by balanced data, both in the training set and in the test set. Balanced data would have allowed a better training phase, with positive effects also on the classifier performances. Nevertheless, we are happy about the results we achieved in TRAC-2 participation and we thank the task organizers for the exciting competition in which we participated. In the future, exploring deep learning techniques for classifying these kinds of text data is certainly necessary.

Figure 1 and Figure 2 show the confusion matrices of both SubTasks classifiers.

As we can see in the SubTask A confusion matrix (Figure 1), CAG class text data are well classified, with the only exception of 15 instances incorrectly classified. The class that achieved the worst performance is NAG, which includes Non-Aggressive texts, but 156 have been classified as CAG and even 74 as OAG. With regard to SubTask B confusion matrix (Figure 2), GEN text data are quite well classified, while there is a big issue with NGEN: slightly more than

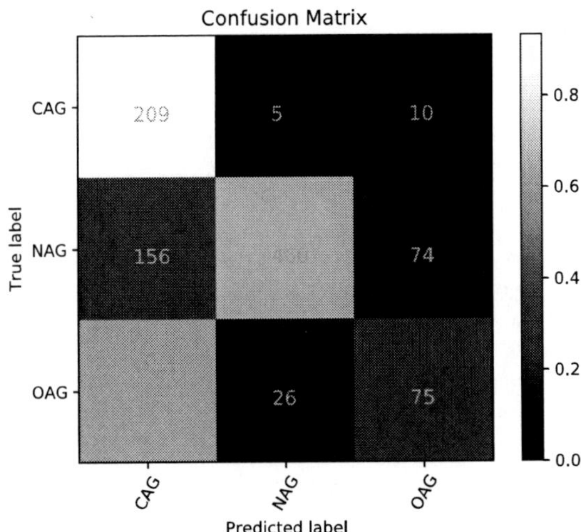

Figure 1: Sub-task EN-A, confusion matrix of the CS-LR-SMO model

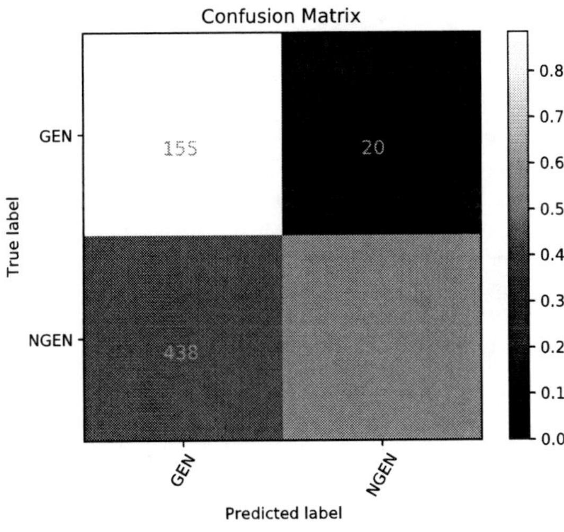

Figure 2: Sub-task EN-B, confusion matrix of the CS-LR-SMO model

half text data have been correctly classified, and this has undermined the performance of our binary classifier.

5. Conclusions

In this paper, we have shown the results achieved during the participation at TRAC-2 shared task workshop, organized as part of LREC 2020. The shared task is organized in two SubTasks: *Aggression Identification task*, for which participant have to build a 3-way classifier to detect if the texts are i) Overtly Aggressive (OAG), ii) Covertly Aggressive (CAG), or iii) Non-Aggressive (NAG) and Sub-task-B: *Misogynistic Aggression Identification task*, for which participants have to build a binary classifier for classifying texts as i) Gendered (GEN) or ii) Non-Gendered (NGEN). We use a hybrid approach based on CS, ML and LR,

which focuses on stylistic features extraction to identify the features that characterize texts belonging to the different categories. With regard to *Aggression Identification task* we achieved 0.629072 of F1-weighted, and with regard to *Misogynistic Aggression Identification task* we achieved 0.673321.

6. Acknowledgements

This research has been partly supported by the PON Ricerca e Innovazione 2014-20 and the POR Campania FSE 2014-2020 funds. Authorship contribution is as follows: Antonio Pascucci is author of Sections 1, 2, and 3. Sections 4 and 5 are in common between Antonio Pascucci and Raffaele Manna. This research has been developed in the framework of two Innovative Industrial PhD projects in Computational Stylometry (CS) by "L'Orientale" University of Naples in cooperation with Expert System Corp. We are grateful to Vincenzo Masucci and Expert System Corp. for providing COGITO© for research and to Prof. Johanna Monti for supervising the research.

7. Bibliographical References

Argamon, S., Šarić, M., and Stein, S. S. (2003). Style mining of electronic messages for multiple authorship discrimination: first results. In *Proceedings of the ninth ACM SIGKDD international conference on Knowledge discovery and data mining*, pages 475–480. ACM.

Aroyehun, S. T. and Gelbukh, A. (2018). Aggression detection in social media: Using deep neural networks, data augmentation, and pseudo labeling. In *Proceedings of the First Workshop on Trolling, Aggression and Cyberbullying (TRAC-2018)*, pages 90–97.

Baayen, H., Van Halteren, H., and Tweedie, F. (1996). Outside the cave of shadows: Using syntactic annotation to enhance authorship attribution. *Literary and Linguistic Computing*, 11(3):121–132.

Basile, V., Bosco, C., Fersini, E., Nozza, D., Patti, V., Pardo, F. M. R., Rosso, P., and Sanguinetti, M. (2019). Semeval-2019 task 5: Multilingual detection of hate speech against immigrants and women in twitter. In *Proceedings of the 13th International Workshop on Semantic Evaluation*, pages 54–63.

Bhattacharya, S., Singh, S., Kumar, R., Bansal, A., Bhagat, A., Dawer, Y., Lahiri, B., and Ojha, A. K. (2020). Developing a multilingual annotated corpus of misogyny and aggression.

Bosco, C., Dell'Orletta, F., Poletto, F., Sanguinetti, M., and Tesconi, M. (2018). Overview of the evalita 2018 hate speech detection task. In *EVALITA 2018-Sixth Evaluation Campaign of Natural Language Processing and Speech Tools for Italian*, volume 2263, pages 1–9. CEUR.

Britannica, E. (2015). Britannica academic. *Encyclopædia Britannica Inc.*

Burnap, P. and Williams, M. L. (2015). Cyber hate speech on twitter: An application of machine classification and statistical modeling for policy and decision making. *Policy & Internet*, 7(2):223–242.

Capozzi, A. T., Lai, M., Basile, V., Poletto, F., Sanguinetti, M., Bosco, C., Patti, V., Ruffo, G., Musto, C., Polignano, M., et al. (2019). Computational linguistics against hate: Hate speech detection and visualization on social media in the" contro l'odio" project. In *6th Italian Conference on Computational Linguistics, CLiC-it 2019*, volume 2481, pages 1–6. CEUR-WS.

Dadvar, M., Trieschnigg, D., Ordelman, R., and de Jong, F. (2013). Improving cyberbullying detection with user context. In *Advances in Information Retrieval*, pages 693–696. Springer.

Daelemans, W. (2013). Explanation in computational stylometry. In *International Conference on Intelligent Text Processing and Computational Linguistics*, pages 451–462. Springer.

Davidson, T., Warmsley, D., Macy, M., and Weber, I. (2017). Automated hate speech detection and the problem of offensive language. In *Eleventh international aaai conference on web and social media*.

De Smedt, T., Jaki, S., Kotzé, E., Saoud, L., Gwóźdź, M., De Pauw, G., and Daelemans, W. (2018). Multilingual cross-domain perspectives on online hate speech. *arXiv preprint arXiv:1809.03944*.

De Vel, O., Anderson, A., Corney, M., and Mohay, G. (2001). Mining e-mail content for author identification forensics. *ACM Sigmod Record*, 30(4):55–64.

Del Vigna, F., Cimino, A., Dell'Orletta, F., Petrocchi, M., and Tesconi, M. (2017). Hate me, hate me not: Hate speech detection on facebook. In *Proceedings of the First Italian Conference on Cybersecurity (ITASEC17)*, pages 86–95.

Dinakar, K., Reichart, R., and Lieberman, H. (2011). Modeling the detection of textual cyberbullying. In *The Social Mobile Web*, pages 11–17.

Fersini, E., Nozza, D., and Rosso, P. (2018). Overview of the evalita 2018 task on automatic misogyny identification (ami). *EVALITA Evaluation of NLP and Speech Tools for Italian*, 12:59.

Fortuna, P. and Nunes, S. (2018). A survey on automatic detection of hate speech in text. *ACM Computing Surveys (CSUR)*, 51(4):1–30.

Hall, M., Frank, E., Holmes, G., Pfahringer, B., Reutemann, P., and Witten, I. H. (2009). The weka data mining software: an update. *ACM SIGKDD explorations newsletter*, 11(1):10–18.

Kumar, R., Ojha, A. K., Malmasi, S., and Zampieri, M. (2018a). Benchmarking aggression identification in social media. In *Proceedings of the First Workshop on Trolling, Aggression and Cyberbullying (TRAC-2018)*, pages 1–11, Santa Fe, New Mexico, USA, August. Association for Computational Linguistics.

Kumar, R., Ojha, A. K., Malmasi, S., and Zampieri, M. (2018b). Benchmarking Aggression Identification in Social Media. In *Proceedings of the First Workshop on Trolling, Aggression and Cyberbulling (TRAC)*, Santa Fe, USA.

Liaw, A., Wiener, M., et al. (2002). Classification and regression by randomforest. *R news*, 2(3):18–22.

Lucisano, P. and Piemontese, M. E. (1988). Gulpease: una formula per la predizione della difficoltà dei testi in lingua italiana. *Scuola e città*, 3(31):110–124.

Malmasi, S. and Zampieri, M. (2017). Detecting hate speech in social media. *arXiv preprint arXiv:1712.06427*.

Menini, S., Moretti, G., Corazza, M., Cabrio, E., Tonelli, S., and Villata, S. (2019). A system to monitor cyberbullying based on message classification and social network analysis. In *Proceedings of the Third Workshop on Abusive Language Online*, pages 105–110.

Musto, C., Semeraro, G., de Gemmis, M., and Lops, P. (2016). Modeling community behavior through semantic analysis of social data: The italian hate map experience. In *Proceedings of the 2016 Conference on User Modeling Adaptation and Personalization*, pages 307–308.

Pascucci, A., Masucci, V., and Monti, J. (2019). Computational stylometry and machine learning for gender and age detection in cyberbullying texts. In *2019 8th International Conference on Affective Computing and Intelligent Interaction Workshops and Demos (ACIIW)*, pages 1–6. IEEE.

Peng, C.-Y. J., Lee, K. L., and Ingersoll, G. M. (2002). An introduction to logistic regression analysis and reporting. *The journal of educational research*, 96(1):3–14.

Platt, J. (1998). Sequential minimal optimization: A fast algorithm for training support vector machines.

Poletto, F., Stranisci, M., Sanguinetti, M., Patti, V., and Bosco, C. (2017). Hate speech annotation: Analysis of an italian twitter corpus. In *4th Italian Conference on Computational Linguistics, CLiC-it 2017*, volume 2006, pages 1–6. CEUR-WS.

Raiyani, K., Gonçalves, T., Quaresma, P., and Nogueira, V. B. (2018). Fully connected neural network with advance preprocessor to identify aggression over facebook and twitter. In *Proceedings of the First Workshop on Trolling, Aggression and Cyberbullying (TRAC-2018)*, pages 28–41.

Ramakrishnan, M., Zadrozny, W., and Tabari, N. (2019). Uva wahoos at semeval-2019 task 6: Hate speech identification using ensemble machine learning. In *Proceedings of the 13th International Workshop on Semantic Evaluation*, pages 806–811.

Risch, J. and Krestel, R. (2018). Aggression identification using deep learning and data augmentation. In *Proceedings of the First Workshop on Trolling, Aggression and Cyberbullying (TRAC-2018)*, pages 150–158.

Ritesh Kumar, Atul Kr. Ojha, S. M. and Zampieri, M. (2020). Evaluating aggression identification in social media. In Ritesh Kumar, et al., editors, *Proceedings of the Second Workshop on Trolling, Aggression and Cyberbullying (TRAC-2020)*, Paris, France, may. European Language Resources Association (ELRA).

Sanguinetti, M., Poletto, F., Bosco, C., Patti, V., and Stranisci, M. (2018). An italian twitter corpus of hate speech against immigrants. In *Proceedings of the Eleventh International Conference on Language Resources and Evaluation (LREC 2018)*.

Schmidt, A. and Wiegand, M. (2017). A Survey on Hate

Speech Detection Using Natural Language Processing. In *Proceedings of the Fifth International Workshop on Natural Language Processing for Social Media. Association for Computational Linguistics*, pages 1–10, Valencia, Spain.

Sprugnoli, R., Menini, S., Tonelli, S., Oncini, F., and Piras, E. (2018). Creating a whatsapp dataset to study pre-teen cyberbullying. In *Proceedings of the 2nd Workshop on Abusive Language Online (ALW2)*, pages 51–59.

Wiegand, M., Siegel, M., and Ruppenhofer, J. (2018). Overview of the GermEval 2018 Shared Task on the Identification of Offensive Language. In *Proceedings of GermEval*.

Xu, J.-M., Jun, K.-S., Zhu, X., and Bellmore, A. (2012). Learning from bullying traces in social media. In *Proceedings of the 2012 conference of the North American chapter of the association for computational linguistics: Human language technologies*, pages 656–666. Association for Computational Linguistics.

Zampieri, M., Malmasi, S., Nakov, P., Rosenthal, S., Farra, N., and Kumar, R. (2019a). Predicting the type and target of offensive posts in social media. *arXiv preprint arXiv:1902.09666*.

Zampieri, M., Malmasi, S., Nakov, P., Rosenthal, S., Farra, N., and Kumar, R. (2019b). Semeval-2019 task 6: Identifying and categorizing offensive language in social media (offenseval). *arXiv preprint arXiv:1903.08983*.

Zheng, R., Li, J., Chen, H., and Huang, Z. (2006). A framework for authorship identification of online messages: Writing-style features and classification techniques. *Journal of the American society for information science and technology*, 57(3):378–393.

Proceedings of the Second Workshop on Trolling, Aggression and Cyberbullying, pages 76–82
Language Resources and Evaluation Conference (LREC 2020), Marseille, 11–16 May 2020
© European Language Resources Association (ELRA), licensed under CC-BY-NC

Aggression Identification in English, Hindi and Bangla Text using BERT, RoBERTa and SVM

Arup Baruah[◇], Kaushik Amar Das[◇], Ferdous Ahmed Barbhuiya[◇], Kuntal Dey[♡]
[◇]IIIT Guwahati, [♡] IBM Research
[◇]Assam India, [♡]New Delhi India
{arup.baruah, kaushikamardas}@gmail.com,
ferdous@iiitg.ac.in, kuntadey@in.ibm.com

Abstract

This paper presents the results of the classifiers that the team 'abaruah' developed for the shared tasks in aggression identification and misogynistic aggression identification. These two shared tasks were held as part of the second workshop on Trolling, Aggression and Cyberbullying (TRAC). Both the subtasks were held for English, Hindi and Bangla language. In our study, we used English BERT (En-BERT), RoBERTa, DistilRoBERTa, and SVM based classifiers for the English language. For Hindi and Bangla language, multilingual BERT (M-BERT), XLM-RoBERTa and SVM classifiers were used. Our best performing models are EN-BERT for English Subtask A (Weighted F1 score of 0.73, Rank 5/16), SVM for English Subtask B (Weighted F1 score of 0.87, Rank 2/15), SVM for Hindi Subtask A (Weighted F1 score of 0.79, Rank 2/10), XLMRoBERTa for Hindi Subtask B (Weighted F1 score of 0.87, Rank 2/10), SVM for Bangla Subtask A (Weighted F1 score of 0.81, Rank 2/10), and SVM for Bangla Subtask B (Weighted F1 score of 0.93, Rank 4/8). It is seen that the superior performance of the SVM classifier was achieved mainly because of its better prediction of the majority class. BERT based classifiers were found to predict the minority classes better.

Keywords: Aggression Identification, Offensive Language, Multilingual, BERT, SVM, RoBERTa

1. Introduction

Partisan antipathy in politics is on the rise. All over the world, societies are getting more and more politically polarized (Thomas Carothers, 2019). It is partly fuelled by the *echo chamber* and *filter bubble* effect of social media. Anger is fast becoming a tool to lure voters. As the world gets polarized, the popularity and convenience of the social media platforms are turning them to a modern-day battlefield. This has led to an increase in aggressive content in social media. Some of the world leaders are also using social media as a platform for displaying their aggressiveness. An example of this is the following tweet addressed to North Korean leader Kim Jong-un by U.S. President Donald Trump, *"Will someone from his depleted and food starved regime please inform him that I too have a Nuclear Button, but it is a much bigger & more powerful one than his, and my Button works!"*

Social media sites are grappling to remove aggressive content from their sites both to promote healthy discussions and also to comply with legal laws. However, the scale involved makes manual moderation a difficult task. The need of the hour is automated methods for detecting aggressive content.

The second workshop on Trolling, Aggression, and Cyberbullying (TRAC-2) (Kumar et al., 2020) is an attempt to promote research in automated detection of aggression in text. This workshop had two shared tasks titled *"Aggression Identification" (Subtask A)* and *"Misogynistic Aggression Identification" (Subtask B)*. Aggression identification is a 3-way classification problem where it is required to determine if a given comment is overtly, covertly or not aggressive. Misogynistic aggression is a binary classification problem where it is required to determine if the comment is gender-based or not. Both the subtasks were held for English, Hindi, and Bangla language.

We participated in both the subtasks for all the three languages. The classifiers we used in this study include En-BERT, M-BERT, RoBERTa, DistilRoBERTa, and XLM-RoBERTa.

2. Related Work

Apart from automatic detection of aggression in text, considerable research has been performed for detection of offensive language, abusive language, hate speech, cyberbullying, profanity, and insults. Fortuna and Nunes (2018) provides definitions of the terms mentioned above, provides statistics of research performed for the detection of hate speech, lists the features, classification methods, and challenges in automated hate speech detection. Schmidt and Wiegand (2017) too discusses the different classification methods, features and the challenges involved in the detection of hate speech.

Davidson et al. (2017) mentions that not all offensive language is hate speech. Their classifier was able to reduce the number of offensive tweets misclassified as hate speech to 5%. Malmasi and Zampieri (2017) worked on differentiating hate speech from profanity by using an SVM classifier trained on features such as character n-grams (2 to 8), word n-grams (1 to 3), and word skip-grams. Malmasi and Zampieri (2018) extended the above work to include Brown cluster features, ensemble classifiers and meta-classifiers in addition to single classifiers.

Zampieri et al. (2019a) introduces a new dataset called Offensive Language Identification Dataset (OLID) where the data has been categorized as offensive or not, targeted or untargeted, and targets individual, group or other. SVM, BiLSTM and CNN classifiers were used in this study to predict the type and target of offensive posts. Zampieri et al. (2019b) summarizes the results from the shared task on

Language	Type	Total	NAG	CAG	OAG	NGEN	GEN	Max Length	Length below 50 words
English	Train	4263	3375 (79.17%)	453 (10.63%)	435 (10.20%)	3954 (92.75%)	309 (7.25%)	806	93.31%
English	Dev	1066	836 (78.42%)	117 (10.98%)	113 (10.60%)	993 (93.15%)	73 (6.85%)	457	93.34%
English	Test	1200	690 (57.50%)	224 (18.67%)	286 (23.83%)	1025 (85.42%)	175 (14.58%)	1390	77.41%
Hindi	Train	3984	2245 (56.35%)	829 (20.81%)	910 (22.84%)	3323 (83.41%)	661 (16.59%)	557	95.41%
Hindi	Dev	997	578 (57.97%)	211 (21.16%)	208 (20.86%)	845 (84.75%)	152 (15.26%)	230	93.98%
Hindi	Test	1200	325 (27.08%)	191 (15.92%)	684 (57.00%)	633 (52.75%)	567 (47.25%)	669	89.92%
Bangla	Train	3826	2078 (54.31%)	898 (23.47%)	850 (22.22%)	3114 (81.39%)	712 (18.61%)	154	98.64%
Bangla	Dev	957	522 (54.55%)	218 (22.78%)	217 (22.68%)	766 (80.04%)	191 (19.96%)	182	98.64%
Bangla	Test	1188	712 (59.93%)	225 (18.94%)	251 (21.13%)	986 (83.00%)	202 (17.00%)	113	99.24%

Table 1: Dataset Statistics

identification and categorization of offensive language held as part of Semantic Evaluation 2019. The best performing system in subtask A of OffensEval 2019 used a BERT based model (Liu et al., 2019b) and obtained a macro F1 score of 0.8286. Zhu et al. (2019) also used a BERT based model and obtained the 3rd rank in subtask A of OffensEval 2019 with a macro F1 score of 0.8136.

The results of the TRAC-1 has been summarized in Kumar et al. (2018). As can be seen, both deep learning (LSTM, BiLSTM, CNN) and traditional machine learning classifiers (SVM, Logistic Regression, Random Forest, Naive Bayes) were used in this shared task.

Similarly, the HASOC [1] (Mandl et al., 2019) workshop organized at FIRE2019 was also aimed at stimulating research the aforementioned areas in Hindi, English and German languages respectively. They note that the most widely used approach was LSTMs coupled with word embeddings. In this workshop, the participants used a wide variety of models such as BERT, SVM, CNN, LSTM with Attention, etc.

3. Data

The dataset for subtask A has been labelled as either overtly aggressive (OAG), covertly aggressive (CAG) or not aggressive (NAG). The dataset for subtask B has been labelled as gendered (GEN) or non-gendered (NGEN). The dataset is further described in Bhattacharya et al. (2020).

Table 1 shows the statistics of the dataset used for the two shared tasks. As can be seen, the dataset is imbalanced with NAG (for subtask A) and NGEN (for subtask B) occurring more frequently in all the three languages. The NGEN category occurred as high as 93.15% in the English development dataset. This, however, is a true reflection of the proportion of aggressive and non-aggressive comments in real life as has been mentioned in Gao et al. (2017). The only exception is the Hindi test dataset. In this dataset, OAG is the most frequently occurring class for subtask A and this dataset is almost balanced for subtask B.

As can be seen, the comments were also of varied length (in terms of the number of words). The longest comment of 1390 words occurred in the English test dataset. However, as can be seen from the table, the majority of the comments were of length less than 50 words.

4. Methodology

4.1. Preprocessing

In our work, before performing tokenization, the text was converted to lower case. This conversion to lower-case was performed through the BERT tokenizer and the TFIDF vectorizer. As mentioned in section 3, except for English and Hindi test set, more than 93% of the comments were of length less than 50 tokens. Hence, for En-BERT and M-BERT, the maximum sequence length of 50 was used. Comments of length beyond 50 tokens were truncated. In the RoBERTa models, the long sentences were split into multiple samples [3].

4.2. Classifiers

4.2.1. English BERT (En-BERT)

English BERT (Devlin et al., 2019) is a bi-directional model based on the transformer architecture. The transformer architecture is an architecture based solely on attention mechanism (Vaswani et al., 2017). The transformer architecture overcomes the inherent sequential nature of Recurrent Neural Networks (RNN) and hence they are more conducive for parallelization.

In our study, we used the uncased large version of En-BERT [2]. This version has 24 layers and 16 attention heads. This

---

[1] https://hasocfire.github.io/hasoc/2019/

[2] https://github.com/google-research/bert

model generates 1024 dimensional vector for each word. We used 1024 dimensional vector of the Extract layer as the representation of the comment. Our classification layer consisted of a single Dense layer.

For subtask A, the dense layer consisted of 3 units and the *softmax* activation function was used. The loss function used was *sparse categorical crossentropy*. For subtask B, the dense layer consisted of 1 unit and the *sigmoid* activation function was used. The loss function used was *binary crossentropy*. The *Adam* optimizer with a learning rate of 2e-5 was used for training the model. The model was trained for 15 epochs. Early stopping with patience of 5 was used for both the subtasks. *Sparse categorical accuracy* was monitored for early stopping.

4.2.2. Multilingual BERT (M-BERT)

Multilingual BERT is BERT trained for multilingual tasks. It was trained on monolingual Wikipedia articles of 104 different languages. It is intended to enable M-BERT fine-tuned in one language to make predictions for another language. In our study, we used the M-BERT model having 12 layers and 12 heads. This model generates 768 dimensional vector for each word. We used the 768 dimensional vector of the Extract layer as the representation of the comment. Just like for the English language subtasks, a single Dense layer was used as the classification model. The hyperparameters used for training the model is the same as mentioned for the English language.

Algorithm 1 Naive Checkpoint Ensemble

1: $A \leftarrow$ True labels
2: $P \leftarrow$ Model predictions at each epoch
3: $N \leftarrow$ Num samples, $C \leftarrow$ Num classes
4: $reverse \leftarrow boolean$
5: **function** ENSEMBLE($P, A, N, C, reverse$)
6:     $models \leftarrow \{\}, val \leftarrow 0$
7:     $Z[N][C] \leftarrow$ Zero Matrix
8:     $\epsilon \leftarrow len(P)$ ▷ Num Epochs
9:     **if** $reverse$ **then**
10:       $range \leftarrow \epsilon$ to 0
11:     **else**
12:       $range \leftarrow 0$ to ϵ
13:     **end if**
14:     **for** $(e \leftarrow range)$ **do**
15:       $temp \leftarrow Z$
16:       $temp \leftarrow temp + P[e]$
17:       **if** $metric(A, temp) > val$ **then**
18:         $Z \leftarrow Z + P$
19:         $models \leftarrow models \cup e$
20:         $val \leftarrow metric(A, temp)$
21:       **else**
22:         continue
23:       **end if**
24:     **end for**
25:     **return** $models, val$
26: **end function**

4.2.3. RoBERTa and DistilRoBERTa

RoBERTa (Liu et al., 2019c) improves upon BERT by adding a few modifications to the original model such as

---

Algorithm 2 Make Prediction

1: $m \leftarrow$ model ids chosen for ensemble
2: $E[N][C] \leftarrow$ Zero Matrix
3: **for** i in m **do**
4:     Load model with weights at epoch i
5:     $p \leftarrow model.predict(samples)$
6:     $E \leftarrow E + p$
7: **end for**
8: $preds \leftarrow$ Index of max element in each row of N

---

training on a larger dataset, dynamically masking out tokens compared to the original static masking, etc. DistilRoBERTa (Sanh et al., 2019) is a compressed version of the same which trains faster and preserves up to 95% of the performance of the original. For both of these models, we make use of the pre-trained *base* versions made available by the HuggingFace Transformers library (Wolf et al., 2019). We make use of the RoBERTa model for English Task A and DistilRoBERTa for English Task B. We use an attention layer (Zhou et al., 2016) on top of the embeddings of the underlying pre-trained model. However, instead of the *tanh* activation function used in the original work, we used $penalized - tanh$ which is demonstrated to work better for NLP tasks (Eger et al., 2019) combined with a cross-entropy loss function. We also do not apply $softmax$ on the output of the classifying layer as done in the original work and instead use $argmax$ directly on the final layer outputs to make the prediction. We make use of the Ranger Optimizer which is a combination of RAdam (Liu et al., 2019a) wrapped with Lookahead (Zhang et al., 2019) to train the model. The entire model is fine-tuned with a tiny learning rate of $1e - 4$ for both of the English classification tasks. For task A and task B, lookahead's (k, α) is set to $(5, 0.5)$ and $(6, 0.5)$ with a weight decay of $1e - 5$ respectively. The models were set to run for 20 epochs with early stopping patience of 4. We made use of a naive checkpoint ensembling method (Chen et al., 2017) where we save the model weights and dev-set predictions (i.e. the final layer output) at each epoch. The method is given in Algorithm 1. The method is called once with $reverse$ set to $True$ and once with $False$. The ensembled model which maximize our chosen metric (weighted–f1) value is chosen. If the ensemble does not improve the metric, we simply choose the best model found during training. Once we have chosen the model, we use Algorithm 2 to make the final prediction on the test set. This Algorithm 2 simply describes adding the weights of the final classifying layer of the model and using argmax along each row to get the prediction. Naive ensembling increases the weighted f1 on the dev–set on English task A from 0.8070 to 0.8124. We did not use it for English task B as it degraded the performance.

4.2.4. XLM-RoBERTa

XLM-RoBERTa (Conneau et al., 2019) is a cross-lingual model that aims to tackle the *curse-of-multilinguality* problem of cross-lingual models. It is inspired by (Liu et al., 2019c) and is trained on up-to 100 languages and outperforms M-BERT in multiple cross-lingual benchmarks.

Similar to Section 4.2.3, we use[3] the *base* version coupled with an attention head classifier, the same optimizer, epochs, and early stopping. Lookahead's (k, α) is set to $(6, 0.5)$ with weight–decay of $1e - 5$. Batch-size is set to $(22, 24)$ for Bangla tasks (A, B) and 32 for both Hindi tasks. This model is used in the sub-tasks of the Hindi and Bangla languages. For the Hindi models, we use the naive checkpoint ensembling method described in Section 4.2.3. This increased the weighted f1 from 0.7146 to 0.7160 for Hindi task A and from 0.8908 to 0.8969 for Hindi task B. Naive ensembling did not yield any performance boosts in Bangla tasks.

4.2.5. SVM

We also used the Support Vector Machine (SVM) model for both the subtasks in all the 3 languages. The SVM model was trained using TF-IDF features of word and character n-grams. Word n-grams of size 1 to 3 and character n-grams of size 1 to 6 were used. The *linear* kernel was used for the classifier and hyperparameter C was set to 1.0.

5. Results

As has been mentioned in section 4, the classifiers we used include En-BERT, RoBERTa, DistilRoBERTa and SVM for the subtasks in the English language, and M-BERT, XLM-RoBERTa and SVM for the subtasks in Hindi and Bangla language.

Table 2 and 3 show the results we obtained on the development and test set respectively. Both the table shows the precision, recall, macro F1, weighted F1, and accuracy. Weighted F1 score is the metric that has officially been used to rank the submissions. As can be seen from table 2, the best performing classifiers on the development set were RoBERTa for English subtask A, En-BERT for English subtask B, XLM-RoBERTa for Hindi subtask A, Bangla subtask A, and Bangla subtask B, and M-BERT for Hindi subtask B.

As can be seen from table 3, the SVM classifier which was not the best on the development set, actually performed well on the test set for English subtask B (ranked 2nd), Hindi subtask A (ranked 2nd), Bangla subtask A (ranked 2nd), and Bangla subtask B (ranked 4th). The other best-performing classifiers are En-BERT for English subtask A (ranked 5th), and XLM-RoBERTa for Hindi subtask B (ranked 2nd). The results of M-BERT for Hindi subtask A are not shown as an error was made for this run (binary classification was performed instead of performing 3-class classification).

It can also be seen from table 3 that for subtask B, the best performance of all the classifiers (SVM, BERT-based, and RoBERTa-based) was obtained for the Bangla language. For subtask B, the SVM classifier had the weighted F1 score of 0.87, 0.84 and 0.92, the RoBERTa-based classifiers had a score of 0.86, 0.87 and 0.92, and the BERT-based classifiers had a score of 0.85, 0.84 and 0.92 for English, Hindi and Bangla language respectively. Even for subtask A, the classifiers obtained better score for the Bangla

language (except for RoBERTa-based classifier which obtained a slightly better score for Hindi language as compared to Bangla language).

The confusion matrices of the classifiers on the test set are shown in table 4 to 9. As can be seen from table 4, the strength of En-BERT which was our best performing classifier for English subtask A, was that it predicted the minority classes better than the other two classifiers. In fact, it was the worst in predicting the majority NAG class. But because of its correct predictions for the minority classes, it was our best performing classifier for this subtask. RoBERTa too predicted the OAG class better than SVM. However, RoBERTa did not perform well in predicting the CAG class. Detecting covertly aggressive comments is very difficult and En-BERT performed better than the other two classifiers in predicting this class.

As can be seen from table 7, SVM which was our best performing classifier for English subtask B, predicted the majority class better than the other two classifiers. SVM, however, was the worst in predicting the minority class. En-BERT again was the best in predicting the minority class. En-BERT also had the best recall score for this subtask.

As mentioned in section 3, for Hindi subtask A, OAG was the majority class. XLM-RoBERTa performed better than SVM in predicting the majority class. However, SVM performed better in predicting the CAG and NAG class and hence was the best performing classifier in this subtask. For Hindi subtask B, the dataset was quite balanced, and in this dataset, XLM-RoBERTa performed the best.

For Bangla subtask A, SVM performed the best in predicting the majority NAG class as well as the CAG class. As such, it was the best performing classifier in this subtask. For Bangla subtask B, SVM again performed better in predicting the majority class. In this subtask, M-BERT and XLM-RoBERTa performed better than SVM in predicting the minority class. The best performing classifier for this subtask was SVM.

6. Error Analysis

On analysis of the predictions made by our classifiers on the development set, we found that our classifiers were not able to handle intentional or unintentional orthographic variations of toxic words and spelling mistakes. For example, both the SVM and En-BERT classifiers wrongly classified the comment *"Fuuck your music"* as not aggressive. This comment has been labelled by the annotators as overtly aggressive. However, after changing the toxic word *'Fuuck'* to *'Fuck'*, both the classifiers were able to make the correct prediction for the comment. Similarly, both the classifiers were not able to handle the spelling mistake for the word *'prostitute'* in the comment *'So sad she is a professional prostatiut'*. The comment was wrongly classified as not gendered. After correcting the spelling mistake, both the classifiers were able to classify the comment correctly.

Annotators have labelled comments such as *'Im homosexual and really proud of it'* and *'I. Gay'* where the user is attributing homosexuality to oneself as not gendered. However, our SVM wrongly classifies these comments as gendered based on the presence of the words *homosexual* and *gay*. So, the SVM classifier has not been able to detect the

---

[3]Code for this particular model available at `https://github.com/cozek/trac2020_submission`

Task	System	Precision (Macro)	Recall (Macro)	F1 (macro)	F1 (weighted)	Accuracy
English A	SVM	0.6415	0.4807	0.5170	0.7729	0.8105
English A	RoBERTa	**0.6418**	0.5883	**0.6106**	**0.8070**	**0.8148**
English A	En-BERT	0.5866	**0.5884**	0.5871	0.7878	0.7858
English B	SVM	0.8060	0.6056	0.6490	0.9244	0.9390
English B	DistilRoBERTa	0.7201	0.6866	0.7016	0.9260	0.9289
English B	En-BERT	**0.8274**	**0.6962**	**0.7423**	**0.9400**	**0.9467**
Hindi A	SVM	**0.6682**	0.6249	0.6409	0.7074	0.7192
Hindi A	XLM-RoBERTa	0.6602	**0.6376**	**0.6472**	**0.7146**	**0.7207**
Hindi A	M-BERT	0.6147	0.6167	0.6151	0.6846	0.6871
Hindi B	SVM	**0.8415**	0.6906	0.7346	0.8765	0.8917
Hindi B	XLM-RoBERTa	0.8125	0.7565	0.7801	0.8908	**0.8959**
Hindi B	M-BERT	0.7977	**0.7781**	**0.7874**	**0.8919**	0.8937
Bangla A	SVM	0.7096	0.6557	0.6747	0.7197	0.7304
Bangla A	XLM-RoBERTa	**0.7203**	**0.7121**	**0.7137**	**0.7539**	**0.7513**
Bangla A	M-BERT	0.6805	0.6891	0.6844	0.7279	0.7252
Bangla B	SVM	**0.8792**	0.7396	0.7826	0.8723	0.8851
Bangla B	XLM-RoBERTa	0.8580	**0.8319**	**0.8439**	**0.9020**	**0.9039**
Bangla B	M-BERT	0.8585	0.7998	0.8242	0.8920	0.8966

Table 2: Dev Set Results

Task	System	Precision (Macro)	Recall (Macro)	F1 (macro)	F1 (weighted)	Accuracy	Rank
English A	SVM	**0.7923**	0.6077	0.6489	0.7173	**0.7450**	
English A	RoBERTa	0.6722	0.5921	0.6130	0.6986	0.7233	
English A	En-BERT	0.6880	**0.6415**	**0.6501**	**0.7289**	0.7350	5th
English B	SVM	**0.7980**	0.6744	0.7121	**0.8701**	**0.8850**	2nd
English B	DistilRoBERTa	0.7277	0.7101	**0.7183**	0.8623	0.8650	
English B	En-BERT	0.6980	**0.7226**	0.7089	0.8503	0.8458	
Hindi A	SVM	**0.7252**	**0.7592**	**0.7363**	**0.7944**	0.7867	2nd
Hindi A	XLM-RoBERTa	0.7129	0.7269	0.7188	0.7927	**0.7892**	
Hindi B	SVM	0.8597	0.8373	0.8395	0.8408	0.8433	
Hindi B	XLM-RoBERTa	**0.8704**	**0.8673**	**0.8683**	**0.8689**	**0.8692**	2nd
Hindi B	M-BERT	0.8395	0.8363	0.8372	0.8379	0.8383	
Bangla A	SVM	**0.8385**	**0.7171**	**0.7586**	**0.8083**	**0.8199**	2nd
Bangla A	XLM-RoBERTa	0.7434	0.7136	0.7264	0.7880	0.7938	
Bangla A	M-BERT	0.7265	0.6945	0.7074	0.7740	0.7820	
Bangla B	SVM	**0.9299**	0.8167	0.8600	**0.9258**	**0.9310**	4th
Bangla B	XLM-RoBERTa	0.8431	0.8617	0.8519	0.9153	0.9141	
Bangla B	M-BERT	0.8619	**0.8648**	**0.8633**	0.9227	0.9226	

Table 3: Official Results on Test Set

	SVM			RoBERTa			En-BERT		
	Pred CAG	Pred NAG	Pred OAG	Pred CAG	Pred NAG	Pred OAG	Pred CAG	Pred NAG	Pred OAG
True CAG	86	135	3	64	132	28	122	83	19
True NAG	3	677	10	26	645	19	48	624	18
True OAG	26	129	131	38	89	159	97	53	136

Table 4: Confusion Matrix on Test Set for English Subtask A

	SVM			XLM-RoBERTa		
	Pred CAG	Pred NAG	Pred OAG	Pred CAG	Pred NAG	Pred OAG
True CAG	121	52	18	101	53	37
True NAG	42	273	10	54	257	14
True OAG	64	70	550	46	49	589

Table 5: Confusion Matrix on Test Set for Hindi Subtask A

	SVM			XLM-RoBERTa			M-BERT		
	Pred CAG	Pred NAG	Pred OAG	Pred CAG	Pred NAG	Pred OAG	Pred CAG	Pred NAG	Pred OAG
True CAG	116	101	8	115	82	28	100	90	35
True NAG	14	691	7	42	647	23	53	645	14
True OAG	16	68	167	33	37	181	26	41	184

Table 6: Confusion Matrix on Test Set for Bangla Subtask A

	SVM		RoBERTa		En-BERT	
	Pred GEN	Pred NGEN	Pred GEN	Pred NGEN	Pred GEN	Pred NGEN
True GEN	66	109	86	89	96	79
True NGEN	29	996	73	952	106	919

Table 7: Confusion Matrix on Test Set for English Subtask B

	SVM		XLM-RoBERTa		M-BERT	
	Pred GEN	Pred NGEN	Pred GEN	Pred NGEN	Pred GEN	Pred NGEN
True GEN	413	154	473	94	453	114
True NGEN	34	599	63	570	80	553

Table 8: Confusion Matrix on Test Set for Hindi Subtask B

	SVM		XLM-RoBERTa		M-BERT	
	Pred GEN	Pred NGEN	Pred GEN	Pred NGEN	Pred GEN	Pred NGEN
True GEN	130	72	158	44	157	45
True NGEN	10	976	58	928	47	939

Table 9: Confusion Matrix on Test Set for Bangla Subtask B

benign use of these words. The En-BERT classifier however correctly classified these comments correctly as not gendered.

Our classifiers were not able to correctly classify comments such as *'There are only 2 genders'* that require world knowledge. The above comment was labelled by the annotators as gendered. However, because of the absence of any toxic words, the above comment was classified by both the SVM and En-BERT classifier as not gendered.

There were also certain comments such as *'Hot'* that were labelled as gendered by the annotators. These comments are ambiguous and can belong to either of the two categories. Most likely, these comments we labelled so based on some contextual information. In the absence of contextual information, our classifiers did not classify these comments correctly.

7. Conclusion

We used BERT, RoBERTa and SVM based classifiers for detection of aggression in English, Hindi and Bangla text. Our SVM classifier performed remarkably well on the test set and obtained 2nd rank in the official results for 3 of the 6 tests and obtained 4th in another. However, on closer analysis, it is seen that the superior performance of the SVM classifier was mainly due to the better prediction of the majority class. BERT based classifiers were found to predict the minority classes better. It was also found that our clas-

sifiers did not handle spelling mistakes and intentional orthographic variations correctly. FastText word embeddings are better in handling orthographic variations. As a future study, it can be checked if FastText embeddings improve performance on this dataset. Another option would be to use automatic methods for correcting grammatical and spelling mistakes. Use of contextual information and world knowledge for automatic detection of aggression needs further investigation.

8. Bibliographical References

Bhattacharya, S., Singh, S., Kumar, R., Bansal, A., Bhagat, A., Dawer, Y., Lahiri, B., and Ojha, A. K. (2020). Developing a multilingual annotated corpus of misogyny and aggression.

Chen, H., Lundberg, S., and Lee, S.-I. (2017). Checkpoint ensembles: Ensemble methods from a single training process.

Conneau, A., Khandelwal, K., Goyal, N., Chaudhary, V., Wenzek, G., Guzmán, F., Grave, E., Ott, M., Zettlemoyer, L., and Stoyanov, V. (2019). Unsupervised cross-lingual representation learning at scale.

Davidson, T., Warmsley, D., Macy, M., and Weber, I. (2017). Automated Hate Speech Detection and the Problem of Offensive Language. In *Proceedings of ICWSM*.

Devlin, J., Chang, M.-W., Lee, K., and Toutanova, K. (2019). BERT: Pre-training of deep bidirectional transformers for language understanding. In *Proceedings of the 2019 Conference of the North American Chapter of the Association for Computational Linguistics*, pages 4171–4186, Minneapolis, Minnesota, June. Association for Computational Linguistics.

Eger, S., Youssef, P., and Gurevych, I. (2019). Is it time to swish? comparing deep learning activation functions across nlp tasks.

Fortuna, P. and Nunes, S. (2018). A Survey on Automatic Detection of Hate Speech in Text. *ACM Computing Surveys (CSUR)*, 51(4):85.

Gao, L., Kuppersmith, A., and Huang, R. (2017). Recognizing Explicit and Implicit Hate Speech Using a Weakly Supervised Two-path Bootstrapping Approach. In *IJC-NLP 2017*, pages 774–782, Taipei, Taiwan.

Kumar, R., Ojha, A. K., Malmasi, S., and Zampieri, M. (2018). Benchmarking Aggression Identification in Social Media. In *Proceedings of the First Workshop on Trolling, Aggression and Cyberbulling (TRAC)*, Santa Fe, USA.

Kumar, R., Ojha, A. K., Malmasi, S., and Zampieri, M. (2020). Evaluating Aggression Identification in Social Media. In Ritesh Kumar, et al., editors, *Proceedings of the Second Workshop on Trolling, Aggression and Cyberbullying (TRAC-2020)*, Paris, France, may. European Language Resources Association (ELRA).

Liu, L., Jiang, H., He, P., Chen, W., Liu, X., Gao, J., and Han, J. (2019a). On the variance of the adaptive learning rate and beyond. *arXiv preprint arXiv:1908.03265*.

Liu, P., Li, W., and Zou, L. (2019b). NULI at SemEval-2019 task 6: Transfer learning for offensive language detection using bidirectional transformers. In *Proceedings of the 13th International Workshop on Semantic Evaluation*, pages 87–91, Minneapolis, Minnesota, USA, June. Association for Computational Linguistics.

Liu, Y., Ott, M., Goyal, N., Du, J., Joshi, M., Chen, D., Levy, O., Lewis, M., Zettlemoyer, L., and Stoyanov, V. (2019c). Roberta: A robustly optimized bert pretraining approach.

Malmasi, S. and Zampieri, M. (2017). Detecting Hate Speech in Social Media. In *Proceedings of the International Conference Recent Advances in Natural Language Processing (RANLP)*, pages 467–472.

Malmasi, S. and Zampieri, M. (2018). Challenges in Discriminating Profanity from Hate Speech. *Journal of Experimental & Theoretical Artificial Intelligence*, 30:1–16.

Mandl, T., Modha, S., Majumder, P., Patel, D., Dave, M., Mandlia, C., and Patel, A. (2019). Overview of the hasoc track at fire 2019: Hate speech and offensive content identification in indo-european languages. In *Proceedings of the 11th Forum for Information Retrieval Evaluation*, FIRE '19, page 14–17, New York, NY, USA. Association for Computing Machinery.

Sanh, V., Debut, L., Chaumond, J., and Wolf, T. (2019). Distilbert, a distilled version of bert: smaller, faster, cheaper and lighter.

Schmidt, A. and Wiegand, M. (2017). A Survey on Hate Speech Detection Using Natural Language Processing.

In *Proceedings of the Fifth International Workshop on Natural Language Processing for Social Media. Association for Computational Linguistics*, pages 1–10, Valencia, Spain.

Thomas Carothers, A. O. (2019). How to Understand the Global Spread of Political Polarization. `https://carnegieendowment.org/2019/10/01/how-to-understand-global-spread-of-political-polarization-pub-79893`. [Online; accessed 15-April-2020].

Vaswani, A., Shazeer, N., Parmar, N., Uszkoreit, J., Jones, L., Gomez, A. N., Kaiser, L., and Polosukhin, I. (2017). Attention is All you Need. In I. Guyon, et al., editors, *Advances in Neural Information Processing Systems 30*, pages 5998–6008. Curran Associates, Inc.

Wolf, T., Debut, L., Sanh, V., Chaumond, J., Delangue, C., Moi, A., Cistac, P., Rault, T., Louf, R., Funtowicz, M., and Brew, J. (2019). Huggingface's transformers: State-of-the-art natural language processing. *ArXiv*, abs/1910.03771.

Zampieri, M., Malmasi, S., Nakov, P., Rosenthal, S., Farra, N., and Kumar, R. (2019a). Predicting the Type and Target of Offensive Posts in Social Media. In *Proceedings of NAACL*.

Zampieri, M., Malmasi, S., Nakov, P., Rosenthal, S., Farra, N., and Kumar, R. (2019b). SemEval-2019 Task 6: Identifying and Categorizing Offensive Language in Social Media (OffensEval). In *Proceedings of The 13th International Workshop on Semantic Evaluation (SemEval)*.

Zhang, M. R., Lucas, J., Hinton, G., and Ba, J. (2019). Lookahead optimizer: k steps forward, 1 step back.

Zhou, P., Shi, W., Tian, J., Qi, Z., Li, B., Hao, H., and Xu, B. (2016). Attention-based bidirectional long short-term memory networks for relation classification. In *Proceedings of the 54th Annual Meeting of the Association for Computational Linguistics (Volume 2: Short Papers)*, pages 207–212, Berlin, Germany, August. Association for Computational Linguistics.

Zhu, J., Tian, Z., and Kübler, S. (2019). UM-IU@LING at SemEval-2019 task 6: Identifying offensive tweets using BERT and SVMs. In *Proceedings of the 13th International Workshop on Semantic Evaluation*, pages 788–795, Minneapolis, Minnesota, USA, June. Association for Computational Linguistics.

Proceedings of the Second Workshop on Trolling, Aggression and Cyberbullying, pages 83–86
Language Resources and Evaluation Conference (LREC 2020), Marseille, 11–16 May 2020
© European Language Resources Association (ELRA), licensed under CC-BY-NC

LaSTUS/TALN at TRAC - 2020 Trolling, Aggression and Cyberbullying

Lütfiye Seda Mut Altın, Àlex Bravo, Horacio Saggion
Large Scale Text Understanding Systems Lab / TALN Research Group
Department of Information and Communication Technologies (DTIC)
Universitat Pompeu Fabra
Tanger 122, Barcelona (08018), Spain
lutfiyeseda.mut01@estudiant.upf.edu,{alex.bravo,horacio.saggion}@upf.edu

Abstract

This paper presents the participation of the LaSTUS/TALN team at TRAC-2020 Trolling, Aggression and Cyberbullying shared task. The aim of the task is to determine whether a given text is aggressive and contains misogynistic content. Our approach is based on a bidirectional Long Short Term Memory network (bi-LSTM). Our system performed well at sub-task A, aggression detection; however underachieved at sub-task B, misogyny detection.

1. Introduction

With millions of users contributing every day, the amount of user-generated text content forms a great amount of data, making the moderation of unwanted content highly difficult. Problematic areas of unwanted text content includes not only aggression but also trolling activities, misogyny and cyberbullying. This type of content has a proven harmful impact especially on mental health of vulnerable groups such as children and youngsters (Kwan et al., 2020). Therefore, systems that can automatically identify inappropriate content gain a lot of interest.

TRAC 2020: Second Workshop on Trolling, Aggression and Cyberbullying (TRAC – 2) shared task aims at identification of aggression and misogyny in text. It is composed of 2 sub-tasks as follows:

Sub-task A: Aggression Identification Shared Task with the classes and labels given below:

- Overtly Aggressive (OAG),

- Covertly Aggressive (CAG),

- Non-aggressive (NAG)

Sub-task B: Misogynistic Aggression Identification Shared Task with the classes and labels given below:

- Gendered (GEN),

- Non-gendered (NGEN)

The shared task is held in three Languages: English, Hindi, Bangla. With our approach, we participated in both sub-tasks only for the English language and submitted three different runs for each sub-task.
The methodology used to create this dataset is described in (Bhattacharya et al., 2020). Example instances from the dataset can be seen below:

–"Homosexuality is against nature. Thats all!" (OAG, GEN)

–"worst video" (CAG, NGEN)

–"That's the truth" (NAG, NGEN)

In this paper, we describe a neural network for text classification for aggression and misogyny identification. The rest of the paper is organized as follows: In section 2, we provide an overview of relevant research for identification of aggression and various related text classification tasks based on the relevant classes. In Section 3 we describe our model structure and specific differences of each run submitted for each sub-task. In Section 4 we provide the results and discuss the performance of the system. In Section 5 we introduce our conclusions.

2. Related Work

Many platforms such as social media sites, forums, blogs, comment and review sections of many web pages and mobile applications are heavily composed of user-generated content. As the way we communicate being substantially transformed into computer mediated communication, the need to filter out detrimental text content such as aggression and hate speech increases.

As a solution to this problem, machine learning and deep learning approaches have been utilised to classify text accordingly. Surveys reviewing previous researches indicated that instead of particular features for hate speech; generic features such as n-grams, part of speech, bag of words or embeddings are mainly used and result in reasonable performance. Moreover, character-level approaches work better than token-level approaches. In addition, lexical resources do not seem to be effective unless combined with other features (Schmidt and Wiegand, 2017), (Fortuna and Nunes, 2018). (Zampieri et al., 2019) emphasized the challenges of distinguishing profanity and threatening language which may not actually contain any swearword or profane language overtly.

Misogyny is defined as hatred, dislike, or mistrust of women, or prejudice against women [1]. One example of online misogyny is observed in the gender-biased job ads. Although, researches claim that gender discrimination in jobs ads tend to decrease (Tang et al., 2017), with the exponential increase in social media content, the need for

---

[1]https://www.dictionary.com/browse/misogyny?s=t

an automated identification mechanism in user generated content continues to increase.

(Cardiff and Shushkevich, 2019) reviewed previous research on automatic misogyny detection and pointed out that classical machine learning models, especially ensembles allow to achieve higher results than the models based on neural networks in some cases however these experiments were executed on relatively small datasets, therefore it is not certain that the results will be the same with an expanded dataset. Additionally, there has been shared tasks organized within this scope including identification of misogyny and also the particular groups such as stereotyping, discredit, dominance, sexual harassment and threats of violence (Fersini et al., 2018b) (IberLEF-2018), (Fersini et al., 2018a) (EVALITA-2018).

3.   Methodology and Data

In our approach, we utilized the same architecture as used in SemEval-2019 Task 6: Identification and Categorization of Offensive Language in Social Media (Altin et al., 2019). This model is composed of a bidirectional Long Short-Term Memory Networks (biLSTM) model with an Attention layer on top. Within the scope of this model, for pre-processing, the instances were tokenized removing punctuation marks and keeping emojis and full hashtags as they can contribute to define the meaning of text.

Then, an embedding layer transforms each element in the tokenized text such as words, emojis and hashtags into a low-dimension vector. The embedding layer, composed of the vocabulary of the task, was randomly initialized from a uniform distribution (between -0.8 and 0.8 values and with 300 dimensions). The initialized embedding layer was updated with the word vectors included in a pre-trained model based on all the tokens, emojis and hashtags from 20M English tweets (Barbieri et al., 2016).

The dataset for English language given by the shared task organizers contains two separate files prepared for training and test. The training dataset contains around 4,000 instances (Bhattacharya et al., 2020) with two given labels for each classification type for aggression and misogyny.

For the agression sub-task we submitted 3 different runs. For the first run we used only the training data provided by the organizers. For the second run we used the additional dataset published with the same task of last year, TRAC-1 dataset (Kumar et al., 2018). For the last run, we used additional dataset from TRAC-1 and changed the optimizer to RmsProp from Adam.

Likewise, for the misogyny sub-task we submitted 3 different runs. For the first run, again we used only the training data provided by the organizers. For the second run, we used only the training dataset and changed optimizer to Nadam. For the last run we used an additional misogyny dataset (Lynn et al., 2019).

4.   Results

Our system ranked 6th in sub-task A and 12th in sub-task B. We have submitted 3 different runs for each sub-task.

For sub-task A, we obtained the best result with the system which used an aditional dataset and RmsProp optimizer instead of Adam. However, the results of all runs were very close to each other. F1 (weighted) scores and accuracies obtained for each run are given in Table 1. Confusion matrix for our best performed submission for sub-task A can be seen in Figure 1. The highest recall belongs to NAG class with 92% whereas recall of other classes are 47% (CAG) and 50% (OAG). With regards to precision, NAG and CAG are similar (both around 78%) where precision of CAG is 52%.

For sub-task B, we obtained the best result with the system which used the basic dataset given and Nadam optimizer instead of Adam. The results of all runs were very close to each other. For sub-task B, F1 (weighted) scores and accuracies obtained for each run are given in Table 2. Confusion matrix for our best performed submission for sub-task B can be seen in Figure 2. Both precision and recall is higher for NGEN class (89% precision and 90% recall) whereas it is much lower for GEN class (38% precision and 34% recall).

Overall, for both sub-tasks, changes in the model for each run did not result in significant difference indicating that different optimizers and additional data did not have much effect on the results. Another point is that the main training dataset is quite unbalanced for both tasks being around 80% of the data labeled as non-Aggressive and around 70% is labeled as non-Gendered. On the other hand, although additional TRAC-1 dataset is more balanced (around 40% labeled as non-Aggressive) that did not improve the result substantially, either.

System	F1 (weighted)	Accuracy
run1	0.7100	0.7308
run2	0.7230	0.7392
run3	**0.7246**	**0.7375**

Table 1: Results for our 3 different submissions for Sub-task A.

System	F1 (weighted)	Accuracy
run1	0.8137	0.8242
run2	**0.8199**	**0.8242**
run3	0.8146	0.8217

Table 2: Results for our 3 different submissions for Sub-task B.

5.   Conclusion

In this paper, we describe the participation of LaSTUS/TALN team to TRAC - 2020 shared task focusing on identification of aggression and misogyny in text. We utilized an architecture based on a bidirectional Long Short

	sub-task A	sub-task B
Best Performer F1 (weighted)	0.8029	0.8716
LaSTUS/TALN F1 (weighted)	0.7246	0.8199
LaSTUS/TALN Ranking / Submissions	6th / 16	12th / 15

Table 3: Comparison of the results with the best performer and rankings

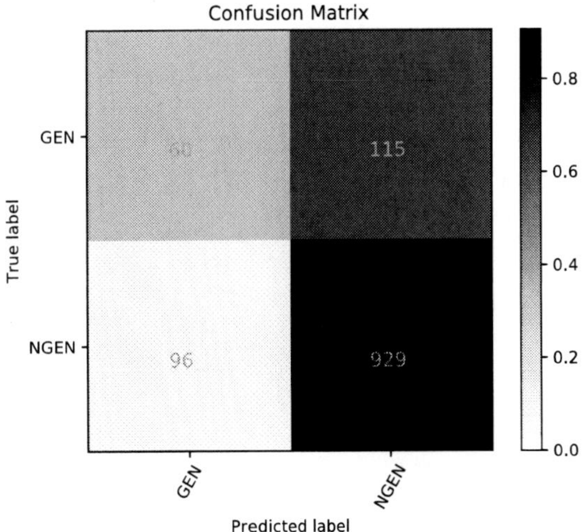

Figure 2: Confusion matrix of our best performed model (Run2) for Sub-task B

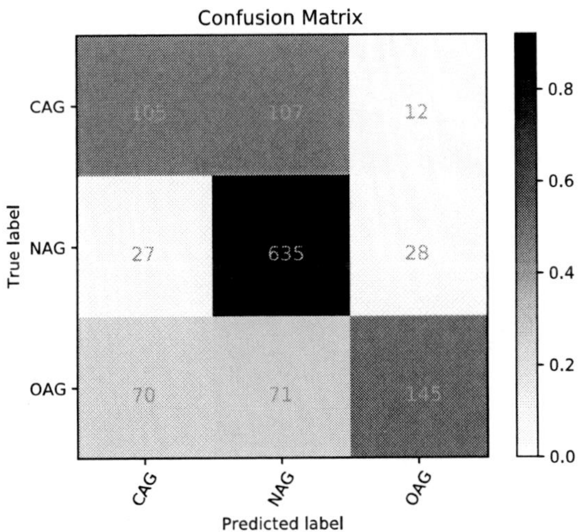

Figure 1: Confusion matrix of our best performed model (Run3) for Sub-task A

Term Memory network (biLSTM) model with an Attention layer on top. Our model performed well in the first task; however the performance was quite poor in the second task indicating that we need to improve our system for future work. Additionally, for future work, data augmentation procedures for a more balanced data can be considered.

6. Bibliographical References

Altin, L. S. M., Serrano, À. B., and Saggion, H. (2019). Lastus/taln at semeval-2019 task 6: Identification and categorization of offensive language in social media with attention-based bi-lstm model. In *Proceedings of the 13th International Workshop on Semantic Evaluation*, pages 672–677.

Barbieri, F., Kruszewski, G., Ronzano, F., and Saggion, H. (2016). How cosmopolitan are emojis? exploring emojis usage and meaning over different languages with distributional semantics. In *Proceedings of the 24th ACM international conference on Multimedia*, pages 531–535.

Bhattacharya, S., Singh, S., Kumar, R., Bansal, A., Bhagat, A., Dawer, Y., Lahiri, B., and Ojha, A. K. (2020). Developing a multilingual annotated corpus of misogyny and aggression.

Cardiff, J. and Shushkevich, E. (2019). Automatic misogyny detection in social media: a survey.

Fersini, E., Nozza, D., and Rosso, P. (2018a). Overview of the evalita 2018 task on automatic misogyny identification (ami). *EVALITA Evaluation of NLP and Speech Tools for Italian*, 12:59.

Fersini, E., Rosso, P., and Anzovino, M. (2018b). Overview of the task on automatic misogyny identification at ibereval 2018. In *IberEval@ SEPLN*, pages 214–228.

Fortuna, P. and Nunes, S. (2018). A Survey on Automatic Detection of Hate Speech in Text. *ACM Computing Surveys (CSUR)*, 51(4):85.

Kumar, R., Ojha, A. K., Malmasi, S., and Zampieri, M. (2018). Benchmarking Aggression Identification in Social Media. In *Proceedings of the First Workshop on Trolling, Aggression and Cyberbulling (TRAC)*, Santa Fe, USA.

Kwan, I., Dickson, K., Richardson, M., MacDowall, W., Burchett, H., Stansfield, C., Brunton, G., Sutcliffe, K., and Thomas, J. (2020). Cyberbullying and children and young people's mental health: a systematic map of systematic reviews. *Cyberpsychology, Behavior, and Social Networking*, 23(2):72–82.

Lynn, T., Endo, P. T., Rosati, P., Silva, I., Santos, G. L., and Ging, D. (2019). Data set for automatic detection of online misogynistic speech. *Data in brief*, 26:104223.

Schmidt, A. and Wiegand, M. (2017). A Survey on Hate Speech Detection Using Natural Language Processing. In *Proceedings of the Fifth International Workshop on Natural Language Processing for Social Media. Association for Computational Linguistics*, pages 1–10, Valencia, Spain.

Tang, S., Zhang, X., Cryan, J., Metzger, M. J., Zheng, H., and Zhao, B. Y. (2017). Gender bias in the job market: A longitudinal analysis. *Proc. ACM Hum.-Comput. Interact.*, 1(CSCW), December.

Zampieri, M., Malmasi, S., Nakov, P., Rosenthal, S., Farra, N., and Kumar, R. (2019). SemEval-2019 Task 6: Identifying and Categorizing Offensive Language in Social Media (OffensEval). In *Proceedings of The 13th International Workshop on Semantic Evaluation (SemEval)*.

Proceedings of the Second Workshop on Trolling, Aggression and Cyberbullying, pages 87–92
Language Resources and Evaluation Conference (LREC 2020), Marseille, 11–16 May 2020
© European Language Resources Association (ELRA), licensed under CC-BY-NC

Spyder: Aggression Detection on Multilingual Tweets

Anisha Datta[1], Shukrity Si[1], Urbi Chakraborty[2], Sudip kumar Naskar[2]
Jalpaiguri Govt. Engineering College, India [1]
Jadavpur University, India [2]
{sukriti.si98, dattaanishadatta, urbichakraborty}@gmail.com, sudip.naskar@cse.jdvu.ac.in

Abstract

In the last few years, hate speech and aggressive comments have covered almost all the social media platforms like facebook, twitter etc. As a result hatred is increasing. This paper describes our (**Team name: Spyder**) participation in the Shared Task on Aggression Detection organised by TRAC-2, Second Workshop on Trolling, Aggression and Cyberbullying. The Organizers provided datasets in three languages – English, Hindi and Bengali. The task was to classify each instance of the test sets into three categories – "Overtly Aggressive" (OAG), "Covertly Aggressive" (CAG) and "Non-Aggressive" (NAG). In this paper, we propose three different models using Tf-Idf, sentiment polarity and machine learning based classifiers. We obtained f1 score of 43.10%, 59.45% and 44.84% respectively for English, Hindi and Bengali.

Keywords: Aggression Detection, Cyberbullying, Tf-Idf, Sentiment polarity, Machine learning

1. Introduction

According to data of smartinsights (https://www.smartinsights.com/social-media-marketing/social-media-strategy/new-global-social-·media-research/), the number of social media users in 2019 was above 3 billion. Due to this huge increase, different types of user generated contents can be seen on social media. Many social media platforms like twitter, facebook, instagram, blogs etc. give users the opportunity to post status, pictures, videos, etc. and anyone can comment and reply to the comments on the posts. The social media posts and comments can be appreciative, affectionate, funny, aggressive, hate-speech or even sarcastic. Due to the huge interaction between people on social media, the incidents of aggression can be seen growing day by day in the form of trolling or hate-speech. The impact of this phenomenon is immense, as it can even lead anyone to commit suicide, two communities to start riot, etc (Phillips, 2015). For this reason, this research topic is of great importance and it has gained popularity among researchers in the last few years. The objective of this research topic is to automatically identify aggressive posts in social media, there by detecting the social media offenders and prevent any undesirable incidents. Research on this topic is very trending and is also a need of the hour.

This workshop focuses on the applications of NLP and Machine Learning to tackle these issues. This includes two shared tasks out of which we have participated on the 1st task as detailed below -

The task was to identify the aggressive posts from the social media texts. The participants were provided with the datasets containing three languages – English, Hindi and Indian-Bengali. People nowadays use multiple languages to write comments or posts on social media. A very important aspect of this task is to handle code-mixing and code-switching in lan-

guages since these are abundantly used in social media platforms. The datasets that we were provided with contain three classes "Overtly Aggressive" (OAG), "Covertly Aggressive" (CAG) and "Non-Aggressive" (NAG) where Overtly means totally aggressive, Covertly means bullying or trolling indirectly containing almost no or less aggressive words and the third one is not aggressive at all.

For our experiments we used three different models for three different languages. We used Tf-Idf vectorizer to vectorize the word-tokens. For English dataset, we used the XGBoost classifier followed by the bagging method. For Hindi dataset, we used the Gradient Boosting classifier and many different types of features like aggressive words lexicon, sentiment scores, parts of speech tags etc. Lastly we used the Gradient Boosting Classifier for Bengali dataset.

The rest of the paper is organized as follows. Section-2 gives a brief account of the related works. Section-3 presents a description of the datasets. In section-4, the system architecture and the feature engineering are explained. Section-5 presents the results and comparison. Section 6 concludes the paper and provides avenues for future work.

2. Related Work

Although aggression detection in text is a relatively new research topic, quite a few research work have been carried out on this topic (AmirHRazavi and Matwin., 2010; Ritesh Kumar and Chennuru, 2018; Ritesh Kumar and Zampieri, 2020). (Duyu Tang and Qin, 2014) showed how positive and negative emoticons can be used for this work. (Kwok and Wang., 2013) used uni-gram model for this task. (Chikashi Nobata and Chang, 2016) used different types of syntactic features and embedding features for aggression detection in text. (Mohammad, 2012) mapped hashtags like 'yuck', 'joy' into different types of emotions and classified the texts. In (Orˇasan, 2018), they used Support Vector

Machine and Random Forest as classifiers and emojis and sentiment scores were used as features. (Nemanja Djuric and Bhamidipati, 2015) used word embeddings which worked better than bag of words to detect aggressive text. (Jan Deriu and Jaggi, 2016) also did the work with the help of emotional sentiment.
However, all the research works mentioned above are based on the English language (Jun-Ming Xu and Bellmore, 2012). These days, with the increasing availability of multi-lingual keypads in the mobile devices and the support for multi-lingual contents in the websites, detecting aggression from multi-lingual texts has become a necessity. (Vinay Singh and Shrivastava, 2018) used CNN and LSTM to detect aggression on Hindi-English code-mixed texts. In (Shukrity Si, 2019), an ensembling method were used with the help of Aggression lexicons, sentiment scores, POS tags and, emoticons on English and Hindi-English code-mixed languages. (Kalika Bali and Vyas, 2014) proposed a model for English-Hindi code-mixed comments from facebook. (Yogarshi Vyas and Choudhury, 2014) proposed a model for Hindi-English codemixed language which is based on the feature - parts of speech. There has also been work on aggression detection in other languages like Chinese (Hui-Po Su and Lin, 2017), Arabian (Hamdy Mubarak and Magdy, 2017), Dutch (Stephan´ Tulkens and Daelemans, 2016), etc.
Our work is based on three languages - English, Hindi and Indian Bengali. There are English-Hindi code-mixing cases too in the datasets. We proposed different models for the different languages and the models are based on machine learning algorithms like XGBoost and Gradient Boosting and features like Tf-Idf, sentiment scores, POS tags and aggressive words lexicon. The methodology is described elaborately in Section 4.

3. Datasets

The TRAC 2020 Shared Task Organizers (Bhattacharya et al., 2020) provided datasets in 3 languages – English, Hindi and Indian Bengali. The English dataset contains 5,120 texts for training and 1,201 texts for testing. The Indian Bengali dataset contains 4,785 texts for training and 1,188 texts for testing (in both Roman and Bangla script). The Hindi dataset contains 4,981 texts for training and 1,200 texts for testing (in both Roman and Devanagari script). Table 1 presents the statistics of the shared task datasets provided by the Organizers.

Table 1: Dataset statistics

Data	*Training*	*Test*
English	5,120	1,201
Hindi	4,981	1,200
Bengali	4,785	1,188

Some examples are shown in figure 1.

English and Codemixed :
It seems like these people want to be famous nothing more they don't care if people die by their hateful talks. *NAG*
Hello mister....kabir singh is a achi cheez...u don't know how many family are destroyed by drinking..... *CAG*
conservatives fuck you all.. *OAG*

Hindi :
"यह एक संवेदनशील,कठोर,सनक, बेपरवाह, दर्द देने वाला,प्रेम कहानी है". *NAG*
कितना आवश्यक है उस भाषा में डिबेट करना जो भाषा आपके पेनलिस्ट्स से आती ही नहीं।. *CAG*
इन लिब्रल्स का भोसड़ा मारू. *OAG*

Bengali :
পতিতাদের চরিত্র রাজনৈতিক নেতাদের থেকে হাজার গুন ভাল । ওদের সততা আছে । টাকা মেরে দেয় না । ওদের আর ঘাটিওনা ভাই ।", *NAG*
রানুদি হাই কোটে গিয়ে ভিখা কোরতো.........., *CAG*
তুই তো খানকি মাগি টাকার মুখ দেখেছিস তাই জন্য এতো গরম", *OAG*

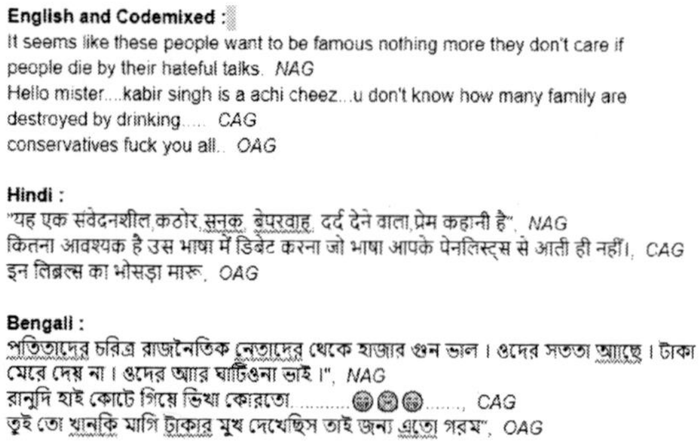

Figure 1: Examples of given texts with categories

The preprocessing steps and further classification process are described as follows.

4. Methodology

Different feature models are used for these 3 different languages in classification process. Though same vectorizing tool is used in all of these three that is Tf-Idf Vectorizer. Three different models are described below.
For English Task-A, we have used Tf-Idf Vectorizer (taking unigram and bigram sequence of words) with 500 maximum words as features. We use XGBoost classifier (with learning rate 0.01 and random state 1) to train the given dataset. Then we have used bagging classifier where the base classifier is also XGBoost (maximum samples=0.5, maximum features=0.5). No extra data is used here for training.
For Bengali dataset, we have used Tf-Idf Vectorizer (max words = 500 , bigram) as feature to vectorize the word tokens. Then we have used Gradient Boosting Classifier for classification. We are using the given dataset and no extra data is used for training here.
For Hindi dataset, we have used Tf-Idf Vectorizer, aggressive word lexicons , sentiment scores(taking compound score from positive and negative scores of individual words) and part of speech tags (as some POS tags are important in classification like-adverbs,adjectives etc.) as features. And we have used Gradient Boosting Classifier for classification. No extra data is used for training here.
Now we describe the vectorizer tool, classification algorithms and other feature models in details.

4.1. Tf-Idf Vectorizer

A machine can't understand raw text data but only number vectors. So the text input must be converted into vector of numbers. There are many tools available in python for this conversion. Bag of Words (BoW), Count Vectorizer, Tf-Idf Vectorizer are some of the examples. Tf-Idf doesn't only count the occurrences of any word in a document, but also gives importance to the words which are more useful in revealing the document's nature. It is the multiplication of Tf (Term Frequency) and Idf (Inverse Document Frequency) which have the formulae as follow -

$$Tf(t) = \frac{frequency\,of\,term\,t\,in\,a\,sentence}{total\,no.\,of\,terms\,in\,that\,sentence}$$

$$Idf(t) = log\frac{no.\,of\,sentences\,in\,a\,document}{total\,no.\,of\,sentences\,which\,contain\,term\,t}$$

By taking the log of the inverse count of term t, the value for the words (terms) occurring much frequently in the document (like stopwords, less important words) gets reduced making the classification task easier.

4.2. XGBoost

XGBoost stands for Extreme Gradient Boosting. We used XGBoost here for the English dataset. It is a new algorithm and an implementation of Gradient Boosted Decision Tree. It is mainly used for better performance and it reduces the execution time also. It has many features such that system features, model features, algorithm features.

4.2.1. System Features

For better and fast performance this feature is included in the XGBoost library. It has out of core computing, distributed computing, cache optimization and parallelization.

- Out of Core Computing - This is a special feature that works for very large dataset. Large dataset generally does not fit into memory. So this feature can overcome this situation.

- Distributed Computing - This feature is used to run very large models which needs a machine-cluster.

- Cache Optimization - It is used for optimizing the algorithm and data structure.

- Parallelization - It uses all CPU cores parallely during the time of training.

4.2.2. Model Features

Model features include regularization methods and different types of gradient boosting algorithm.

- Stochastic Gradient Boosting - It is a special form of Gradient Boosting Machine that sub-samples the column and row.

- Regularization - It includes L1 and L2 regularization which help to overcome overfitting.

4.2.3. Algorithm Features

This feature is included to increase the efficiency of available resources and computational time. To do this it uses block structure, continued training and sparse aware method.

4.2.4. Bagging with XGBoost

Then we used bagging classifier keeping XGBoost as our base classifier.

Bagging is one type of ensembling method that is used for better prediction. For bagging, the original dataset is divided into many random subsets. Then the base classifier is fitted (here XGBoost) into the subsets.

Then the output is given by aggregating (voting or averaging) their individual predictions. This method is known as bagging and with this we can minimize the variance of the model. We used bagging classifer with the help of XGBoost to classify the English task.

4.3. Gradient Boosting Machine

Gradient Boosting machine (GBM) was used for Hindi and Bengali dataset. Weak learner by training can become a strong learner - on this assumption GBM works. Gradient Boosting Classifier is mainly consisting of three major components - a loss function, a weak learner and an additive model. On training the loss function is optimized, the weak learner is used to predict on the basis of the task and the additive model is used so that the weak learner can minimize the loss function.

- Loss Function - In supervised learning, error should always be minimized during the training. To calculate the error first we have to take a function, it is called loss function. Loss function is generally taken on the basis of problem statement. The main criteria of a loss function is that it must be differentiable. For classification, we can use logarithmic loss and for regression, squared error can be used. For our task, we used logarithmic loss as our loss function.

- Weak Learner - For Gradient Boosting, Decision Tree is taken into consideration for weak learner. The learner should be greedy and that is why tree is chosen here. Tree are constructed in a greedy way. Trees generally choose the best split points to minimize the scores. And later an additive model is added with this weak learner.

- Additive Model - Additive model is used to minimize the error of loss function. For this algorithm, trees are added but one at a time and for this, the trees should not be changed. Gradient Descent method is also used here and it helps to minimize the error during the addition of trees. After the errors are calculated the weights are updated for minimizing the error. The new output is added to the old output of the existing tree and the process is continued. In this way, Gradient Boosting is heading towards a better result.

4.4. Aggressive Word Lexicon

For doing the task, we observed the dataset very carefully and we observed that the texts contain many bad words and slang languages. We considered these as an important feature and named these as aggressive word features. So, we made a lexicon of these aggressive words which can be used to write hate comments and used it to build our model. Here is some examples of aggressive words.

e.g - "chutiya", "jhant", "   " etc.

These types of words are frequently used in texts labelled as 'OAG'. So, this feature is very important to identify the 'OAG' class in our task. We used this lexicon for Hindi dataset only.

4.5. Sentiment Score

Observing the dataset, we can say that aggression is one kind of sentiment and for this, we used sentiment score as one of our features. Generally if the sentiment of a text is very negative, then there is a high chance that the text would be OAG. Because, OAG text contains many slang words which belongs to negative sentiment category. We used this feature for Hindi dataset. Hindi-sentiwordnet is used to get the sentiment score of each word present in the dataset. There are three types of sentiment in sentiwordnet - positive, negative and neutral. We tagged all the tokens accordingly this and used sentiment score as a feature.

4.6. POS Tag

POS tag represents part of speech tag. We observed that adjectives and adverbs are highly used in case of OAG and CAG. Higher the present of adjective and adverb higher the chance of the text is to be a OAG or CAG. We used this feature for Hindi dataset and to do this sentiwordnet was used. There are four parts of speech in sentiwordnet - noun, verb, adjective and adverb. We tagged the word-tokens according to their parts of speech and constructed a feature matrix and used it to build our model.

5. Results and Discussion

In this section, we will discuss about all our of results in details. Table 2 shows the result of English dataset. We got the weighted F1 score of 43.10% and accuracy of 58% for this model.

The performance of our model is not so good in the

System	F1 (weighted)	Accuracy
Bagging (XGBoost)	0.4310	0.58

Table 2: Results for Sub-task EN-A

shared task competition. The comparison with other models is shown in Table 3.

Table 3: Comparison Table for English Dataset

	Julian	Sdhanshu	krishan thvs	Our Model
F Score	80.29	75.92	44.17	43.10

From the table, we can clearly see that our performance is very poor. So we need many modifications in our model and we will discuss about the poor performance of our model in the end of this section. Table 4 shows the result of Hindi dataset. We got the F1 score of 59.45% and accuracy of 62.08%. The comparison with other models in this dataset is shown in Table 5.

System	F1 (weighted)	Accuracy
GBM	0.5945	0.6208

Table 4: Results for Sub-task HIN-A

Table 5: Comparison Table for Hindi Dataset

	Julian	abaruah	bhanu prakash2708	Our Model
F Score	81.27	79.43	14.06	59.45

The performance of our model for Hindi dataset is slightly better than the previous one. But still it needs lot of modification.
The result for Bengali dataset is shown in Table 6. We got the F1 score of 44.84% and accuracy of 59.76%. The comparison with other models for this Bengali

System	F1 (weighted)	Accuracy
GBM	0.4484	0.5976

Table 6: Results for Sub-task BEN-A

dataset is shown in Table 7.
Our performance on Bengali dataset is also not good and we will modify our model for better performance.

Confusion matrices are given to visualize the results for all of the three languages. This matrix gives the actual measurement to test the performance of our model. It compares between the true (actual result) and predicted (model prediction) classes. As for binary classification, the confusion matrix looks like the Table 8.

Here TP means True Positive (predicted as true and actually it is true), FP means False Positive (predicted as true but actually it is false), FN means False Negative (predicted as false but actually it is true) and TN means True Negative (predicted as false and actually it is false).

In our model, this is 3-class classification and so the confusion matrix is of 3*3 matrix. The confusion matrix for the Bengali dataset is shown in figure 2. The confusion matrix for the English dataset is shown in figure 3.
The confusion matrix for the Hindi dataset is shown in figure 4.
This model gives good results but these could be better if we could modify our model in some ways more. There are some modifications that can be done as follows-
(1) We can use extra resources like aggressive words lexicon for Bengali and English datasets as well. It will help to distinguish the aggressive texts from others like in Hindi dataset.
(2) We have used bagging classifier (ensembling

Table 7: Comparison Table for Bengali Dataset

	Julian	*abaruah*	*saikesav 564*	*Our Model*
F Score	82.18	80.82	46.84	44.84

Predicted(row)/ True(col)	Posi- tive	Nega- tive
Pos	TP	FP
Neg	FN	TN

Table 8: Confusion Matrix of Binary Classification

method) in case of English data only with base classifier as XGBoost. But this method can be applied to other two datasets as well for improvement.
(3) We have used only machine learning classifiers for this 3-class classification. But we can implement deep learning models also. Although the datasets are not very large and it might not give good results, but we can try this in future for more exploration.

6. Conclusion

After observing the results we can come to a conclusion. The performances of our models is poor and all models need many modifications for better performance. We observed that deep learning methods like LSTM, RNN or CNN-LSTM with pre-trained word embedding methods like glove gave good results for some researches. As we did not use any deep learning technique in our work we can use it and results can be better for this. We will work on this task in future to modify the models and a general model have to be made which can work fine for datasets of any language.

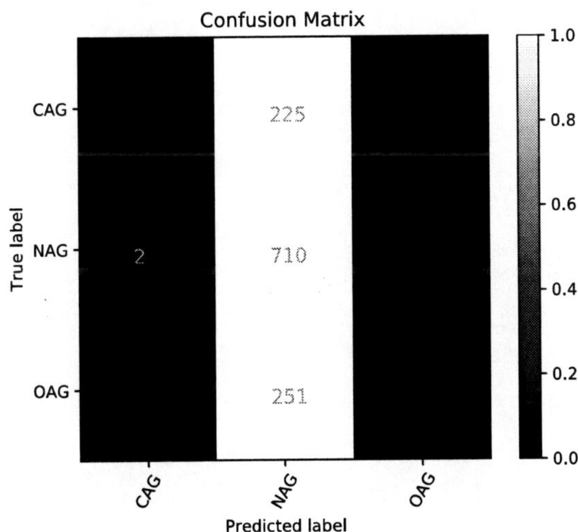

Figure 2: Confusion Matrix for Sub-task BEN-A)

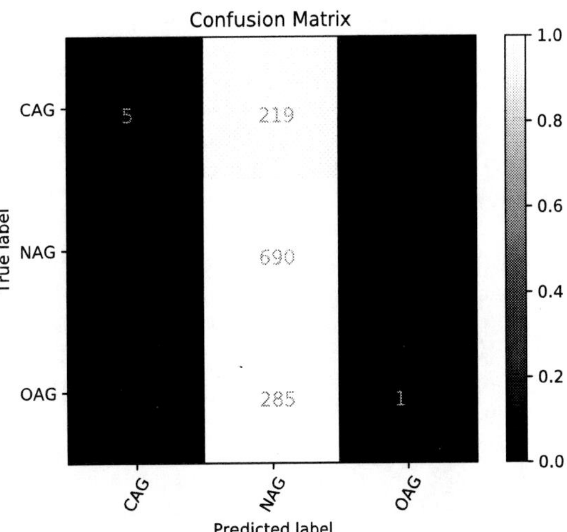

Figure 3: Confusion Matrix for Sub-task EN-A

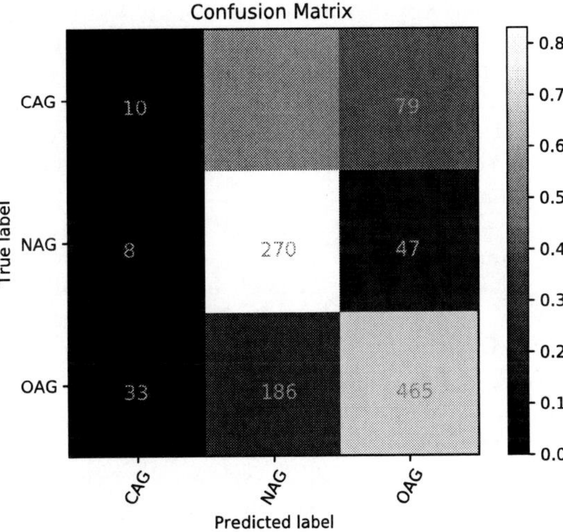

Figure 4: Confusion Matrix for Sub-task HIN-A

This can be done in future.

7. Bibliographical References

AmirHRazavi, DianaInkpen, S. and Matwin., S. (2010). Offensive language detection using multi-level classification. In Canadian Conference on Artificial Intelligence, pages 16–27. Springer.

Bhattacharya, S., Singh, S., Kumar, R., Bansal, A., Bhagat, A., Dawer, Y., Lahiri, B., and Ojha, A. K. (2020). Developing a multilingual annotated corpus of misogyny and aggression.

Chikashi Nobata, Joel Tetreault, A. T. Y. M. and Chang, Y. (2016). Abu-sive language detection in online user content. In Proceedings of the 25th International Conference on World Wide Web, pages 145–153. International World Wide Web Conferences Steering Committee.

Duyu Tang, Furu Wei, N. Y. M. Z. T. L. and Qin, B. (2014). Learning sentiment-specific word embedding for twitter sentiment classification. In Proceedings of the 52nd Annual Meeting of the Association for Computational Linguistics (Volume 1: Long Papers), volume 1, pages 1555–1565.

Hamdy Mubarak, K. D. and Magdy, W. (2017). Abusive language detection on arabic social media. In Proceedings of the First Workshop on Abusive Language Online, pages 52–56.

Hui-Po Su, Zhen-Jie Huang, H.-T. C. and Lin, C.-J. (2017). Rephrasing profanity in chinese text. In Proceedings of the First Workshop on Abusive Language Online, pages 18–24..

Jan Deriu, Maurice Gonzenbach, F. U. A. L. V. D. L. and Jaggi, M. (2016). Swisscheese at semeval-2016 task 4: Sentiment classification using an ensemble of convolutional neural networks with distant supervision. In Proceedings of the 10th International Workshop on Semantic Evaluation, number EPFL-CONF-229234, pages 1124–1128.

Jun-Ming Xu, Kwang-Sung Jun, X. Z. and Bellmore, A. (2012). Learning from bullying traces in social media. In Proceedings of the 2012 conference of the North American chapter of the association for computational linguistics: Human language technologies, pages 656– 666. Association for Computational Linguistics.

Kalika Bali, Jatin Sharma, M. C. and Vyas, Y. (2014). i am borrowing ya mixing?" an analysis of english-hindi code mixing in facebook. In Proceedings of the First Workshop on Computational Approaches to Code Switching, pages 116–126.

Kwok, I. and Wang., Y. (2013). Locate the hate: Detecting tweets against blacks. In Twenty-Seventh AAAI Conference on Artificial Intelligence.

Mohammad, S. M. (2012). emotional tweets. In Proceedings of the First Joint Conference on Lexical and Computational Semantics-Volume 1: Proceedings of the main conference and the shared task, and Volume 2: Proceedings of the Sixth International Workshop on Semantic Evaluation, pages 246–255. Associa-tion for Computational Linguistics.

Nemanja Djuric, Jing Zhou, R. M. M. G. V. R. and Bhamidipati, N. (2015). Hate speech detection with comment embeddings. In Proceedings of the 24th International Conference on World Wide Web Companion, pages 29–30. International World Wide Web Con-ferences Steering Committee.

Orăasan, C. (2018). Aggressive language identification using word embeddings and sentiment features. Proceedings of the First Workshop on Trolling, Aggression and Cyberbullying, pages 113–119.

Phillips, W. (2015). This is why we can't have nice things: Mapping the relationship between online trolling and mainstream culture. Mit Press.

Ritesh Kumar, Guggilla Bhanodai, R. P. and Chennuru, M. R. (2018). Trac-1 shared task on aggression identification: Iit(ism)@coling'18.

Ritesh Kumar, Atul Kr. Ojha, S. M. and Zampieri, M. (2020). Evaluating aggression identification in social media. In Ritesh Kumar, et al., editors, *Proceedings of the Second Workshop on Trolling, Aggression and Cyberbullying (TRAC-2020)*, Paris, France, may. European Language Resources Association (ELRA).

Shukrity Si, Anisha Datta, S. B. S. K. N. (2019). Aggression detection on multilingual social media text. 10th ICCCNT - 2019.

Stephan´ Tulkens, Lisa Hilte, E. L. B. V. and Daelemans, W. (2016). A dictionary-based approach to racism detection in dutch social media. In Proceedings of the Workshop Text Analytics for Cybersecurity and Online Safety (TA-COS), Portoroz, Slovenia.

Vinay Singh, Aman Varshney, S. S. A. D. V. and Shrivastava, M. (2018). Aggression detection on social media text using deep neural networks. Empirical Methods in Natural Language Processing (EMNLP-2018).

Yogarshi Vyas, Spandana Gella, J. S. K. B. and Choudhury, M. (2014). Pos tagging of english-hindi code-mixed social media content. In Proceedings of the 2014 Conference on Empirical Methods in Natural Language Processing (EMNLP), pages 974–979.

Proceedings of the Second Workshop on Trolling, Aggression and Cyberbullying, pages 93–98
Language Resources and Evaluation Conference (LREC 2020), Marseille, 11–16 May 2020

BERT of all trades, master of some

Denis Gordeev [1], Olga Lykova[2]
[1]Russian Presidential Academy of National Economy and Public Administration,
[2]National Research Nuclear University MEPhI
Moscow, Russia
gordeev-di@ranepa.ru, OVLykova@mephi.ru

Abstract

This paper describes our results for TRAC 2020 competition held together with the conference LREC 2020. Our team name was **Ms8qQxMbnjJMgYcw**. The competition consisted of 2 subtasks in 3 languages (Bengali, English and Hindi) where the participants' task was to classify aggression in short texts from social media and decide whether it is gendered or not. We used a single BERT-based system with two outputs for all tasks simultaneously. Our model placed first in English and second in Bengali gendered text classification competition tasks with 0.87 and 0.93 in F1-score respectively.

Keywords: aggression, classification, BERT, neural network, Transformer, NLP

1. Introduction

Aggression, hate speech and misogyny detection is a rampant problem nowadays on the Internet. Thousands of people of all ages and nations face it every day. However, the problem is far from being solved. Many research initiatives have been devoted to its investigation. Given the overwhelming amount of information that social media users output every second, it is incomprehensible to monitor and moderate all of it manually. So it becomes useful to make at least semi-automatic predictions about whether a message contains aggression. Shared tasks and competitions are of great utility in this problem because they provide data that can be used to research new ways of aggression expression and allow different methods to be compared in a uniform and impartial way. TRAC 2020 is one of such initiatives (Ritesh Kumar and Zampieri, 2020).

This paper is devoted to our system's solution for TRAC 2020 competition held together with LREC 2020 conference [1]. TRAC 2020 competition consisted of 2 sub-tasks in 3 languages: Bengali, English and Hindi. In the first sub-task participants needed to make a system that would label texts into three classes: 'Overtly Aggressive', 'Covertly Aggressive' and 'Non-aggressive'. In the second task the contestants' aim was to label the same texts as gendered or not. The dataset contained 18681 texts in total, approximately 6000 texts for each language.

We used a single BERT-based system with two Linear layer outputs for all subtasks and languages simultaneously. Our model took first place in English gendered text classification and second place in Bengali gendered text classification.

2. Related Work

Many researchers have paid attention to the problem of aggression detection on the Internet. However, hate and offensive speech are not homogeneous. There are various types of it that are aimed at different social groups and that use distinct vocabulary. Davidson et al. collected a hate speech dataset exploring this problem (Davidson et al., 2017). The authors relied on heavy use of crowd-sourcing. First, they used a crowd-sourced hate speech lexicon to collect tweets with hate speech keywords. Then they resorted again to crowd-sourcing to label a sample of these tweets into three categories: those containing hate speech, containing only offensive language, and those with neither. Later analysis showed that hate speech can be reliably separated from other types of offensive language. They find that racist and homophobic tweets are more likely to be classified as hate speech but sexist tweets are generally classified as offensive. Malmasi together with Zampiere explored this dataset even further (Malmasi and Zampieri, 2017). They have found that the main challenge for successful hate speech detection lies in indiscriminating profanity and hate speech from each other.

Many works have been devoted to hate speech detection. Thus, it seems that there should be a lot of available data exploring this problem for various languages. However, as the survey by Fortuna and Nunes (Fortuna and Nunes, 2018) showed most authors do not publish the data they collected and used. Therefore, competitions and shared tasks releasing annotated datasets that let explorers study the problem of hate speech detection carry even greater importance. Among such competitions, we can name the previous TRAC competition (Kumar et al., 2018) and Offenseval (Zampieri et al., 2019). The first TRAC shared task on aggression identification was devoted to a 3-way classification between 'Overtly Aggressive', 'Covertly Aggressive' and 'Non-aggressive' Facebook text data in Hindi and English. Offenseval was very similar in nature but it contained texts only in English. It consisted of 3 subtasks: binary offence identification, binary categorization of offence types and offence target classification.

The best model at the previous TRAC competition used an LSTM-model (Aroyehun and Gelbukh, 2018). They

---

[1]available at github.com/InstituteForIndustrialEconomics/trac2

used preprocessing techniques to remove non-English characters and various special symbols. They also resorted to back-translation into 4 intermediate languages: French, Spanish, German, and Hindi.

Private initiatives also do not keep out of this problem. For example, there were held several challenges on machine learning competition platform Kaggle devoted to aggression investigation in social media, among them: Jigsaw Toxic Comment Classification Challenge [2] and Jigsaw Unintended Bias in Toxicity Classification [3]. The best solutions on Kaggle used a bunch of various techniques to improve the model score. Among such techniques were various types of pseudo-labelling such as back-translation and new language modelling subtasks.

There are few competitions that have the data labelled in more than two languages at the same time. However, the latest advances in machine translation show us that simultaneous multiple language learning may vastly improve the scores of the models (Arivazhagan et al., 2019). The researchers trained a single neural machine translation model on more than one billion sentence pairs, from more than 100 languages to and from English. The resulting massively multilingual, massive neural machine translation model demonstrated large quality improvements on both low- and high-resource languages and showed great efficacy on cross-lingual downstream transfer tasks.

Unsupervised cross-lingual language model learning also shows promising results. Some researchers have shown that pretraining of multilingual language models at scale leads to significant performance gains for a wide range of cross-lingual transfer tasks (Conneau et al.,). The authors trained a Transformer-based masked language model on one hundred languages, using more than two terabytes of filtered CommonCrawl data. Their model outperformed previous state-of-the-art solutions in a variety of cross-lingual tasks without hurting single-language performance.

However, even the most modern and sophisticated solutions are far from solving this problem. According to the survey by Fortuna and Nunes (Fortuna and Nunes, 2018) even human annotators have a tendency to disagree while labelling hate speech datasets. Detecting hate speech requires knowledge about social structure and culture. Even some websites may vary in what can be considered hate speech. Moreover, social phenomena and language are in constant evolution especially among young users which makes it challenging to track all racial and minority insults. Hate speech may also be very subtle and contain no offensive vocabulary or slurs.

3. TRAC-2 dataset

TRAC 2020 competition dataset contained around 18000 texts in 3 languages (see Table 2): Bengali, English and

Language	Class	Example
English	NAG	Best topic for Law Students!
English	CAG	Arundhati Roy has biggest bowls
English	OAG	One word for u bhaad me jaa chudail
English	NGEN	She is wrong.
English	GEN	I love u sakib but opu sotiya
Hindi	NAG	bro house of card ka review karona
Hindi	CAG	"Liberal bhi hai, Tolerant bhi hai!!!" LoL
Hindi	OAG	Feminism ki maa chod dee
Hindi	NGEN	Amrit Anand अबअ तो जउङअए हइइ हअइ उनअको बोलो जउङअनाए
Hindi	GEN	@Nareshkumar Ravanaboina teri ma ka bhosda
Bengali	NAG	Dada taratari
Bengali	CAG	Basa niye bhore dite habe sali ke
Bengali	OAG	Ei mahila manasika rogi
Bengali	NGEN	Dada taratari
Bengali	GEN	Kena? Ranu mandala apanara bala chirache.

Table 1: Text Examples for all languages and classes.

Dataset	English	Hindi	Bengali
Train	4263	3984	3826
Development	1066	997	957
Test	1200	1200	1188
Total	6529	6181	5971

Table 2: Number of texts for each language and dataset

Hindi. Hindi and Bengali texts could be written both in Roman and Bangla or Devanagari script within a single text (see Table 3). Moreover, many texts were written in two languages at the same time. It should also be noted that texts labelled as English contained a lot of names and words from non-English languages (most probably Hindi) and were hard to comprehend without knowledge of Hindi or Bengali (see Table 1).

The authors of the competition split texts in all languages into training, validation and test datasets. Each text had one label for each of the subtasks. The first subtask was a 3-way classification of aggression in social media texts. The classes were 'Overtly Aggressive', 'Covertly Aggressive' and 'Non-aggressive'. The second task was a binary classification between "gendered" and "not gendered" texts.

Languages differed in their class distributions. In Subtask A Hindi and Bengali had a larger ratio of covertly aggressive texts than English both in the train and development datasets (see Fig. 1). The numbers for Subtask B are similar. English had a much lower ratio of gendered texts than Hindi or Bengali (see Fig. 2). Moreover, it should be noted

---

[2]https://www.kaggle.com/c/jigsaw-toxic-comment-classification-challenge

[3]https://www.kaggle.com/c/jigsaw-unintended-bias-in-toxicity-classification

Language	Examples
Bengali	best giris jain a katha
English	no gay gene discovered recently
Hindi	Negative positive दोनों म h sir
Hindi	Please logic mat ghusao

Table 3: Examples of script usage for different languages.

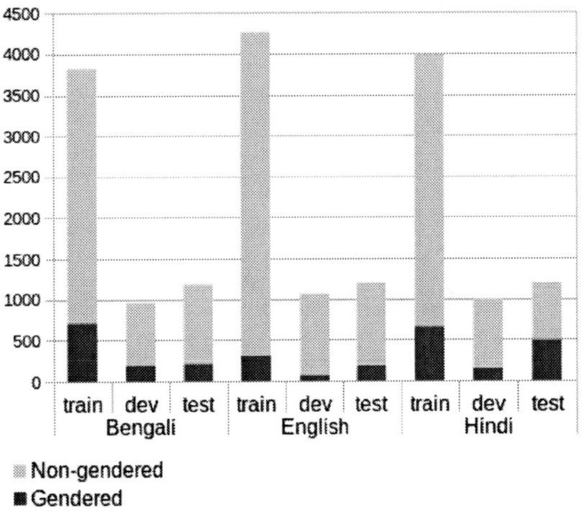

Figure 2: Class distribution (Subtask B)

4. BERT model with multiple outputs

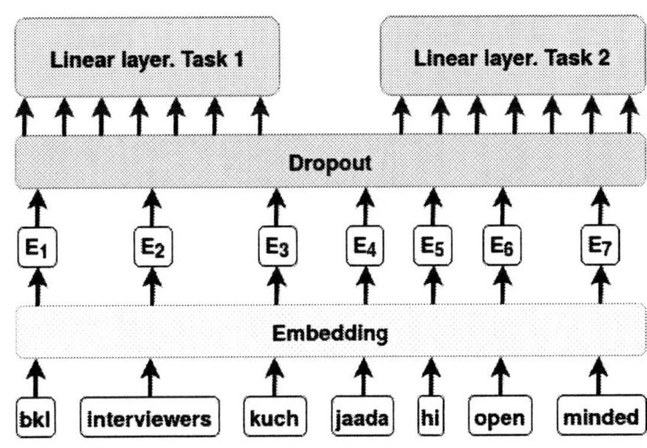

Figure 5: Our multitask model depiction

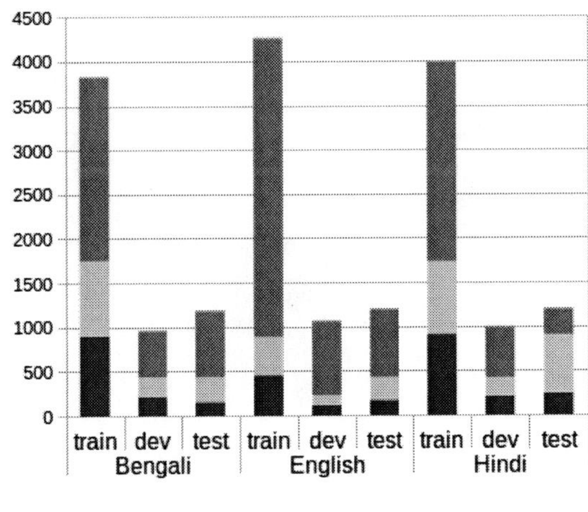

Figure 1: Class distribution (Subtask A)

that the distribution for Subtask B was rather skewed. For example, the number of gendered texts for English in the training dataset was 13 times higher than that of the non-gendered ones (for Bengali and Hindi the numbers are 4.4 and 5 respectively). For all languages class distributions between train and development datasets did not differ much. However, test distributions (which were unknown during the competition) do not look the same as the train dataset. For example, Hindi as well as English had many more gendered texts in the test (0.17 vs 0.70 and 0.07 vs 0.17 ratios respectively). For subtask A, Hindi also had some peculiarities with overtly aggressive texts being the majority in the test dataset while neutral texts dominated the train and development datasets.

In this task, we wanted to experiment with a single model that works with multiple languages at once. We could have used an embedding-based approach with Word2Vec (Mikolov et al., 2013) or FastText (Joulin et al., 2016) input and a neural network classifier to classify aggression in texts (Gordeev, 2016). However, pre-trained language models are usually trained for one language at a time and either require augmentation via back-translation (Aroyehun and Gelbukh, 2018) or training a new word embedding model for several languages at once. Fortunately, it is possible to overcome this using multilingual language models such as BERT (Devlin et al., 2018).

BERT is a Transformer-based model (Vaswani et al., 2017). We used a multilingual uncased BERT model provided

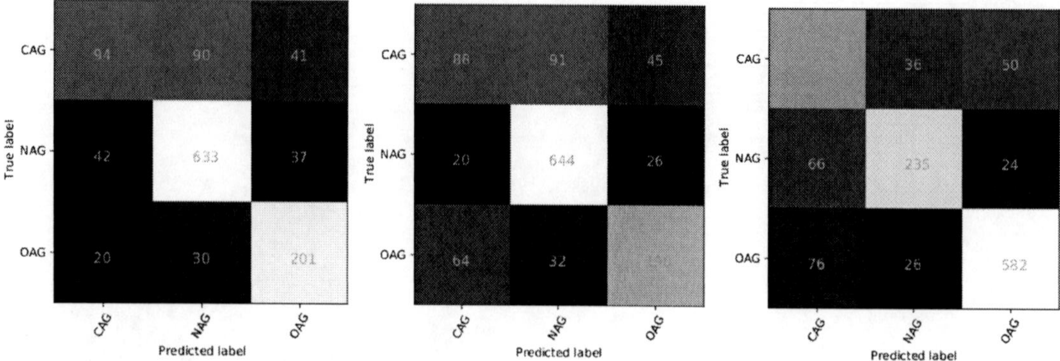

Figure 3: Subtask A. Confusion matrices for the final test dataset. Provided in the following order: Bengali, English, Hindi (the 4th, 3rd and 4th places in the leaderboard respectively)

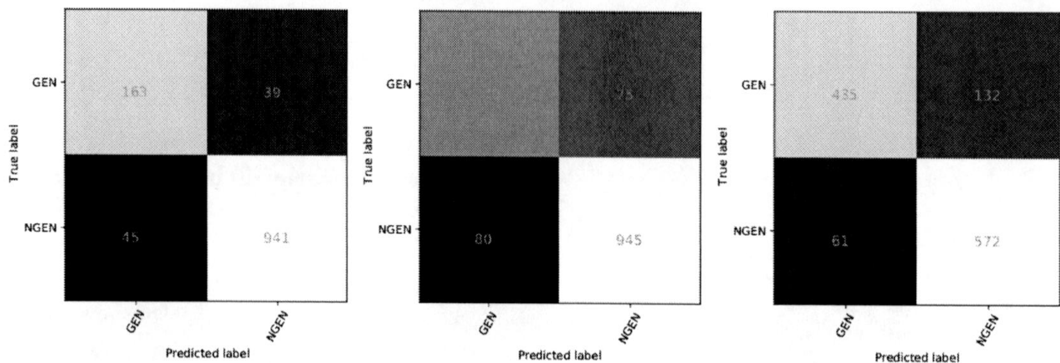

Figure 4: Subtask B. Confusion matrices for the final test dataset. Provided in the following order: Bengali, English, Hindi (the 2nd, 1st and 3rd places in the leaderboard respectively)

by Hugging Face (Wolf et al., 2019). We used PyTorch framework to create our model. BERT was trained using Wikipedia texts in more than 100 languages. All texts were tokenized using byte-pair encoding (BPE) which allows limiting the vocabulary size compared to Word2vec and other word vector models. The training consisted in predicting a random masked token in the sentence and a binary next sentence prediction. We did not fine-tune the language model using the text data provided by the organizers. Information about the text language was not included in the model. We also did not perform any text augmentation or pre-processing besides standard byte-pair encoding. All texts longer than 510 tokens were truncated. Two tokens marking the beginning and the end of the sequence were added to each input text ("[CLS]" and "[SEP]"). Texts shorter than 510 tokens were padded with zeroes. All tokens excluding special ones were masked with ones, while all other tokens were masked with zeroes.

On top of BERT, we added a Dropout layer to fight overfitting. The Dropout probability was equal to 0.1. On top of the Dropout Layer, two softmax layers were added for each of the subtasks. Their dimensions were 3 and 2 respectively, equal to the number of classes. Target values were one-hot encoded. All texts were selected randomly out of the training and validation datasets. Cross entropy loss function was used for each of the outputs. The final loss function was calculated just as the sum of these two output losses. Half precision training was used via Apex library [4]. We used a single Nvidia V100 GPU to train our model. The training batch size was made equal to 16. The model was trained for 10 epochs.

We used the same training, validation and test datasets as they were provided by the organizers. The validation data was applied only to hyperparameter tuning and was not included in the training dataset.

Our team members have only knowledge of the English language and absolutely no familiarity with Hindi or Bengali.

5. Results

The results of our system are provided in Table 4. All in all we took first place in the gendered classification for English and the second place for the same task in Bengali. The results of our model were better for binary gendered classification than for 3-way aggression labelling. It might be due to the fact that we did not weight our loss function

---

[4]https://github.com/NVIDIA/apex

Task	F1 (weighted)	Accuracy	Rank
Bengali-A	0.7716	0.7811	4
Bengali-B	0.9297	0.9293	2
English-A	0.7568	0.7683	3
English-B	0.8716	0.8708	1
Hindi-A	0.7761	0.7683	4
Hindi-B	0.8381	0.8392	3

Table 4: Results for all tasks

and both tasks contributed equally to the result. While it might be a better idea to give more emphasis to the target that has more potential values. We also did not use any early stopping or other similar techniques. Given that the model was trained for 10 epochs, it might have been not enough for 3-way classification. A more challenging task might require more epochs to converge, thus, in future research we will also check the balance for early stopping between two targets. Moreover, we could have enhanced individual subtask predictions by using values inferred by our model for another target. We hope to also try it in future research.

As can be seen from confusion matrices for subtask A (see Fig. 3) for all languages, our model had difficulties in distinguishing covertly expressed aggression and misclassified it in almost half of the cases. It seems only logical that it should be the most challenging class to predict because in many cases it may be difficult even for humans to correctly recognize subtle aggression, especially on the Internet where there are few non-verbal indicators.

Confusion matrices for the second subtask for all languages can be seen in Figure 4. Our results for the English dataset, where we had almost a half of gendered texts misclassified, were worse than for Bengali. However, given the skewed class distribution for English, this class turned out to be challenging for all of the 15 participants and our model outperformed other solutions. In Bengali all systems including ours had higher results than for all other languages. It may be attributed to the dataset peculiarities or for some features of the Bengali language which make it easy to recognize gendered texts (e.g. for English with its lack of genders and cases in nouns, it might be a more challenging problem given the results of the competition). The lower performance of our model for Hindi might show that our system might have overfitted to the class distributions from the train set.

6. Conclusion

This paper describes our results for TRAC 2020 competition held together with the conference LREC 2020. Competition consisted of 2 subtasks where participants had to classify aggression in texts and decide if it is gendered or not for 3 languages: Bengali, English and Hindi. We used a single BERT-based system with two outputs for all tasks simultaneously. Our model took the first place in English gendered text classification and the second place in Bengali gendered text classification. Thus, cross-lingual multitask

BERT finetuning can be considered a promising approach even for non-IndoEuropean languages. In future work we will check the balance for early stopping between two targets and weighting schemes for simultaneous subtask training which might improve the results of our model.

7. References

Arivazhagan, N., Bapna, A., Firat, O., Lepikhin, D., Johnson, M., Krikun, M., Chen, M. X., Cao, Y., Foster, G., Cherry, C., Macherey, W., Chen, Z., and Wu, Y. (2019). Massively Multilingual Neural Machine Translation in the Wild: Findings and Challenges. *arxiv.org*.

Aroyehun, S. T. and Gelbukh, A. (2018). Aggression Detection in Social Media: Using Deep Neural Networks, Data Augmentation, and Pseudo Labeling. *Proc. First Work. Trolling, Aggress. Cyberbullying*, pages 90–97.

Conneau, A., Khandelwal, K., Goyal, N., Chaudhary, V., Wenzek, G., Guzmán, F., Grave, E., Ott, M., Zettlemoyer, L., and Stoyanov, V.). Unsupervised Crosslingual Representation Learning at Scale. Technical report.

Davidson, T., Warmsley, D., Macy, M., and Weber, I. (2017). Automated Hate Speech Detection and the Problem of Offensive Language. In *Proc. ICWSM*.

Devlin, J., Chang, M.-W., Lee, K., and Toutanova, K. (2018). BERT: Pre-training of Deep Bidirectional Transformers for Language Understanding. oct.

Fortuna, P. and Nunes, S. (2018). A Survey on Automatic Detection of Hate Speech in Text. *ACM Comput. Surv.*, 51(4):85.

Gordeev, D. (2016). Detecting state of aggression in sentences using cnn. In *Lect. Notes Comput. Sci. (including Subser. Lect. Notes Artif. Intell. Lect. Notes Bioinformatics)*, volume 9811 LNCS, pages 240–245.

Joulin, A., Grave, E., Bojanowski, P., and Mikolov, T. (2016). Bag of Tricks for Efficient Text Classification. jul.

Kumar, R., Ojha, A. K., Malmasi, S., and Zampieri, M. (2018). Benchmarking Aggression Identification in Social Media. In *Proc. First Work. Trolling, Aggress. Cyberbulling*, Santa Fe, USA.

Malmasi, S. and Zampieri, M. (2017). Detecting Hate Speech in Social Media. In *Proc. Int. Conf. Recent Adv. Nat. Lang. Process.*, pages 467–472.

Mikolov, T., Chen, K., Corrado, G., and Dean, J. (2013). Efficient estimation of word representations in vector space. In *Proc. Int. Conf. Learn. Represent. (ICLR 2013)*, pages 1–12, jan.

Ritesh Kumar, Atul Kr. Ojha, S. M. and Zampieri, M. (2020). Evaluating aggression identification in social media. In Ritesh Kumar, et al., editors, *Proceedings of the Second Workshop on Trolling, Aggression and Cyberbullying (TRAC-2020)*, Paris, France, may. European Language Resources Association (ELRA).

Vaswani, A., Shazeer, N., Parmar, N., Uszkoreit, J., Jones, L., Gomez, A. N., Kaiser, Ł., and Polosukhin, I. (2017). Attention is all you need. In *Adv. Neural Inf. Process. Syst.*, volume 2017-Decem, pages 5999–6009.

Wolf, T., Debut, L., Sanh, V., Chaumond, J., Delangue,

C., Moi, A., Cistac, P., Rault, T., Louf, R., Funtowicz, M., and Brew, J. (2019). HuggingFace's Transformers: State-of-the-art Natural Language Processing.
ArXiv, abs/1910.0.

Zampieri, M., Malmasi, S., Nakov, P., Rosenthal, S., Farra,
N., and Kumar, R. (2019). SemEval-2019 Task 6: Iden-
tifying and Categorizing Offensive Language in Social
Media (OffensEval). In *Proc. 13th Int. Work. Semant.
Eval.*

Proceedings of the Second Workshop on Trolling, Aggression and Cyberbullying, pages 99–105
Language Resources and Evaluation Conference (LREC 2020), Marseille, 11–16 May 2020
© European Language Resources Association (ELRA), licensed under CC-BY-NC

SAJA at TRAC 2020 Shared Task: Transfer Learning for Aggressive Identification with XGBoost

Saja Khaled Tawalbeh, Mahmoud Hammad, Mohammad AL-Smadi

Jordan University of Science and Technology
Irbid, Jordan
sajatawalbeh91@gmail.com, {m-hammad, masmadi}@just.edu.jo

Abstract

This paper describes the participation of the SAJA team to the TRAC 2020 shared task on aggressive identification in the English text. we have developed a system based on transfer learning technique depending on universal sentence encoder (USE) embedding that will be trained in our developed model using xgboost classifier to identify the aggressive text data from English content. A reference dataset has been provided from TRAC 2020 to evaluate the developed approach. The developed approach achieved in sub-task EN-A 60.75% F1 (weighted) which ranked fourteenth out of sixteen teams and achieved 85.66% F1 (weighted) in sub-task EN-B which ranked six out of fifteen teams.

Keywords: aggression identification, social media, NLP, USE, transfer learning, XGBoost

1. Introduction

In today's time, the advances in the web and the communication technologies is one of the main reasons to increase the impact of the nasty content on social media, blogs, and other websites. Detecting aggressive and insulting content is gained recent attention according to the negative effects on its users. For instance, demeaning comments, incidents of aggression, trolling, cyberbullies, hate speech, insulting, and toxic utterance have negative impact of users. Unfortunately, during the recent years, the percentage of using toxic utterance has been increased. Consequently, led to problems affecting real societies.

In 2018 the first shared task on aggression identification has been announced (Kumar et al., 2018). (Davidson et al., 2017) presented work for aggression classification by performing the logistic regression classifier depending on several hand-crafted features. (Djuric et al., 2015) focused on the embedding that has been learnt from an input text using paragraph2vec (Le and Mikolov, 2014) to train the logistic regression classifier. In 2013, (Kwok and Wang, 2013) developed a Naive Bayes classifier based on unigram features. (Bhattacharya et al., 2020) the second shared task on aggression identification will behold on Trolling, Aggression, and Cyberbullying (TRAC 2020) focusing on three languages as a Multilingual shared task. It aims to classify social media posts into one of three labels (Overtly aggressive 'OAG', Covertly aggressive 'CAG', Non-aggressive 'NAG'). Moreover, to classify social media posts as binary classifications into (gendered 'GEN' or non-gendered 'NGEN').

The major contribution of this paper is to describe our participation of the SAJA team to the TRAC 2020 shared task on aggressive identification and more precisely we participate in English language. We have developed a system based on transfer learning technique depending on universal sentence encoder (USE) embedding that will be trained in our developed model using XGBoost classifier to identify the aggressive text data from English content.

Several approaches have been performed to solve the provided task. We mentioned the best-reported results according to the evaluation step. A reference dataset has been provided from TRAC 2020 to evaluate the developed approach. The developed approach achieved in sub-task EN-A 60.75% F1 (weighted) and achieved 85.66% F1 (weighted) in sub-task EN-B.

We discuss the problem statement in section 2. Section 3 contains details about our methodology and the used dataset. In Section 4, we discuss the results and Section 5 concludes our work.

2. Related Work

Micro-blogging is considered as one of the most popular social network applications. In recent years, the rapid of using social media to express the users feeling and share their ideas. On the other hand, the uses of aggressive, hate speech, and offensive language obviously has been increased gradually.

Present comprehensive studies for hate speech detection by (Schmidt and Wiegand, 2017) and (Fortuna and Nunes, 2018), (Davidson et al., 2017) presenting the Hate Speech Detection dataset. Additionally, (Spertus, 1997) consider as the earliest efforts in hate speech detection, had been presented a decision tree-based classifier with 88.2% accuracy. Moreover, Offensive identification for sentences have been tried for several languages behind the English such that, Arabic (Mubarak et al., 2017) and (Al-Hassan and Al-Dossari, 2019), German (Ross et al., 2017), (Fišer et al., 2017), and (Su et al., 2017).

In particular, Zampieri et al. (2019a) OLID dataset presented last year for offensive language detection (Zampieri et al., 2019b). (Mohaouchane et al., 2019) presents several neural networks namely: (i) CNN, (ii) Bi-LSTM, (iii) Bi-LSTM with attention mechanism, (iv) Combined CNN and LSTM on Arabic language. Moreover, the dataset has been used is Arabic YouTube comments. The best performing model was CNN with 84.05% F1-score. In (Liu et al., 2019) Proposed a fine-tuned technique for the Bidirectional Encoder Representation from Transformer (BERT) to solve the shared task of identifying and categorizing offensive language in social media at SemEval 2019. Several features were used such as word unigrams and word2vec. (Pelicon et al., 2019) Adds LSTM neural network architecture to perform fine-tuned a BERT. Several automatically and manually crafted features were used namely: word embeddings, TFIDF, POS sequences, BOW, the length of the longest punctuation sequence, and the sentiment of the tweets. (Mahata et al., 2019) Proposed an ensemble technique consist of CNN, Bidirectional LSTM with attention, and Bidirectional LSTM + Bidirectional GRU to tackle the shared SemEval 2019 - Task 6 Identifying and Categorizing Offensive Language. The train data used to obtain a set of heuristics as features. (Han et al., 2019) Presented two approaches namely: bidirectional with GRU and probabilistic model modified sentence offensiveness calculation (MSOC) for the same Task Identifying and Categorizing Offensive Language. Word2vec embedding used as a feature. (Swamy et al., 2019) Introduced an ensemble approach consist of L1-regularised Logistic Regression, L2-regularised Logistic Regression, Linear SVC, and LSTM neural network. Several features were used, for instance, GloVe embedding, word/character n-grams by TF-IDF, POS tags, sentiment Score and count features for URLs, mentions, hashtags, punctuation marks.

In 2018 shared task TRAC 1 has been released, (Ramiandrisoa and Mothe, 2018) have been developed an approach to detect aggressive language for English language. Three approaches have been developed based on machine learning and deep learning models. Several features have been used (i.e Part-Of-Speech, emoticonssentiment frequency and logistic regression built with document vectorization using Doc2vec). (Samghabadi et al., 2018) discussing the lexical and semantic features for English and Hindi languages. (Roy et al., 2018) presented an ensemble solution depending on CNN and SVM for English and Hindi languages. Word embedding, n-grams, and Tf-Idf vectors have been discussed. (Nikhil et al., 2018) demonstrate LSTM approach with an attention unit according to the remarkable results for this approach in NLP tasks. It performs for English and Hindi language as well. Moreover, (Aroyehun and Gelbukh, 2018) presents an investigation between deep learning and traditional machine learning (i.e NB and SVM) to achieve the best efficient model. The remarkable point in this paper to improve the overall performance, the augmented data and pseudo labeled method have been used during the training step.

3. Data and Methodology

Shared task on Aggression Identification focused on the English language which provided to identifying the aggressive language thought the social media content.

3.1. Task Description

The shared task TRAC 2020 (Ritesh Kumar and Zampieri, 2020; Bhattacharya et al., 2020), is a multilingual task, which provides two subtasks namely: A- aggression identification shared task, it represents a classification task to classify a given text into three classes between (1) Overtly Aggressive where it represents the human behavior meant to hurt a community through the verbal, physical and psychological attitude. (2) Covertly Aggressive where it represents the hidden aggressive attack consist of the negative ironic emotions and (3) Non-aggressive. Table 1 represents the aggressive type cases. B- misogynistic aggression identification shared task, it represents a binary classification that aims to classify a given text to gendered or non-gendered.

Type	Cases
Overtly Aggressive (OAG)	verbal attack directly pointed towards any group or individuals, abusive words or comparing in a derogatory manner, supporting false attack
Covertly Aggressive (CAG)	foucus on figurative words aims to attack(individual, nation, religion), Praising someone by criticizing group irrespective of being right or wrong.
Non Aggressive (NAG)	In this case, the absence of the intention to be aggressive.

Table 1: The classes of the Aggressive including their cases for sub-task EN-A

3.2. Dataset

This shared task represents a multilingual dataset Bhattacharya et al. (2020) which contains three languages namely: English, Bangla, and Hindi. In this paper, we participate in the English language for both subtasks A and B. The shared task provides three files train, validation, and test file which consists of 5000 annotated rows from social media that have been represented for both subtasks. Tables 2 and 3 provide more details about the distribution of the provided dataset.

Table 4 represents examples of the provided dataset for both subtasks.

3.3. Data Pre-processing

The pre-processing step on a text is crucial processes, especially social network datasets such that, Facebook and Twitter where posts and tweets are noisy and contain a lot of slang language. In order to have a clean version of the provided dataset to remove the unnecessary noise, for instance, special character, punctuation marks (*,@#-(—),

Dataset File	Total	Count of Labels sub-task EN-A
Train Set	4263	OAG= 435
		CAG= 453
		NAG= 3375
Validation Set	1066	OAG= 113
		CAG= 117
		NAG= 836
Test Set	1200	-

Table 2: Represents the distribution of the provided dataset for the English language for suntask A

Dataset File	Total	Count of Labels sub-task EN-B
Train Set	4263	NGEN= 3954
		GEN= 309
Validation Set	1066	NGEN= 993
		GEN= 73
Test Set	1200	-

Table 3: Represents the distribution of the provided dataset for the English language for sub-task EN-B

ID	Original Text	Label sub-task EN-A	Label sub-task EN-B
C68.872	Nice video..	NAG	NGEN
C10.689	She is a traitor of India	OAG	NGEN
C32.128	"Wrong message for youth. Fight, dont be a coward"	CAG	NGEN
C65.70	Hot	NAG	GEN

Table 4: Examples that represents the dataset for both sub-tasks

ID	Original Text	Processed Text	Label sub-task EN-A	Label sub-task EN-B
C68.872	Nice video..	nice video	NAG	NGEN
C10.689	She is a traitor of India	she is a traitor of india	OAG	NGEN
C32.128	"Wrong message for youth. Fight, dont be a coward"	wrong message for youth fight do not be a coward	CAG	NGEN
C65.70	Hot	hot	NAG	GEN

Table 5: Data pre-processing performed on the available dataset for both subtasks

URLs, and user mentions. Whereas, pre-processing step is required to improve the analysis process applied to the raw tweets. We have been done various pre-processing to achieve a clean version of the provided dataset, such that, each tweet was normalized. and then tokenized. The normalization is a necessary process since some words are written on shortcut format (i.e. dont returned to (do not)). Finally, numbers and non-English characters were also removed. The following are examples of pre-processing step have been shown in table 5 for the provided dataset.

3.4. Embeddings

Recently, word embeddings widely used in NLP applications and their research, where word embedding aims to obtain the vector representation of the input of textual data to input numeric for deep neural networks. Word embeddings tend to capture the semantic features for each word and the linguistic relationship among them, whereas these embeddings help to improve system performance in several NLP domains (e.g text mining). Since 2003 (Bengio et al., 2003) has been started to generate word embedding using neural probabilistic language model, then Word2Vec by (Mikolov et al., 2013), Glove (Pennington et al., 2014), AraVec (Soliman et al., 2017) and the recent model ElMo Embedding by (Peters et al., 2018), BERT contextual embedding (Devlin et al., 2018), and Universal Sentence Encoder USE (Cer et al., 2018). The distributional linguistic hypothesis it's the main intuition of word embedding idea, whereas each model has its own way to capture the semantic meaning or the idea of how they trained. Consequently, each model can capture different semantic attributes compared to other models. In this research, we depend on pretrained sentence USE embedding to trained the developed model. It is a language representation model and sentence embedding provided by Google which aims to extract the sentence embeddings from the provided dataset. Moreover, it will become one of the state of art model for most of NLP research.

3.5. Proposed Model-(XGB-USE)

The transformer and contextual embedding added much progress in the NLP research area. In addition, it outperforms the deep learning approaches according to the promising results achieved. The transformer considered an encoder-decoder architecture applied to attention mechanisms tasks. More particularly, Google has been released Universal Sentence Encoder (USE) Cer et al. (2018) which aims to map an input sentence to vector representations, this kind of representation aims to capture the meaning of the sentence. Moreover, Google has been released a pre-trained USE embedding using TensorFlow Hub Module [1] to extract the embedding directly and find the semantic similarities for the provided sentences.

The proposed model based on transfer learning architecture that has used in common especially in image classification and computer vision (Litjens et al., 2017). Moreover, as we mentioned earlier, the applied transformers show significant results compared to deep learning approaches. For instance, USE developers created several versions of the pre-trained models such as multilingual USE to represent the semantic relationships among text as well as it could be applied as an independent classifier in different NLP domains (i.g. aggressive identification). Moreover, the extracted embedding dimension for USE is 512. In this research, we used USE2 pre-trained model to extract the sentence embedding based on transfer learning architecture to tackle the shared task problem. The XGboost, distributed gradient boosting library (XGB) classifier (Chen and Guestrin, 2016) have been built to be highly efficient. The XGB has been used as a text transfer learning model powered by the USE embedding whereas XGB considered as a powerful classifier compared to other machine learning classifiers as well as compared to deep learning. It becomes a popular method to solve NLP tasks. The reason why XGB has been used as follows: a) XGB considered as a regularized boosting technique prepared to prevent overfitting, b) it has a structure to handle the missing values, c) it is fast compared to others gradient boosting.

As we mentioned above for the sake of this research, the XGB classifier approach has been developed based on transfer learning with Universal Sentence Encoder (XGB-USE). This developed approach performed to solve the aggressive identification for the English language. USE embedding has been extracted from the pre-trained model with 512 dimensions for each input sentence before they prepared to train step using XGB. Table 6 provides more details about the value of each parameter have been used during the training step, which represents the best parameters are used. The XGB-USE architecture shown as depicted in Figure 1.

For BERT-GRU training procedure, we fine-tuned the BERT by excluding the last 3 layers as well as adding the Gaussian Noise layer followed by GRU (Chung et al., 2014) layer consist of 300 neurons, and global average pooling aims to extract the discriminative features from the past layer aims to pass them to the next layer. L2 regularization and Dropout have been used to prevent overfitting. The last layer used to predict the output predictions with a dense layer of 1 neuron, sigmoid activation function, and TruncatedNormal kernal initializers. we trained TRAC 2020 dataset without any external resources, however, in the future we will try an external dataset for the

---

parameter	Value
Embedding dimension (USE)	512
# of Estimators	3000
Sub-sample	0.3
max_depth	5
gamma	0.2
objective	(multi:softmax/ for sub-task EN-A) (binary:logistic/ for sub-task EN-B)
booster	gbtree
num_class	3 for sub-task EN-A

Table 6: The XGB classifier parameters used by grid search in the training phase

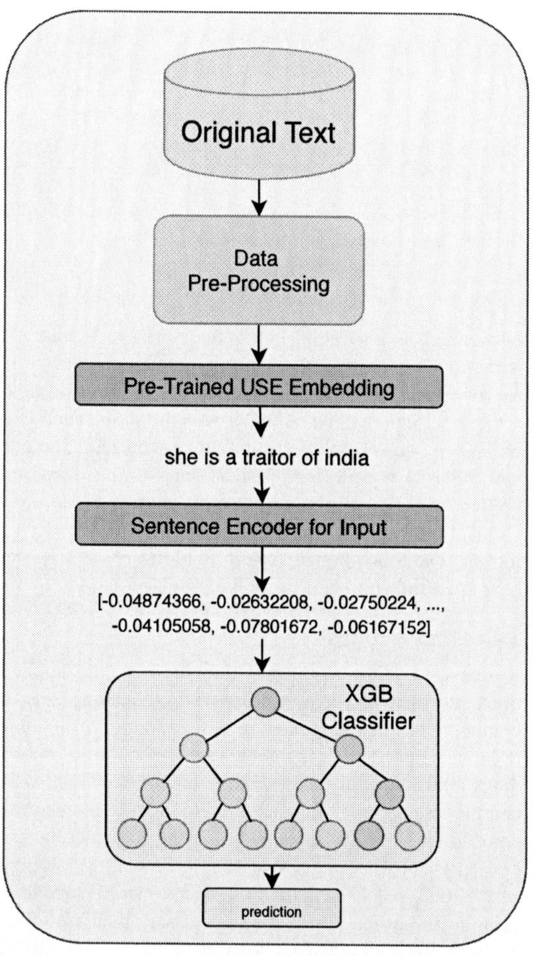

Figure 1: The architecture of our system (XGB-USE)

experimentation step. The the best parameter as follows: batch size= 16, optimizer= Adam, learning rate= 2e-5, and finally BERT max length= 40.

4. Results

4.1. Evaluation Measures

In order to evaluate the implemented approach, weighted F1 has been used according to the provided shared task. Moreover, the accuracy has been included to used for the comparison as well.

4.2. Discussion

Focusing on both sub-task EN-A and B for English language to tackle the problem of aggressive identification, table 7 presents the reported results for our proposed approaches for sub-task EN-A aggression identification shared task. The best results achieved with XGB-USE approach including the hyper-parameter that discussed above, where it achieves 0.6075 F1 (weighted) and 0.6833 accuracy. Moreover, the second approach has been used for the same sub-task achieves 0.5965 F1 (weighted) and 0.6758 accuracy where XGB-USE-PLL approach the same main approach including the pseudo label testing. The last approach using the fine-tuning BERT embedding with GRU where it achieves 0.5461 F1 (weighted) and 0.6392 accuracy. It's obvious that the XGB-USE had the best results according to F1 (weighted) and accuracy

System	F1 (weighted)	Accuracy
XGB-USE	**0.6075**	**0.6833**
XGB-USE-PLL	0.5965	0.6758
BERT-GRU	0.5461	0.6392

Table 7: Results for Sub-task EN-A (where PLL pseudo label testing, USE universal sentence encoder, and XGB XGBoot classifier)

For sub-task EN-B misogynistic aggression identification shared task, table 8 presents the reported results for our proposed approaches. The best results achieved with XGB-USE approach including the hyper-parameter that discussed above, where it achieves 0.8567 F1 (weighted) and 0.8758 accuracy. Moreover, the second approach has been used for the same sub-task achieves 0.8547 F1 (weighted) and 0.8825 accuracy where XGB-USE-PLL approach the same main approach including the pseudo label testing as a feature. The last approach using the fine-tuning BERT embedding with GRU where it achieves 0.8180 F1 (weighted) and 0.8433 accuracy. It's obvious that the XGB-USE had the best results according to F1 (weighted) and accuracy

System	F1 (weighted)	Accuracy
XGB-USE	**0.8567**	**0.8758**
XGB-USE-PLL	0.8547	0.8825
BERT-GRU	0.8180	0.8433

Table 8: Results for Sub-task EN-B (where PLL pseudo label testing, USE universal sentence encoder, and XGB XGBoot classifier)

4.3. Results and Findings

In order to show the reported results for focusing on sub-task A table 9 shows the reported results for the top teams.

The best results achieve with 0.8029 F1 (weighted) presented by (Julian) team compared to our team (SAJA) achieved 0.6075 F1 (weighted).

Team	F1 (weighted)
Julian	0.8029
sdhanshu	0.7592
Ms8qQxMbnjJMgYcw	0.7568
zhixuan	0.7393
SAJA	0.6075

Table 9: Results for Sub-task EN-A compared to other teams.

For sub-task EN-B, table 10 shows the reported results for the top teams as well. The best results achieve with 0.8715 F1 (weighted) presented by (Ms8qQxMbnjJMgYcw) team compared to our team (SAJA) achieved 0.8566 F1 (weighted). We can see all the results are close to each other. We are ranking number six in this sub-task.

Team	F1 (weighted)
Ms8qQxMbnjJMgYcw	0.8715
abaruah	0.8701
na14	0.8579
sdhanshu	0.8578
SAJA	0.8566

Table 10: Results for Sub-task EN-B compared to other teams.

The figure 2 shows the confusion matrix of our best model of sub-task EN-A all for the three classes, it's clear that the XGB-USE model is performing well at classifying the non-aggressive (NAG) inputs compared to other classes. However, figure3 represents the confusion matrix for sub-task EN-B obviously the XGB-USE model is performing better for detecting the non-gendered 'NGEN' class compared to gendered 'GEN' class.

5. Conclusion

In this paper, we presented our participation to TRAC 2020 shared task on aggression identification in the English language for both sub-task EN-A and EN-B. Combination of transformers have been developed to solve the provided problem, XGB-USE has been used as the main approach for this paper which extracts the USE embeddings to performs transfer learning using XGB classifier. We have been ranked fourteenth out of sixteen teams for sub-task EN-A. For sub-task EN-B, we have been ranked six out of fifteen teams which are encouraging results especially the difference between our results and the top ranked teams are very close.

This paper shows that the developed model produced great results compared to deep learning approaches and transfer learning with BERT transformers. We have used a reference dataset that provided for the TRAC 2020 shared task on aggression identification multilingual languages. The

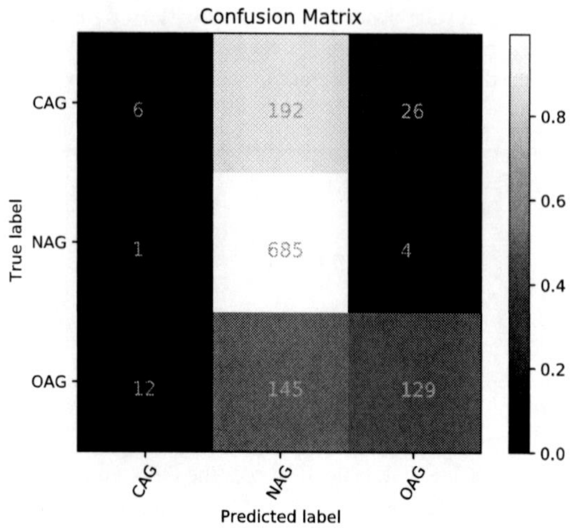

Figure 2: Sub-task EN-A, the confusion matrix for XGB-USE approach

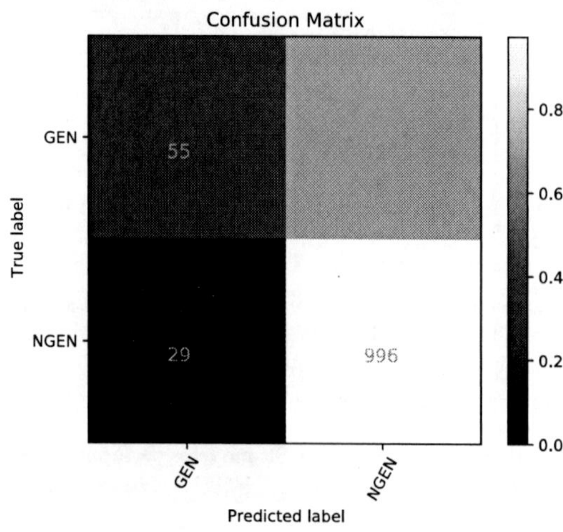

Figure 3: Sub-task EN-B, the confusion matrix for XGB-USE approach

best-reported results for sub-task EN-A achieved 0.6075 F1 (weighted) and 0.8567 F1 (weighted) for sub-task EN-B.

In the future, we will use several features and analyze them to get the best features for aggression detection. Moreover, we will study the impact of data augmentation types on the performance of various ML models.

Acknowledgements

This research is partially funded by Jordan University of Science and Technology.

6. Bibliographical References

Al-Hassan, A. and Al-Dossari, H. (2019). Detection of hate speech in social networks: a survey on multilingual corpus. In *6th International Conference on Computer Science and Information Technology*.

Aroyehun, S. T. and Gelbukh, A. (2018). Aggression detection in social media: Using deep neural networks, data augmentation, and pseudo labeling. In *Proceedings of the First Workshop on Trolling, Aggression and Cyberbullying (TRAC-2018)*, pages 90–97.

Bengio, Y., Ducharme, R., Vincent, P., and Jauvin, C. (2003). A neural probabilistic language model. *Journal of machine learning research*, 3(Feb):1137–1155.

Bhattacharya, S., Singh, S., Kumar, R., Bansal, A., Bhagat, A., Dawer, Y., Lahiri, B., and Ojha, A. K. (2020). Developing a multilingual annotated corpus of misogyny and aggression.

Cer, D., Yang, Y., Kong, S.-y., Hua, N., Limtiaco, N., John, R. S., Constant, N., Guajardo-Cespedes, M., Yuan, S., Tar, C., et al. (2018). Universal sentence encoder. *arXiv preprint arXiv:1803.11175*.

Chen, T. and Guestrin, C. (2016). Xgboost: A scalable tree boosting system. In *Proceedings of the 22nd acm sigkdd international conference on knowledge discovery and data mining*, pages 785–794.

Chung, J., Gulcehre, C., Cho, K., and Bengio, Y. (2014). Empirical evaluation of gated recurrent neural networks on sequence modeling. *arXiv preprint arXiv:1412.3555*.

Davidson, T., Warmsley, D., Macy, M., and Weber, I. (2017). Automated hate speech detection and the problem of offensive language. In *Eleventh international aaai conference on web and social media*.

Devlin, J., Chang, M.-W., Lee, K., and Toutanova, K. (2018). Bert: Pre-training of deep bidirectional transformers for language understanding. *arXiv preprint arXiv:1810.04805*.

Djuric, N., Zhou, J., Morris, R., Grbovic, M., Radosavljevic, V., and Bhamidipati, N. (2015). Hate speech detection with comment embeddings. In *Proceedings of the 24th international conference on world wide web*, pages 29–30.

Fišer, D., Erjavec, T., and Ljubešić, N. (2017). Legal framework, dataset and annotation schema for socially unacceptable online discourse practices in slovene. In *Proceedings of the first workshop on abusive language online*, pages 46–51.

Fortuna, P. and Nunes, S. (2018). A Survey on Automatic Detection of Hate Speech in Text. *ACM Computing Surveys (CSUR)*, 51(4):85.

Han, J., Wu, S., and Liu, X. (2019). jhan014 at SemEval-2019 task 6: Identifying and categorizing offensive language in social media. In *Proceedings of the 13th International Workshop on Semantic Evaluation*, pages 652–656, Minneapolis, Minnesota, USA, June. Association for Computational Linguistics.

Kumar, R., Ojha, A. K., Malmasi, S., and Zampieri, M. (2018). Benchmarking aggression identification in social media. In *Proceedings of the First Workshop on*

Trolling, Aggression and Cyberbullying (TRAC-2018), pages 1–11.

Kwok, I. and Wang, Y. (2013). Locate the hate: Detecting tweets against blacks. In *Twenty-seventh AAAI conference on artificial intelligence*.

Le, Q. and Mikolov, T. (2014). Distributed representations of sentences and documents. In *International conference on machine learning*, pages 1188–1196.

Litjens, G., Kooi, T., Bejnordi, B. E., Setio, A. A. A., Ciompi, F., Ghafoorian, M., Van Der Laak, J. A., Van Ginneken, B., and Sánchez, C. I. (2017). A survey on deep learning in medical image analysis. *Medical image analysis*, 42:60–88.

Liu, P., Li, W., and Zou, L. (2019). NULI at SemEval-2019 task 6: Transfer learning for offensive language detection using bidirectional transformers. In *Proceedings of the 13th International Workshop on Semantic Evaluation*, pages 87–91, Minneapolis, Minnesota, USA, June. Association for Computational Linguistics.

Mahata, D., Zhang, H., Uppal, K., Kumar, Y., Shah, R. R., Shahid, S., Mehnaz, L., and Anand, S. (2019). MIDAS at SemEval-2019 task 6: Identifying offensive posts and targeted offense from twitter. In *Proceedings of the 13th International Workshop on Semantic Evaluation*, pages 683–690, Minneapolis, Minnesota, USA, June. Association for Computational Linguistics.

Mikolov, T., Sutskever, I., Chen, K., Corrado, G. S., and Dean, J. (2013). Distributed representations of words and phrases and their compositionality. In *Advances in neural information processing systems*, pages 3111–3119.

Mohaouchane, H., Mourhir, A., and Nikolov, N. S. (2019). Detecting offensive language on arabic social media using deep learning. In *2019 Sixth International Conference on Social Networks Analysis, Management and Security (SNAMS)*, pages 466–471. IEEE.

Mubarak, H., Darwish, K., and Magdy, W. (2017). Abusive language detection on arabic social media. In *Proceedings of the First Workshop on Abusive Language Online*, pages 52–56.

Nikhil, N., Pahwa, R., Nirala, M. K., and Khilnani, R. (2018). Lstms with attention for aggression detection. In *Proceedings of the First Workshop on Trolling, Aggression and Cyberbullying (TRAC-2018)*, pages 52–57.

Pelicon, A., Martinc, M., and Kralj Novak, P. (2019). Embeddia at SemEval-2019 task 6: Detecting hate with neural network and transfer learning approaches. In *Proceedings of the 13th International Workshop on Semantic Evaluation*, pages 604–610, Minneapolis, Minnesota, USA, June. Association for Computational Linguistics.

Pennington, J., Socher, R., and Manning, C. (2014). Glove: Global vectors for word representation. In *Proceedings of the 2014 conference on empirical methods in natural language processing (EMNLP)*, pages 1532–1543.

Peters, M. E., Neumann, M., Iyyer, M., Gardner, M., Clark, C., Lee, K., and Zettlemoyer, L. (2018). Deep contextualized word representations. *arXiv preprint arXiv:1802.05365*.

Ramiandrisoa, F. and Mothe, J. (2018). Irit at trac 2018. In *Proceedings of the First Workshop on Trolling, Aggression and Cyberbullying (TRAC-2018)*, pages 19–27, Santa Fe, New Mexico, USA, August. Association for Computational Linguistics.

Ritesh Kumar, Atul Kr. Ojha, S. M. and Zampieri, M. (2020). Evaluating aggression identification in social media. In Ritesh Kumar, et al., editors, *Proceedings of the Second Workshop on Trolling, Aggression and Cyberbullying (TRAC-2020)*, Paris, France, may. European Language Resources Association (ELRA).

Ross, B., Rist, M., Carbonell, G., Cabrera, B., Kurowsky, N., and Wojatzki, M. (2017). Measuring the reliability of hate speech annotations: The case of the european refugee crisis. *arXiv preprint arXiv:1701.08118*.

Roy, A., Kapil, P., Basak, K., and Ekbal, A. (2018). An ensemble approach for aggression identification in english and hindi text. In *Proceedings of the First Workshop on Trolling, Aggression and Cyberbullying (TRAC-2018)*, pages 66–73.

Samghabadi, N. S., Mave, D., Kar, S., and Solorio, T. (2018). Ritual-uh at trac 2018 shared task: aggression identification. *arXiv preprint arXiv:1807.11712*.

Schmidt, A. and Wiegand, M. (2017). A Survey on Hate Speech Detection Using Natural Language Processing. In *Proceedings of the Fifth International Workshop on Natural Language Processing for Social Media. Association for Computational Linguistics*, pages 1–10, Valencia, Spain.

Soliman, A. B., Eissa, K., and El-Beltagy, S. R. (2017). Aravec: A set of arabic word embedding models for use in arabic nlp. *Procedia Computer Science*, 117:256–265.

Spertus, E. (1997). Smokey: Automatic recognition of hostile messages. In *Aaai/iaai*, pages 1058–1065.

Su, H.-P., Huang, Z.-J., Chang, H.-T., and Lin, C.-J. (2017). Rephrasing profanity in chinese text. In *Proceedings of the First Workshop on Abusive Language Online*, pages 18–24.

Swamy, S. D., Jamatia, A., Gambäck, B., and Das, A. (2019). NIT_Agartala_NLP_Team at SemEval-2019 task 6: An ensemble approach to identifying and categorizing offensive language in twitter social media corpora. In *Proceedings of the 13th International Workshop on Semantic Evaluation*, pages 696–703, Minneapolis, Minnesota, USA, June. Association for Computational Linguistics.

Zampieri, M., Malmasi, S., Nakov, P., Rosenthal, S., Farra, N., and Kumar, R. (2019a). Predicting the Type and Target of Offensive Posts in Social Media. In *Proceedings of NAACL*.

Zampieri, M., Malmasi, S., Nakov, P., Rosenthal, S., Farra, N., and Kumar, R. (2019b). SemEval-2019 Task 6: Identifying and Categorizing Offensive Language in Social Media (OffensEval). In *Proceedings of The 13th International Workshop on Semantic Evaluation (SemEval)*.

Proceedings of the Second Workshop on Trolling, Aggression and Cyberbullying, pages 106–112
Language Resources and Evaluation Conference (LREC 2020), Marseille, 11–16 May 2020
© European Language Resources Association (ELRA), licensed under CC-BY-NC

FlorUniTo@TRAC-2: Retrofitting Word Embeddings on an Abusive Lexicon for Aggressive Language Detection

Anna Koufakou, Valerio Basile, Viviana Patti
Florida Gulf Coast University, University of Turin, University of Turin
akoufakou@fgcu.edu, valerio.basile@unito.it, viviana.patti@unito.it

Abstract

This paper describes our participation to the TRAC-2 Shared Tasks on Aggression Identification. Our team, FlorUniTo, investigated the applicability of using an abusive lexicon to enhance word embeddings towards improving detection of aggressive language. The embeddings used in our paper are word-aligned pre-trained vectors for English, Hindi, and Bengali, to reflect the languages represented in the shared task datasets. The embeddings are retrofitted to a multilingual abusive lexicon, HurtLex. We experimented with an LSTM model using the original as well as the transformed embeddings and different language and setting variations. Overall, our systems placed toward the middle of the official rankings based on weighted F1 score. Furthermore, the results on the development and test sets show promise for this novel avenue of research.

Keywords: embeddings, retrofitting, abusive lexicon

1. Introduction

Abusive language is a broad term encompassing several linguistic patterns linked to phenomena such as offensive language, aggressive language or hate speech. Abusive language is a strong signal to detect problematic use of languages, e.g., in cases of cyberbullying, misogyny, racism, or trolling. *Aggressive language* is any form of natural language written or spoken with the intention of hurt. It is typically offensive, although a growing number of studies are recently modeling covert, or implicit, abuse (Caselli et al., 2020).

In the Natural Language Processing (NLP) field, the automatic detection of abusive language, and related phenomena such as aggressiveness and offensiveness, is traditionally approached in a supervised fashion, with or without the support of language resources such as lexicons and dictionaries. A large part of recent research in many NLP tasks has employed deep learning based on word or character embeddings, for example, see Gambäck and Sikdar (2017), Pavlopoulos et al. (2017), Mishra et al. (2018), and Zhang et al. (2018), among others. Abusive language detection is no exception, as highlighted by the characteristics of the participating systems to the most recent and popular evaluation campaigns for offensive language (Zampieri et al., 2019) and hate speech detection (Basile et al., 2019).

In this paper, we describe the systems we submitted for detecting aggression in the context of the TRAC-2 shared task (Kumar et al., 2020) This task was designed as a two-fold open challenge on detecting aggression in English, Hindi, and Bengali social media posts and then detecting misogynistic aggression in the same posts. Our systems utilize word embeddings that are retrofitted to an abusive language lexicon (Bassignana et al., 2018) and then used by an Long Short-Term memory (LSTM) network model to predict labels. We retrofitted the word embeddings so that words that are found in the same categories in the lexicon end up closer together in the vector space. The retrofitting technique has been applied before for semantic lexicons, however it has never been applied to hate or abusive lexicons or similar.

2. Related Work

Recent related work in this field has focused on various tasks in different languages, for example: abuse (Waseem et al., 2017), gender- or ethnic-based hate speech (Basile et al., 2019), misogyny (Fersini et al., 2018) and aggression (Kumar et al., 2018), among others. The methods in recent literature utilize deep learning based on a plethora of models (e.g. RNNs or CNNs or BERT, see for instance Mishra and Mishra (2019) on Hate Speech Identification) and have used character or word embeddings, subword units, etc. A recent survey is given by Mishra et al. (2019).

Language resources also provide substantial support to tasks like abusive language detection (Wiegand et al., 2018), misogyny identification (Pamungkas et al., 2018a; Pamungkas et al., 2018b) or hate speech detection (Davidson et al., 2017). **HurtLex**[1] (Bassignana et al., 2018) is a multilingual lexicon of offensive words, created by semi-automatically translating a handcrafted resource in Italian by linguist Tullio De Mauro (called *Parole per Ferire*, "words to hurt" (De Mauro, 2016)) into 53 languages. Lemmas in HurtLex are associated to 17 non-mutually exclusive categories, plus a binary macro-category indicating whether the lemma reflects a stereotype. The number of lemmas in any language of HurtLex is in the order of thousands, depending on the language, and they are divided into the four principal parts of speech: noun, adjective, verb, and adverb. The lexicon includes *conservative* entries with a higher level of confidence of being offensive, and *inclusive* entries. In this work, we employ HurtLex version 1.2, comprising 8,228 entries for English, 2,209 for Hindi, and 994 for Bengali. It should be noted that code-switching is a phenomenon in HurtLex, with many English lemmas present in the Hindi and Bengali lexicons.

Retrofitting. Although embeddings have been shown to be successful in the wider field of NLP and specifically in abusive language detection, they do not take into account semantic relationships among words, such as synonyms or antonyms. One well-cited technique that addresses this issue is the retrofitting technique proposed by Faruqui et al.

---

[1] https://github.com/valeriobasile/hurtlex

(2015). This technique uses belief propagation to transform the original embeddings based on relationships it finds in a lexicon so that words that are related end up closer together in the vector space. The original paper used semantic lexicons such as the Paraphrase database (Ganitkevitch et al., 2013, PPDB) to extract synonym relationships, while in this paper we utilize an abusive lexicon and leverage its categorization of the words. Earlier work of an author of this paper examined the use of retrofitting in the context of abusive language detection (Koufakou and Scott, 2019; Koufakou and Scott, 2020), but that work used semantic lexicons, rather than an abusive lexicon. Outside of this field, retrofitting has been successfully applied in other applications, for example the classification of cancer pathology reports by Alawad et al. (2018), utilizing medical resources for a lexicon.

More recently, other methods have been presented that are related to retrofitting: for example, Mrkšić et al. (2017) proposed ATTRACT-REPEL, which utilizes the semantic lexicon to use antonym in addition to synonym relationships. Such methods, however, are based on opposition relations, which are unfit to be adapted to a resource like a hate lexicon. Therefore, we found that the retrofitting method is the most efficient and easy to implement for our purpose, being applicable to a hate lexicon with slight modifications.

3. Methodology and Data

The multilingual annotated data provided by the TRAC-2 workshop organizers are described in Bhattacharya et al. (2020). They included data in three different languages: English, Hindi, and Bengali. The shared task comprises two sub-tasks: sub-task A was Aggression Identification and sub-task B was Misogynistic Aggression Identification. For sub-task A, the data provided were labeled as "Overtly Aggressive" (OAG), "Covertly Aggressive" (CAG) and "Non-aggressive" (NAG). The data came as 5,000 annotated records from social media each in Bangla (in both Roman and Bangla script), Hindi (in both Roman and Devanagari script) and English for training and validation (development set). The data for sub-task B were the same records as for sub-task A with annotations for "Gendered" (GEN) or "Non-Gendered" (NGEN).

We used the TRAC-2 data for all experiments, and also augmented the train set with training data from TRAC-1 (Kumar et al., 2018), the first edition of the shared task, when applicable. For example, we used the English train data from TRAC-1 and English train data from TRAC-2 for sub-task A English. In contrast, we did not use any additional train data for the Bengali tasks (A or B), as it was not available in TRAC-1. Table 1 shows the distribution of the three labels for each of the sets we used for training (train) and validation (dev) related to sub-task A. As shown in the table, the 'Non Aggressive' (NAG) label is the vast majority for all sets, except in the case of the augmented Hindi train dataset (denoted in the table as HIN train++).

Table 2 shows the distribution of GEN versus NGEN labels for the data and sub-task B. As we see in Table 2, the data are very imbalanced with the 'Non Gendered' (NGEN) class as the vast majority label. For this sub-task, we only

Set	OAG	CAG	NAG	Total
EN train	435	453	3,375	4,263
EN train++	3,143	4,693	8,426	16,262
EN dev	113	117	836	1,066
HIN train	910	829	2,245	3,984
HIN train++	5,766	5,698	4,520	15,984
HIN dev	208	211	578	997
BEN train	850	898	2,078	3,826
BEN dev	217	218	522	957

Table 1: Label distribution for datasets used in Sub-task A: Aggression Identification. ++ denotes that the train set from TRAC-2 was augmented with the equivalent TRAC-1 train set.

Set	GEN	NGEN	Total
EN train	309	3,954	4,263
EN dev	73	993	1,066
HIN train	661	3,323	3,984
HIN dev	152	845	997
BEN train	712	3,114	3,826
BEN dev	191	766	957

Table 2: Label distribution for datasets used in Sub-task B: Misogyny Identification. Only TRAC-2 data was used.

used TRAC-2 data, as TRAC-1 did not have specific gender labels for their data.

For our experiments, we started with pre-processing and tokenizing the text. For pre-processing the text, we used the Ekphrasis tool (Baziotis et al., 2017) and regular expressions adapted from Raiyani et al. (2018), a paper from TRAC-1. We also normalized emojis[2] and applied basic tokenization. We applied pre-trained embedddings to the resulting vocabulary. The embeddings that worked the best for the data according to our experimentation were the models provided by FastText[3]. We specifically used the 25-dimensional[4] aligned version of the word embeddings in English, Hindi, and Bengali, in order to encode code-switched messages.

A few examples of the data provided by the shared task that show the code-switching and different labels are included below:

jitne wrong kah rhe hn wo sare bi sexual hn.because its prove that all homophofic are always homosexual (from the English train set, NAG, and GEN)

Bhai I just hope that jab aapki beti college ke pehle din entrance exam me rank laake admission le tab koi chutiya bewdaa class me jaake ye na bole ki wo meri property hai,sab durr rehna usse. (from the Hindi train set, OAG and NGEN)

---

[2] https://pypi.org/project/emoji
[3] https://fasttext.cc
[4] We started experimenting with larger embeddings, but, due to time constraints, we participated to the shared task with the 25-dimensional setting. We are currently carrying out further experiments with larger models.

We experimented with retrofitting these embeddings to the
HurtLex lexicon (Bassignana et al., 2018). In particular,
we considered the relationship between words that belong
to the same category in HurtLex, and applied retrofitting
based on such symmetric relation. We only considered
"conservative" entries in HurtLex, which are supposed to
contain less ambiguous terms and therefore less noise, although inducing a smaller coverage.

For each word in our vocabulary, we looked up the relative lemma in HurtLex and found the unique categories the
word belongs to. We then created a set of words, which is
the union of all words in these categories. This set of words
becomes the lexicon for retrofitting. Finally, for all the vectors corresponding to these words, we applied a retrofitting
process using code similar to the code found online provided by the original paper[5]. We kept all constants and
steps in the method the same as in the original code.

As the data came in three different languages, we experimented with different combinations of languages for the
embeddings: for example, we applied English-only pre-
trained embeddings to English data, as well as English and
Hindi pre-trained embeddings to English data. Also, as
Hurtlex contains lexicons for different languages, we were
able to experiment with English, Hindi, and Bengali combinations for the retrofitting as well. For example, we used
English and Hindi word aligned vectors, for all terms that
have a match in our vocabulary. We then retrofitted these
vectors using first Hurtlex English and then Hurtlex Hindi
as the lexicon.

We implemented our models with the Keras library for
Python. First we used an Embedding Layer with Trainable set to True, which fed into an LSTM with 8 nodes.
This was followed by a dropout of 0.5, and finally a dense
layer with softmax or sigmoid activation, corresponding to
the sub-task. As loss functions, we used categorical cross
entropy or binary entropy according to the sub-task, Adam
optimizer, 10 epochs, and batch size of 64 (if we used only
the TRAC-2 train set) or 256 (if we augmented the train set
with the equivalent TRAC-1 train set).

Among the submissions for Sub-task A in Bengali, we also
introduced a baseline system based on a Support Vector
Machine trained on unigrams and TF-IDF, for comparison,
since three runs were allowed for submission.

4. Results

We participated to both sub-tasks in all three languages
provided by the shared task. In all settings, our systems
ranked toward the middle of the official rankings based on
weighted F1 score.

4.1. Sub-task A: Aggression Identification

In sub-task A, our systems ranked 9th out of 16 in English,
and 5th out of 10 in Hindi and Bengali. Table 3 shows the

---

[5]https://github.com/mfaruqui

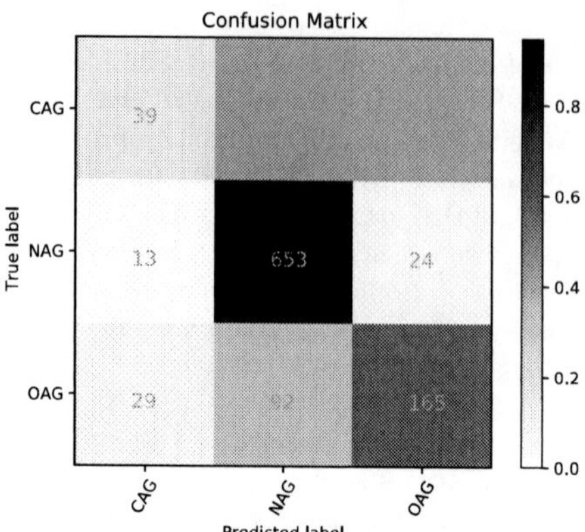

Figure 1: Confusion matrix for our best run in Sub-task
EN-A (EN+HIN embeddings, no retrofitting).

results of all the runs we submitted. We included accuracy
as well as macro-averaged F1 score in order to get a clearer
picture of the experimental results. We also provided the
weighted F1 for the best system as it was provided by the
organizers of the task (weighted F1 was the only metric provided for other systems).

In this task, we used several combinations of pre-trained
word embeddings from FastText, and retrofitted them on
HurtLex extracting the categories of words in one or more
language at a time. The combinations that worked better
during development, therefore subject to the final submission to the shared task, all involved English, even on the
Hindi and Bengali data, probably because the beneficial effect of the larger coverage of resources in such language.
For example, using only Bengali FastText word-aligned
vectors covered only 25 percent of the vocabulary in the
BEN-A sub-task data, but after adding the English FastText
word-aligned vectors the coverage of the vocabulary was
60 percent.

Moreover, for some runs, we concatenated the training set
of TRAC-1 to the training data, which proved beneficial in
the Hindi case according to weighted F1 and to English according to macro F1. We observed that the performance on
the development set was always improved by augmenting
the train set with the TRAC-1 data. Additionally, the effect
of retrofitting in this task is mixed, sometimes helping the
performance, while other times lowering it.

Another interesting observation comes from the confusion
matrices. For English sub-task A (see Figure 1), the matrix shows NAG ('Non Aggressive') as the large majority,
which is what we observed in the TRAC-2 train and development sets (see Table 1). In contrast, for Hindi sub-task
A, the confusion matrix (see Figure 2) shows that OAG
('Overtly Aggressive') is the larger class. Moreover, our
best models are slightly biased towards overt aggression in
English and Bengali (Figures 1 and 3), but biased towards
covert aggression in Hindi (Figure 2).

Language	System			F1	F1	Accuracy
	Embeddings	HurtLex	Augmented with	(weighted)	(macro)	
English	EN+HIN			**.677**	.564	**.714**
	EN+HIN	EN+HIN		.622	.512	.670
	EN+HIN	EN+HIN	TRAC-1	.676	**.585**	.676
	Best TRAC-2 system			.802	-	-
Hindi	EN+HIN			.725	**.650**	.714
	EN+HIN	EN+HIN		.705	.629	.695
	EN+HIN	EN+HIN	TRAC-1	**.726**	.649	**.720**
	Best TRAC-2 system			.813	-	-
Bengali	none (SVM)			.742	.671	.758
	EN+BEN			**.746**	**.672**	**.763**
	EN+BEN	EN+BEN		.730	.644	.750
	Best TRAC-2 system			.821	-	-

Table 3: Results for Sub-task A: Aggression Identification.

Language	System		F1	F1	Accuracy
	Embeddings	HurtLex	(weighted)	(macro)	
English	EN	EN	.830	.628	.847
	EN	EN (5 cat.)	.829	.620	.848
	EN+HIN	EN+HIN (5 cat.)	**.838**	**.649**	**.852**
	Best TRAC-2 system		.871		
Hindi	EN+HIN		.770	.768	**.774**
	EN+HIN	EN+HIN (5 cat.)	**.771**	**.769**	**.774**
	HIN	HIN (5 cat.)	.762	.760	.765
	Best TRAC-2 system		.878		
Bengali	EN+BEN		**.869**	.761	.872
	EN+BEN	EN+BEN (5 cat.)	.867	.748	**.877**
	BEN	BEN (5 cat.)	.860	.736	.870
	Best TRAC-2 system		.939		

Table 4: Results for Sub-task B: Misogynistic Aggression Identification.

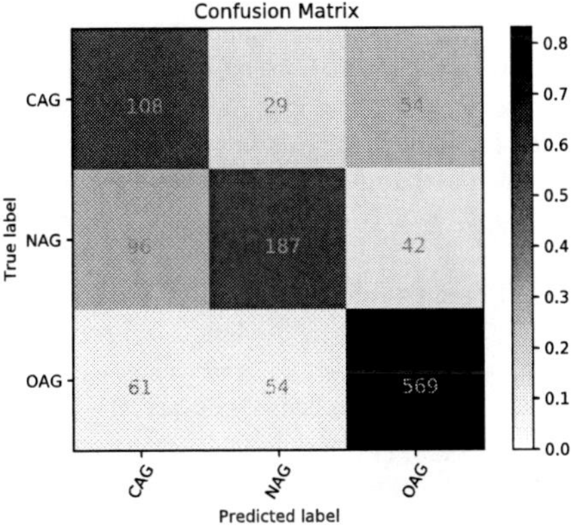

Figure 2: Confusion matrix for our best run in Sub-task HIN-A (EN+HIN embeddings, retrofitted on EN+HIN Hurtlex, additional data from TRAC-1).

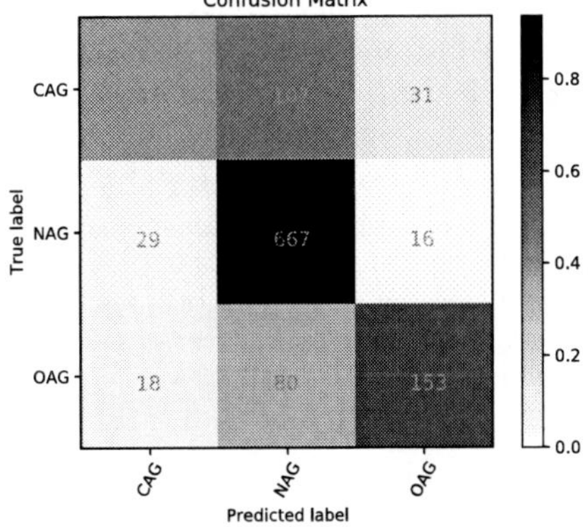

Figure 3: Confusion matrix for our best run in Sub-task BEN-A (EN+BEN embeddings, no retrofitting).

4.2. Sub-task B: Misogynistic Aggression Identification

Similarly to the previous section, Table 4 shows the results of all the systems we submitted for sub-task B. In sub-task B, our systems ranked 9th out of 15 for English, 6th out of 10 for Hindi, and 7th out of 8 for Bengali (all the rankings were based on weighted F1 score).

For this sub-task, as the focus is on gender, we explored using only categories in the HurtLex lexicon that relate to gender and misogyny. This is denoted in the Tables as "5 cat." which stands for "5 categories". This approach was

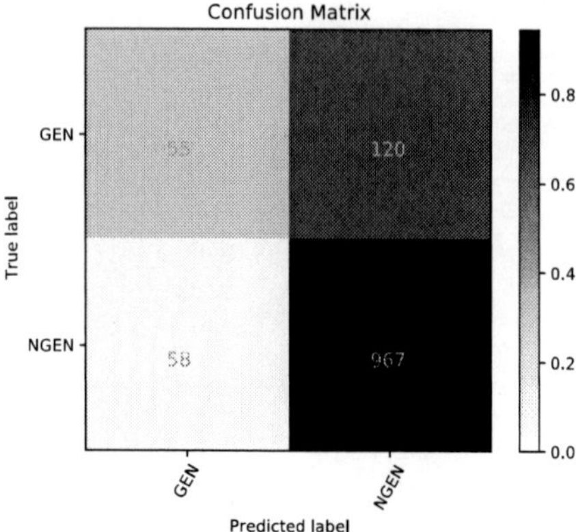

Figure 4: Confusion matrix for our best run in Sub-task EN-B (EN+HIN embeddings, retrofitted on 5 categories of EN+HIN HurtLex).

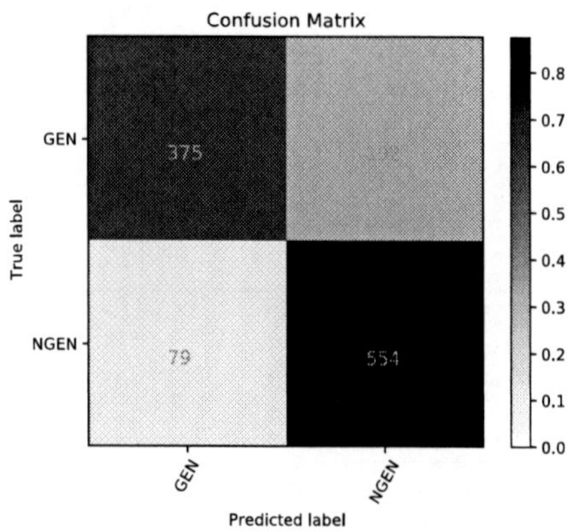

Figure 5: Confusion matrix for our best run in Sub-task HIN-B (EN+HIN embeddings, retrofitted on 5 categories of EN+HIN HurtLex).

inspired by Pamungkas et al. (2018b), who also explored the application of a selection of HurtLex categories to automatic misogyny identification.

Specifically, the categories we selected from HurtLex are the following, as in the aforementioned studies (Pamungkas et al., 2018a; Pamungkas et al., 2018b):

- ASF: female genitalia

- ASM: male genitalia

- DDF: physical disabilities and diversity

- DDP: cognitive disabilities and diversity

- PR: words related to prostitution

From the results, we observe that retrofitting using these categories in HurtLex leads to the best performance for English and Hindi when both English and Hindi parts of HurtLex are used as the lexicons for retrofitting, but not for Bengali (possibly due to the smaller coverage of the resource for this language).

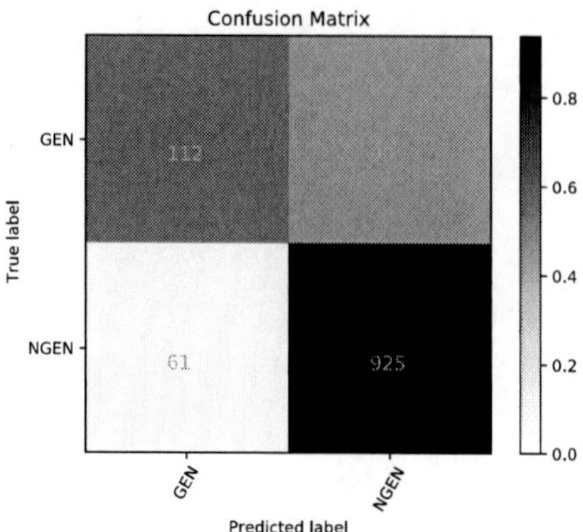

Figure 6: Confusion matrix for our best run in Sub-task BEN-B (EN+BEN embeddings, no retrofitting).

Looking more closely into the predictions of our best runs for this sub-task, the confusion matrices depicted in Figures 4–6 show a similar situation. In all three languages, our classifiers are quite conservative with respect to the *gendered* class, with roughly twice as many (depending on the language) GEN→NGEN misclassifications than NGEN→GEN.

5. Conclusion

In this report, we presented our systems submitted to the TRAC-2 shared task on aggression identification. We participated to both sub-tasks (aggression and gendered aggression) in the three languages proposed by the organizers. The main novelty of our proposed approach is the use of a multilingual abusive lexicon, and the implementation of a retrofitting technique on pre-trained embeddings based on such lexicon. Although our methods yielded mixed results in the general aggression identification task (Sub-task A) compared to the method without retrofitting, we show that our approach is indeed beneficial when focused on a more narrow scope, namely misogynistic aggression identification.

Despite differences in coverage, the resources used by our models are available for all the languages proposed in this shared task, as well as many more languages. We even found that the different languages actually inform each other, especially in presence of code-switched data.

Future work includes exploring the effect of altering the retrofitting method and its parameters for its application to abusive lexicons as well as experimenting with different data and models. Given the success of using the categorized lexicon HurtLex for some of the subtasks, we also plan to explore the direct coding of lexical-level features based on the lexicon, in a complementary approach to retrofitting.

Acknowledgements

The work of V. Basile and V. Patti is partially funded by Progetto di Ateneo/CSP 2016 (*Immigrants, Hate and Prejudice in Social Media*, S1618_L2_BOSC_01).

6. Bibliographical References

Alawad, M., Hasan, S. S., Christian, J. B., and Tourassi, G. (2018). Retrofitting word embeddings with the umls metathesaurus for clinical information extraction. In *2018 IEEE International Conference on Big Data (Big Data)*, pages 2838–2846. IEEE.

Basile, V., Bosco, C., Fersini, E., Nozza, D., Patti, V., Pardo, F. M. R., Rosso, P., and Sanguinetti, M. (2019). Semeval-2019 task 5: Multilingual detection of hate speech against immigrants and women in twitter. In *Proceedings of the 13th International Workshop on Semantic Evaluation*, pages 54–63.

Bassignana, E., Basile, V., and Patti, V. (2018). Hurtlex: A multilingual lexicon of words to hurt. In Elena Cabrio, et al., editors, *Proceedings of the Fifth Italian Conference on Computational Linguistics (CLiC-it 2018), Torino, Italy, December 10-12, 2018*.

Baziotis, C., Pelekis, N., and Doulkeridis, C. (2017). Datastories at semeval-2017 task 4: Deep lstm with attention for message-level and topic-based sentiment analysis. In *Proceedings of the 11th International Workshop on Semantic Evaluation (SemEval-2017)*, pages 747–754, Vancouver, Canada, August. Association for Computational Linguistics.

Bhattacharya, S., Singh, S., Kumar, R., Bansal, A., Bhagat, A., Dawer, Y., Lahiri, B., and Ojha, A. K. (2020). Developing a multilingual annotated corpus of misogyny and aggression.

Caselli, T., Basile, V., Mitrović, J., Kartoziya, I., and Granitzer, M. (2020). I Feel Offended, Don't Be Abusive! Implicit/Explicit Messages in Offensive and Abusive Language. In *Proceedings of LREC*.

Davidson, T., Warmsley, D., Macy, M., and Weber, I. (2017). Automated Hate Speech Detection and the Problem of Offensive Language. In *Proceedings of Eleventh International AAAI conference on Web and Social Media*.

De Mauro, T. (2016). Le parole per ferire. *Internazionale*. 27 settembre 2016.

Faruqui, M., Dodge, J., Jauhar, S. K., Dyer, C., Hovy, E., and Smith, N. A. (2015). Retrofitting word vectors to semantic lexicons. In *Proceedings of the 2015 Conference of the North American Chapter of the Association for Computational Linguistics: Human Language Technologies*, pages 1606–1615, Denver, Colorado, May–June. Association for Computational Linguistics.

Fersini, E., Nozza, D., and Rosso, P. (2018). Overview of the EVALITA 2018 Task on Automatic Misogyny Identification (AMI). In *Proceedings of Sixth Evaluation Campaign of Natural Language Processing and Speech Tools for Italian. Final Workshop (EVALITA 2018)*. CEUR-WS.org.

Gambäck, B. and Sikdar, U. K. (2017). Using Convolutional Neural Networks to Classify Hate-speech. In *Proceedings of the First Workshop on Abusive Language Online*, pages 85–90.

Ganitkevitch, J., Van Durme, B., and Callison-Burch, C. (2013). Ppdb: The paraphrase database. In *Proceedings of the 2013 Conference of the North American Chapter of the Association for Computational Linguistics: Human Language Technologies*, pages 758–764.

Koufakou, A. and Scott, J. (2019). Exploring the use of lexicons to aid deep learning towards the detection of abusive language. In *Proceedings of the 2019 Workshop on Widening NLP, collocated with ACL*, pages 129–131.

Koufakou, A. and Scott, J. (2020). Lexicon-enhancement of embedding-based approaches towards the detection of abusive language. In *Proceedings of the Second Workshop on Trolling, Aggression and Cyberbullying (TRAC-2020)*.

Kumar, R., Ojha, A. K., Malmasi, S., and Zampieri, M. (2018). Benchmarking Aggression Identification in Social Media. In *Proceedings of the First Workshop on Trolling, Aggression and Cyberbulling (TRAC-2018)*, Santa Fe, USA.

Kumar, R., Ojha, A. K., Malmasi, S., and Zampieri, M. (2020). Evaluating aggression identification in social media. In Ritesh Kumar, et al., editors, *Proceedings of the Second Workshop on Trolling, Aggression and Cyberbullying (TRAC-2020)*, France, May. European Language Resources Association (ELRA).

Mishra, S. and Mishra, S. (2019). 3idiots at hasoc 2019: Fine-tuning transformer neural networks for hate speech identification in indo-european languages. In *FIRE*.

Mishra, P., Yannakoudakis, H., and Shutova, E. (2018). Neural character-based composition models for abuse detection. In *Proceedings of the 2nd Workshop on Abusive Language Online (ALW2)*, pages 1–10.

Mishra, P., Yannakoudakis, H., and Shutova, E. (2019). Tackling online abuse: A survey of automated abuse detection methods. *arXiv preprint arXiv:1908.06024*.

Mrkšić, N., Vulić, I., Séaghdha, D. Ó., Leviant, I., Reichart, R., Gašić, M., Korhonen, A., and Young, S. (2017). Semantic specialization of distributional word vector spaces using monolingual and cross-lingual constraints. *Transactions of the association for Computational Linguistics*, 5:309–324.

Pamungkas, E. W., Cignarella, A. T., Basile, V., and Patti, V. (2018a). Automatic identification of misogyny in english and italian tweets at evalita 2018 with a multilingual hate lexicon. In *Sixth Evaluation Campaign of Natural Language Processing and Speech Tools for Italian (EVALITA 2018)*. CEUR-WS.org.

Pamungkas, E. W., Cignarella, A. T., Basile, V., and Patti, V. (2018b). *14-ExLab@UniTo* for AMI at ibereval2018: Exploiting lexical knowledge for detecting misogyny in english and spanish tweets. In *Proceedings of the Third Workshop on Evaluation of Human Language Technologies for Iberian Languages (IberEval 2018) co-located with 34th Conference of the Spanish Society for Natural Language Processing (SEPLN 2018), Sevilla, Spain, September 18th, 2018*, volume 2150 of *CEUR Workshop Proceedings*, pages 234–241. CEUR-WS.org.

Pavlopoulos, J., Malakasiotis, P., and Androutsopoulos, I. (2017). Deep learning for user comment moderation. In *Proceedings of the First Workshop on Abusive Language (ALW1)*, pages 25–35, Vancouver, BC, Canada, August. Association for Computational Linguistics.

Raiyani, K., Gonçalves, T., Quaresma, P., and Nogueira, V. B. (2018). Fully connected neural network with advance preprocessor to identify aggression over facebook and twitter. In *Proceedings of the First Workshop on Trolling, Aggression and Cyberbullying (TRAC-2018)*, pages 28–41.

Waseem, Z., Davidson, T., Warmsley, D., and Weber, I. (2017). Understanding Abuse: A Typology of Abusive Language Detection Subtasks. In *Proceedings of the First Workshop on Abusive Langauge Online (ALW1)*.

Wiegand, M., Ruppenhofer, J., Schmidt, A., and Greenberg, C. (2018). Inducing a lexicon of abusive words – a feature-based approach. In *Proceedings of the 2018 Conference of the North American Chapter of the Association for Computational Linguistics: Human Language Technologies*, June.

Zampieri, M., Malmasi, S., Nakov, P., Rosenthal, S., Farra, N., and Kumar, R. (2019). SemEval-2019 Task 6: Identifying and Categorizing Offensive Language in Social Media (OffensEval). In *Proceedings of the 13th International Workshop on Semantic Evaluation (SemEval)*.

Zhang, Z., Robinson, D., and Tepper, J. (2018). Detecting Hate Speech on Twitter Using a Convolution-GRU Based Deep Neural Network. In *Lecture Notes in Computer Science*. Springer Verlag.

Proceedings of the Second Workshop on Trolling, Aggression and Cyberbullying, pages 113–119
Language Resources and Evaluation Conference (LREC 2020), Marseille, 11–16 May 2020
© European Language Resources Association (ELRA), licensed under CC-BY-NC

AI_ML_NIT_Patna @ TRAC - 2: Deep Learning Approach for Multi-lingual Aggression Identification

Kirti Kumari and Jyoti Prakash Singh
National Institute of Technology Patna
Patna, Bihar, India
kirti.cse15@nitp.ac.in, jps@nitp.ac.in

Abstract

This paper describes the details of developed models and results of team AI_ML_NIT_Patna for the shared task of TRAC - 2. The main objective of the said task is to identify the level of aggression and whether the comment is gendered based or not. The aggression level of each comment can be marked as either Overtly aggressive or Covertly aggressive or Non-aggressive. We have proposed two deep learning systems: Convolutional Neural Network and Long Short Term Memory with two different input text representations, FastText and One-hot embeddings. We have found that the LSTM model with FastText embedding is performing better than other models for Hindi and Bangla datasets but for the English dataset, the CNN model with FastText embedding has performed better. We have also found that the performances of One-hot embedding and pre-trained FastText embedding are comparable. Our system got 11th and 10th positions for English Sub-task A and Sub-task B, respectively, 8th and 7th positions, respectively for Hindi Sub-task A and Sub-task B and 7th and 6th positions for Bangla Sub-task A and Sub-task B, respectively among the total submitted systems.

Keywords: Cyber-aggression, Misogyny, ComMA Project, LSTM, CNN

1. Introduction

The emergence of Internet, social networks and microblogging sites have changed our lifestyles the way we communicate, share, mingle, interact, advertise and do businesses. In India, five most popular social media platforms are Facebook, WhatsApp, YouTube, Twitter and Instagram. YouTube is the most popular social media for video sharing in which we can share educational, entertaining and informational video without paying any cost. All these changes have made our society a virtual place where most of the interactions are taking place through the electronic media. But such changes do not have only positive but also some detrimental effects such as cyber-aggression (Kumari et al., 2019a), cyberbullying (Kumari et al., 2019b; Kumari and Singh, 2020), hate speech (Schmidt and Wiegand, 2017; Fortuna and Nunes, 2018), misogynistic aggression, cyberstalking and cyber-crime. A large number of negative incidents are regularly occurring on social media creating a need for continuous monitoring of social media posts to overcome such harmful effects. The identification of cyber-aggression and misogynistic aggression can help to manage such problems. Among the most challenging issues in the identification of cyber-aggression and misogynistic aggression are multi-linguality, multi-modality and different posting styles of social media platforms. In the last few years, the research community has mainly been engaged in addressing these issues by considering these (multi-linguality, multi-modality and different posting styles of social media platforms) challenges and have provided some sociotechnical solutions. Among these efforts are the works of the popular shared tasks of TRAC - 1[1] and HASOC - 2019[2] that considered the challenges of identification of cyber-aggression and hate speech on multi-lingual and multiple platforms' comments. In both of the shared tasks, the organizers were mainly focussed on English and Hindi code-mixed comments of Facebook and Twitter and at the same time HASOC - 2019 shared task also considered the English-German code-mixed comments. Similarly, in the current shared task TRAC - 2[3] which comes under Communal and Misogynistic Aggression in Hindi-English-Bangla (ComMA) Project have considered the challenge of multi-linguality for three Indian languages, Hindi-English-Bangla code-mixed comments of YouTube (Ritesh Kumar and Zampieri, 2020). In this shared task, there are two sub-tasks: (a) Sub-task A- Level of Aggression Identification (overtly aggressive, covertly aggressive or non-aggressive) and (b) Sub-task B- Misogyny Aggression Identification (gendered or non-gendered), for each three code-mixed (English, Hindi and Bangla) languages.

In this contribution, we analyze multi-lingual YouTube comments of three popular Indian languages (Hindi-English-Bangla) provided by TRAC - 2 organizers. We have worked for each dataset and each subtask. For this, we have implemented two popular deep learning models: Convolutional Neural Network (CNN) and Long Short Term Memory (LSTM), and two embedding techniques: One-hot and pre-trained FastText embeddings as input representation for these deep learning models. We have found that single-layer CNN and single-layer LSTM networks have performed better than multi-layered CNN and multi-layered LSTM networks and the LSTM model is performing better than the CNN model for Hindi and Bangla datasets but for English dataset, CNN model is performing better than LSTM model. We have also found that as an input representation, pre-trained FastText embedding is better than other pre-trained embedding methods and the perfor-

---

[1] First Workshop on Trolling, Aggression and Cyberbullying (TRAC - 1) at COLING - 2018

[2] Hate Speech and Offensive Content Identification in Indo-European Languages at FIRE - 2019

[3] Second Workshop on Trolling, Aggression and Cyberbullying (TRAC - 2) at LREC - 2020

mance of One-hot embedding is similar to the performance of pre-trained FastText embedding.

The rest of the paper is framed as follows. The related works are briefly presented in Section 2. Our proposed framework for Cyber-aggression and Misogyny aggression detection is presented in Section 3. The finding of the proposed systems and analysis of the results are presented in Section 4. Finally, we conclude the paper in Section 5 by pointing out the future direction.

2. Related Work

Identification of aggression in social media is closely related to cyberbullying, hate speech, offensive and abusive language identification. In this section, we have briefly discussed some recently published relevant papers on aggression, cyberbullying, hate speech, offensive, and abusive language identification.

Burnap and Williams (2015) used ensemble techniques to detect racism type hate speech on Twitter and achieved a weighted F1-Score of 0.77 by voted ensemble of Random Forest, Support Vector Machine (SVM) and Logistic Regression classifiers. Malmasi and Zampieri (2017) analyzed methods for detecting hate speech of English tweets by differentiating hate speech from general profanity. They used character n-grams, word n-grams and word skip-grams features and got an accuracy of 0.78. Davidson et al. (2017) created a dataset for abusive language identification and categorizes the tweets among hate, offensive or neither (neither hate nor offensive). They have reported that the racist and the homophobic tweets generally come under hate class and the sexist tweets generally come under offensive class. They used Logistic Regression, Naive Bayes, Decision Trees, Random Forests and SVM to classify the tweets in three classes and concluded that the comment which does not have any abusive word is very difficult to detect. Malmasi and Zampieri (2018) discussed the challenges appearing in the process of identification of hate speech in social media and distinguished hate speech from profanity. Their claimed accuracy was 0.80 by using ensemble methods. Zampieri et al. (2019a) created a dataset of 14,000 English tweets for three different tasks and named the dataset as Offensive Language Identification Dataset (OLID). They also described the similarities and dissimilarities between OLID and earlier datasets for aggression detection, hate speech detection and similar tasks. These three different tasks were - Task 1: Offensive language detection (the tweet is either offensive or not-offensive), Task 2: Type of offense (Targeted insult or Un-targeted insult) and Task 3: Target of insult or threat (either individual or group or other). Zampieri et al. (2019b) analyzed all the submitted systems of the OffensEval 2019 tasks on the OLID dataset and highlighted the issues in separating the comments having profanity from those threatening comments which do not carry profane language.

Some recent works (Chatzakou et al., 2017; Chen et al., 2018; Raiyani et al., 2018; Modha et al., 2018; Samghabadi et al., 2018; Risch and Krestel, 2018) tried to solve Cyber-aggression issues. The works by Chatzakou et al. (2017) and Chen et al. (2018) are focussed on a particular platform (Twitter) and standard English text for aggression detection, which is not equally applicable to multi-lingual cases and for other social media platforms. Chatzakou et al. (2017) found improved accuracy after combining user and network-based features with text-based features. They got overall precision and recall of 0.72 and 0.73, respectively. Chen et al. (2018) used Convolutional Neural Network (CNN) and sentiment analysis method and reported an accuracy of 0.92. Some researchers of TRAC - 1 shared task (Raiyani et al., 2018; Risch and Krestel, 2018; Modha et al., 2018; Samghabadi et al., 2018) worked on the aforesaid challenges and achieved limited success due to the provided data being very noisy, unbalance and multi-lingual. Some participants (Risch and Krestel, 2018; Modha et al., 2018; Samghabadi et al., 2018) tried ensemble learning methods with various machine learning classifiers and many deep learning models and achieved better performance. The other group of researchers (Risch and Krestel, 2018; Aroyehun and Gelbukh, 2018) applied data augmentation with the help of machine translation using different languages (French, German, Spanish and Hindi) by preserving the meaning of comments with different wording and found better training result for such enlarged dataset. Raiyani et al. (2018) used three layers of dense system architecture with One-hot encoding. They found that simple three-layers of the fully connected neural network model with One-hot encoding performed better than complex deep learning models, but their system suffered from false-positive cases and they omitted the words not found in the vocabulary. Kumari and Singh (2019) proposed a four-layered CNN model with three different embedding techniques: One-hot, GloVe and FastText embeddings to detect different classes of abusive language for multi-lingual text comments of Facebook and Twitter on HASOC - 2019 shared task. They found that FastText and One-hot embeddings performed better than other pre-trained models. The work Kumari and Singh (2019) motivated us to adopt a similar approach for TRAC - 2 shared tasks because here also the tasks are multi-lingual and the data provided are noisy. In this paper, we have addressed the multi-lingual issue of social media post considering YouTube comments in Indian scenario by applying two deep learning models with different types of word embeddings.

3. Methodology and Data

This section presents the descriptions of used datasets and proposed methods. First, we discuss the three different datasets in Section 3.1 and then we explain the details of the proposed approach in Section 3.2.

3.1. Dataset Description

We have used the datasets of the shared task of TRAC - 2[4]. The provided datasets are of English, Hindi and Bangla. The shared task contains two subtasks: Sub-task A (Aggression Identification) and Sub-task B (Misogyny Aggression Identification). Sub-task A is a three-class problem, where the comments are classified into Overtly Aggressive (OAG), Covertly Aggressive (CAG) and Non-Aggressive (NAG) classes. The comment having direct aggression is

---

[4]https://sites.google.com/view/trac2/home

labelled as OAG comment, the comment having indirect aggression is labelled as CAG comment and the comment that does not have any type of aggression is labelled as NAG comment. Sub-task B is misogyny aggression identification, which is a binary classification task and is labelled as Gendered (GEN) and Non-gendered (NGEN). The comment in which attack is because of someone being a woman, or a man or a transgender is labelled as GEN otherwise the comment is labelled as NGEN. For the training of the proposed models for English and the Hindi Sub-task A, we have also used TRAC - 1 (Kumar et al., 2018) datasets. The organizers of TRAC - 2 shared tasks have provided three sets (Training, Validation and Test sets) of datasets for each language. The class-wise description of all the three datasets of TRAC - 2 is given in Table 1 where S refers the number of samples in each class. The class information has been given only for Training and Validation (or Dev) sets but this information has not been given for Test sets at the time of competition. The more detailed explanation of data collection and labelling is discussed in Bhattacharya et al. (2020). The comments are code-mixed Hindi-English and Bangla-English. These comments are having lots of Emojis. We have not done any pre-processing of data.

3.2. Proposed Method

In this subsection, we describe our best three runs for both the subtasks (Sub-task A and Sub-task B) of each (English, Hindi and Bangla) dataset in detail. First, we have implemented Convolutional Neural Network (CNN) with pre-trained FastText (Joulin et al., 2016) embedding as input representation for the CNN model and have named the system as Run1_CNN_FastText. Then, we have tried One-hot embedding as input representation for the CNN model and have named the system as Run2_CNN_One-hot. But we have found that pre-trained FastText embedding is performing better than One-hot embedding in the validation phase. Therefore, next, we have tried Long Short Term Memory (LSTM) with pre-trained FastText (Joulin et al., 2016) embedding and have named the system as Run3_LSTM_FastText. In the following paragraphs, we discuss the systems in detail.

3.2.1. Input Representation

The deep learning model takes input as the embedding layer, which encodes each token in the dataset used by the model. We have experimented with three popular embedding techniques: pre-trained GloVe, FastText and One-hot embeddings. In One-hot embedding, we assigned each distinct word/token of the dataset with a unique index value (integer value). Then each comment is represented by a one-dimensional vector of the vocabulary size of the dataset. We have used embedding dimension 300 for both pre-trained GloVe and FastText embeddings and the embedding dimension of the size of vocabulary for One-hot embedding. Since all the comments are not of equal length so we have used padding to make them equal. We have padded each comment to the average length of the comments. We have used post padding to make comment length 26, 35 and 30 for English, Hindi and Bangla datasets, re-

Table 1: Class-wise description of all the three datasets of TRAC - 2

Dataset	Set	Sub-task	Class	S
English	Training	A	OAG	435
			CAG	453
			NAG	3375
		B	GEN	309
			NGEN	3954
		Both A and B	Total	4263
	Dev	A	OAG	113
			CAG	117
			NAG	836
		B	GEN	73
			NGEN	993
		Both A and B	Total	1066
	Test	A	OAG	286
			CAG	224
			NAG	690
		B	GEN	175
			NGEN	1025
		Both A and B	Total	1200
Hindi	Training	A	OAG	910
			CAG	829
			NAG	2245
		B	GEN	661
			NGEN	3323
		Both A and B	Total	3984
	Dev	A	OAG	208
			CAG	211
			NAG	578
		B	GEN	152
			NGEN	845
		Both A and B	Total	997
	Test	A	OAG	684
			CAG	191
			NAG	325
		B	GEN	567
			NGEN	633
		Both A and B	Total	1200
Bangla	Training	A	OAG	850
			CAG	898
			NAG	2078
		B	GEN	712
			NGEN	3114
		Both A and B	Total	3826
	Dev	A	OAG	217
			CAG	218
			NAG	522
		B	GEN	191
			NGEN	766
		Both A and B	Total	957
	Test	A	OAG	251
			CAG	225
			NAG	712
		B	GEN	202
			NGEN	986
		Both A and B	Total	1188

spectively. The comment having larger length is truncated up to average length and the comment having smaller than average length is appended zeros to make the length equal to average length. While experimenting, we have found that pre-trained FasText embedding is performing better than pre-trained GloVe embedding and we have also found that the performance of One-hot embedding is comparable to the performance of pre-trained FastText embedding. So, we are reporting the best three runs for the TRAC - 2 shared task obtained by pre-trained FastText and One-hot embeddings.

3.2.2. Deep Learning Models

We have done experiments with two popular deep learning models: Convolutional Neural Network (CNN) and Long Short Term Memory (LSTM). In the CNN model, we have implemented one convolutional layer with 128 filters having a filter size of 3 and Rectified Linear Unit (ReLU) as an activation function. Then we have used one max-pooling layer of size 5 followed by flatten layer. After that, we have applied two dense layers of size 256 and 2 or 3 depending upon subtask (the size of last dense layer is 3 for Sub-task A and 2 for Sub-task B) with activation function as ReLU in the first dense layer. We have used dropout of 0.5 in between two dense layers and in between max-pooling and flatten layer.

For the LSTM model, we have implemented one layer of LSTM with 192 LSTM units with both dropout and recurrent_dropout value of 0.2 followed by one dense layer of size 3 or 2 depending upon subtask as is done for CNN model. We have applied the Categorical_crossentropy and Binary_crossentropy as loss function for Sub-task A and Sub-task B, respectively, and Adam is used as optimizer function for both CNN and LSTM models. In both CNN and LSTM models, we have applied Softmax (for Sub-task A) or Sigmoid (for Sub-task B) for the last dense layer depending on the type of problem. We have trained every system for 100 epochs with a batch size of 100.

We have trained our systems with training sets and validated with validation (Dev set) sets of the datasets provided by TRAC - 2 but for Sub-task A of English and Hindi dataset, we have trained our systems with both TRAC - 1 and TRAC - 2 datasets. We have repeated the experiments with varying number of layers of CNN and LSTM networks but did not get any improvement in performance. So, we have decided to use a single-layer CNN and single-layer LSTM networks.

4. Results

This section presents the results and analysis of validation and test sets of all the three datasets provided by TRAC - 2 organizers in terms of weighted F1-Score (as a primary performance metric) and accuracy. In this section, F1-Score refers to weighted F1-Score in all the tables. The validation results for subtasks of each dataset are shown in Table 2. The best three runs for each test set on each dataset are shown in Tables 3 and 4 for Sub-task A and for Sub-task B, respectively, where Acc stands for Accuracy. Each table shows the results obtained by the best three systems for each dataset either Sub-task A or Sub-task B.

Table 2: Validation results of the best three systems for Dev sets

Dataset	Sub-task	System	F1-Score
English	A	CNN_FastText	0.74
		CNN_One-hot	0.76
		LSTM_FastText	0.73
	B	CNN_FastText	0.92
		CNN_One-hot	0.91
		LSTM_FastText	0.92
Hindi	A	CNN_FastText	0.63
		CNN_One-hot	0.63
		LSTM_FastText	0.63
	B	CNN_FastText	0.82
		CNN_One-hot	0.80
		LSTM_FastText	**0.84**
Bangla	A	CNN_FastText	0.64
		CNN_One-hot	0.63
		LSTM_FastText	**0.66**
	B	CNN_FastText	0.79
		CNN_One-hot	0.80
		LSTM_FastText	**0.85**

Table 3: Results of the best three systems for test sets of Sub-task A

Dataset	System	F1-Score	Acc
English	**Run1_CNN_FastText**	**0.6602**	**0.6667**
	Run2_CNN_One-hot	0.5997	0.6392
	Run3_LSTM_FastText	0.5952	0.6092
Hindi	Run1_CNN_FastText	0.5964	0.5775
	Run2_CNN_One-hot	0.6370	0.6125
	Run3_LSTM_FasText	**0.6547**	**0.6367**
Bangla	Run1_CNN_FastText	0.7037	0.7088
	Run2_CNN_One-hot	0.7002	0.6987
	Run3_LSTM_FastText	**0.7175**	**0.7306**

From the Table 3 and Table 4, it is observed that the CNN model with FastText embedding is performing better than the other two models for English dataset and the LSTM models with FastText embedding is performing better than the other two models for Hindi and Bangla datasets. Figures 1, 2, 3, 4, 5 and 6 show the confusion matrix of the best results obtained by us for the different datasets for both the subtasks.

We have found that the LSTM model is performing better than the CNN model for Hindi and Bangla datasets whereas the CNN model is performing better than the LSTM model for the English dataset. The reason behind this is that LSTM is preserving long-term dependency of comment when comments are usually longer as in the case of Hindi and Bangla dataset. Our other finding is that FastText embedding is performing better than the other embeddings especially when the data is noisy. This is because FastText embedding is capable of preserve semantics information in solving the issues related to Emoji and out of vocabulary words but One-hot embedding does not consider the semantics information.

Table 4: Results of the best three systems for test sets of Sub-task B

Dataset	System	F1-Score	Acc
English	**Run1_CNN_FastText**	**0.8227**	**0.8383**
	Run2_CNN_One-hot	0.8099	0.8158
	Run3_LSTM_FastText	0.8199	0.8450
Hindi	Run1_CNN_FastText	0.6957	0.6983
	Run2_CNN_One-hot	0.6645	0.6758
	Run3_LSTM_FastText	**0.7363**	**0.7425**
Bangla	Run1_CNN_FastText	0.7834	0.7702
	Run2_CNN_One-hot	0.8211	0.8140
	Run3_LSTM_FastText	**0.8793**	**0.8847**

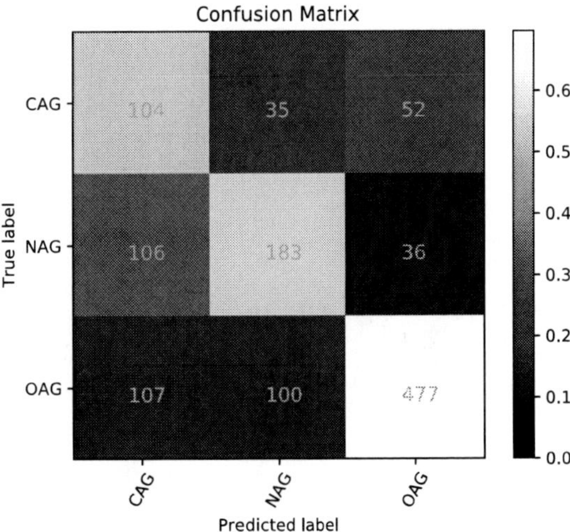

Figure 3: Confusion Matrix of the LSTM_FastText model for test set of Hindi Sub-task A

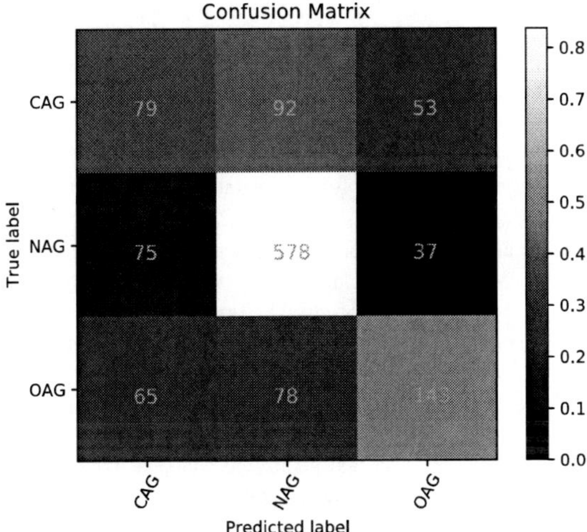

Figure 1: Confusion Matrix of the CNN_FastText model for test set of English Sub-task A

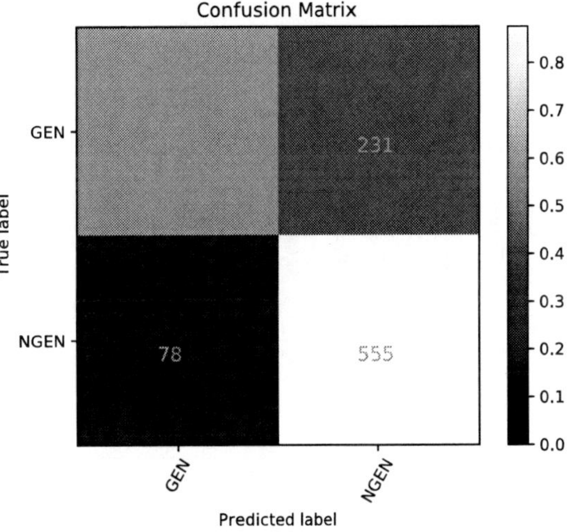

Figure 4: Confusion Matrix of the LSTM_FastText model for test set of Hindi Sub-task B

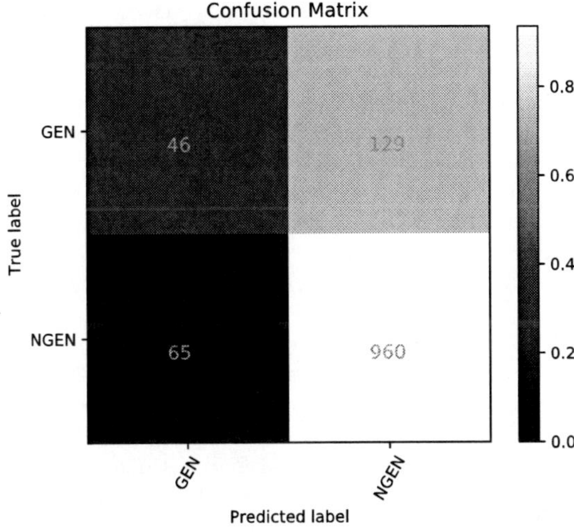

Figure 2: Confusion Matrix of the CNN_FastText model for test set of English Sub-task B

5. Conclusion

In this paper, we have established the challenges of the TRAC - 2 shared task. Then we have discussed the summary of similar works. Thereafter, we have described the proposed deep learning methods (to combat the issues) which consist of two popular deep learning models: Convolutional Neural Network (CNN) and Long Short Term Memory (LSTM), and two embedding techniques: One-hot and pre-trained FastText embeddings. We have used two different methods for input representation: One-hot and FastText embeddings for deep learning models, and our results show that FastText embedding is performing better than other embeddings in every case. To get better results,

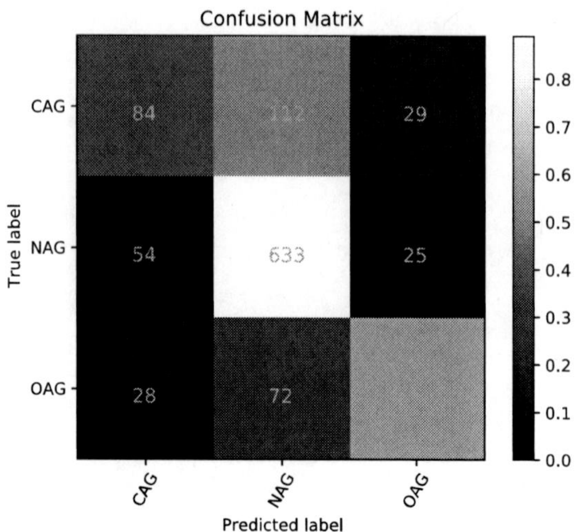

Figure 5: Confusion Matrix of the LSTM_FastText model for test set of Bangla Sub-task A

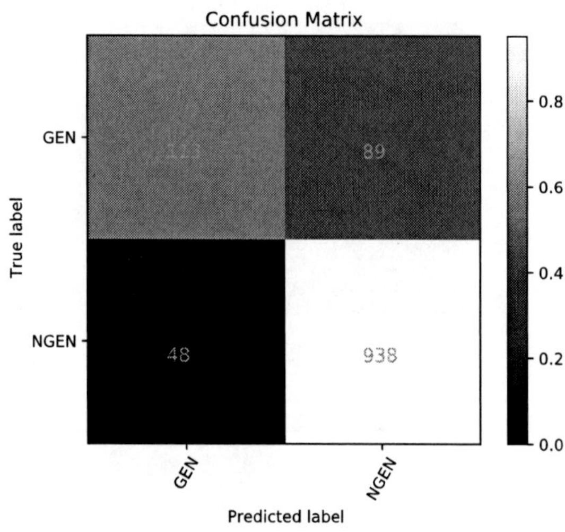

Figure 6: Confusion Matrix of the LSTM_FastText model for test set of Bangla Sub-task B

we have tried several systems and have concluded that a single layer of CNN or LSTM networks perform better for the classification of YouTube comments. We have found that the LSTM model is performing better than the CNN model except for the English dataset. We have achieved weighted F1-Score: 66% and 82% for English Sub-task A and Sub-task B, respectively, 65% and 74%, respectively for Hindi Sub-task A and Sub-task B, and 72% for Bangla Sub-task A and 88% for Sub-task B.

The future system may integrate active learning and unsupervised learning to overcome the burden of labelling efforts.

Acknowledgements

The first author would like to acknowledge the Ministry of Electronics and Information Technology (MeitY), Government of India for the financial support during the research work through Visvesvaraya Ph.D. Scheme for Electronics and IT.

Bibliographical References

Aroyehun, S. T. and Gelbukh, A. (2018). Aggression detection in social media: Using deep neural networks, data augmentation, and pseudo labeling. In *Proceedings of the First Workshop on Trolling, Aggression and Cyberbullying (TRAC-2018)*, pages 90–97.

Bhattacharya, S., Singh, S., Kumar, R., Bansal, A., Bhagat, A., Dawer, Y., Lahiri, B., and Ojha, A. K. (2020). Developing a multilingual annotated corpus of misogyny and aggression.

Burnap, P. and Williams, M. L. (2015). Cyber hate speech on twitter: An application of machine classification and statistical modeling for policy and decision making. *Policy & Internet*, 7(2):223–242.

Chatzakou, D., Kourtellis, N., Blackburn, J., De Cristofaro, E., Stringhini, G., and Vakali, A. (2017). Mean birds: Detecting aggression and bullying on twitter. In *Proceedings of the 2017 ACM on web science conference*, pages 13–22. ACM.

Chen, J., Yan, S., and Wong, K.-C. (2018). Verbal aggression detection on twitter comments: convolutional neural network for short-text sentiment analysis. *Neural Computing and Applications*, pages 1–10.

Davidson, T., Warmsley, D., Macy, M., and Weber, I. (2017). Automated Hate Speech Detection and the Problem of Offensive Language. In *Proceedings of ICWSM*.

Fortuna, P. and Nunes, S. (2018). A Survey on Automatic Detection of Hate Speech in Text. *ACM Computing Surveys (CSUR)*, 51(4):85.

Joulin, A., Grave, E., Bojanowski, P., Douze, M., Jégou, H., and Mikolov, T. (2016). Fasttext.zip: Compressing text classification models. *CoRR*, abs/1612.03651:1–13.

Kumar, R., Ojha, A. K., Malmasi, S., and Zampieri, M. (2018). Benchmarking Aggression Identification in Social Media. In *Proceedings of the First Workshop on Trolling, Aggression and Cyberbulling (TRAC)*, Santa Fe, USA.

Kumari, K. and Singh, J. P. (2019). AI_ML_NIT Patna at HASOC 2019: Deep learning approach for identification of abusive content. In *Proceedings of the 11th annual meeting of the Forum for Information Retrieval Evaluation (FIRE 2019, December 2019)*, pages 328–335.

Kumari, K. and Singh, J. P. (2020). Identification of cyberbullying on multi-modal social media posts using genetic algorithm. *Transactions on Emerging Telecommunications Technologies*, doi:10.1002/ett.3907.

Kumari, K., Singh, J. P., Dwivedi, Y. K., and Rana, N. P. (2019a). Aggressive social media post detection system containing symbolic images. In *Conference on e-Business, e-Services and e-Society*, pages 415–424. Springer.

Kumari, K., Singh, J. P., Dwivedi, Y. K., and Rana, N. P. (2019b). Towards cyberbullying-free social media in smart cities: a unified multi-modal approach. *Soft Computing*, `doi:10.1007/s00500-019-04550-x`.

Malmasi, S. and Zampieri, M. (2017). Detecting Hate Speech in Social Media. In *Proceedings of the International Conference Recent Advances in Natural Language Processing (RANLP)*, pages 467–472.

Malmasi, S. and Zampieri, M. (2018). Challenges in Discriminating Profanity from Hate Speech. *Journal of Experimental & Theoretical Artificial Intelligence*, 30:1–16.

Modha, S., Majumder, P., and Mandl, T. (2018). Filtering aggression from the multilingual social media feed. In *Proceedings of the First Workshop on Trolling, Aggression and Cyberbullying (TRAC-2018)*, pages 199–207.

Raiyani, K., Gonçalves, T., Quaresma, P., and Nogueira, V. B. (2018). Fully connected neural network with advance preprocessor to identify aggression over facebook and twitter. In *Proceedings of the First Workshop on Trolling, Aggression and Cyberbullying (TRAC-2018)*, pages 28–41.

Risch, J. and Krestel, R. (2018). Aggression identification using deep learning and data augmentation. In *Proceedings of the First Workshop on Trolling, Aggression and Cyberbullying (TRAC-2018)*, pages 150–158.

Ritesh Kumar, Atul Kr. Ojha, S. M. and Zampieri, M. (2020). Evaluating aggression identification in social media. In Ritesh Kumar, et al., editors, *Proceedings of the Second Workshop on Trolling, Aggression and Cyberbullying (TRAC-2020)*, Paris, France, may. European Language Resources Association (ELRA).

Samghabadi, N. S., Mave, D., Kar, S., and Solorio, T. (2018). Ritual-uh at trac 2018 shared task: Aggression identification. In *Proceedings of the First Workshop on Trolling, Aggression and Cyberbullying (TRAC-2018)*, pages 12–18.

Schmidt, A. and Wiegand, M. (2017). A Survey on Hate Speech Detection Using Natural Language Processing. In *Proceedings of the Fifth International Workshop on Natural Language Processing for Social Media. Association for Computational Linguistics*, pages 1–10, Valencia, Spain.

Zampieri, M., Malmasi, S., Nakov, P., Rosenthal, S., Farra, N., and Kumar, R. (2019a). Predicting the Type and Target of Offensive Posts in Social Media. In *Proceedings of NAACL*.

Zampieri, M., Malmasi, S., Nakov, P., Rosenthal, S., Farra, N., and Kumar, R. (2019b). SemEval-2019 Task 6: Identifying and Categorizing Offensive Language in Social Media (OffensEval). In *Proceedings of The 13th International Workshop on Semantic Evaluation (SemEval)*.

Proceedings of the Second Workshop on Trolling, Aggression and Cyberbullying, pages 120–125
Language Resources and Evaluation Conference (LREC 2020), Marseille, 11–16 May 2020
© European Language Resources Association (ELRA), licensed under CC-BY-NC

Multilingual Joint Fine-tuning of Transformer models for identifying Trolling, Aggression and Cyberbullying at TRAC 2020

Sudhanshu Mishra[1], Shivangi Prasad[2], Shubhanshu Mishra[2]
[1]Indian Institute of Technology Kanpur, [2]University of Illinois at Urbana Champaign
sdhanshu@iitk.ac.in, sprasad6@illinois.edu, mishra@shubhanshu.com

Abstract

We present our team '3Idiots' (referred as 'sdhanshu' in the official rankings) approach for the Trolling, Aggression and Cyberbullying (TRAC) 2020 shared tasks. Our approach relies on fine-tuning various Transformer models on the different datasets. We also investigated the utility of task label marginalization, joint label classification, and joint training on multilingual datasets as possible improvements to our models. Our team came second in English sub-task A, a close fourth in the English sub-task B and third in the remaining 4 sub-tasks. We find the multilingual joint training approach to be the best trade-off between computational efficiency of model deployment and model's evaluation performance. We open source our approach at https://github.com/socialmediaie/TRAC2020.

Keywords: Aggression Identification, Misogynistic Aggression Identification , BERT, Transformers, Neural Networks.

1. Introduction

The internet has become more accessible in recent years, leading to an explosion in content being produced on social media platforms. This content constitutes public views, and opinions. Furthermore, social media has become an important tool for shaping the socio-economic policies around the world. This utilization of social media by public has also attracted many malicious actors to indulge in negative activities on these platforms. These negative activities involve, among others, misinformation, trolling, displays of aggression, as well as cyberbullying behaviour (Mishra et al., 2014). These activities have led to derailment and disruption of social conversation on these platforms. However, efforts to moderate these activities have revealed the limits of manual content moderation systems, owing to the the scale and velocity of content production. This has allowed more and more platforms to move to automated methods for content moderation. However, simple rule based methods do not work for subjective tasks like hate-speech, trolling, and aggression identification. These limitations have moved the automated content moderation community to investigate the usage of machine learning based intelligent systems which can identify the nuance in language to perform the above mentioned tasks more efficiently.

In this work, we utilize the recent advances in information extraction systems for social media data. In the past we have used information extraction for identifying sentiment in tweets (Mishra and Diesner, 2018) (Mishra et al., 2015), enthusiastic and passive tweets and users (Mishra et al., 2014) (Mishra and Diesner, 2019), and extracting named entities (Mishra, 2019) (Mishra and Diesner, 2016). We extend a methodology adopted in our previous work (Mishra and Mishra, 2019) on on Hate Speech and Offensive Content (HASOC) identification in Indo-European Languages (Mandl et al., 2019). In our work on HASOC, we investigated the usage of monolingual and multilingual transformer (Vaswani et al., 2017) models (specifically Bidirectional Encoder Representation from Transformers (BERT) (Devlin et al., 2019)) for hate speech identification. In this work, we extend our analysis to include a

newer variant of transformer model called XLM-Roberta (Conneau et al., 2019). In this year's TRAC (Ritesh Kumar and Zampieri, 2020) shared tasks, our team '3Idiots' (our team is referred as 'sdhanshu' in the rankings(Ritesh Kumar and Zampieri, 2020)) experimented with fine-tuning different pre-trained transformer networks for classifying aggressive and misogynistic posts. We also investigated a few new techniques not used before, namely, joint multitask multilingual training for all tasks, as well as marginalized predictions based on joint multitask model probabilities. Our team came second in English sub-task A, a close fourth in the English sub-task B and third in the remaining 4 sub-tasks. We open source our approach at https://github.com/socialmediaie/TRAC2020.

2. Related Work

The shared tasks in this year's TRAC focused on Aggression and Misogynistic content classification(Ritesh Kumar and Zampieri, 2020), the related work in this field focuses on a more general topic that is hate speech and abusive content detection. The abusive content identification tasks are are challenging due to the lack of large amounts of labeled datasets. The currently available datasets lack variety and uniformity. They are usually skewed towards specific topics in hate speech like racism, sexism. A good description of the various challenges in abusive content detection can be found here. (Vidgen et al., 2019) The recent developments in the field of Natural Language Processing (NLP) have really spearheaded research in this domain. One of the most remarkable developments in NLP was the introduction of transformer models (Vaswani et al., 2017) using different attention mechanisms, which have become state of the art in many NLP tasks beating recurrent neural networks and gated networks. These transformer models can process longer contextual information than the standard RNNs. One of the main state of the art models in many NLP tasks are Bidirectional Encoder Representation from Transformers (BERT) models (Devlin et al., 2019). The open source transformers library by HuggingFace Inc. (Wolf et al., 2019) has made fine-tuning pre-trained transformer models easy. In a 2019 task on Hate Speech and Offensive Content (HASOC) identification in Indo-European Languages (Mandl et al., 2019), we had the opportunity to try out different BERT models (Mishra and Mishra, 2019). Our models performed really well in the HASOC shared task, achieving first position on 3 of the 8 sub-tasks and being within top 1% for 5 of the 8 sub-tasks. This motivated us to try similar methods in this year's TRAC (Ritesh Kumar and Zampieri, 2020) shared tasks using other transformer models using our framework from HASOC based on the HuggingFace transformers library[1].

3. Data

The data-set provided by the organizers consisted of posts taken from Twitter and YouTube. They provided us with training and dev datasets for training and evaluation of our models for three languages, namely **English (ENG)**, **Hindi (HIN)** and **Bengali (IBEN)**. For both the sub-tasks, the same training and dev data-sets were used with different fine-tuning techniques. The **Aggression Identification** sub-task (task - A) consisted of classifying the text data into **'Overtly Aggressive' (OAG)**, **'Covertly Aggressive' (CAG)** and **'Non-Aggressive' (NAG)** categories. The **Misogynistic Aggression Identification** sub-task (task - B) consisted of classifying the text data into **'Gendered' (GEN)** and **'Non-gendered' (NGEN)** categories. For further details about the shared tasks, we refer to the TRAC website and the shared task paper (Ritesh Kumar and Zampieri, 2020). The data distribution for each language and each sub-task is mentioned in Table 1.

Lang	task A			task B		
	train	dev	test	train	dev	test
ENG	4263	1066	1200	4263	1066	1200
HIN	3984	997	1200	3984	997	1200
IBEN	3826	957	1188	3826	957	1188

Table 1: Distribution of number of tweets in different datasets and splits.

4. Methodology

Our methods used for the TRAC (Ritesh Kumar and Zampieri, 2020) shared tasks are inspired from our previous work (Mishra and Mishra, 2019) at HASOC 2019 (Mandl et al., 2019). For the different shared tasks we fine-tuned different pre-trained transformer neural network models using the HuggingFace transformers library.

4.1. Transformer Model

For all of the sub-tasks we used different pre-trained transformer neural network models. The transformer architecture was proposed in (Vaswani et al., 2017). It's effectiveness has been proved in numerous NLP tasks like machine translation, sequence classification and natural language generation. A transformer consists of a set of stacked encoders and decoders with different attention mechanisms.

Like any encoder-decoder model, it takes an input sequence produces a latent representation which is passed on to the decoder which gives an output sequence. A major change in the transformer architectures was that the decoder is supplied with all of the hidden states of the encoder. This helps the model to gain contextual information for even large sequences. To process the texts we utilized the model specific tokenizers provided in the HuggingFace transformers library to convert the texts into a sequence of tokens which are then utilised to generate the features for the model. We utilised similar training procedures like the one used in our HASOC 2019 submission code[2]. We investigated with two variants of transformer models, namely BERT (both monolingual and multilingual) (Devlin et al., 2019) and XLM-Robert (Conneau et al., 2019). While, for BERT we tested its in English, and multilingual versions, whereas, for XLM-Roberta we tried only the multilingual model. There are many other variants of transformers but we could not try them out because of GPU memory constraints, as these models require GPUs with very large amounts of RAM.

4.2. Fine-Tuning Techniques

For the TRAC shared tasks we investigated the following fine-tuning techniques on the different transformer models.

- **Simple fine-tuning:** In this approach we simply fine tune an existing transformer model for the specific language on the new classification data.

- **Joint label training (C):** In our approach during the HASOC (Mishra and Mishra, 2019) shared tasks we had to tackle the problem of data sparsity as the different tasks did not have enough data samples, which makes the training of deep learning models very difficult. To tackle this issue, we had combined the labels of the different shared tasks, which enabled us to train a single model for both the tasks. We tried the same approach for TRAC (Ritesh Kumar and Zampieri, 2020) ,although, here both tasks had the same dataset, so this did not result in an increase in the size of the dataset but it did enable us to train a single model capable of handling both the tasks. We combined the labels of the 2 sub-tasks and trained a single model for the classification. The predicted outputs were **NAG-GEN, NAG-NGEN, CAG-GEN, CAG-NGEN, OAG-GEN** and **OAG-NGEN** respectively, taking the argmax of the outputs produces the corresponding label for each task. To get the output of the respective tasks is trivial, we just have to separate the labels by the '-' symbol, where the first word corresponds to sub-task A and second word corresponds to sub-task B. The models using this technique are labeled with **(C)** in the results table below.

- **Marginalization of labels (M):** While using the previous method, in HASOC (Mishra and Mishra, 2019) we just took the respective probability of the combined label and made our decision on the basis of that probability. A limitation of this approach is that it does not guarentee consistency

---

lang	task	model	run_id	Macro-F1		Weighted-F1		rank
				dev	train	dev	train	
ENG	**A**	**bert-base-multilingual-uncased (ALL)**	**9**	0.611	0.903	0.798	0.957	1
		bert-base-uncased (C)	**4 (C)**	0.596	0.902	0.795	0.956	2
		bert-base-uncased (M)	**4 (M)**	0.595	0.900	0.795	0.956	3
		bert-base-cased (C)	**3 (C)**	0.571	0.912	0.786	0.961	4
		bert-base-uncased	**2**	0.577	0.948	0.784	0.979	5
		bert-base-cased (M)	**3 (M)**	0.568	0.908	0.782	0.960	6
		bert-base-multilingual-uncased (ALL) (M)	**9 (M)**	0.555	0.865	0.780	0.939	7
		bert-base-multilingual-uncased (ALL) (C)	**9 (C)**	0.550	0.871	0.778	0.941	8
		bert-base-cased	**1**	0.563	0.966	0.774	0.987	9
		xlm-roberta-base	**5**	0.531	0.676	0.772	0.862	10
		xlm-roberta-base (C)	**6 (C)**	0.515	0.640	0.762	0.835	11
		xlm-roberta-base (ALL)	**9**	0.512	0.610	0.762	0.823	12
		xlm-roberta-base (M)	**6 (M)**	0.518	0.634	0.761	0.830	13
HIN	**A**	**bert-base-multilingual-uncased**	**5**	0.637	0.846	0.708	0.881	1
		bert-base-multilingual-uncased (ALL) (C)	**9 (C)**	0.628	0.903	0.696	0.924	2
		bert-base-multilingual-uncased (ALL) (M)	**9 (M)**	0.626	0.899	0.695	0.921	3
		bert-base-multilingual-uncased (ALL)	**9**	0.626	0.939	0.694	0.952	4
		bert-base-multilingual-uncased (C)	**3 (C)**	0.616	0.849	0.688	0.884	5
		bert-base-multilingual-uncased (M)	**3 (M)**	0.611	0.848	0.684	0.884	6
		xlm-roberta-base (ALL)	**9**	0.598	0.698	0.672	0.753	7
		xlm-roberta-base	**2**	0.394	0.388	0.527	0.509	8
		xlm-roberta-base (C)	**4 (C)**	0.245	0.240	0.426	0.406	9
		xlm-roberta-base (M)	**4 (M)**	0.245	0.240	0.426	0.406	9
IBEN	**A**	**bert-base-multilingual-uncased (ALL)**	**9**	0.698	0.933	0.737	0.945	1
		xlm-roberta-base (M)	**4 (M)**	0.694	0.758	0.732	0.796	2
		xlm-roberta-base (C)	**4 (C)**	0.692	0.757	0.731	0.796	3
		bert-base-multilingual-uncased (M)	**3 (M)**	0.686	0.856	0.729	0.879	4
		bert-base-multilingual-uncased (C)	**3 (C)**	0.684	0.860	0.728	0.883	5
		bert-base-multilingual-uncased	**5**	0.680	0.903	0.726	0.918	6
		bert-base-multilingual-uncased (ALL) (C)	**9 (C)**	0.686	0.893	0.726	0.912	7
		bert-base-multilingual-uncased (ALL) (M)	**9 (M)**	0.683	0.893	0.723	0.913	8
		xlm-roberta-base (ALL)	**9**	0.663	0.728	0.710	0.767	9
		xlm-roberta-base	**2**	0.584	0.631	0.646	0.691	10

Table 2: Results of sub-task A for each model and each language.

in relative ranks of labels for that subtasks when combined with labels from other subtasks, i.e. $p(\textbf{NAG-GEN}) > p(\textbf{CAG-GEN})$ does not guarentee that $p(\textbf{NAG-NGEN}) > p(\textbf{CAG-NGEN})$. Hence, we introduce a marignalized post processing of label to get the total probablity assigned to labels of a given subtasks by marignalizing probabilities across all other subtask labels. This can be done very easily by just summing the combined labels of a particular task label, **Eg.** the probabilities of **CAG-GEN** and **CAG-NGEN** can be added to get the probability of the label **CAG** for **sub-task A**. This provides a stronger signal for each task label. Then, finally taking the argmax of the marginalized labels of the respective tasks, determines the output label for that task. The models using this technique are labeled with **(M)** in the results table below. We only use this approach for post-processing the label probabilities of the joint model. In future we plan to investigate using this marginalized approach during the training phase.

- **Joint training of different languages (ALL):** This was a technique that we previously did not experiment with in HASOC (Mishra and Mishra, 2019). Currently we do not have models dedicated to many languages, e.g., there are specific pre-trained BERT (Devlin et al., 2019) models for the English language but no such model for Hindi exists. For those languages, our only choice is to utilize a multilingual or cross-lingual model. Furthermore, as the data consisted of social-media posts, which predominantly consists of sentences containing a mix of different languages, we expected the cross-lingual models to perform better than the others. An obvious advantage of using a multi-lingual model is that it can process data from multiple languages, therefore we can train a single model for all of the different languages for each sub-task. To do so we combined the datasets of the three languages into a single dataset, keeping track of which text came from which language. This can easily be done by flagging the respective id with the respective

lang	task	model	run_id	Macro-F1		Weighted-F1		rank
				dev	train	dev	train	
ENG	B	bert-base-uncased (M)	4 (M)	0.757	0.920	0.943	0.978	1
		xlm-roberta-base (ALL)	9	0.765	0.878	0.941	0.968	2
		bert-base-multilingual-uncased (ALL) (M)	9 (M)	0.760	0.939	0.940	0.983	3
		bert-base-uncased (C)	4 (C)	0.734	0.914	0.939	0.977	4
		bert-base-cased (C)	3 (C)	0.729	0.931	0.939	0.982	5
		bert-base-multilingual-uncased (ALL) (C)	9 (C)	0.752	0.936	0.938	0.983	6
		bert-base-cased (M)	3 (M)	0.727	0.935	0.938	0.983	7
		bert-base-uncased	2	0.737	0.991	0.938	0.998	8
		bert-base-multilingual-uncased (ALL)	9	0.751	0.987	0.937	0.996	9
		xlm-roberta-base	5	0.734	0.915	0.936	0.978	10
		xlm-roberta-base (M)	6 (M)	0.728	0.807	0.934	0.948	11
		xlm-roberta-base (C)	6 (C)	0.711	0.813	0.933	0.952	12
		bert-base-cased	1	0.700	0.982	0.929	0.995	13
HIN	B	bert-base-multilingual-uncased	6	0.780	0.974	0.891	0.986	1
		bert-base-multilingual-uncased (ALL)	9	0.778	0.990	0.888	0.994	2
		bert-base-multilingual-uncased (ALL) (C)	9 (C)	0.783	0.932	0.888	0.962	3
		bert-base-multilingual-uncased (ALL) (M)	9 (M)	0.778	0.931	0.886	0.962	4
		bert-base-multilingual-uncased (M)	3 (M)	0.760	0.844	0.882	0.916	5
		bert-base-multilingual-uncased (C)	3 (C)	0.750	0.847	0.874	0.917	6
		xlm-roberta-base (ALL)	9	0.745	0.831	0.870	0.909	7
		xlm-roberta-base	2	0.459	0.455	0.778	0.759	8
		xlm-roberta-base (C)	4 (C)	0.459	0.455	0.778	0.759	8
		xlm-roberta-base (M)	4 (M)	0.459	0.455	0.778	0.759	8
IBEN	B	bert-base-multilingual-uncased (ALL)	9	0.849	0.987	0.905	0.992	1
		bert-base-multilingual-uncased (ALL) (M)	9 (M)	0.849	0.943	0.904	0.965	2
		bert-base-multilingual-uncased (ALL) (C)	9 (C)	0.846	0.943	0.902	0.966	3
		bert-base-multilingual-uncased	6	0.830	0.975	0.894	0.985	4
		bert-base-multilingual-uncased (M)	3 (M)	0.827	0.924	0.892	0.954	5
		bert-base-multilingual-uncased (C)	3 (C)	0.824	0.923	0.890	0.953	6
		xlm-roberta-base (ALL)	9	0.792	0.845	0.873	0.908	7
		xlm-roberta-base (M)	4 (M)	0.783	0.835	0.869	0.903	8
		xlm-roberta-base (C)	4 (C)	0.783	0.833	0.868	0.902	9
		xlm-roberta-base	2	0.714	0.743	0.830	0.855	10

Table 3: Results of sub-task B for each model and each language.

language name. This increases the size of the dataset which is beneficial for training deep learning models. We then fine-tuned the pre-trained multilingual model for our dataset. After training, we can separate the dataset based on their language id. Thus resulting in a single model that is able to classify data from all of the three languages. This can be especially useful in deploying situations as this results in models which are resource friendly. The models using this technique are labeled with (**ALL**) in the results table below.

- **Combining the above three techniques:** Finally, we also experimented with combining all of the above three techniques. This results in a single model that can be used for all of the six sub-tasks. Thus, this technique is very efficient in terms of resources used and flexibility. The models using this technique are labeled either (**ALL**) (**M**) or (**ALL**) (**C**) in the results table below, based on the presence and absence of the marignalization approach, respectively.

4.3. Training

For training our models we used the standard hyperparameters as mentioned in the transformers models. We used the Adam optimizer (with $\epsilon = 1e-8$) for five epochs, with a training/eval batch size of 32. Maximum allowable length for each sequence is 128. We use a learning rate of $5e-5$ with a weight decay of 0.0 and a max gradient norm of 1.0. All models were trained using Google Colab's [3] GPU runtimes.

4.4. Results and Experiments

For each language and each sub-task we experimented with different pre-trained transformer language models present in the transformers library using the various fine-tuning techniques mentioned in the previous section. The different models with their respective dev and training weighted-F1 and macro-F1 scores for sub-task A and sub-Task B are given in **Table 2** and **Table 3** respectively. The table fol-

---

[3]https://colab.research.google.com/

lang	task	model	weighted-F1		rank		Overall
			dev	test	dev	test	Rank
ENG	**A**	**bert-base-multilingual-uncased (ALL)**	0.798	0.728	1	3	-
		bert-base-uncased (C)	0.795	0.759	2	2	-
		bert-base-uncased (M)	0.795	0.759	3	1	**2**
		Overall Best Model****	-	0.802	-	-	**1***
HIN	**A**	**bert-base-multilingual-uncased**	0.708	0.778	1	3	-
		bert-base-multilingual-uncased (ALL) (C)	0.696	0.779	2	1	**3**
		bert-base-multilingual-uncased (ALL) (M)	0.695	0.778	3	2	-
		Overall Best Model****	-	0.812	-	-	**1***
IBEN	**A**	**bert-base-multilingual-uncased (ALL)**	0.737	0.780	1	1	**3**
		xlm-roberta-base (M)	0.732	0.772	2	2	-
		xlm-roberta-base (C)	0.731	0.772	3	3	-
		Overall Best Model****	-	0.821	-	-	**1***
ENG	**B**	**bert-base-uncased (M)**	0.978	0.857	1	1	**4**
		xlm-roberta-base (ALL)	0.968	0.844	2	2	-
		bert-base-multilingual-uncased (ALL) (M)	0.983	0.843	3	3	-
		Overall Best Model****	-	0.871	-	-	**1***
HIN	**B**	**bert-base-multilingual-uncased**	0.986	0.837	1	3	-
		bert-base-multilingual-uncased (ALL)	0.994	0.849	2	1	**3**
		bert-base-multilingual-uncased (ALL) (C)	0.962	0.843	3	2	-
		Overall Best Model****	-	0.878	-	-	**1***
IBEN	**B**	**bert-base-multilingual-uncased (ALL)**	0.992	0.927	1	1	**3**
		bert-base-multilingual-uncased (ALL) (M)	0.965	0.926	2	2	-
		bert-base-multilingual-uncased (ALL) (C)	0.902	0.925	3	3	-
		Overall Best Model****	-	0.938	-	-	**1***

Table 4: Test results of the submitted models

lows the following convention to describe the fine-tuning technique used in each experiment. We submitted the top three models based on the weighted-F1 scores on the dev dataset.

- **No label:** This represents the simple fine-tuning approach.
- **(C):** Joint label training
- **(M):** Marginalization of labels
- **(ALL):** Joint training of different languages.
- **(ALL) (C):** Joint training of different languages with joint label training.
- **(ALL) (M):** Joint training of different languages with joint label training and marginalization of labels.

4.5. External Evaluation

We were only provided with the weighted-F1 scores of the three submitted models in each task. Hence, only those results are mentioned in Table 4. Based on the final leaderboard, our models were ranked second in 1/6 task, third in 4/6 tasks, and 4/6 in 1/6 tasks.

5. Discussion

On the basis of the various experiments conducted using the many transformer models, we see that most of them give a similar performance, being within $2-3\%$ of the best model. Exception being the **xlm-roberta-base** (Liu et al., 2019) model which showed appreciable variations. It performed extremely poorly in the Hindi sub-tasks, but with the joint training with different languages its performance increased significantly. Using the joint label training technique it performed really well in the Bengali sub-tasks whilst also being the bottom performer with the other techniques. One important thing to notice is that the joint training with different language fine-tuning technique (**ALL**) works really well. It was a consistent top performing model in our experiments, being the best for Bengali. In most cases, we can see that the (**ALL**) models were better than the base model without any marginalization or joint-training. The marginalization scheme does not change the results much from the joint label training approach. A major benefit of using joint training with different languages, is that is significantly reduces the computational cost of the usage of our models, as we have to only train a single model for multiple tasks and languages, so even if there is a slight performance drop in the (**ALL**) (**C**) or (**M**) model compared to the single model, usage of the (**ALL**) (**C**) or (**M**) model should still be preferred for its computational efficiently. Our team came second in English sub-task A, a close fourth in the English sub-task B and third in the remaining 4 sub-tasks.

6. Conclusion

From the experiments conducted for this year's TRAC (Ritesh Kumar and Zampieri, 2020) shared tasks, we see that the (**ALL**) models provide us with an extremely powerful approach which gives us a single model capable of classifying texts across all the six shared sub-tasks. We have presented our team 3Idiots's (our team is referred as 'sdhanshu' in the rankings(Ritesh Kumar and Zampieri, 2020)) approach based on fine-tuning monolingual and multi-lingual transformer networks to classify social media posts in three different languages for Trolling, Aggression and Cyber-bullying content. We open source our approach at: https://github.com/socialmediaie/TRAC2020

7. Bibliographical References

Conneau, A., Khandelwal, K., Goyal, N., Chaudhary, V., Wenzek, G., Guzmán, F., Grave, E., Ott, M., Zettlemoyer, L., and Stoyanov, V. (2019). Unsupervised cross-lingual representation learning at scale. *arXiv preprint arXiv:1911.02116*.

Devlin, J., Chang, M.-W., Lee, K., and Toutanova, K. (2019). BERT: Pre-training of deep bidirectional transformers for language understanding. In *Proceedings of the 2019 Conference of the North American Chapter of the Association for Computational Linguistics: Human Language Technologies, Volume 1 (Long and Short Papers)*, pages 4171–4186, Minneapolis, Minnesota, June. Association for Computational Linguistics.

Liu, Y., Ott, M., Goyal, N., Du, J., Joshi, M., Chen, D., Levy, O., Lewis, M., Zettlemoyer, L., and Stoyanov, V. (2019). Roberta: A robustly optimized bert pretraining approach. *arXiv preprint arXiv:1907.11692*.

Mandl, T., Modha, S., Patel, D., Dave, M., Mandlia, C., and Patel, A. (2019). Overview of the HASOC track at FIRE 2019: Hate Speech and Offensive Content Identification in Indo-European Languages. In *Proceedings of the 11th annual meeting of the Forum for Information Retrieval Evaluation*, December.

Mishra, S. and Diesner, J. (2016). Semi-supervised Named Entity Recognition in noisy-text. In *Proceedings of the 2nd Workshop on Noisy User-generated Text (WNUT)*, pages 203–212, Osaka, Japan. The COLING 2016 Organizing Committee.

Mishra, S. and Diesner, J. (2018). Detecting the Correlation between Sentiment and User-level as well as Text-Level Meta-data from Benchmark Corpora. In *Proceedings of the 29th on Hypertext and Social Media - HT '18*, pages 2–10, New York, New York, USA. ACM Press.

Mishra, S. and Diesner, J. (2019). Capturing Signals of Enthusiasm and Support Towards Social Issues from Twitter. In *Proceedings of the 5th International Workshop on Social Media World Sensors - SIdEWayS'19*, pages 19–24, New York, New York, USA. ACM Press.

Mishra, S. and Mishra, S. (2019). 3Idiots at HASOC 2019: Fine-tuning Transformer Neural Networks for Hate Speech Identification in Indo-European Languages. In *Proceedings of the 11th annual meeting of the Forum for Information Retrieval Evaluation*.

Mishra, S., Agarwal, S., Guo, J., Phelps, K., Picco, J., and Diesner, J. (2014). Enthusiasm and support: alternative sentiment classification for social movements on social media. In *Proceedings of the 2014 ACM conference on Web science - WebSci '14*, pages 261–262, Bloomington, Indiana, USA, jun. ACM Press.

Mishra, S., Diesner, J., Byrne, J., and Surbeck, E. (2015). Sentiment Analysis with Incremental Human-in-the-Loop Learning and Lexical Resource Customization. In *Proceedings of the 26th ACM Conference on Hypertext & Social Media - HT '15*, pages 323–325, New York, New York, USA. ACM Press.

Mishra, S. (2019). Multi-dataset-multi-task Neural Sequence Tagging for Information Extraction from Tweets. In *Proceedings of the 30th ACM Conference on Hypertext and Social Media - HT '19*, pages 283–284, New York, New York, USA. ACM Press.

Ritesh Kumar, Atul Kr. Ojha, S. M. and Zampieri, M. (2020). Evaluating aggression identification in social media. In Ritesh Kumar, et al., editors, *Proceedings of the Second Workshop on Trolling, Aggression and Cyberbullying (TRAC-2020)*, Paris, France, may. European Language Resources Association (ELRA).

Vaswani, A., Shazeer, N., Parmar, N., Uszkoreit, J., Jones, L., Gomez, A. N., Kaiser, L., and Polosukhin, I. (2017). Attention is all you need. *CoRR*, abs/1706.03762.

Vidgen, B., Harris, A., Nguyen, D., Tromble, R., Hale, S., and Margetts, H. (2019). Challenges and frontiers in abusive content detection. In *Proceedings of the Third Workshop on Abusive Language Online*, pages 80–93, Florence, Italy, August. Association for Computational Linguistics.

Wolf, T., Debut, L., Sanh, V., Chaumond, J., Delangue, C., Moi, A., Cistac, P., Rault, T., Louf, R., Funtowicz, M., and Brew, J. (2019). Huggingface's transformers: State-of-the-art natural language processing.

Proceedings of the Second Workshop on Trolling, Aggression and Cyberbullying, pages 126–131
Language Resources and Evaluation Conference (LREC 2020), Marseille, 11–16 May 2020
© European Language Resources Association (ELRA), licensed under CC-BY-NC

Aggression and Misogyny Detection using BERT: A Multi-Task Approach

Niloofar Safi Samghabadi[♠1]**, Parth Patwa**[◇1]**, Srinivas PYKL**[◇]**,
Prerana Mukherjee**[◇]**, Amitava Das**[♣]**, Thamar Solorio**[♠]
♠ Department of Computer Science, University of Houston
◇ Indian Institute of Information Technology, Sri City
♣Wipro Research Lab
{nsafisamghabadi, tsolorio}@uh.edu
{parthprasad.p17, srinivas.p, prerana.m}@iiits.in
amitava.das2@wipro.com

Abstract

In recent times, the focus of the NLP community has increased towards offensive language, aggression, and hate-speech detection. This paper presents our system for TRAC-2 shared task on "Aggression Identification" (sub-task A) and "Misogynistic Aggression Identification" (sub-task B). The data for this shared task is provided in three different languages - English, Hindi, and Bengali. Each data instance is annotated into one of the three aggression classes - Not Aggressive, Covertly Aggressive, Overtly Aggressive, as well as one of the two misogyny classes - Gendered and Non-Gendered. We propose an end-to-end neural model using attention on top of BERT that incorporates a multi-task learning paradigm to address both sub-tasks simultaneously. Our team, "na14", scored 0.8579 weighted F1-measure on the English sub-task B and secured 3rd rank out of 15 teams for the task. The code and the model weights are publicly available at https://github.com/NiloofarSafi/TRAC-2.

Keywords: Aggression, Misogyny, Abusive Language, Hate-Speech Detection, BERT, NLP, Neural Networks, Social Media

1. Introduction

Social media and the internet are overabundant with data. The number of users on the internet has increased by 83% from 2014 to 2019. In 2019, more than 500 million tweets and 4 billion Facebook messages were posted daily[2]. Social Media has become an important and influential means of communication as it is easily accessible and provides a lot of freedom to users. Some users misuse this by engaging in trolling, cyberbullying, or by sharing aggressive, hateful, misogynistic content. Aggressive words, abusive language, or hate-speech is used to harm the identity, status, mental health, or prestige of the victim (Beran and Li, 2005; Culpeper, 2011). This type of anti-social behavior causes disharmony in society. Hence, it is becoming quite alarming, and it is crucial to address this problem.

Aggression is a feeling of anger that results in hostile behavior and readiness to attack. According to Kumar et al. (2018c), aggression can either be expressed in a direct, explicit manner (Overtly Aggressive) or an indirect, sarcastic manner (Covertly Aggressive). Hate-speech is used to attack a person or a group of people based on their color, gender, race, sexual orientation, ethnicity, nationality, religion (Nockleby, 2000). Misogyny or Sexism is a subset of hate-speech (Waseem and Hovy, 2016) and targets the victim based on gender or sexuality (Davidson et al., 2017; Bhattacharya et al., 2020).

It is essential to identify aggression and hate-speech in social networks to protect online users against such attacks, but it is quite time-consuming to do so manually. Hence, social media companies and government agencies are focusing on building a system that can automate the identification process. However, it is difficult to draw a dis-

tinguishing line between acceptable content and aggressive/hateful content due to the subjectivity of the definitions and different perceptions of the same content by different people, which makes it harder to build an automated AI system. Facebook published its audit report[3] on civil rights, which explains its strategy to tackle abusive and hateful content. The report claims that building a complete automation system to detect hate-speech is not possible, and content moderation is unavoidable. This point brings many researchers to focus on building hate-speech/aggression detection systems since a large amount of such data is diffused in social networks. To this end, several workshops have been organized, including 'Abusive Language Online' (ALW) (Roberts et al., 2019), 'Trolling, Aggression and Cyberbullying' (TRAC) (Kumar et al., 2018b), and Semantic Evaluation (SemEval) shared task on Identifying Offensive Language in Social Media (OffensEval) (Zampieri et al., 2020).

This paper presents our system for TRAC-2 Shared Task on "Aggression Identification" (sub-task A) and "Misogynistic Aggression Identification" (sub-task B), in which we propose a BERT (Devlin et al., 2018) based architecture to detect misogyny and aggression using a multi-task approach. The proposed model uses attention mechanism over BERT to get relative importance of words, followed by Fully-Connected layers, and a final classification layer for each sub-task, which predicts the class.

2. Related Work

Hate-speech: The interest of NLP researchers in hate-speech, aggression, and sexism detection has increased recently. Kwok and Wang (2013) proposed a supervised ap-

---

[1]These authors contributed equally.

[2]https://blog.microfocus.com/how-much-data-is-created-on-the-internet-each-day/

[3]https://www.theverge.com/interface/2019/7/2/20678231/facebook-civil-rights-audit-hate-speech-moderators

proach to detect anti-black hate-speech in social media platforms using Twitter data. They categorized the text into binary labels racist vs. non-racist and achieved a classification accuracy of 76%. Burnap and Williams (2015) utilized ensemble based classifier results to forecast cyberhate proliferation using statistical approaches. The classifier captured the grammatical dependencies between words in Twitter data to anticipate the behavior to give antagonistic responses. Nobata et al. (2016) curated a corpus of user comments for abusive language detection and resorted to machine learning based approaches to detect subtle hate-speech. Schmidt and Wiegand (2017), give a detailed survey on hate-speech detection works. Gambäck and Sikdar (2017) used convolutional layers on word vectors to detect hate-speech. Other recent works (Zhang et al., 2018; Agrawal and Awekar, 2018; Dadvar and Eckert, 2018) also use deep learning based techniques to detect hate-speech. BERT Based approaches also have become popular recently (Nikolov and Radivchev, 2019; Mozafari et al., 2019; Risch et al., 2019).

Sexism: Recently, misogynistic and sexist comments, posts, or tweets on social media platforms have become quite predominant. Jha and Mamidi (2017) provided an analysis of sexist tweets and further categorize them as hostile, benevolent, or other. Sharifirad and Matwin (2019) also provided an in-depth analysis of sexist tweets and categorize them based on the type of harassment. Frenda et al. (2019) performed linguistic analysis to detect misogyny and sexism in tweets. Parikh et al. (2019) introduced the first work on multi-label classification for sexism detection and also provided the largest dataset on sexism categorization. They built a BERT based neural architecture with distributional and word level embeddings to perform the classification task.

Aggression: The first Shared Task on Aggression Identification (Kumar et al., 2018a) aimed to identify aggressive tweets in social media posts and provided datasets in Hindi and English. Samghabadi et al. (2018) used lexical and semantic features along with logistic regression for the task and obtained 0.59 and 0.63 F1 scores on Hindi and English Facebook datasets, respectively. Orasan (2018) utilized machine learning (SVM, random forest) on word embeddings for aggressive language identification. Raiyani et al. (2018) used fully connected layers on highly pre-processed data. Aroyehun and Gelbukh (2018) used data augmentation along with deep learning for aggression identification and achieved 0.64 F1 score on the English dataset. Risch and Krestel (2018) also employed a similar technique and got 0.60 F1 score for English.

3. Data

The datasets for this shared task are provided by (Bhattacharya et al., 2020) in three different languages: English, Hindi, and Bengali. For sub-task A, the data has been labeled with one out of three possible tags:

Not Aggressive (NAG): Texts which are not aggressive. E.g. *"hats off brother"*.

Covertly Aggressive (CAG): Texts that express aggression in an indirect, sarcastic manner. E.g., *"You are not wrong, you are just ignorant."*.

Overtly Aggressive (OAG): Texts which express aggression in a direct, straightforward, and explicit way. E.g., *"Liberals are retards"*.

For sub-task B, there are two classes:

Gendered (GEN): Texts that target a person or a group of people based on gender, sexuality, or lack of fulfillment of stereotypical gender roles. E.g., *"Homosexuality should be banned"*.

Non-gendered (NGEN): Texts that are not gendered. E.g.. *"you are absolutely true bro...but even politicians supports them"*.

Although the perception of aggression and misogyny can vary from person to person, we found some annotations that are highly improbable. The following are some examples that are mislabeled as NAG:

- *"This lady from BJP is crazy this is how u react man such a foolish and ignorant lady"*

- *"What a lousy moderator arnab is. Falthu show"*,

- *"Ha yaar bahut hi chutya movie tha.sab log keh raha tha badia movie tha isliye dekha bt bilkul jhaand tha"* (It was a stupid movie. Everyone was saying it is good so I saw but it is completely stupid)

- *"Brother puri movie bta di chutiya he kya"* (brother you spoiled the entire movie are you an idiot)

Some examples of comments mislabeled as NGEN:

- *"true feminist is Cancer"*

- *"Breif description but feminist is like urban terrorist and they will never understand"*

- *"Feminists are the next threat to our country"*

- *"chutiya hai ye feminists"* (these feminists are idiots)

Table 1 shows statistics over the train and validation data for both sub-tasks across all available languages. From this table, we can easily find out that for both sub-tasks A and B, the train and dev sets are highly skewed towards NAG and NGEN classes, respectively.

Table 2 indicates the co-occurrence of sub-task A and sub-task B labels. NAG mostly co-occurs with NGEN. The ratio of GEN to NGEN in OAG is greater than that in NAG and CAG. Overall, in all three languages, we can observe that as the directness of aggression increases (NAG<CAG<OAG), the percentage of GEN examples also increases. In Hindi and Bengali, OAG examples are more likely to be tagged as GEN than NGEN. Based on these observations, we can say that these two sub-tasks are related.

4. System Architecture

As we saw that the sub-tasks are related to each other, we create a unified deep neural architecture, following a multi-task approach. Figure 1 illustrates the overall architecture of our proposed model. Our proposed model consists of the following modules:

language	split	size	sub-task A			sub-task B	
			NAG	CAG	OAG	GEN	NGEN
English	train	4263	3375 (79.17%)	453 (10.63%)	435 (10.20%)	309 (7.25%)	3954 (92.75%)
	dev	1066	836 (78.42%)	117 (10.98%)	113 (10.60%)	73 (6.85%)	993 (93.15%)
	test	1200	690 (57.50%)	224 (18.67%)	286 (23.83%)	175 (14.58%)	1025 (85.42%)
Hindi	train	3984	2245 (56.35%)	829 (20.81%)	910 (22.84%)	661 (16.59%)	3323 (83.41%)
	dev	997	578 (57.97%)	211 (21.17%)	208 (20.86%)	152 (15.25%)	845 (84.75%)
	test	1200	325 (27.08%)	191 (15.92%)	684 (57.00%)	567 (47.25%)	633 (52.42%)
Bengali	train	3826	2078 (54.31%)	898 (23.47%)	850 (22.22%)	712 (18.61%)	3114 (81.39%)
	dev	957	522 (54.55%)	218 (22.78%)	217 (22.67%)	191 (19.96%)	766 (80.04%)
	test	1188	712 (59.93%)	225 (18.94%)	251 (21.13%)	202 (17.00%)	986 (83.00%)

Table 1: Data statistics.

language	split	total	NAG-GEN	NAG-NGEN	CAG-GEN	CAG-NGEN	OAG-GEN	OAG-NGEN
English	train	4263	134	3241	35	418	140	295
	dev	1066	38	798	9	108	26	87
Hindi	train	3984	32	2213	79	750	550	260
	dev	997	11	567	26	185	115	93
Bengali	train	3826	129	1949	129	769	454	395
	dev	957	37	485	31	187	123	94

Table 2: Co-occurrence between sub-task labels.

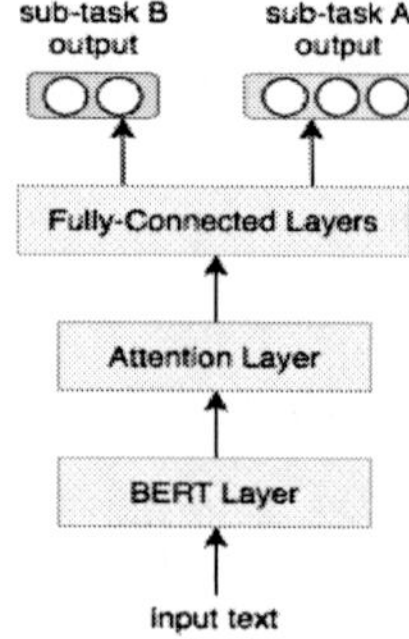

Figure 1: Overall architecture of the proposed model.

BERT Layer: We pass the input sequence of tokens to the BERT model (Devlin et al., 2018) to extract contextualized information.

Attention Layer: We feed the output of BERT layer to the attention mechanism proposed in Bahdanau et al. (2014). This layer computes the weighted sum of $r = \sum_i \alpha_i h_i$ to aggregate hidden representations (h_i) of all tokens in a sequence to a single vector. To measure the relative importance of words, we calculate the attention weights α_i as follows:

$$\alpha_i = \frac{exp(score(h_i, e))}{\Sigma_{i'} exp(score(h_{i'}, e))} \tag{1}$$

where the $score(.)$ function is defined as:

$$score(h_i, e) = v^T tanh(W_h h_i + b_h) \tag{2}$$

where W_h is the weight matrix, and v and b_h are the parameters of the network.

Fully-Connected Layers: We pass the output of the attention layer to Fully Connected (linear) layers for dimen-

sion reduction. There are two linear layers with 500 and 100 neurons, respectively.

Classification Layer: We feed the output of linear layers to two separate classification layers, one for predicting aggression class, and another for misogyny identification. For both cases, we use a linear layer with a softmax activation on top, which gives a probability score to the classes. The number of output neurons is three and two for sub-tasks A and B, respectively.

4.1. Experimental Setups

For pre-processing, we use the BERT tokenizer for text tokenization. Then, we truncate the posts to 200 tokens, and left-pad the shorter sequence with zeros. For initializing weights of the BERT layer, we use "bert_based_uncased" pre-trained weights for English and "bert_base_multilingual_cased" for Hindi and Bengali. To compute the loss between predicted and actual labels, we use Binary Cross Entropy. We calculate the sum of losses for both sub-tasks A and B. Additionally, for addressing the imbalance problem in the corpora, we add information about class weights to the loss functions for both outputs. We update the network weights using Adam optimizer (Kingma and Ba, 2014) with a learning rate of $1e^{-5}$; however, we do not fine-tune the BERT layer. We train the model over 200 epochs using training data and save the best model based on the F1 score obtained on the validation set. We train our models on Nvidia Tesla P40 GPU having 24 GB memory, where each epoch takes around 1.5 minutes to be completed. The code and the model weights are publicly available[1].

5. Results

Table 3 shows the weighted F1 score and accuracy of our system on all the sub-tasks. Weighted F1 score is used as

---

[1]https://github.com/NiloofarSafi/TRAC-2

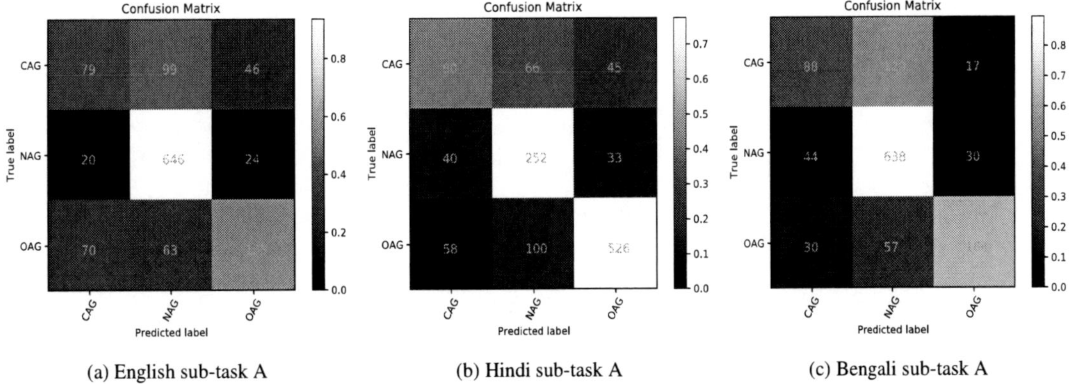

<table>
<tr><td>(a) English sub-task A</td><td>(b) Hindi sub-task A</td><td>(c) Bengali sub-task A</td></tr>
</table>

Figure 2: Heatmap of confusion matrices of our best performing systems for sub-task A across all languages.

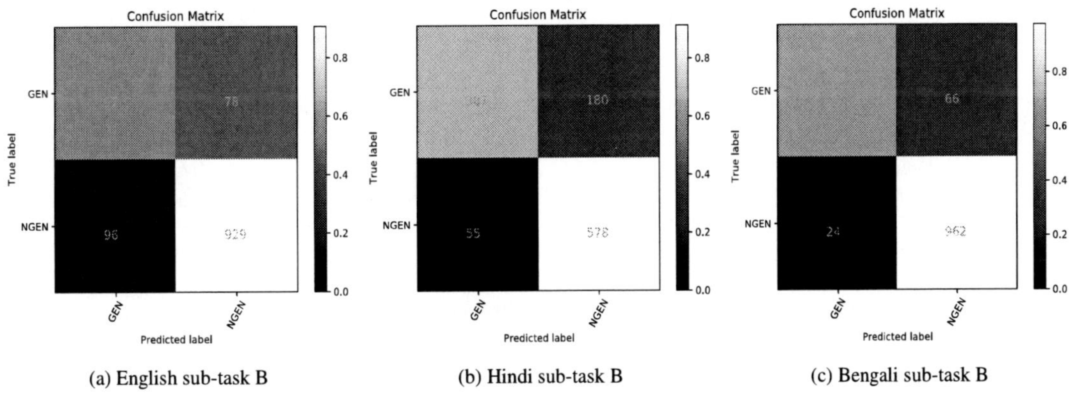

<table>
<tr><td>(a) English sub-task B</td><td>(b) Hindi sub-task B</td><td>(c) Bengali sub-task B</td></tr>
</table>

Figure 3: Heatmap of confusion matrices of our best performing systems for sub-task B across all languages.

the official metric to rank the participants by the organizers. Based on the table, misogyny is easier to detect as compared to aggression across all available languages. The possible reason could be its binary and relatively straightforward nature as compared to sub-task A, which includes three classes. Our best score is achieved on English sub-task B, where we secured 3rd rank out of 15 teams. Our system lags behind the best performance on EN-B (0.8715 F1), and BEN-B (0.9365 F1) by 0.0136 and 0.0159, respectively, which shows our system is competitive and comparable to them.

Sub-task	F1 (weighted)	Accuracy
ENG-A	0.7143	0.7317
HIN-A	0.7183	0.7150
BEN-A	0.7369	0.7492
ENG-B	0.8579	0.8550
HIN-B	0.8008	0.8042
BEN-B	0.9206	0.9242

Table 3: Results of BERT model on all sub-tasks.

Figure 2 illustrates the confusion matrices of sub-task A for all three languages. Overall, CAG examples are more likely to be wrongly predicted as NAG than OAG. This could be due to the lack of abusive or explicit words in CAG instances. We further investigate this possibility in Section 5.1. In Hindi, OAG-NAG confusion (100) is high and is significantly more than that in English and Bengali. The reason could be that for Hindi corpus, the majority of the train instances are tagged as NAG (56.35%), whereas in its test data, the majority of the instances are labeled as OAG (57.00%).

Figure 3 shows the confusion matrices for sub-task B on all three languages. Similar to OAG-NAG, we can see that GEN-NGEN confusion for Hindi test data is higher than that in other languages. It can be explained by table 1, where we can see that for Hindi sub-task B, the distribution of classes across the test data is significantly different from the training and dev sets.

Language	Sub-task A			Sub-task B	
	NAG	CAG	OAG	GEN	NGEN
English	0.86	0.40	0.60	0.53	0.91
Hindi	0.68	0.43	0.82	0.77	0.83
Bengali	0.84	0.45	0.71	0.75	0.96

Table 4: Class-wise F1 score for both sub-tasks across all three languages.

Table 4 indicates the class-wise performance of our system

S.no	sub-task	text	actual	predicted
a	ENG-A	*Also Veere Di Wedding Fake Feminist Piece Of Shit...*	NAG	OAG
b	ENG-A	*oneitis - that's what kabir singh had with that girl in the movie ... dumb as fuck*	NAG	OAG
c	HIN-A	*Maha Chutiyapay ki film he Kabir Singh... It's totally bullshit movie...* (Kabir Singh is a very stupid film... it's totally bullshit movie...)	NAG	OAG
d	HIN-A	*Mujhe bhi jand lagi movie lakin maine chutiyo ke samne jaban nahi kholi or na hi kholuga* (I also found this movie stupid, but I didn't open my mouth in front of idiots and won't do so.)	NAG	OAG
e	ENG-B	*neha gupta ur are a crook if there are no evidence den how u can file a false compaint????*	GEN	NGEN
f	ENG-B	*kapil why are u listening to these chutiaasssss....give them shut up call...insane idiots*	GEN	NGEN
g	HIN-B	*Bhadwa hai rajdeep ...* (Rajdeep is an idiot.)	GEN	NGEN
h	HIN-B	*Kaunsi charas ya afeem phoonk ke aayi hai ye. Gandee aurat. Aurat ke naam pe dhabba.* (Which weed or poppy has she smoked? Dirty lady. Blot on the name of a woman.)	NGEN	GEN

Table 5: Instances where predicted label seems more accurate than given label.

on all the sub-tasks. For sub-task A, the performance is least for CAG across all the languages, which shows that it is the most challenging aggression class to identify. OAG and CAG scores are least for English as compared to the other two languages because the percentage of training examples for those two classes is lower in English as compared to other languages. NAG is the easiest to detect in English and Bengali, whereas OAG is the easiest to detect in Hindi. With regards to sub-task B, the performance is better on NGEN than GEN for all the three languages. The difference between the F1 score on NGEN and GEN is significantly more in English than in Hindi and Bengali. This can be attributed to the lower percentage of GEN examples in English than in the other two languages.

5.1. Error Analysis

We analyze the mistakes of our model on the validation set to see where it goes wrong. We found several instances where the actual tag is CAG, but our model classifies them as NAG. Some of those examples are listed as follows:

- *"Fat shaming is good. Why not?"*

- *"**Gay people rely on straight people to produce more gay people**"*

- *"They have no right to live"*

- *"Inko hospital bejo..ye mentally hille hue log han"* *(Send them to hospital, they are mentally disturbed people.)*

- *"Bhai aap na sirf review kariye baki ki baatein na hi kare toh accha h ?" (Brother you only do review, it's better of you don't talk about other things.)*

From these examples, we can see that due to the indirect/sarcastic nature and lack of profanity in CAG, it is confused with NAG. This flags CAG as the most difficult class to detect.

We also found some instances where the predicted labels seem more likely to be correct than the annotated labels.

Table 5 shows such examples. In that, examples a-d are from sub-task A and are labeled as NAG, but as they include abusive and explicit words, the predicted label OAG seems more accurate. Examples e-g are labeled as GEN, but they are targeted towards a specific person not based on gender. So the model prediction NGEN is correct. Example h attacks a woman based on her gender, and hence the model predicts it as GEN.

6. Conclusion

In this paper, we present our multi-task deep neural model to identify misogyny and aggression for three different corpora - English, Hindi, and Bengali. The analysis of the label co-occurrence across the two sub-tasks shows that aggression identification and misogyny identification are related. Analysis of the results shows that CAG is often confused with NAG and is the most challenging aggression class to detect.

For future work, instead of employing BERT as a feature extractor, we plan to fine-tune it using the training data. We also plan to explore more sentiment features for better identification of the implicit forms of aggression (CAG).

7. Bibliographical References

Agrawal, S. and Awekar, A. (2018). Deep learning for detecting cyberbullying across multiple social media platforms. In *European Conference on Information Retrieval*. Springer.

Aroyehun, S. T. and Gelbukh, A. (2018). Aggression detection in social media: Using deep neural networks, data augmentation, and pseudo labeling. In *Proceedings of the First Workshop on Trolling, Aggression and Cyberbullying (TRAC-2018)*.

Bahdanau, D., Cho, K., et al. (2014). Neural machine translation by jointly learning to align and translate. *arXiv preprint arXiv: 1409.0473*.

Beran, T. and Li, Q. (2005). Cyber-harassment: A study of a new method for an old behavior. *JECR*, 32(3).

Bhattacharya, S., Singh, S., Kumar, R., Bansal, A., Bhagat, A., Dawer, Y., Lahiri, B., and Ojha, A. K. (2020). Developing a multilingual annotated corpus of misogyny and aggression. *arXiv preprint arXiv:2003.07428*.

Burnap, P. and Williams, M. L. (2015). Cyber hate speech on twitter: An application of machine classification and statistical modeling for policy and decision making. *Policy & Internet*, 7(2).

Culpeper, J. (2011). *Impoliteness: Using language to cause offence*, volume 28. Cambridge University Press.

Dadvar, M. and Eckert, K. (2018). Cyberbullying detection in social networks using deep learning based models; a reproducibility study. *arXiv preprint arXiv:1812.08046*.

Davidson, T., Warmsley, D., Macy, M., and Weber, I. (2017). Automated Hate Speech Detection and the Problem of Offensive Language. In *Proceedings of ICWSM*.

Devlin, J., Chang, M., Lee, K., and Toutanova, K. (2018). BERT: pre-training of deep bidirectional transformers for language understanding. *CoRR*, abs/1810.04805.

Frenda, S., Ghanem, B., Montes-y Gómez, M., and Rosso, P. (2019). Online hate speech against women: Automatic identification of misogyny and sexism on twitter. *Journal of Intelligent & Fuzzy Systems*, 36(5).

Gambäck, B. and Sikdar, U. K. (2017). Using Convolutional Neural Networks to Classify Hate-speech. In *Proceedings of the First Workshop on Abusive Language Online*.

Jha, A. and Mamidi, R. (2017). When does a compliment become sexist? analysis and classification of ambivalent sexism using twitter data. In *Proceedings of the Second Workshop on NLP and Computational Social Science*.

Kingma, D. P. and Ba, J. (2014). Adam: A method for stochastic optimization. *arXiv preprint arXiv:1412.6980*.

Kumar, R., Ojha, A. K., Malmasi, S., and Zampieri, M. (2018a). Benchmarking Aggression Identification in Social Media. In *Proceedings of the First Workshop on Trolling, Aggression and Cyberbulling (TRAC)*.

Ritesh Kumar, et al., editors. (2018b). *Proceedings of the First Workshop on Trolling, Aggression and Cyberbullying (TRAC-2018)*. Association for Computational Linguistics.

Kumar, R., Reganti, A. N., Bhatia, A., and Maheshwari, T. (2018c). Aggression-annotated corpus of hindi-english code-mixed data. *CoRR*, abs/1803.09402.

Kwok, I. and Wang, Y. (2013). Locate the hate: Detecting Tweets Against Blacks. In *Twenty-Seventh AAAI Conference on Artificial Intelligence*.

Mozafari, M., Farahbakhsh, R., and Crespi, N. (2019). A bert-based transfer learning approach for hate speech detection in online social media. In *Proceedings of the International Conference on Complex Networks and Their Applications*. Springer.

Nikolov, A. and Radivchev, V. (2019). Nikolov-radivchev at SemEval-2019 task 6: Offensive tweet classification with BERT and ensembles. In *Proceedings of the 13th International Workshop on Semantic Evaluation*.

Nobata, C., Tetreault, J., Thomas, A., Mehdad, Y., and Chang, Y. (2016). Abusive Language Detection in Online User Content. In *Proceedings of the 25th International Conference on World Wide Web*.

Nockleby, J. T. (2000). Hate speech. *Encyclopedia of the American constitution*.

Orasan, C. (2018). Aggressive language identification using word embeddings and sentiment features. *Proceedings of the First Workshop on Trolling, Aggression and Cyberbullying*.

Parikh, P., Abburi, H., Badjatiya, P., Krishnan, R., Chhaya, N., Gupta, M., and Varma, V. (2019). Multi-label categorization of accounts of sexism using a neural framework. *arXiv preprint arXiv:1910.04602*.

Raiyani, K., Gonçalves, T., Quaresma, P., and Nogueira, V. B. (2018). Fully connected neural network with advance preprocessor to identify aggression over Facebook and twitter. In *Proceedings of the First Workshop on Trolling, Aggression and Cyberbullying (TRAC-2018)*.

Risch, J. and Krestel, R. (2018). Aggression identification using deep learning and data augmentation. In *Proceedings of the First Workshop on Trolling, Aggression and Cyberbullying (TRAC-2018)*.

Risch, J., Stoll, A., Ziegele, M., and Krestel, R. (2019). hpiDEDIS at GermEval 2019: Offensive language identification using a german BERT model. In *Proceedings of the 15th Conference on Natural Language Processing*.

Ritesh Kumar, Atul Kr. Ojha, S. M. and Zampieri, M. (2020). Evaluating aggression identification in social media. In Ritesh Kumar, et al., editors, *Proceedings of the Second Workshop on Trolling, Aggression and Cyberbullying (TRAC-2020)*, Paris, France, may. European Language Resources Association (ELRA).

Sarah T. Roberts, et al., editors. (2019). *Proceedings of the Third Workshop on Abusive Language Online*. Association for Computational Linguistics.

Samghabadi, N. S., Mave, D., Kar, S., and Solorio, T. (2018). Ritual-uh at TRAC 2018 shared task: Aggression identification. *CoRR*, abs/1807.11712.

Schmidt, A. and Wiegand, M. (2017). A Survey on Hate Speech Detection Using Natural Language Processing. In *Proceedings of the Fifth International Workshop on Natural Language Processing for Social Media*.

Sharifirad, S. and Matwin, S. (2019). When a tweet is actually sexist. A more comprehensive classification of different online harassment categories and the challenges in NLP. *CoRR*, abs/1902.10584.

Waseem, Z. and Hovy, D. (2016). Hateful symbols or hateful people? predictive features for hate speech detection on twitter. In *Proceedings of the NAACL Student Research Workshop*.

Zampieri, M., Nakov, P., Rosenthal, S., Atanasova, P., Karadzhov, G., Mubarak, H., Derczynski, L., Pitenis, Z., and Çöltekin, c. (2020). SemEval-2020 Task 12: Multilingual Offensive Language Identification in Social Media (OffensEval 2020). In *Proceedings of SemEval*.

Zhang, Z., Robinson, D., and Tepper, J. (2018). Detecting Hate Speech on Twitter Using a Convolution-GRU Based Deep Neural Network. In *Lecture Notes in Computer Science*. Springer Verlag.

Proceedings of the Second Workshop on Trolling, Aggression and Cyberbullying, pages 132–136
Language Resources and Evaluation Conference (LREC 2020), Marseille, 11–16 May 2020
© European Language Resources Association (ELRA), licensed under CC-BY-NC

Automatic Detection of Offensive Language in Social Media: Defining Linguistic Criteria to build a Mexican Spanish Dataset

María José Díaz-Torres[*], **Paulina Alejandra Morán-Méndez**[*]
Luis Villaseñor-Pineda[††], **Manuel Montes-y-Gómez**[†]
Juan Aguilera[†], **Luis Meneses-Lerín**[‡]
[*]Facultad de Lenguas, Universidad de las Américas Puebla, México,
{maria.diazto, paulina.moranmz}@udlap.mx
[†]Laboratorio de Tecnologías del Lenguaje, Instituto Nacional de Astrofísica, Óptica y Electrónica, Mexico,
{villasen, mmontesg, jaguilera}@inaoep.mx
[‡]Centre de Recherche en Linguistique Française GRAMMATICA, Université d'Artois, France,
luis_meneses_lerin@yahoo.fr

Abstract

Phenomena such as bullying, homophobia, sexism and racism have transcended to social networks, motivating the development of tools for their automatic detection. The challenge becomes greater when speakers make use of popular sayings, colloquial expressions and idioms which may contain vulgar, profane or rude words, but not always have the intention to offend; a situation often found in the Mexican Spanish variant. Under these circumstances, the identification of the offense goes beyond the lexical and syntactic elements of the message. This first work aims to define the main linguistic features of aggressive, offensive and vulgar language in social networks in order to establish linguistic-based criteria to facilitate the identification of abusive language. For this purpose, a Mexican Spanish Twitter corpus was compiled and analyzed. The dataset included words that, despite being rude, need to be considered in context to determine they are part of an offense. Based on the analysis of this corpus, linguistic criteria were defined to determine whether a message is offensive. To simplify the application of these criteria, an easy-to-follow diagram was designed. The paper presents an example of the use of the diagram, as well as the basic statistics of the corpus.
Keywords: aggressiveness detection, corpus annotation, text classification, Spanish

1. Introduction

As of today, social media platforms such as Facebook, Twitter and YouTube have facilitated and encouraged interpersonal communication. Through them, people interact and share their opinions through posts, messages and comments online. Unfortunately, since these platforms guarantee to some extent the freedom of expression of their users, they can and often use these means to attack or offend other persons. This situation leads to safety issues: online aggression and abuse not only create mental and psychological health problems for the victims but have also been proved to cause self-harm and even suicide (Kumar et al., 2018). Some of the major challenges for detecting abusive language in social networks are the speed and volume of online communication. Every second, approximately 6,000 tweets are published, which is equivalent to more than 500 million tweets per day[1], making manual monitoring impossible. The previous scenario has motivated the development of methods for the automatic detection of abusive messages. Current methods are of two main kinds: supervised (Burnap and Williams, 2016; Plaza-del Arco et al., 2019) which require labeled data for learning a classification model, and, unsupervised (Gitari et al., 2015; Wiegand et al., 2018; Guzmán-Falcón, 2018), which detect hostile messages by searching for words in a given lexicon of profane words. Both kinds of approaches have their own advantages and disadvantages. In particular, the creation of supervised learning methods for offensive language detection requires of large, accurate, manually annotated resources. Nevertheless, most corpora available are in English (Pamungkas and Patti, 2019), which greatly hinders this task in low-resource languages. Annotation criteria for this type of datasets have only seldom been detailed (Ousidhoum et al., 2019), and, moreover, the labeling of offensive and non-offensive messages is commonly a costly and highly subjective task due to several socio-cultural and domain dependent issues. A greater challenge is posed by the richness of colloquial expressions and vulgar language that characterizes communication in social networks, since the identification of offenses goes beyond the lexical and syntactic elements of the message, and requires the annotator to understand the context beyond individual terms. With this motivation, through the present research we sought to define the main linguistic features that characterize abusive language manifested in social networks. As a first step, our work departs from the fact that the language used in social networks is abundant in colloquial expressions, commonly composed of rude or profane words, but they are not used to offend. Hence, the interest of this work is the definition of an annotation scheme with enough elements to discriminate these situations. To this end, we defined the concepts of offensive, aggressive and vulgar language, based on Austin's Speech Acts theory (Austin, 1962), with the aim of establishing criteria to facilitate their identification and thus define an accurate, fine-grained and linguistic-based annotation scheme.

2. Related Work

The task of automatically detecting aggressive content aimed at individuals or communities has recently been studied in different academic forums. However, most of them focus on the English language (Álvarez-Carmona et al.,

---

[1]Internet Live Stats, 2019 - www.internetlivestats.com/twitter-statistics

2018). In 2017, the 1st Workshop on Abusive Language Online (ALW1) was organized, where different approaches were presented for the detection of abusive language in social networks, focusing particularly on written communications in English and German (Waseem et al., 2017a). Subsequently, more workshops of the same court emerged, but due to the lack of consensus on a definition for "offensive language", the scope of the task was narrowed to more specific and identifiable behaviors. This was the case of the recent First Workshop on Trolling, Aggression and Cyberbullying (TRAC-2018) (Kumar et al., 2018). In this workshop, the phenomena of online aggression such as trolling and cyberbullying were discussed.

By the same token, issues such as racism (Tulkens et al., 2016), sexism (Lee et al., 2010), and bullying (Samghabadi et al., 2017) have been studied in this line of research. Along the definitions proposed for these abusive behaviors we can find certain patterns, such as the presence of curse words, discriminatory vocabulary, derogatory adjectives and the explicit mention of others; manifested through names, pronouns, and user tags (Waseem et al., 2017b).

With respect to the efforts made for Mexican Spanish, the last two years, the evaluation forum "Authorship and Aggressiveness Analysis in Twitter: a case study in Mexican Spanish" (MEX-A3T) has been held. This forum -which took place within the IberEval 2018 (Álvarez-Carmona et al., 2018) and IberLEF 2019 (Aragón et al., 2019) conferences- evaluated an aggressiveness detection task in Mexican Spanish tweets. The results confirmed the complexity of this task, and the need for well-defined criteria to differentiate offensive, aggressive and vulgar language. Therefore, the goal of the present research was to establish criteria to facilitate the identification of offensive language and thus define a detailed, linguistic-based annotation scheme.

3. Data Collection

To collect data, we considered Twitter as the source media since it is open and its anonymity allows people to write judgments or assessments about other people, including offenses or aggressions. The interest of this first work is the definition of criteria to distinguish the offense or the aggression when using the same vocabulary. That is, it is necessary to collect messages that, despite using the same words (*i.e.* rude words), it is the context that determines whether a word is used to offend, or is part of a colloquial expression that is not intended to offend. To build the corpus, we collected tweets from August to November of 2017. We used some rude words and controversial hashtags to narrow the search. We collected a set of 143 terms that served as seeds for extracting the tweets, which includede words classified as vulgar and non-colloquial in the *Diccionario de Mexicanismos de la Academia Mexicana de la Lengua*, as well as words and hashtags identified by the *Instituto Nacional de las Mujeres* as related to violence and sexual harassment against women on Twitter (Guzmán-Falcón, 2018). Table 1 shows examples of these seed words.

To ensure their origin, the tweets were collected considering their geolocation. We considered Mexico City as the center and extracted all tweets that were within a radius of

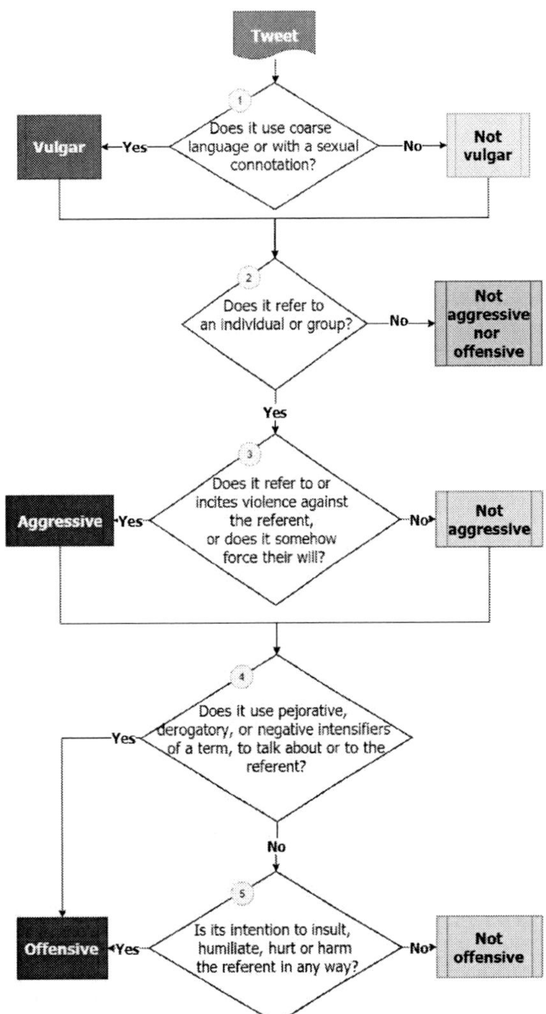

Figure 1: Annotation flowchart for abusive language categorization

500km. Finally, nearly 10,500 tweets in Mexican Spanish were collected and analyzed to define the annotation scheme.

4. Annotation Scheme

The creation of the annotation scheme and the annotation task itself were part of an incremental and complementary process. Two linguists from our research team studied the abusive language phenomenon through the literature and analyzed the collected tweets, to arrive to a typology that identified the defining characteristics of vulgar, aggressive and offensive language. Then, the linguists wrote the annotation diagram and used it to classify the corpus. For the purpose of creating said linguistic-based annotation scheme, first, it was necessary to arrive at a definition for the concepts of offensive, aggressive, vulgar language. Having a conceptualization of each term is a critical task, since it allows to establish linguistic criteria for the iden-

Table 1: Sample of the vocabulary applied for the recovery of tweets.

Spanish	English Translation
luchona	*hard-working woman (single mother; derogatory)*
pendejo(a)	*asshole (masc./fem.)*
prieto(a)	*dark-skinned (masc./fem.; derogatory)*
vergazos	*strong blow (vulgar)*
golfas	*whores*
puta	*slut*
lameculos	*ass kisser*

tification and classification of these linguistic phenomena. Once the theoretical framework on these linguistic manifestations was outlined, we looked for the lexical and semantic elements representative of the aggressive, offensive or vulgar messages.

4.1. Offensive, Aggressive and Vulgar Language

In order to identify the most characteristic features of aggressive, offensive and vulgar language, we first studied the definitions formulated in several academic forums and workshops. Among the proposed conceptualizations, recurrent linguistic characteristics can be found: the presence of rudeness, discriminatory vocabulary, derogatory adjectives and the mention of others, which is manifested through names, pronouns, and user tags (Waseem et al., 2017b). Beyond these lexical and syntactic elements, the pragmatic aspect of the messages is crucial to qualify them as aggressive, offensive or vulgar. According to the Speech Acts theory (Austin, 1962), the production of a statement performs three types of actions or acts at the same time: the locutionary act, the linguistic expression itself, its syntactic structure and the literal meaning semantic; the illocutionary act, the force or intention of the expression provided by the speaker; and the perlocutionary act, the consequence or effect of the statement on the interlocutor. The second act is the one that interests the detection of abusive language, since the illocutionary force of a message is its underlying purpose, which could go from asking a question, an invitation, a reminder, to a warning, a promise, or a threat, among many others. This wide range of intentions is delineated in the classification of illocutionary speech acts by (Searle, 1976). It is important to emphasize that the illocutionary force of a speech act always depends on the context of the expression (Fromkin et al., 2011), and since tweets provide very little context other than the linguistic expression itself, the annotators must rely on their sociopragmatic knowledge of the language to identify the illocutionary force of the message. That is the reason why linguistic variation must be taken into account for the definition of these concepts. Linguistic variation is the intrinsic characteristic of all languages that refers to the systematic differences in pronunciation, vocabulary and grammar of different social and regional groups of speakers of a language (Holmes and Wilson, 2017). This is a relevant phenomenon for any natural language processing task, and in the case of abusive language detection it should be considered not only because of the distinctive lexical and syntactic characteristics of the

dialect, but also because these patterns convey social meanings (Wardhaugh, 2011), which would affect the way of expressing aggressiveness.

After revising the literature on the subject and analyzing the definitions of other related linguistic manifestations such as hate speech, cyberbullying, and racism, an offensive, aggressive and vulgar language typology was reached:

- Offensive language: aims at insulting or humiliating a group or individual, usually using derogatory or derogatory terms. An example from the corpus is: *No es que estés gorda, lo gordo se quita. Es tu cara de caballo.* This tweet humiliates a woman, makes fun of her body and compares her to an animal.

- Aggressive language: seeks to harm or hurt a group or individual by referring to or inciting violence. An example from the corpus is: *pero estas gorda... aprovecha tu fin pendeja que el lunes te violo.* This tweet involves insults and a rape threat.

- Vulgar language: it involves profanity, with sexual connotation and sometimes double entendre, but may or may not refer to an individual or collective. An example from the corpus is: *Martes con de M de Mamando onvre se arreglan las cosas... creo... eso dicen..* This tweet uses obscene vocabulary and is sexually explicit.

5. Diagram Description

Our annotation scheme was designed as a flowchart, for the purpose of supporting abusive language categorization into aggressive, offensive and vulgar in a clear, visual way. It was devised with the goal to be easy to read and useful for annotators without strong linguistics knowledge, to account for the diversity of backgrounds in the field of natural language processing. The typology portrays each concept as a non-exclusive quality of the message or tweet. This way, the tool allows for a better characterization of the texts when considering the possibility of a tweet belonging to one, two or even all classes, which represents more accurately the nature of these messages in social networks. The flowchart presents questions regarding the form and function of the message, about the presence of insults, derogatory, or sexually-charged vocabulary, but most prominently it is concerned on the illocutionary force of the message; that is, the intention and target of the tweet. As shown in Fig. 1, the labeling process begins with the selection of a tweet, and the first question that asks if the tweet uses coarse language or with a sexual connotation. If the answer is yes, this indicates the message is vulgar, otherwise it is not. Following, the annotator is asked whether the tweet refers to an individual or to a group of people, or not. This question serves to make an early discard of aggressiveness and offensiveness, since these classes, unlike vulgar language, require of a target to qualify as such. If the message does not have a specific referent, the labeling process ends there. On the contrary, if the answer is positive, then the next question concerns aggressiveness, and asks if the tweet incites violence or tries to force the will of its referent. Finally, to determine if the message is offensive, the diagram

Table 2: Examples showing the use of the proposed scheme. The number in parentheses refers to the question in the annotation flowchart.

Message	Vulgar?	Aggressive?	Offensive?
Lo más rico de coger no es lo que tú sientes; sino ver al cabrón retorcerse de placer... #Bottom #Sex #Coger *The best part about sex is not the feeling you get, but watching the man shiver of pleasure... #Bottom #Sex #Fuck*	Yes (1)	No (3)	No (5)
@USUARIO Estoy hasta la puta madre jajajajajaja *@USER I've fucking had it hahahahaha*	Yes (1)	No (3)	No (5)
Vrg que feas botas *Holy fuck those are some ugly boots*	Yes (1)	No (2)	No (3)
Lloran cuando las golpean, ah pero en la calle andan de golfas :) #MujerGolpeada-HombreFeliz *They cry when they're beaten, oh but they're out whoring on the street :) #Beaten-WomanHappyMan*	No (1)	Yes (3)	Yes (4)
Tu no por qué eres MACHORRA!! *Not you because you're a BUTCH!!*	No (1)	No (3)	Yes (4)
Te recomiendo que te vayas comprando tus Tampax joto agachón!!! *I recommend you buy tampons bitch boy!!!*	No (1)	No (3)	Yes (5)
Ya me tienes hasta la madre pendejo. Al chile el martes el Richi y yo te vamos a partir la madre. *I'm fucking sick of you asshole. I swear on Tuesday Richi and I are going to fuck you up.*	Yes (1)	Yes (3)	Yes (5)

directs the annotator to observe if the tweet uses pejorative, derogatory or negative intensifiers of a term to refer to its target; if the tweet seeks to humiliate or insult its referent. Be any of these questions answered affirmatively, the tweet shall be labeled as offensive.

It should be noted that each of these classifications, vulgar, aggressive, and offensive, are non-exclusive qualities of the tweet. That is the reason why the flowchart continues after every decision, with the exception of the message having no referent. Table 2 shows examples that correspond to each of the categories.

6. Towards automatic detection of abusive language

This research work generated two digital linguistic resources: a linguistic annotation scheme for the classification of offensive, aggressive and vulgar language; and a corpus of offensive language in Mexican Spanish. As it was previously explained, the scheme was designed based on an abusive language typology, which served to annotate the dataset. This obtained a Kappa coefficient of inter-evaluator agreement of 0.91, which means that as a result we had a consistent annotation when making use of the proposed scheme while annotating the corpus with both of the evaluators. Clearly, the high level of agreement is because they labelled the corpus at the time of analysis. A second exercise with new annotators is needed to confirm the applicability of the proposed scheme.

Table 3 shows the general characteristics of this corpus: the distribution of the messages in the offensive and non-offensive classes, as well as the size of their vocabularies. Using this corpus, a first classification exercise was carried out. To do this, a traditional method for text classification

was applied[2]. The objective of this exercise was to observe the strong overlap between both classes. As mentioned in previous sections, the collection of messages was done with a single set of seed words. Consequently, the common vocabulary between the two classes is high. However, although many of the messages in the non-offensive class use the same rude words, they are not considered offenses or aggressions.

Table 3: Corpus' distribution.

Class	Tweets	Vocabulary	Tweet size
Non-offensive	7,460	13,696	16.1±5.9
Offensive	3,015	7,365	16.3±5.8
Total	**10,475**	**17,067**	**16.1±5.9**

Table 4 shows the results obtained. As it can be seen, the non-offensive class achieves greater F1-measure, an effect expected by the imbalance in the classes. On the other hand, as expected, the classifier does not correctly discriminate between the two classes, because this simple representation (*i.e.* unigrams) does not consider the entire context.

Table 4: Offensive detection results, Acc=0.77±0.06 (stratified 10-fold cross validation).

Class	Precision	Recall	F1-measure
Non-offensive	0.83±0.05	0.86±0.06	0.84±0.04
Offensive	0.63±0.13	0.56±0.18	0.58±0.14

---

[2]A unigram based representation with frequency weights; frequency threshold $>=$ 10; SVM classifier (linear kernel, C = 1).

7. Conclusions

This research work focuses on the annotation process of corpora for the detection of abusive language. The proposed annotation scheme provides specific criteria to identify aggressive, offensive and vulgar language based on its linguistic characteristics and intent of the message. This initial scheme took special care to include in the analysis messages that, despite the use of rude words, are not considered offensive. On the other hand, the collected corpus of abusive language is representative of the variant of Mexican Spanish, encouraging the creation of more resources in our language and giving visibility to one of its many dialects. Our contribution encourages the emergence of proposals for automatic methods that will be able to obtain better results thanks to a more accurate dataset, consistent with the reality of this online language phenomenon. Lastly, it should be noted that the diagram will be made available, and our corpus will be made available through the MEX-A3T 2020 forum[3]. Any future participant in the forum will have access to the dataset presented in this work.

8. Acknowledgements

We would like to thank CONACyT for partially supporting this work under grants CB-2015-01-257383 and the Thematic Networks program (Language Technologies Thematic Network).

9. Bibliographical References

Álvarez-Carmona, M. Á., Guzmán-Falcón, E., Montes-y Gómez, M., Escalante, H. J., Villasenor-Pineda, L., Reyes-Meza, V., and Rico-Sulayes, A. (2018). Overview of mex-a3t at ibereval 2018: Authorship and aggressiveness analysis in mexican spanish tweets. In *Notebook Papers of 3rd SEPLN Workshop on Evaluation of Human Language Technologies for Iberian Languages (IBEREVAL), Seville, Spain*, volume 6.

Aragón, M. E., Álvarez-Carmona, M. Á., Montes-y Gómez, M., Escalante, H. J., Villasenor-Pineda, L., and Moctezuma, D. (2019). Overview of mex-a3t at iberlef 2019: Authorship and aggressiveness analysis in mexican spanish tweets. In *Notebook Papers of 1st SEPLN Workshop on Iberian Languages Evaluation Forum (IberLEF), Bilbao, Spain*.

Austin, J. (1962). How to do things with words, 2nd edn, jo urmson and m. *Sbasa (eds)*.

Burnap, P. and Williams, M. L. (2016). Us and them: identifying cyber hate on twitter across multiple protected characteristics. *EPJ Data Science*, 5(1):11.

Fromkin, V., Rodman, R., and Hyams, V. (2011). An introduction to language, 9e. *Boston, MA: Wadsworth, Cengage Learning*.

Gitari, N. D., Zuping, Z., Damien, H., and Long, J. (2015). A lexicon-based approach for hate speech detection. *International Journal of Multimedia and Ubiquitous Engineering*, 10(4):215–230.

Guzmán-Falcón, E. (2018). *Detección de lenguaje ofensivo en Twitter basada en expansión automática de lexicones*. Tesis de maestría en ciencias computacionales, Instituto Nacional de Astrofísica, Óptica y Electrónica.

Holmes, J. and Wilson, N. (2017). *An introduction to sociolinguistics*. Routledge.

Kumar, R., Ojha, A. K., Zampieri, M., and Malmasi, S. (2018). Proceedings of the first workshop on trolling, aggression and cyberbullying (trac-2018). In *Proceedings of the First Workshop on Trolling, Aggression and Cyberbullying (TRAC-2018)*.

Lee, T. L., Fiske, S. T., Glick, P., and Chen, Z. (2010). Ambivalent sexism in close relationships:(hostile) power and (benevolent) romance shape relationship ideals. *Sex Roles*, 62(7-8):583–601.

Ousidhoum, N., Lin, Z., Zhang, H., Song, Y., and Yeung, D.-Y. (2019). Multilingual and multi-aspect hate speech analysis. *arXiv preprint arXiv:1908.11049*.

Pamungkas, E. W. and Patti, V. (2019). Cross-domain and cross-lingual abusive language detection: A hybrid approach with deep learning and a multilingual lexicon. In *Proceedings of the 57th Annual Meeting of the Association for Computational Linguistics: Student Research Workshop*, pages 363–370.

Plaza-del Arco, F. M., Molina-González, M. D., Martín-Valdivia, M. T., and Lopez, L. A. U. (2019). Sinai at semeval-2019 task 6: Incorporating lexicon knowledge into svm learning to identify and categorize offensive language in social media. In *Proceedings of the 13th International Workshop on Semantic Evaluation*, pages 735–738.

Samghabadi, N. S., Maharjan, S., Sprague, A., Diaz-Sprague, R., and Solorio, T. (2017). Detecting nastiness in social media. In *Proceedings of the First Workshop on Abusive Language Online*, pages 63–72.

Searle, J. R. (1976). A classification of illocutionary acts. *Language in society*, 5(1):1–23.

Tulkens, S., Hilte, L., Lodewyckx, E., Verhoeven, B., and Daelemans, W. (2016). The automated detection of racist discourse in dutch social media. *Computational Linguistics in the Netherlands Journal*, 6:3–20.

Wardhaugh, R. (2011). *An introduction to sociolinguistics*, volume 28. John Wiley & Sons.

Waseem, Z., Chung, W. H. K., Hovy, D., and Tetreault, J. (2017a). Proceedings of the first workshop on abusive language online. In *Proceedings of the First Workshop on Abusive Language Online*.

Waseem, Z., Davidson, T., Warmsley, D., and Weber, I. (2017b). Understanding abuse: A typology of abusive language detection subtasks. *arXiv preprint arXiv:1705.09899*.

Wiegand, M., Ruppenhofer, J., Schmidt, A., and Greenberg, C. (2018). Inducing a lexicon of abusive words– a feature-based approach. In *Proceedings of the 2018 Conference of the North American Chapter of the Association for Computational Linguistics: Human Language Technologies, Volume 1 (Long Papers)*, pages 1046–1056.

---

[3]sites.google.com/view/mex-a3t/

Proceedings of the Second Workshop on Trolling, Aggression and Cyberbullying, pages 137–143
Language Resources and Evaluation Conference (LREC 2020), Marseille, 11–16 May 2020
© European Language Resources Association (ELRA), licensed under CC-BY-NC

Offensive Language Detection Explained

Julian Risch,[1] Robin Ruff,[2,3] Ralf Krestel[1,2]

[1]Hasso Plattner Institute, University of Potsdam, [2]University of Passau, [3]Karlsruhe Institute of Technology
[1]Prof.-Dr.-Helmert-Str. 2-3, 14482 Potsdam, Germany
[2]Innstraße 41, 94032 Passau, Germany
[3]Kaiserstraße 12, 76131 Karlsruhe, Germany
julian.risch@hpi.de, upnub@student.kit.edu, ralf.krestel@uni-passau.de

Abstract

Many online discussion platforms use a content moderation process, where human moderators check user comments for offensive language and other rule violations. It is the moderator's decision which comments to remove from the platform because of violations and which ones to keep. Research so far focused on automating this decision process in the form of supervised machine learning for a classification task. However, even with machine-learned models achieving better classification accuracy than human experts in some scenarios, there is still a reason why human moderators are preferred. In contrast to black-box models, such as neural networks, humans can give explanations for their decision to remove a comment. For example, they can point out which phrase in the comment is offensive or what subtype of offensiveness applies. In this paper, we analyze and compare four attribution-based explanation methods for different offensive language classifiers: an interpretable machine learning model (naive Bayes), a model-agnostic explanation method (LIME), a model-based explanation method (LRP), and a self-explanatory model (LSTM with an attention mechanism). We evaluate these approaches with regard to their explanatory power and their ability to point out which words are most relevant for a classifier's decision. We find that the more complex models achieve better classification accuracy while also providing better explanations than the simpler models.

Keywords: neural networks, offensive language detection, explanation methods

1. The Need for Explanations

Online news platforms (e.g., New York Times), question answering platforms (e.g., Stack Overflow), collaborative projects (e.g., Wikipedia), and social networks (e.g., Facebook): all these social media platforms have one thing in common. They provide a discussion space for users, where content moderators are employed to keep a respectful tone, and foster fruitful discussions. Moderators ensure that the platform's discussion rules are adhered to, including the ban of offensive language. They enforce these rules by partially or entirely removing a user comment.

Typically, a platform's rules are listed in the form of guidelines, and they overlap considerably with the "netiquette", the basic rules about communication over the Internet. However, that does not mean all users have these rules in mind when they post comments. Moderators on online discussion platforms, therefore, explain why they intervene. For example, they replace a removed comment with the following text: "Removed. Please refrain from insults." or "Removed. Please refrain from insinuations and personal attacks.". In case they ultimately close a comment section, they post a final comment, for example, stating: "This comment section has been closed due to (racist) generalizations, baseless assumptions up to conspiracy theories and extreme polemics.". On the one hand, the idea behind these explanations is transparency. On the other hand, they aim to educate users to adhere to the discussion rules.

Research on comment classification focuses on supervised machine learning approaches and often uses black-box models. For example, there is research on detecting hate speech (Gao and Huang, 2017), racism/sexism (Waseem and Hovy, 2016) or offensive/aggressive/abusive language (Struß et al., 2019; Kumar et al., 2018). However, to support moderators, semi-automated comment moderation

in the form of a pre-classification of comments (Risch and Krestel, 2018) is not enough. Black-box models lack the ability to give explanations for their automated decisions. Therefore, they cannot be properly applied to comment moderation. Users and moderators are skeptical about an incomprehensible automation. Explanations help to build trust and increase the acceptance of machine-learned classifiers. Only then can a fair and transparent moderation process be ensured.

There are two more reasons for explanations in general. First, there are legal reasons to utilize machine-learned classifiers only if they can give explanations for their decisions. For example, under certain circumstances, the General Data Protection Regulation (GDPR) in the EU grants users the right to "obtain an explanation of the decision reached" if they are significantly affected by automated decision-making, e.g., if a credit application is refused.[1] A second reason is that explanations help to reveal the strengths and weaknesses of a model. They could also benefit the task of identifying a potential bias in a model's decisions. Researchers can then work on improving the models based on these insights.

Contributions The main contribution of this paper is the evaluation and comparison of attribution-based explanation methods for offensive language detection. To this end, we use a word deletion task to compare an interpretable machine learning model (naive Bayes), a model-agnostic explanation method (LIME), a model-based explanation method (LRP), and a self-explanatory model (LSTM with an attention mechanism). In a second experiment, we use the explanatory power index (EPI) as a metric to evaluate the approaches. Further, we take into account the classifi-

---

[1]https://eur-lex.europa.eu/eli/reg/2016/679/oj

cation accuracy of each approach and discuss strengths and weaknesses in the application context of automated content moderation. Based on this discussion, we give directions for future work.

Outline In the following, we summarize related work on explanation methods in Section 2 and describe which of these methods and what classifiers we implement for offensive language detection in Section 3. Section 4 evaluates the methods with the help of a word deletion task and the explanatory power index (EPI), while Section 5 discusses the results. We conclude with a summary of the contributions and an outlook on future work in Section 6.

2. Related Work

There is plenty of research on offensive language detection, and the classification accuracy for this task drastically increased in recent years — not least due to deep learning approaches for natural language processing. However, one aspect of this classification task has gone mostly unnoticed: the need for explaining classification results.

More precisely, research on explanation methods distinguishes explainability from interpretability. The former refers to locally comprehending individual decisions, while the latter refers to globally comprehending the decision function (Došilović et al., 2018; Monroe, 2018; Montavon et al., 2017). Unfortunately, there is no universal definition of these two terms. The definition used in this paper is:

- A decision function f is called explainable if the decision $f(x)$ for each single input $x \in X$ (in domain X) can be explained in understandable terms to humans.

- A decision function f is called interpretable if the whole function f (for the whole domain X) can be explained in understandable terms to humans.

In the field of image classification, CNN-based explanation methods are prominent. For example, DeConvNet (Zeiler and Fergus, 2014) inverts the convolutional operations to gain explanations and an approach by Simonyan et al. (2014) applies sensitivity analysis to achieve similar results. There have been several follow-up papers that compare these two approaches and propose combinations (Kindermans et al., 2018; Springenberg et al., 2015).

Explanation methods for text classification are rarely studied. For example, Nguyen (2018) compares human evaluation and automatic evaluation for explanation methods. The comparison uses the twenty newsgroups dataset and a dataset of movie reviews. To the best of our knowledge, the only publication on explanation methods in the field of offensive language detection is by Carton et al. (2018). The authors use an attention mechanism to generate explanations for the detection of personal attacks.

An empirical study by Chakrabarty et al. (2019) shows the importance of contextual or self-attention for abusive language detection. Whether attention weights can also be used as explanations is under discussion (Wiegreffe and Pinter, 2019; Jain and Wallace, 2019). In this paper, we consider a long short-term memory (LSTM) neural network (Hochreiter and Schmidhuber, 1997; Gers et al., 1999) with an attention mechanism (Yang et al., 2016) as an

example of a self-explanatory model. The inherent attention weights provide attribution-based explanations. Further, we consider a naive Bayes classifier, which is an example of an interpretable model. A classification result (and the entire model) can be understood with the help of the discrete conditional probabilities in the classifier. The relevance of a word w is the probability that the class c is predicted given w:

$$P(c|w) = \frac{P(c) \cdot P(w|c)}{P(w)}$$

The attention-based LSTM and the naive Bayes classifier are two a priori explainable models. We also consider two post-hoc explanation methods in our paper: layerwise relevance propagation (LRP) and local interpretable model-agnostic explanations (LIME). We describe these two methods in the following. The idea behind LRP (Bach et al., 2015) is to backpropagate the relevance scores from the output layer to the input layer of a neural network. To this end, the relevance of each input value (feature) is derived from the neuron activations in the output layer. This procedure makes LRP a *model-based* explanation method. The idea behind LIME (Ribeiro et al., 2016) is to use a local approximation of the classifier f at a point x and its neighborhood. This local approximation needs to be an interpretable classifier and a good approximation of f in the local neighborhood of point x. The authors evaluate their *model-agnostic* explanation method with text and image classification tasks.

3. Explanation Methods

For our comparative study, we implement a variety of classifiers for offensive language detection and suitable explanation methods. To train the classifiers, we use a dataset of toxic comments published by Google Jigsaw in the context of a Kaggle challenge.[2] The Python code for all classifiers, a web application to visualize the explanations, and the training and evaluation procedures are published online.[3]

3.1. Classifiers

There are four different classifiers that we implement and pair with different attribution-based explanation methods. First, there is a multinomial naive Bayes classifier, which serves as a baseline. It is interpretable by default and provides explanations in the form of conditional probabilities. Further, we implement a support vector machine (SVM) and a long short-term memory (LSTM) neural network. The input to the SVM is a TF-IDF vector representation of the unigrams in the comment text. GloVe word embeddings (Pennington et al., 2014) serve as the input to the neural network.

Both the SVM and the LSTM network are paired with the two explanation methods LRP and LIME. To this end, we adapt the LRP implementation by Arras et al.[4] and the

---

[2]https://www.kaggle.com/c/
jigsawtoxic-comment-classification-challenge
[3]https://hpi.de/naumann/projects/
repeatability/text-mining.html
[4]https://github.com/ArrasL/LRP_for_LSTM/

Table 1: Absolute and relative frequency of the six class labels in the training dataset and test dataset. The class distribution is highly imbalanced.

Class	Training Set		Test Set	
Toxic	19,235	9.56%	2,149	9.61%
Severe Toxic	1,757	0.87%	205	0.92%
Obscene	10,922	5.43%	1,218	5.45%
Threat	617	0.31%	72	0.32%
Insult	10,178	5.06%	1,126	5.04%
Identity Hate	1,906	0.95%	211	0.94%

LIME implementation by Ribeiro et al.[5]. To generate explanations for SVM and LSTM with the model-agnostic method LIME, we first sample perturbations of the input text by randomly deleting words. For each sample, we calculate the class probabilities with the SVM and the LSTM by applying a softmax function as the final calculation step. The default ridge regression algorithm is used to train an interpretable linear model. This model learns the word relevance scores bases on the classified samples.

Last but not least, we implement an LSTM network with an attention mechanism, which is an example of a self-explanatory model. It uses attention weights on the word level (not on the sentence level) and implements the architecture by Yang et al. (2016).

3.2. Dataset

The *toxic comments* dataset contains about 220,000 comments, each labeled with regard to six non-exclusive classes: *toxic, severe toxic, insult, threat, obscene,* and *identity hate.* Table 1 shows the class distribution in the training set and test set. Note that a comment is always labeled as toxic if one of the other labels applies. Even if none of the other labels apply, it can still be labeled as toxic.

3.3. Training Procedure

The GloVe word embeddings are trained from scratch on the training and test set. We restrict the input length of the basic LSTM network and the LSTM network with an attention mechanism to a maximum of 250 words. Further, we use 50 LSTM units, which means the output of this layer is 50-dimensional. The training of the networks runs for five, respectively, three epochs with the Adam optimizer until the validation loss increases.

The task on our dataset is a multi-label classification task. Our network architecture addresses this multi-label task by sharing the same LSTM layer across all class labels. However, for each label, an independent fully-connected layer follows after the output of the last LSTM unit. The attention mechanism is also trained for each label individually and fits in between the LSTM output and the following fully-connected layer.

SVM and naive Bayes use stemming to reduce the vocabulary size. They are trained according to a one-against-all scheme to conform to the multi-label classification task. The trained models therefore can be seen as six independent

[5]https://github.com/marcotcr/lime

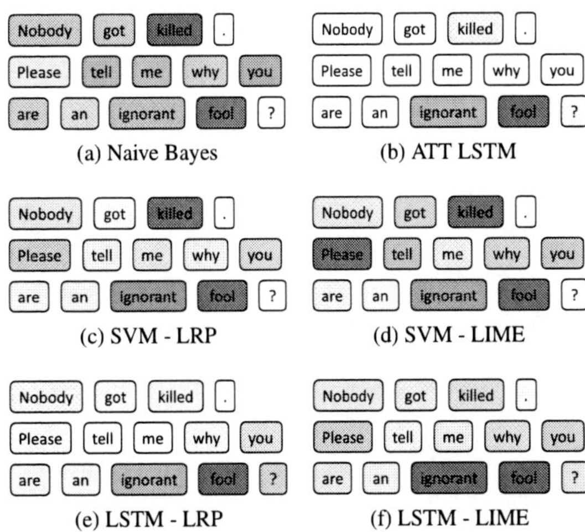

Figure 1: This heatmap visualizes positive (red) and negative (blue) word relevance scores generated by combinations of different classifiers and explanation methods.

binary naive Bayes classifiers, respectively, six independent binary SVMs. The SVM uses a linear kernel. There is only one hyperparameter to choose, which is the regularization term c. We set $C = 0.6$ and thereby relax the penalty for misclassifications.

3.4. Heatmap Visualization

To give an example of the explanations, Figure 1 and Figure 2 visualize the word relevance scores generated by the different explanation methods for two toxic comments. The conditional probabilities of the naive Bayes approach and the attention weights of the attention-based LSTM define positive word relevance scores between 0 and 1. In contrast to that, LIME and LRP define unbound relevance scores, which can also be negative. A negative word relevance score means that the respective word indicates the absence of a particular class rather than its presence. Because the attention weights are class-independent, these weights can only explain the predicted class. All other methods can also be used to explain a class that was not predicted by the classifier. This property can be used to analyze which words speak in favor of a not predicted class.

In Figure 1, the naive Bayes classifier marks the words *killed* and *fool* as most relevant for the decision to classify this comment as toxic. Similarly, the SVM classifier with LRP and LIME mark these two words. In contrast to that, the word *killed* is less relevant for the LSTM classifiers (with and without attention). Only the naive Bayes and the SVM classifiers use stemming but not the LSTM classifiers. The stemming collapses *killed* to *kill*. Therefore, our naive Bayes and SVM classifiers cannot distinguish the active form of the verb from other words with the same stem. In this particular context, the non-stemmed word is not toxic. The stemming misleads the classifiers to wrongly explain the toxicity of the comment with this word.

The attention mechanism highlights the words *ignorant* and *fool*. The word *killed* is marked as slightly relevant and all

139

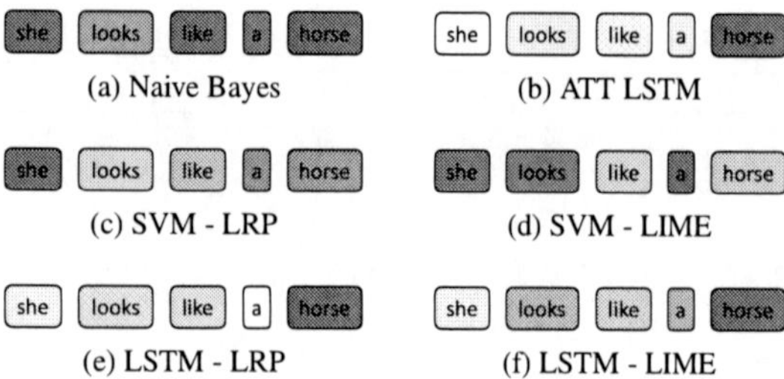

Figure 2: This heatmap visualizes positive (red) and negative (blue) word relevance scores generated by combinations of different classifiers and explanation methods.

other words as irrelevant. This explanation aligns with an explanation a human would give. In general, we find that the attention mechanism gives meaningful explanations for toxic comments. For non-toxic comments, however, its explanations can be misleading. The attention mechanism distributes a relevance score of one among the words — even if there is nothing toxic in the comment. To our surprise, the attention mechanism often marks punctuation as relevant in non-toxic comments.

The basic LSTM approach marks only a few words as relevant, and most words have relevance close to zero. These sparse explanations are suitable for our dataset, as there is typically a small set of toxic words, which explains the toxicity of the entire comment. In Figure 1c to 1f, LIME and LRP assign negative relevance scores to the word *Please*. This negative relevance score means that this word speaks against the toxicity of the comment.

The heatmaps in Figure 2 visualize the word relevance scores of another comment. Only the basic LSTM classifies this short comment correctly. It contains no swear words, but it is still offensive. The negatively connoted association of a person with an animal falls into the category of dehumanizing language. Without the full context, none of the single words explains the toxicity of the comment. Therefore, it is difficult to provide an attribution-based explanation.

4. Evaluation

The following evaluation is three-fold. First, we compare the different classification approaches (naive Bayes, SVM, LSTM, and LSTM with attention mechanism) with regard to their classification performance on the toxic comments dataset. Second, we pair the approaches with attribution-based explanation methods and evaluate the generated explanations based on a word deletion task. The third part of the evaluation uses the explanatory power index (EPI) by Arras et al. (2017).

4.1. Classification Performance

To evaluate the classification performance of the different classifiers, we use a multi-label classification task on the toxic comments dataset. Due to the imbalanced class distribution of this dataset, we refrain from using accuracy as the evaluation metric and instead use precision, recall, and F1-score. Table 2 lists the results on the test set and

Table 2: Precision (P), Recall (R) and F1-score of the classifiers on the toxic comments dataset (in percent). Bold font indicates best F1-score per class.

Class	Metric	NB	SVM	LSTM	ATT
Toxic	P	69.87	83.22	81.66	84.54
	R	63.89	65.98	68.36	69.74
	F1	66.75	73.60	74.42	**76.43**
Severe Toxic	P	14.45	52.11	56.96	58.33
	R	92.20	18.05	21.95	07.69
	F1	24.98	26.81	**31.69**	13.59
Obscene	P	51.89	85.64	81.09	86.15
	R	75.70	67.57	71.84	67.13
	F1	61.57	75.54	**76.19**	75.46
Threat	P	03.95	72.41	31.43	89.29
	R	59.72	29.17	15.28	35.21
	F1	07.41	41.58	20.56	**50.51**
Insult	P	48.41	78.43	72.67	77.64
	R	75.75	57.82	69.18	59.56
	F1	59.07	66.56	**70.88**	67.40
Identity Hate	P	11.72	64.47	55.36	65.77
	R	73.46	23.22	29.38	49.75
	F1	20.21	34.15	38.39	**56.64**

shows that the naive Bayes baseline is weakest, followed by the SVM approach. The basic LSTM network and the LSTM network with attention mechanism overall achieve similar F1-score with larger differences in the less populated classes *severe_toxic*, *threat*, and *identity_hate*. For the following evaluation of explanation methods, we consider a binary classification task based on the *toxic* class label only. All classifiers achieve their best performance for this most frequent label.

4.2. Word Deletion Task

We consider a word deletion task to evaluate whether explanation methods correctly identify which input words are most relevant for the classifier's output. It is based on an idea by Arras et al. (2017). The task evaluates whether the words that the explanation points out to be relevant for the classification indeed have a strong influence on it. Each explanation method, therefore, needs to calculate a relevance score for each input word. The word with the highest relevance is deleted, and it is checked whether the model's classification result changes with the perturbed input.

Given the set of true positives (toxic comments that are correctly identified as toxic), we use each explanation method to calculate word relevance scores for each comment. For each method, we then delete the most relevant words from each comment. If the word is indeed relevant for the classifier's decision, the classification most likely changes for the perturbed comment. Step-by-step, we delete more and more words with decreasing relevance scores. An explanation method is considered to provide good relevance scores if the classification changes for a large number of comments after deleting only a few words.

Figure 3 shows how the accuracy quickly drops as more and

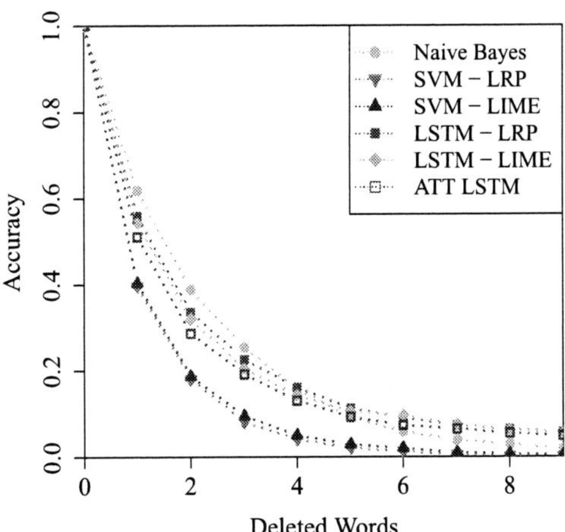

Figure 3: Correct classifications into the *toxic* class change to *non-toxic* if the most relevant input words are deleted. This result shows that the word relevance scores successfully mirror a word's influence on the classification result.

Table 3: Explanatory Power Index (EPI) for classifiers and explanation methods. Hyperparameter k denotes the number of nearest neighbors that maximizes the EPI.

Classifier	Explanation Method	EPI	k
Naive Bayes	Conditional Probability	82.29	3
SVM	TF-IDF	87.59	25
	LRP	93.38	19
	LIME	93.14	19
LSTM	GloVe	84.74	15
	LRP	**99.67**	3
	LIME	99.48	9
ATT LSTM	Attention Mechanism	92.04	11

more words are deleted. By deleting four words, more than 80% of the comments that were previously correctly classified as toxic (true positives) are classified as non-toxic. This result confirms that the classifiers detect those words that often constitute the toxicity of a comment (e.g., swear words).

Further, Figure 3 suggests that SVMs provide better explanations than LSTMs. This suggestion is misleading and reveals one limitation of the experiment. Each method starts with its own set of true positives. Therefore each line in the plot corresponds not only to a different explanation method but also to a slightly different dataset. While the overlap of the sets is relatively large, the LSTM network's set of true positives is slightly larger (almost a superset). It also contains some of the more difficult samples of toxic comments, which are correctly classified by the LSTM but misclassified by the naive Bayes approach. One idea to get rid of this problem is to use the intersection of all sets of true positives. The resulting comments are unanimously correctly classified. However, when we further explored this idea, we found that this set is rather small and, more importantly, it contains only the most simple comments — the comments that *all* classifiers detect correctly as toxic.

Still, for those comments that it classifies correctly, the SVM classifier definitely provides the best explanations according to the word deletion experiment. However, the true positives of the LSTM approach also contain comments whose toxicity can only be detected with context. A comment that contains a single swear word is easier to perturb to be classified as non-toxic than a comment that is toxic in its entirety.

4.3. Explanatory Power Index

Arras et al. (2017) propose a three-step approach to quantify the explanatory power of a text classifier with their explanatory power index (EPI). We follow this approach and first calculate one document summary vector per comment in the test set based on each combination of a classifier and an explanation method. The document summary vector is either calculated as a weighted average of the comment's GloVe word embeddings or as the comment's weighted TF-IDF vector representation. We compare a variety of approaches for weighting the words based on word relevance scores.

In the second step, we perform a k-nearest neighbor (kNN) classification on these document summary vectors based on each classifier's predictions. This step is repeated ten times on different random splits of the data and with different values of k. The classification accuracy of the KNN classifier is averaged for each k over the ten runs. The EPI is defined as the maximum achieved classification accuracy. We limit the dataset to all toxic comments and a random sample of non-toxic comments of the same size. This downsampling reduces the data to a balanced set of $4,300$ comments and allows to properly use accuracy as the evaluation metric. Intuitively speaking, the EPI mirrors how good the document summary vectors capture the semantic similarity of documents of the same class by clustering them closer to each other in the high-dimensional vector space.

Table 3 lists the EPI for the different classifiers paired with the respective explanation methods. The results show that weighting a document's bag-of-words vector representation with conditional probabilities from the naive Bayes baseline has the weakest explanatory power. Its performance is followed by the other two baselines: the SVM approach with TF-IDF weights and the basic LSTM approach with averaged GloVe vectors to obtain document summary vectors. The explanatory power of the basic LSTM classifier combined either with LIME or LRP is superior to all other methods. Although the LSTM with attention mechanism achieves slightly better classification results (F1-score of 76.4% vs. 74.4%), the attention weights are not as suited for explanations as word relevance scores generated with LIME or LRP for the basic LSTM network.

5. Discussion

LIME and LRP achieve similar results in our experiments. However, they strongly differ in their computational costs. The runtime to generate explanations with LIME is about 40 times higher than with LRP. This difference is because

LRP needs only one backpropagation run to propagate the relevance scores from the output layer to the input (word) layer. In contrast to that, LIME requires perturbing a large set of samples. These samples need to come from the local neighborhood of the comment to be explained. Fore example, they need to have many words in common. The more samples are used, the more stable are the explanations.

In the word deletion experiment, LIME has an unfair advantage over the other explainability methods due to the way it is trained. The perturbation in its training process is similar to the perturbation in the word deletion task. Therefore, LIME is tailored to this task.

A downside of the attention mechanism is that it cannot provide class-specific word relevance scores. Strictly speaking, the attention weights — and thus also the derived relevance scores — do not refer to the word level. The weights instead refer to the hidden states in the sequence of LSTM units. The attention mechanism explains which states are most relevant for the network's final output. The activation of a hidden state is the result of processing a subsequence of the input word sequence — regardless of the actual classification output (toxic/non-toxic). The heatmap visualizations in Figure 1b and Figure 2b show that the attention mechanism distributes the relevance only among a few words, more precisely, hidden states. One reason for that is that a single hidden state actually captures information gained from a sequence of input words.

A limitation of attribution-based explanations for offensive language detection seems to be a focus on words that are toxic regardless of the context. This limitation might render them inappropriate for the detection of implicit offensive language. The latter defines offensiveness that is not directly expressed but only arises from the context, uses irony or sarcasm, or can be inferred from metaphors, comparisons, or ascribed properties (Struß et al., 2019).

In the application scenario of content moderation on an online platform, a classifier that achieves slightly worse accuracy might be preferable if it provides explanations. The reason for this trade-off is not only the importance of transparency of the moderation process and acceptance by the user community. Explanations also facilitate the maintenance of a trained classification model. As the topics of online news articles and the corresponding user discussions change daily, adaptation is necessary — also adaptation of machine-learned models.

For example, on one day, an offensive comment might be removed from the platform. However, on the next day, the same comment might be the legitimate center of the discussion because it is a quotation by a well-known politician. In industry applications in general, explanations can support software developers and maintainers to understand machine-learned models and the associated software better.

6. Conclusions

Besides the need for automated offensive language detection, there is also a need for understanding these automated decisions. To this end, we studied explanation methods and compared four different approaches to make offensive language detection explainable: an interpretable machine learning algorithm (naive Bayes), a model-agnostic explanation method (LIME), a model-based explanation method (LRP), and a self-explanatory model (LSTM network with an attention mechanism).

In future work, we plan to generate explanations for users on online discussion platforms. The goal there is to make content moderation more comprehensible by using a fine-grained classifier (insult, threat, profanity, etc.) together with highlighting the most relevant input words as explanations. We also envision either selecting pre-defined text blocks or generating text as explanations and plan to compare these approaches to the explanations that a human moderator would provide. Last but not least, we are working on a journal article as an extended version of this paper (Risch et al., 2020).

7. Bibliographical References

Arras, L., Horn, F., Montavon, G., Müller, K.-R., and Samek, W. (2017). What is relevant in a text document?: An interpretable machine learning approach. *PLOS ONE*, 12(8):1–23.

Bach, S., Binder, A., Montavon, G., Klauschen, F., Müller, K.-R., and Samek, W. (2015). On pixel-wise explanations for non-linear classifier decisions by layer-wise relevance propagation. *PLOS ONE*, 10(7):1–46.

Carton, S., Mei, Q., and Resnick, P. (2018). Extractive adversarial networks: High-recall explanations for identifying personal attacks in social media posts. In *Proceedings of the Conference on Empirical Methods in Natural Language Processing (EMNLP)*, pages 3497–3507. ACL.

Chakrabarty, T., Gupta, K., and Muresan, S. (2019). Pay "attention" to your context when classifying abusive language. In *Proceedings of the Workshop on Abusive Language Online (ALW@ACL)*, pages 70–79. ACL.

Došilović, F. K., Brčić, M., and Hlupić, N. (2018). Explainable artificial intelligence: A survey. In *International Convention on Information and Communication Technology, Electronics and Microelectronics (MIPRO)*, pages 0210–0215. IEEE.

Gao, L. and Huang, R. (2017). Detecting online hate speech using context aware models. In *Proceedings of the International Conference on Recent Advances in Natural Language Processing (RANLP)*, pages 260–266. INCOMA Ltd.

Gers, F. A., Schmidhuber, J., and Cummins, F. (1999). Learning to forget: Continual prediction with LSTM. *Neural Computation*, 12:2451–2471.

Hochreiter, S. and Schmidhuber, J. (1997). Long short-term memory. *Neural Computation*, 9:1735–1780.

Jain, S. and Wallace, B. C. (2019). Attention is not Explanation. In *Proceedings of the Conference of the North American Chapter of the Association for Computational Linguistics (NAACL)*, pages 3543–3556. ACL.

Kindermans, P.-J., Schütt, K. T., Alber, M., Müller, K.-R., Erhan, D., Kim, B., and Dähne, S. (2018). Learning how to explain neural networks: PatternNet and PatternAttribution. In *Proceedings of the International Conference on Learning Representations (ICLR)*, pages 1–16.

Kumar, R., Reganti, A. N., Bhatia, A., and Maheshwari, T. (2018). Aggression-annotated Corpus of Hindi-

English Code-mixed Data. In *Proceedings of the International Conference on Language Resources and Evaluation (LREC)*. ELRA.

Monroe, D. (2018). AI, explain yourself. *Communications of the ACM*, 61(11):11–13.

Montavon, G., Lapuschkin, S., Binder, A., Samek, W., and Müller, K.-R. (2017). Explaining nonlinear classification decisions with deep taylor decomposition. *Pattern Recognition*, 65:211–222.

Nguyen, D. (2018). Comparing automatic and human evaluation of local explanations for text classification. In *Proceedings of the Conference of the North American Chapter of the Association for Computational Linguistics (NAACL)*, pages 1069–1078. ACL.

Pennington, J., Socher, R., and Manning, C. D. (2014). Glove: Global vectors for word representation. In *Empirical Methods in Natural Language Processing (EMNLP)*, pages 1532–1543.

Ribeiro, M. T., Singh, S., and Guestrin, C. (2016). ”why should I trust you?”: Explaining the predictions of any classifier. In *Proceedings of the International Conference on Knowledge Discovery and Data Mining (KDD)*, pages 1135–1144.

Risch, J. and Krestel, R. (2018). Delete or not delete? semi-automatic comment moderation for the newsroom. In *Proceedings of the Workshop on Trolling, Aggression and Cyberbullying (TRAC@COLING)*, pages 166–176.

Risch, J., Ruff, R., and Krestel, R. (2020). Explaining offensive language detection. *Journal for Language Technology and Computational Linguistics (JLCL)*, 34(1):1–19.

Simonyan, K., Vedaldi, A., and Zisserman, A. (2014). Deep Inside Convolutional Networks: Visualising Image Classification Models and Saliency Maps. In *Workshop Proceedings of the International Conference on Learning Representations (ICLR)*, pages 1–8.

Springenberg, J. T., Dosovitskiy, A., Brox, T., and Riedmiller, M. A. (2015). Striving for simplicity: The all convolutional net. In *Workshop Proceedings of the International Conference on Learning Representations (ICLR)*, pages 1–14.

Struß, J. M., Siegel, M., Ruppenhofer, J., Wiegand, M., and Klenner, M. (2019). Overview of germeval task 2, 2019 shared task on the identification of offensive language. In *Proceedings of the Conference on Natural Language Processing (KONVENS)*.

Waseem, Z. and Hovy, D. (2016). Hateful symbols or hateful people? predictive features for hate speech detection on twitter. In *Proceedings of the NAACL Student Research Workshop*, pages 88–93.

Wiegreffe, S. and Pinter, Y. (2019). Attention is not not explanation. In *Proceedings of the Conference on Empirical Methods in Natural Language Processing and the International Joint Conference on Natural Language Processing (EMNLP-IJCNLP)*, pages 11–20. ACL.

Yang, Z., Yang, D., Dyer, C., He, X., Smola, A., and Hovy, E. (2016). Hierarchical attention networks for document classification. In *Proceedings of the Conference of the North American Chapter of the Association for Computational Linguistics (NAACL)*, pages 1480–1489.

Zeiler, M. D. and Fergus, R. (2014). Visualizing and understanding convolutional networks. In *European Conference on Computer Vision (ECCV)*, pages 818–833. Springer.

Proceedings of the Second Workshop on Trolling, Aggression and Cyberbullying, pages 144–149
Language Resources and Evaluation Conference (LREC 2020), Marseille, 11–16 May 2020

Detecting Early Signs of Cyberbullying in Social Media

Niloofar Safi Samghabadi♠, A. Pastor López-Monroy♣, Thamar Solorio♠
♠Department of Computer Science, University of Houston, USA
♣Department of Computer Science, Mathematics Research Center (CIMAT), Mexico
nsafisamghabadi@uh.edu, pastor.lopez@cimat.mx, tsolorio@uh.edu

Abstract

Nowadays, the amount of users' activities on online social media is growing dramatically. These online environments provide excellent opportunities for communication and knowledge sharing. However, some people misuse them to harass and bully others online, a phenomenon called cyberbullying. Due to its harmful effects on people, especially youth, it is imperative to detect cyberbullying as early as possible before it causes irreparable damages to victims. Most of the relevant available resources are not explicitly designed to detect cyberbullying, but related content, such as hate speech and abusive language. In this paper, we propose a new approach to create a corpus suited for cyberbullying detection. We also investigate the possibility of designing a framework to monitor the streams of users' online messages and detects the signs of cyberbullying as early as possible.

Keywords: Cyberbullying Detection, Text Mining, Early Text Categorization

1. Introduction

In recent years, the internet has become the primary communication tool worldwide.[1] There are several social media platforms where people can share information and interact with each other in a virtually unlimited space. Although such platforms are beneficial for online users to develop their social skills and learn about new ideas and issues, they also put them under the risk of harassment, bullying, and cyber-attacks. Cyberbullying is defined as the use of information/communication technologies (ICT's) to harm others by sending or posting negative, harmful, false, or mean content to them *intentionally* and *repeatedly*. The most vulnerable groups targeted by this phenomenon are teens and pre-teens (Livingstone et al., 2010). Previous research shows that there is a statistically significant relationship between low self-esteem and experiences with cyberbullying (Patchin and Hinduja, 2010). Relevantly, cyberbullying victims have been reported to face various psychological and physical disorders that sometimes may lead them to harm themselves (Xu et al., 2012). Therefore, it is extremely important to detect cyberbullying incidents before they cause irreparable damages to the victims.

Several works have been done towards finding cyberbullying traces on social media by detecting online hateful and aggressive comments. Still, most of these efforts are focused on offline settings and only detect the event after it took place. Therefore, none of these methods can be used for prevention.

In this research, we aim to detect early signs of cyberbullying using *as few textual evidence as possible* by providing *timely* predictions. The main contributions of this work are listed as follows:

- A new methodology for creating a cyberbullying corpus and the first dataset suited for the task of early cyberbullying prediction.

- A new strategy to detect cyberbullying events as early as possible and the first evaluation framework that takes both the performance and the earliness of the predictions into account.

2. Related Research

Although there are several works on detecting different types of online aggression (Wulczyn et al., 2016; Nobata et al., 2016; Van Hee et al., 2018; Qian et al., 2018; Mishra et al., 2019a; Mishra et al., 2019b), only a few of them address cyberbullying detection. Dinakar et al. (2012) construct a common sense knowledge base - BullySpace - with knowledge about bullying situations and a wide range of common daily topics. Xu et al. (2012) study bullying traces and formulate cyberbullying detection as different Natural Language Processing (NLP) tasks. For instance, they use latent topic modeling to analyze the topics commonly discussed in bullying comments. Some previous works investigate cyberbullying on Instagram and Vine (Hosseinmardi et al., 2014; Hosseinmardi et al., 2015; Rafiq et al., 2018). For instance, Hosseinmardi et al. (2015) use a combination of textual, user-level, and image-related features to find cyberbullying incidents on Instagram media sessions. There are also a few studies that use time-related information to detect cyberbullying by using several different temporal features (Soni and Singh, 2018) and modeling the structure of a social media session with a hierarchical attention model (Cheng et al., 2019).

The main limitation of the previous systems is that they are built using an offline settings, and cannot detect cyberbullying in its early stages. Concerning this problem, early text categorization strategies could be a solution to model the dynamics of online conversations and provide timely predictions based on little evidence. Early text categorization is an emerging research topic which is being more popular, by reason of the specialized forums such as eRisk-CLEF.[2] eRisk started from 2017, and have emphasized topics such as detecting the early signs of depression (Losada et al.,

---

[1]http://www.gallup.com/poll/179288/
new-era-communication-americans.aspx

[2]https://erisk.irlab.org

Q: didn't you used to make yourself throw up or something? It obviously didn't work because you're still over weight	
A: you're ignorant.	
Q: I'm not trying to be!!!! you're just better off dead so go right ahead. Nobody's holding you back honey. We won't miss you.	
A: thanks for the clarification	
Q: glad I could help! Let me know when you're dead so I can spit on your grave!!! :-)	
A: ok	
Q: Fucking bulimic bitch	
A: yeah totally!!	
Q: tell your mom I said hi when you see her in hell!!! She's so proud of how you've turned out. Just kidding	
A: she's definitely in heaven. and she's my god mother. and I know she loves me	
Q: oh look here your best friend coming to the rescue how cute. She secretly thinks you're worthless too. Nobody actually cares! They just say they do. Oh silly Meaghan so naive. You need serious help. Maybe you should ask your pointer and middle fingers? They've seemed to help you this far	
A: please just stop.	

Table 1: Parts of a cyberbullying instance in our corpus.

2017a), anorexia (Losada et al., 2018; Losada et al., 2019), and self-harm (Losada et al., 2019) with monitoring the threads of online messages collected from Reddit.[3]

In this research, we investigate the possibility of employing the early text classification approach to tackle the problem of cyberbullying detection. We first introduce a new dataset suited for the task. Then, we conduct initial experiments to detect cyberbullying incidents as early as possible.

3. Data Collection

Abusive language detection can be considered as the initial step towards finding cyberbullying incidents. Cyberbullying happens when the victim receives several offensive messages repeatedly. Therefore, at least parts of the users' conversations should be monitored to detect such episodes. We collect our data from ask.fm.[4] This platform became the largest Q&A network in the world in 2017, reaching 215 million registered users. [5] ask.fm is a semi-anonymous social network that allows people to send comments/questions to any other user anonymously. This anonymity option provides the possibility for the attackers to freely harass users by sending lots of invective messages to their pages. Typically in ask.fm, the data consists of question-answer pairs in users' timeline.

Figure 1 shows the corpus creation scheme. We collect a large amount of ask.fm data, including the full history of question-answer pairs for 3K users. The question field includes a question/comment posted by the other users, and the answer field consists of the reply to that question/comment provided by the owner of the account. As we mentioned earlier, for finding the cyberbullying incidents,

we may look for the threads of messages that include high ratio of abusive comments. We use our previous system for abuse detection on ask.fm (Samghabadi et al., 2017). We utilize the ask.fm corpus proposed in the same work for training the model and label each row of our data automatically. To make the cyberbullying instances, we create a fixed-length sliding window and move it through the whole history of question-answer pairs per user. For each window sample, we calculate the ratio of offensive questions/comments that the user received inside the window. If it is greater than a pre-defined threshold, we consider the window as a *potential* cyberbullying event. Additionally, we check whether we can expand the potential negative window by adding more question-answer pairs to it, yet keeping the inside negativity rate greater than the defined threshold. This step is crucial to capture the whole cyberbullying episode. Finally, since automatic labeling is likely to be noisy, we asked two annotators to manually check the resulting windows to assure that they represent real cyberbullying incidents. A window is tagged as cyberbullying, where both annotators agree that it includes a cyberbullying incident. Figure 1 shows some parts of a cyberbullying instance in our corpus. We empirically fixed the minimum window size and negativity threshold to 20 and 40%, respectively (i.e., the potential cyberbullying windows include at least 20 question-answer pairs from a specific user's timeline, and at least 40% of questions are labeled as offensive).

For the non-cyberbullying instances, we apply the same method, but inversely. In this case, we look for the windows that have the negativity ratio less than the defined threshold. We create bins of various negativity ratios (e.g., 0%-5%, 5%-10%, etc.) and make sure to add a fair number of samples from each category to our data. As for the false-positive examples, we also add the window samples that are labeled as highly negative but are not annotated as cyberbullying after manual checking (e.g., when two users send negative comments toward each other in the third user's timeline)

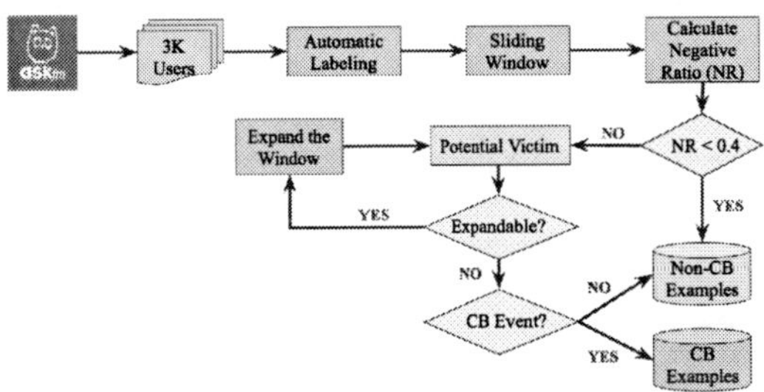

Figure 1: Overall process of building the new corpus.

Table 2 shows the distribution of the data in terms of the number of users in each class. Since *cyberbullying is a rare event*, we keep the ratio of positive to negative examples 1:10 to be closer to the real case scenarios. Finally, we divide all training and test examples to 10 different chunks to make the corpus suitable for early text classification. For every instance, each chunk contains 10% of all the question-answer pairs for that user.

---

[3] https://www.reddit.com

[4] https://ask.fm

[5] https://en.wikipedia.org/wiki/Ask.fm#2016\OT1\textendashpresent:_Purchased_by_Noosphere_and_new_cryptocurrency_plans

Class	training	test	Total
cyberbullying	19	8	27
non-cyberbullying	190	80	270
Total	209	88	297

Table 2: Statistics for our ask.fm data.

4. Methodology

Early text classification aims at developing a predictive model that is capable of determining the class that a document belongs to as early as possible, using partial information (Escalante et al., 2015). In this scenario, the instances (conversations) are read sequentially in chunks of texts that are fed into a classifier in an incremental fashion to obtain the prediction at chunk t. In our case, at every time t, we only have access to question-answer pairs in the first t chunks of test data to make the predictions. However, the training is done as usual (using all 10 chunks per instance). The intuition behind this scenario is to learn the overall pattern of a conversation and to investigate how helpful this pattern is to detect cyberbullying in the early stages of the conversation. This is the most standard framework for early prediction according to different forums such as eRisk (Losada et al., 2017a; Losada et al., 2019).

4.1. Feature Engineering

We use the following features to extract the information from the text:

Lexical: We use word n-grams (n = 1, 2, 3) and char n-grams (n = 3, 4, 5) as they are proven to be effective lexical representation for abuse and hate speech detection. For word n-gram features, we build a vocabulary that only considers top 10K features ordered by term frequency across the corpus. We weigh each term with its term frequency-inverse document frequency (TF-IDF).

Word Embeddings: The idea behind this approach is to map the words to a vector space model to improve lexical semantic modeling (Le and Mikolov, 2014). We use the pre-trained Google News word2vec model, including embeddings for about 3 million words. We create our feature vector by averaging the word embeddings of all the words in each post.

Style and Writing density (WR): This category extracts the stylistic properties of the text, and consists of the number of words, characters, all uppercase words, exclamations, question marks, as well as average word length, sentence length, and words per sentence.

LIWC (Linguistic Inquiry and Word Count): LIWC2007 (Pennebaker et al., 2007)) extracts different language dimensions like different emotions (e.g., sadness, anger, etc.), self-references, and casual words in each text. To create this feature set, we use a normalized count of words separated by any of the LIWC categories.

DeepMoji: The emojis are used to better understand the textual message by suggesting pictures that may help to represent it better. DeepMoji (Felbo et al., 2017) is a deep learning model that is pre-trained on a large set of Twitter data. Given an input text, this model provides an output representation for 64 frequently used online emojis. This representation shows how relevant each of those emojis is to the given input. We apply this pre-trained model on our data and extract the last hidden representation as the feature set for each post.

5. Experiments and Results

In the experiments, for each instance in our corpus, we have ten chunks, any of which includes 10% of question-answer pairs in that conversation. The first chunk contains the oldest 10% of the question-answer pairs, the second chunk consists of the second oldest 10%, and so forth.

5.1. Experimental Setup

In our chunk-by-chunk setting, we consider all questions and all answers within a chunk as the separate documents. Then, we extract the features from each document instead of a single post. The reason for separating questions and answers is that we believe these two categories of posts reflect two different views (i.e., commenters vs. account holder). We concatenate question-based and answer-based feature vectors to get a single representation for each instance. Then we feed these final representations to a linear SVM classifier. For each set of features, we tune the C parameter of the classifier with a grid search over values $\{0.1, 1, 2, 5, 10\}$.

5.2. Evaluation

For evaluating our early predictive model, we report the performance of the different methods using increasing amounts of textual evidence (chunk-by-chunk evaluation). More specifically, we evaluate the model in 10 consecutive iterations across the test set. In the first iteration, we generate a document representation starting with the first chunk, and then for each next iteration, we incrementally add one more chunk of data. The model makes predictions incrementally, as well. This chunk-by-chunk evaluation is a strategy that has been used to evaluate early classification models (Escalante et al., 2015; Errecalde et al., 2017; Losada et al., 2017b; Losada et al., 2018; López Monroy et al., 2018). As for the evaluation metric, we report F1-score for the cyberbullying class (the class of interest). We use this metric because the corpus is highly imbalanced towards the non-cyberbullying class.

5.3. Classification Results

Table 3 shows the classification results in terms of F1-score for the cyberbullying class. The results of WR and LIWC features are not included in the table due to the very low performance of the model using these features. Even combining these features with the other ones does not improve the performance. However, they seem to be helpful for the task of abusive language detection (Samghabadi et al., 2017). This contradiction indicates that in practice, there are some differences between the two tasks of abusive language and cyberbullying detection.

Based on the results, the best F1 measure is obtained from DeepMoji features using eight chunks of data. Even in earlier chunks, this method works significantly better than the other approaches. It shows that emoji-based representation for cyberbullying and non-cyberbullying instances are

Feature	ch1	ch2	ch3	ch4	ch5	ch6	ch7	ch8	ch9	ch10
Unigram	0.46	0.54	0.66	**0.76**	0.61	0.71	0.71	0.61	0.61	0.67
Bigram	0.00	0.20	0.00	0.20	0.36	0.36	**0.40**	0.40	0.22	0.40
Trigram	0.00	0.20	0.22	0.22	0.40	0.54	0.54	**0.61**	0.50	0.33
Char 3gram	0.40	0.22	0.40	0.40	**0.54**	0.36	0.40	0.54	0.54	0.54
Char 4gram	0.22	0.22	0.22	0.22	**0.40**	0.40	0.40	0.40	0.40	0.40
Char 5gram	0.00	0.22	0.22	0.22	0.22	**0.40**	0.40	0.40	0.40	0.40
Word2Vec	0.43	**0.59**	0.47	0.53	0.53	0.57	0.50	0.50	0.50	0.36
Unigram + Word2Vec	0.67	0.61	0.67	0.67	**0.71**	0.71	0.71	0.71	0.61	0.66
DeepMoji	0.73	0.78	0.75	0.80	0.88	0.82	0.82	**0.93**	0.75	0.77

Table 3: F1-score for the chunk-by-chunk evaluation for the positive class. The bold values show the best performance gained for each feature set.

likely to be entirely different. We further analyze this result in Section 5.4..

Taking into account that the average number of question-answer pairs in each chunk of the test data is 4, unigram+Word2Vec and DeepMoji features show very promising results in the earlier chunks (considering only a few question-answer pairs). Overall, it seems that adding more information to the test data decreases the performance of the system after a while (especially in the last two chunks). Even for the Word2Vec feature, we get the best performance using only the first two chunks of the data. The reason could be the distribution of the offensive messages in a cyberbullying episode. These events are usually started with a couple of questions/comments from the attacker(s), and as they go forward, one or more users get involved in the conversation as the victim's bystanders. Some of these users try to encourage the victim to stay strong, and some others start defending the victim by posting aggressive comments targeting the attacker(s). This information possibly confuses the classifier when it gets access to the later chunks. To sum up, Table 3 shows that we can successfully adapt the early text categorization approach to the cyberbullying detection task, where the system shows better performance using less evidence.

5.4. Analysis

Figure 2 illustrates the flow of emojis for a non-cyberbullying and a cyberbullying instance in our corpus. It helps us to understand better why DeepMoji representation helps detect early signs of cyberbullying. For making this figure, we choose 6 out of 64 emojis from the output of the DeepMoji model. We try to select an emoji set that covers various emotions (e.g., happiness, sadness, anger). Then, we plot the probability of each emoji to be related to the textual data we have available in each chunk.

Based on Figure 2a, in a non-cyberbullying thread, we have a mixture of the emojis (i.e., overall, no emoji is dominant). But in a cyberbullying one (Figure 2b), negative emojis like ● and ☁ are almost dominant, specifically in the first few chunks. It is interesting to see that laughing face (😄) is also showing a higher probability in this case. So, we can conclude that probably in this instance, the attacker(s) makes fun of the victim.

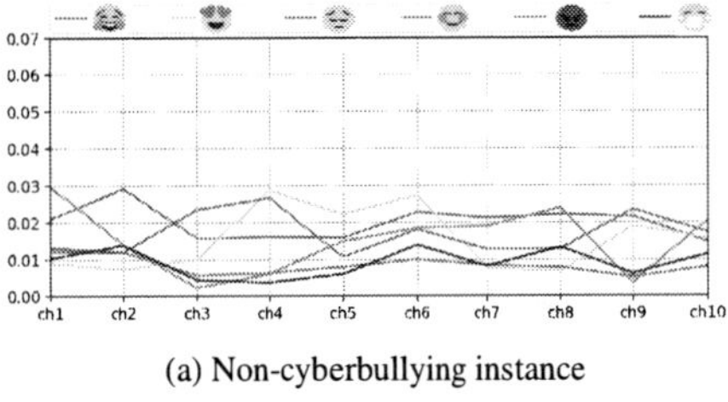

(a) Non-cyberbullying instance

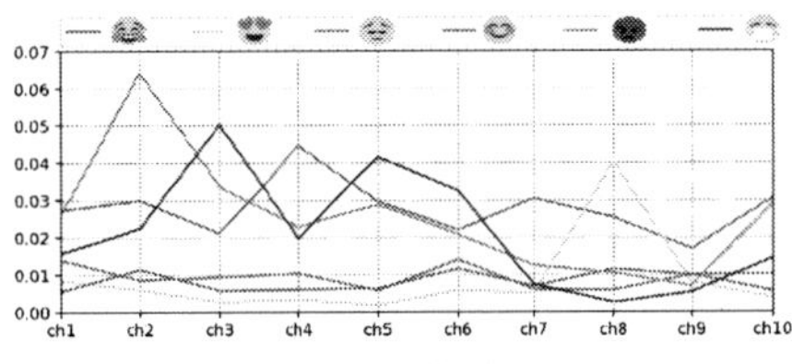

(b) Cyberbullying instance

Figure 2: Flow of Emojis.

6. Conclusion

In this paper, we present a new approach to create a linguistic resource for detecting the early signs of cyberbullying. We start by automatically labeling all rows of data. Then, we move a sliding window through the history of each user's interactions to find the potential cyberbullying cases based on the ratio of received abusive messages. Finally, each of these possible cyberbullying instances is annotated manually to make sure that it includes a cyberbullying incident. We follow the same process to label the non-cyberbullying class. Furthermore, we use a simple set of lexical, semantic, and stylistic features to train an SVM classifier for cyberbullying detection. This system is evaluated over the different chunks of test data iteratively. The final results demonstrate that early text classification scenarios can be successfully adapted to detect cyberbullying at the early stages.

For future work, we plan to enrich our ask.fm corpus by collecting more users. Also, instead of chunk-by-chunk evaluation, we plan to examine the post-by-post evaluation that is closer to the real case scenario. Our ultimate goal is to design a sequential decision-making module, which can provide accurate and timely predictions on whether to label a conversation as cyberbullying based on the current information, or wait for more evidence.

7. Bibliographical References

Cheng, L., Guo, R., Silva, Y., Hall, D., and Liu, H. (2019). Hierarchical attention networks for cyberbullying detection on the instagram social network. In *Proceedings of the 2019 SIAM International Conference on Data Mining*, pages 235–243. SIAM.

Dinakar, K., Jones, B., Havasi, C., Lieberman, H., and Picard, R. (2012). Common sense reasoning for detection, prevention, and mitigation of cyberbullying. *ACM Transactions on Interactive Intelligent Systems (TiiS)*, 2(3):18.

Errecalde, M. L., Villegas, M. P., Funez, D. G., Ucelay, M. J. G., and Cagnina, L. C. (2017). Temporal variation of terms as concept space for early risk prediction.

Escalante, H. J., Montes-y Gómez, M., Villaseñor-Pineda, L., and Errecalde, M. L. (2015). Early text classification: a naïve solution. *arXiv preprint arXiv:1509.06053*.

Felbo, B., Mislove, A., Søgaard, A., Rahwan, I., and Lehmann, S. (2017). Using millions of emoji occurrences to learn any-domain representations for detecting sentiment, emotion and sarcasm. In *2017 Conference on Empirical Methods in Natural Language Processing-Conference on Empirical Methods in Natural Language Processing*. Association for Computational Linguistics.

Hosseinmardi, H., Ghasemianlangroodi, A., Han, R., Lv, Q., and Mishra, S. (2014). Analyzing negative user behavior in a semi-anonymous social network. *CoRR abs*, 1404.

Hosseinmardi, H., Mattson, S. A., Rafiq, R. I., Han, R., Lv, Q., and Mishra, S. (2015). Detection of cyberbullying incidents on the instagram social network. *arXiv preprint arXiv:1503.03909*.

Le, Q. V. and Mikolov, T. (2014). Distributed representations of sentences and documents. In *ICML*, volume 14, pages 1188–1196.

Livingstone, S., Haddon, L., Görzig, A., and Ólafsson, K. (2010). Risks and safety on the internet. *The Perspective of European Children. Final Findings from the EU Kids Online Survey of*, pages 9–16.

López Monroy, A. P., González, F. A., Montes, M., Escalante, H. J., and Solorio, T. (2018). Early text classification using multi-resolution concept representations. In *Proceedings of the 2018 Conference of the North American Chapter of the Association for Computational Linguistics: Human Language Technologies, NAACL-HLT-2018, Volume 1 (Long Papers)*, pages 1216–1225. Association for Computational Linguistics.

Losada, D. E., Crestani, F., and Parapar, J. (2017a). Clef 2017 erisk overview: Early risk prediction on the internet: Experimental foundations. In *CLEF (Working Notes)*.

Losada, D. E., Crestani, F., and Parapar, J. (2017b). erisk 2017: Clef lab on early risk prediction on the internet: Experimental foundations. In *International Conference of the Cross-Language Evaluation Forum for European Languages*, pages 346–360. Springer.

Losada, D. E., Crestani, F., and Parapar, J. (2018). Overview of erisk 2018: Early risk prediction on the internet (extended lab overview). In *Proceedings of the 9th International Conference of the CLEF Association, CLEF*.

Losada, D. E., Crestani, F., and Parapar, J. (2019). Overview of erisk 2019 early risk prediction on the internet. In *International Conference of the Cross-Language Evaluation Forum for European Languages*, pages 340–357. Springer.

Mishra, P., Del Tredici, M., Yannakoudakis, H., and Shutova, E. (2019a). Abusive language detection with graph convolutional networks. *arXiv preprint arXiv:1904.04073*.

Mishra, P., Del Tredici, M., Yannakoudakis, H., and Shutova, E. (2019b). Author profiling for hate speech detection. *arXiv preprint arXiv:1902.06734*.

Nobata, C., Tetreault, J., Thomas, A., Mehdad, Y., and Chang, Y. (2016). Abusive language detection in online user content. In *Proceedings of the 25th International Conference on World Wide Web*, WWW '16, pages 145–153, Republic and Canton of Geneva, Switzerland. International World Wide Web Conferences Steering Committee.

Patchin, J. W. and Hinduja, S. (2010). Cyberbullying and self-esteem. *Journal of School Health*, 80(12):614–621.

Pennebaker, J. W., Booth, R. J., and Francis, M. E. (2007). Liwc2007: Linguistic inquiry and word count. *Austin, Texas: liwc.net*.

Qian, J., ElSherief, M., Belding, E., and Wang, W. Y. (2018). Leveraging intra-user and inter-user representation learning for automated hate speech detection. In *Proceedings of the 2018 Conference of the North American Chapter of the Association for Computational Linguistics: Human Language Technologies, Volume 2 (Short Papers)*, pages 118–123, New Orleans, Louisiana, June. Association for Computational Linguistics.

Rafiq, R. I., Hosseinmardi, H., Han, R., Lv, Q., and Mishra, S. (2018). Scalable and timely detection of cyberbullying in online social networks. In *Proceedings of the 33rd Annual ACM Symposium on Applied Computing*, pages 1738–1747. ACM.

Samghabadi, N. S., Maharjan, S., Sprague, A., Diaz-Sprague, R., and Solorio, T. (2017). Detecting nastiness in social media. In *Proceedings of the First Workshop on Abusive Language Online*, pages 63–72.

Soni, D. and Singh, V. (2018). Time reveals all wounds: Modeling temporal characteristics of cyberbullying. In *Twelfth International AAAI Conference on Web and Social Media*.

Van Hee, C., Jacobs, G., Emmery, C., Desmet, B., Lefever, E., Verhoeven, B., De Pauw, G., Daelemans, W., and Hoste, V. (2018). Automatic detection of cyberbullying in social media text. *PloS one*, 13(10).

Wulczyn, E., Thain, N., and Dixon, L. (2016). Ex machina: Personal attacks seen at scale. *CoRR*, abs/1610.08914.

Xu, J.-M., Jun, K.-S., Zhu, X., and Bellmore, A. (2012). Learning from bullying traces in social media. In *Proceedings of the 2012 Conference of the North American Chapter of the Association for Computational Linguistics: Human Language Technologies*, NAACL HLT '12,

pages 656–666, Stroudsburg, PA, USA. Association for
Computational Linguistics.

Lexicon-Enhancement of Embedding-based Approaches
Towards the Detection of Abusive Language

Anna Koufakou, Jason Scott
Florida Gulf Coast University
Fort Myers, Florida, USA
akoufakou@fgcu.edu

Abstract

Detecting abusive language is a significant research topic, which has received a lot of attention recently. Our work focuses on detecting personal attacks in online conversations. As previous research on this task has largely used deep learning based on embeddings, we explore the use of lexicons to enhance embedding-based methods in an effort to see how these methods apply in the particular task of detecting personal attacks. The methods implemented and experimented with in this paper are quite different from each other, not only in the type of lexicons they use (sentiment or semantic), but also in the way they use the knowledge from the lexicons, in order to construct or to change embeddings that are ultimately fed into the learning model. The sentiment lexicon approaches focus on integrating sentiment information (in the form of sentiment embeddings) into the learning model. The semantic lexicon approaches focus on transforming the original word embeddings so that they better represent relationships extracted from a semantic lexicon. Based on our experimental results, semantic lexicon methods are superior to the rest of the methods in this paper, with at least 4% macro-averaged F1 improvement over the baseline.

Keywords: Abusive Language Online, Personal Attacks, Embeddings, Lexicons

1.   Introduction

The pervasiveness of social media and the increase in online interactions in recent years has also led to a surge of online abusive behavior, which can be exhibited in different forms: toxic comments, aggression, hate speech, trolling, cyberbullying, etc. Online abuse influences individuals and communities in many ways, from leading users to quit a particular online site, to move away from their home, or to even commit suicide. Governments as well as social media platforms are under pressure to detect and remove abusive posts and users. On the other hand, online communities thrive on free speech and would be damaged by flagging and removing innocent users. Many efforts have been made for these tasks, including automated systems as well as employing human moderators.

At a first glance, NLP models can learn linguistic patterns in conversations and detect offensive speech using features such as swear words or racial/sexist slurs. This becomes a difficult research problem as online conversational text contains casual language, abbreviations, misspellings, slang, etc. Additionally, there are gray areas which make it hard to determine if a comment is actually offensive or abusive.

Methods employing word or character embeddings have been used successfully in many NLP tasks such as sentiment analysis or classification. A great part of the current research in the field of abuse detection in online conversations is based on deep learning with embeddings; for example, see (Gamback and Sikdar, 2017; Pavlopoulos et al., 2017; Gunasekara and Nejadgholi, 2018; Mishra et al., 2018; Zhang et al., 2018) among others.

In this study, we explore different ways of using lexicons to enhance deep learning methods that use embeddings and how they apply to the task of detecting abusive language. Specifically, we apply Convolutional Neural Networks to automatically identify comments which contain personal attacks (Wulczyn et al., 2017). Our research follows two very different ways in the literature to employ lexicons.

First, we look at the use of sentiment lexicons, a form of sentiment dictionary associating words with sentiments. We choose to follow the work by (Shin et al., 2017) which uses sentiment lexicon-based embeddings alongside word embeddings and integrates them in its convolutional model in different ways. Second, we explore semantic lexicons, which contain semantic relationships between words (for example, synonyms or antonyms). These methods essentially transform the word embeddings themselves so that they better reflect the semantic relationships of the words, based on the semantic lexicon. To the best of our knowledge, none of these ideas or the specific methods we use in this paper have been applied towards the detection of abusive language or related tasks. Our experiments show that the semantic lexicon based methods outperform the baseline CNN, while the sentiment lexicon methods perform the same or lower than the baseline. Additionally, the semantic lexicon methods offer an efficient and flexible approach to enhance embeddings (as also discussed in Vulić et al., 2018).

The following sections give an overview of related work, describe our corpus and the different approaches implemented and applied in this paper, and present our experimentation and results, followed by concluding remarks.

2.   Related Work

Related work has focused on many tasks in the field of abuse detection, for example, detecting hate speech (e.g., Saleem et al., 2017), abuse (e.g., Waseem et al., 2017), gender- or ethnic-based abuse (e.g., Basile et al., 2019), and aggression (e.g., Kumar et al., 2018), among others.

There has been much work in literature with the Wikipedia Toxicity corpora used in our paper (see Section 3). The creators of these corpora, Wulczyn et al. (2017), explored character as well as n-gram based models with logistic regression and multi-layer perceptron models.

Gunasekara et al. (2018) used a related dataset from a Kaggle challenge[1] targeting a multi-label classification task. Some papers (e.g. Brassard-Gourdeau et al., 2019) focused on the Toxicity corpus, not the Personal Attacks corpus, which we use. Similarly to our work, Brassard-Gourdeau et al. (2019) utilized sentiment lexicons. They used the sum of the sentiment score of each word in the comment, which is quite different from the sentiment lexicon approaches we employed in this paper.

Recent research, such as (Pavlopoulos et al., 2017; Mishra et al., 2018; Kumar et al., 2019; Bodapati et al., 2019), included experimental results with the Personal Attacks corpus. Pavlopoulos et al. (2017) used a Recursive Neural Network (RNN) along with an attention mechanism. Mishra et al. (2018) built on the previous work by using character n-grams; their best algorithm achieved an F1 macro of 87.44 on the Personal Attacks data. Bodapati et al. (2019) compared different methods such as fasttext, CNN, and BERT using various combinations of word, character, and subword units and reported that they achieved state-of-the-art F1 macro (89.5) on the Personal Attacks data with BERT fine tuning. These papers either followed different preprocessing (for example, removed stop words or used bigrams) or a different experimentation setup (for example, artificially balanced the dataset or used a different split on the data), etc. Therefore, we cannot directly compare their results with ours. Ultimately, the goal of our paper is to explore the impact of using sentiment and semantic lexicons to enhance embedding-based methods, achieved by comparing these methods with our CNN baseline (see Section 4).

To the best of our knowledge, none of the sentiment or semantic lexicon ideas in this work have been applied towards abuse detection. Note that an early draft of this work with preliminary results was shown in (Koufakou and Scott, 2019). In the current paper, we present additional algorithms, extensive experimentation and results, and an in-depth examination of the results and our observations.

Beyond abusive language detection, one of the semantic lexicon approaches we used, retrofitting (Faruqui et al., 2015), has been successfully applied to the classification of pathology reports by (Alawad et al., 2018).

3. Corpus

For this paper, we focus on data released from the Wikipedia Detox Project[2] (Wulczyn et al., 2017). We obtain the data from figshare[3]. The three corpora included in the release are Personal Attacks, Aggression, and Toxicity; we focus on the Personal Attacks corpus. This contains more than a 100k comments from English Wikipedia labeled by approximately 10 annotators via Crowdflower on whether or not it contained a personal attack. The data also contains additional fields, such as the type of attack; we use only the comment text and whether it contained an attack or not (label).

First, we apply basic preprocessing to the comment text, for example: force lowercase, remove multiple periods or spaces, but keep the main punctuation. We do not remove stop words or fix spelling errors. We then extract single tokens (unigrams). Finally, we remove any records that ended up empty after the preprocessing. The resulting dataset contains a total of 115,841 text comments, each with annotations by about 10 human workers which indicated whether or not each worker believed the comment contained a personal attack. A comment in our data is labeled as an attack if at least 5 annotators labeled it as an attack. As a result, the dataset has the record and label characteristics shown in Table 1.

4. Approaches

In this section, we describe our baseline model, the sentiment lexicon approaches, and the semantic lexicon approaches. Figure 1 displays diagrams for the two different approaches explored in this paper.

4.1 Baseline

As our baseline, we employ a convolutional neural network (CNN) (Kim, 2014). This choice was made to follow (Shin et al., 2017) discussed in the next section. Additionally, in early experiments, our CNN did better on our data than other models we tried (e.g. RNN or GRU).

We first extract words from our corpus (as described in Section 3) and then create a word embedding matrix, which is the input to the model (see Section 5.1 for the embeddings we use in our experiments).

Word embeddings are first passed through an embedding layer, kept static in our experiments, before being fed as input into the convolutional layers. The window sizes of the convolutional filters are 3, 4, and 5: using multiple filters enables us to extract multiple features. We use Rectified Linear Unit (ReLU) as the activation function.

The feature maps generated by the convolutions are passed through a max pooling layer, which gives the maximum value from each feature map. The results are concatenated and passed to a soft-max fully connected layer to produce the classification.

4.2 Sentiment Lexicon Approaches

Sentiment lexicons generally associate each term in the lexicon with a positive or negative score. A term in the lexicon might be associated with a positive or negative label or it might be given an emotion (e.g. angry or happy) or it might have a continuous sentiment score.

For this section, we experiment with techniques from the paper by Shin et al. (2017). Figure 1(a) shows an overview of the sentiment lexicon approaches. These ideas involve creating sentiment embeddings from sentiment lexicons and then integrating the sentiment embeddings to the model (CNN) in different ways. For each word w in the corpus, we search for w in each sentiment lexicon; then, we construct a sentiment lexicon embedding by concatenating all the lexicon values corresponding to w.

Attack	14,205	12.3%
Not Attack	101,636	87.7%
Total	115,841	100.0%

Table 1: The resulting Personal Attack dataset

---

[1] https://www.kaggle.com/c/jigsaw-toxic-comment-classification-challenge
[2] https://meta.wikimedia.org/wiki/Research:Detox/Data_Release
[3] https://figshare.com/projects/Wikipedia_Talk/16731

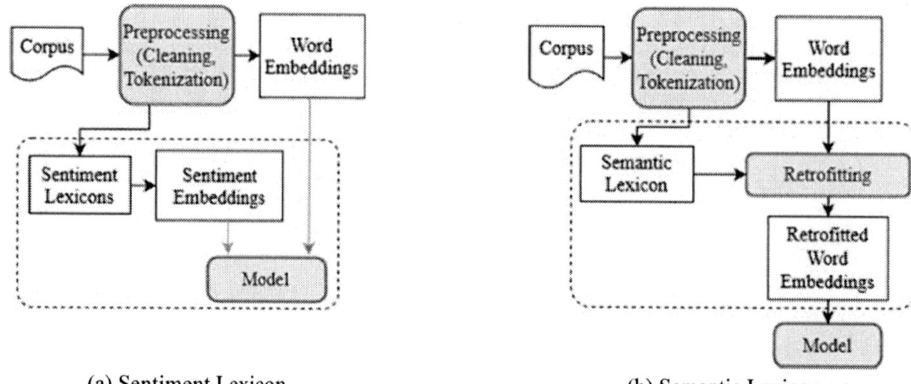

(a) Sentiment Lexicon   (b) Semantic Lexicon

Figure 1. Block diagrams of the sentiment lexicon approaches versus the semantic lexicon approaches. The dashed-line rectangle indicates difference from the baseline. Grayed out lines for (a) indicate that the embeddings are used in different ways by the model (e.g., embeddings are concatenated or they pass through separate convolutions)

If w is not found in a lexicon, the value for that lexicon in the resulting embedding is 0. The lexicon embedding is a vector of dimensionality l, where l is the total number of sentiment lexicons. Finally, the word and sentiment lexicon embeddings are used by the model in different ways, described next.

The three approaches with sentiment lexicons based on (Shin et al., 2017) are briefly introduced below – the reader is referred to the original paper for more details:

Naive Concatenation (NC): This approach does not require any changes to the baseline model, as all of the modifications are on the embedding preparation stage. As described earlier, we extract sentiment lexicon entries for each word in our corpus. The entry from each lexicon is appended to the word embedding as an additional dimension before being fed into the embedding input layer. If l is the sentiment lexicon embedding dimensionality and m is the word embedding dimensionality, the resulting embedding for this approach is an $(l+m)$-dimensional combined embedding (word + sentiment).

Separate Convolution (SC): This approach does change the network from the baseline by adding a second input layer, and a second, parallel set of convolutional layers for the lexicon embeddings. The network has two inputs: one for the word embeddings and one for the lexicon embeddings, while the data input to each is, as before, the encoded text comments. The matrix of word embeddings and matrix of lexicon information each separately pass through convolutional layers, then are concatenated before continuing through the softmax layer of the network, as before.

Embedding Attention Vector (EAV): This approach utilizes the idea of attention. First, an attention matrix is constructed by performing multiple convolutions on the document matrix. Then, the attention vector is created by performing max pooling on each row of the attention matrix. The Embedding Attention Vector (EAV) is created by multiplying the transposed document matrix to the attention vector. EAVs are created for word and for lexicon embeddings. Finally, the resulting EAVs are appended to the penultimate layer of the network to serve as additional information for the softmax layer.

4.3   Semantic Lexicon Approaches

Semantic lexicons contain semantic relationships among the terms in the lexicon, for example synonyms. The main idea behind semantic lexicon-enhanced embeddings is that embeddings of words that are linked in the semantic lexicon should have similar vector representations (Faruqui et al., 2015).

The techniques presented in this section are quite different from the sentiment-lexicon approaches in the previous section: the techniques in this section use semantic knowledge to enhance (or transform) the word embeddings themselves rather than use the lexicon information in the learning process.

The block diagram in Figure 1(b) illustrates the semantic lexicon methods. The figure only refers to the first method in this section (retrofitting) for simplicity: any of the other methods can substitute it in the diagram. As shown in the diagram, the word embeddings pass through a retrofitting algorithm, resulting in the transformed embeddings (Retrofitted Word Embeddings) that are then fed into the model. These methods do not change the model itself, only the embeddings.

The three semantic lexicon approaches employed in this paper are briefly introduced below – the reader is referred to the original papers for more details:

Retrofitting: The first method in this section focuses on enhancing the word embeddings by "retrofitting" them to a semantic lexicon, as proposed by Faruqui et al. (2015). This method extracts synonym relationships from a semantic lexicon and "retrofits" the word embeddings based on belief propagation so that the vectors for synonym words are closer together in the vector space.

ATTRACT-REPEL (AR): While the Retrofitted embeddings focus on synonym relationships, more recent methods explore antonyms as well. The second method we explore is ATTRACT-REPEL (AR) proposed by Mrkšić et al. (2017). The key idea of this work is a process to fine tune pre-trained word embeddings also based on semantic constraints extracted from semantic lexicons. Given the initial vector space and collections of ATTRACT (synonym) and REPEL (antonym) constraints, the model gradually modifies the

152

space to bring the designated word vectors closer together (synonyms) or further apart (antonyms).

Post-Specialized: Another issue for the semantic lexicon approaches is that semantic lexicons cover a small portion of the words in the corpus. This means that part of the word vectors resulting from retrofitting or AR (see above) are unchanged compared to the original word vectors, as a fraction of the words in the vocabulary are not found in the semantic lexicon.

This was addressed by the third method we explore, called Post-Specialized Word Embeddings, proposed by Vulić et al. (2018). This method extends the fine-tuning or specialization of embeddings to words not found in the external semantic lexicons. Essentially, it learns a mapping function based on the transformation of the "seen" words (e.g., the transformation from the original vectors into the AR vectors) and then applies this mapping to the vector space of the "unseen" words. The mapping is implemented as a deep feed-forward NN with non-linear activations.

5. Experiments

5.1 Experimental Setup

For our implementation, we use TensorFlow executed on Google Cloud TPUs on the TensorFlow Research Cloud[4], using a free trial of Cloud TPUs. We evaluate the network after 10,000 TPU steps of training with a randomly shuffled and batched training dataset, a learning rate of 0.001, dropout of 0.5, Adam optimizer, and 90-10 training-test split.

For the sentiment lexicon approaches (see section 4.2), we use the code provided online by Shin[5], though we had to make several modifications to adapt it to TPU-based code, handle old versions issues, etc.

For the semantic lexicon approaches (see section 4.3), we first construct our word embeddings as described in the next section. Then, we run the code provided by the authors of the corresponding papers[6] (with the parameters and lexical constraints/lexicons they provide) in order to "retrofit" or "specialize" our word embeddings as applicable. Finally, we use the resulting embeddings as input into the model.

5.2 Embeddings

We first pre-process the data, tokenize and generate word embeddings (see section 3 for our preprocessing and tokenization). Since the comments vary in length, we set the max document length to 400. Early on, we experimented with various types of embeddings (fasttext, pre-trained, etc.) and we saw that we obtain good results using gensim word2vec[7] on all tokenized sentences of our corpus (minimum word occurrences and iterations is set to 5). For all of our experiments, we use dimensionality of 200 or 300 (also used in the original papers) and report the best result.

Lexicon	Type	Coverage
AFINN-96	Sentiment	3.3%
NRC	Sentiment	11.1%
MSOL-June15-09	Sentiment	38.8%
Bing-Liu	Sentiment	10.2%
PPDB-XL	Semantic	67.5%

Table 2: The coverage for the vocabulary in our corpus by each lexicon we use

Specifically for the Post-Specialized method (Vulić et al., 2018), we are unable to run the code using our own word embeddings (trained on our corpus, as described above), so we utilize the SGNS-BOW2 embeddings as provided with the post-specialization code[6] (Skip-Gram Negative Sampling, pre-trained on the Polyglot Wikipedia, 300-d). We see that this set of vectors covers about 90% of our vocabulary.

5.3 Lexicons

In this paper, we utilize the following sentiment lexicons for the sentiment lexicon methods (see section 4.2):

- **AFINN-96[8]:** The AFINN-96 sentiment lexicon (Nielsen, 2011) contains 3,382 words rated between -5 (most negative) and 5 (most positive).
- **NRC[9]:** The National Research Council Emotion Lexicon (Mohammad et al., 2013), commonly referred to as NRC EmoLex, contains 14,182 words labeled with eight emotions (anger, fear, etc.) and sentiment polarity (negative or positive).
- **MSOL-June15-09[10]:** The Macquarie Semantic Orientation Lexicon, or MSOL, contains a total of 76,400 entries either labeled as positive or negative (Mohammad, et al., 2009). It has 51,208 single-word entries.
- **Bing-Liu[11]:** The Bing-Liu Opinion contains 6,789 positive or negative words. The list was originally compiled as part of a study on mining and summarizing customer reviews but subsequently grew into a larger lexicon (Hu and Liu, 2004).

The sentiment lexicons above are preprocessed into lexicon embeddings using python code we wrote. Each lexicon is reduced to a key-value pairing of a word or phrase with its polarity value, which is -1 for negative polarity, 1 for positive polarity, or 0 for neutral. As described in section 4.2, every matching entry between our vocabulary and each sentiment lexicon is used to build the sentiment lexicon embeddings, following the work in the original paper by (Shin et al., 2017).

For retrofitting (Faruqui et al., 2015), we utilize the PPDB-XL[12] lexicon, as it was shown to have superior performance in the original paper and it had the best performance in our early trials. This lexicon is based on the paraphrase database (Ganitkevitch et al., 2013) with more than 220 million

---

[4] https://www.tensorflow.org/tfrc

[5] https://github.com/emorynlp/doc-classify

[6] https://github.com/mfaruqui/
https://github.com/nmrksic/attract-repel
https://github.com/cambridgeltl/post-specialisation

[7] https://radimrehurek.com/gensim/models/word2vec.html

[8] https://github.com/fnielsen/afinn

[9] http://saifmohammad.com/WebPages/lexicons.html

[10] https://www.saifmohammad.com/Lexicons

[11] http://www.cs.uic.edu/~liub/FBS/opinion-lexicon-English.rar

[12] http://paraphrase.org/#/download

paraphrase pairs of English; of these, 8 million are lexical (single word to single word) paraphrases. For the rest of the semantic lexicon approaches (AR and Post-Specialized, see section 4.3), we use the lexical constraints as they are provided with the code of the respective paper.

We also provide the coverage of the vocabulary in our corpus by each lexicon we use (see Table 2). From the table, the coverage by the semantic lexicon is good, while for any sentiment lexicons, the word coverage is low. It is important to note that the sentiment lexicon percentages are similar to percentages in original paper for the related algorithms by (Shin et al., 2017).

5.4 Experimental Results and Discussion

Table 3 shows our results for the sentiment lexicon methods (see section 4.2) and the semantic lexicon methods (see section 4.3) versus our baseline (CNN, per the description in section 4.1).

We present results averaged over 10 different runs and reported accuracy, precision, recall, F1-score, and macro averaged F1-score (or F1-macro). As our dataset is very imbalanced (see Table 1), accuracy is not a good metric for comparison. The F1-score is the harmonic mean of the precision and recall. The macro averaged F1-score is the average of the F1-score for each class, averaged without taking class distribution into consideration. The macro-averaged F1 is better suited for showing the effectiveness of algorithms on smaller classes, which is important as we are interested in the small percentage of personal attacks in the data.

Overall, the sentiment lexicon techniques from (Shin et al., 2017) do not make a difference to the baseline or do worse than the baseline. For example, the baseline CNN with embeddings trained on our data has an F1-macro of 90.1 and all the sentiment lexicon methods have F1-macro from 85.7 to 90. Even through the low coverage of the words in our corpus by the sentiment lexicons (see Table 2) might seem

like the likely reason for this, we note that the lexicon coverage in our paper is similar to the one reported in the original paper for these methods (Shin et al., 2017). One thing that we thought might improve the performance of these methods was to introduce more sentiment lexicons; however, we do not see a difference in performance from using one lexicon to using all four, so we do not further pursue this line of work (see section 0 for the sentiment lexicons we use and their coverage for our corpus). Extending our work to hate lexicons such as Hatebase[13] or HurtLex[14] is a line of future work.

On the other hand, all semantic lexicon approaches perform better than the baseline. The best performing semantic lexicon approach is the Post-Specialized Embeddings (Vulić et al., 2018) with a 95.1 F1-macro, followed closely by the other two semantic-based approaches (around 94 F1-macro) versus 90.1 for the baseline CNN with embeddings trained on our corpus. It is noteworthy that the Post-Specialized experiments in Table 3 use pre-trained embeddings (SGNS-BOW2), while the other two methods (Retrofitted and AR) use the respective techniques on the embeddings trained on our corpus (see section 5.2 for more information on the embeddings we used in our experiments).

A combination of the sentiment with the semantic lexicon approaches does not seem to yield better results: for example, applying first Naïve Concatenation (NC) of sentiment lexicon and word embeddings (see section 4.2) and then using the resulting embeddings in the Retrofitting approach (see section 4.3) shows no difference from the metrics shown in Table 3 for Retrofitted embeddings.

From the semantic lexicon approaches, it is noteworthy that the Retrofitting approach is the simplest of the semantic lexicon approaches, still it performs quite well (see Table 2). In order to explore the transformation of the words from our corpus in the vector space, we look at different word vectors before and after they are retrofitted to the semantic lexicon (Faruqui et al., 2015). All the results in the following discussion are according to cosine similarity.

Approach	Embeddings	Model	Accuracy	Precision	Recall	F1	F1-macro
Baseline	Word Embeddings	CNN	95.9 ± 0.2	85.3 ± 0.8	80.1 ± 0.7	82.6 ± 0.6	90.1 ± 0.3
Sentiment Lexicon	Sentiment + Word Embeddings (Shin et al., 2017)	NC CNN	95.9 ± 0.1	87.6 ± 0.8	76.8 ± 1.1	82.4 ± 0.5	90.0 ± 0.3
		SC CNN	95.1 ± 0.1	85.1 ± 0.9	73.3 ± 1.4	78.7 ± 0.5	88.0 ± 0.3
		EAV CNN	95.0 ± 0.1	83.9 ± 1.0	67.3 ± 1.6	75.5 ± 0.8	85.7 ± 0.4
Semantic Lexicon	Retrofitted Word Embeddings (Faruqui et al., 2015)	CNN	97.6 ± 0.1	93.8 ± 0.2	86.6 ± 1.0	90.0 ± 0.5	94.3 ± 0.3
	ATTRACT-REPEL Word Embeddings (Mrkšić et al., 2017)	CNN	97.4 ± 0.0	93.2 ± 0.4	85.9 ± 0.5	89.4 ± 0.1	94.0 ± 0.1
	Post-Specialized (on SGNS-BOW2) Word Embeddings (Vulić et al., 2018)	CNN	**98.0** ± 0.0	**95.3** ± 0.2	**87.7** ± 0.7	**91.4** ± 0.4	**95.1** ± 0.2

Table 3: Results for our baseline, sentiment lexicon and semantic lexicon approaches (best results in **bold**)

---

[13] https://hatebase.org

[14] https://github.com/valeriobasile/hurtlex

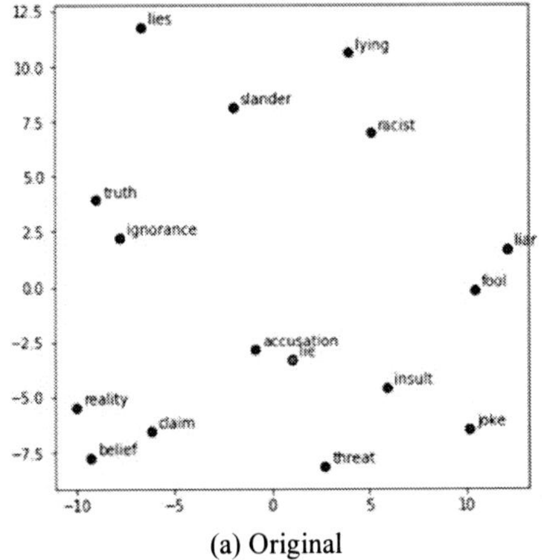
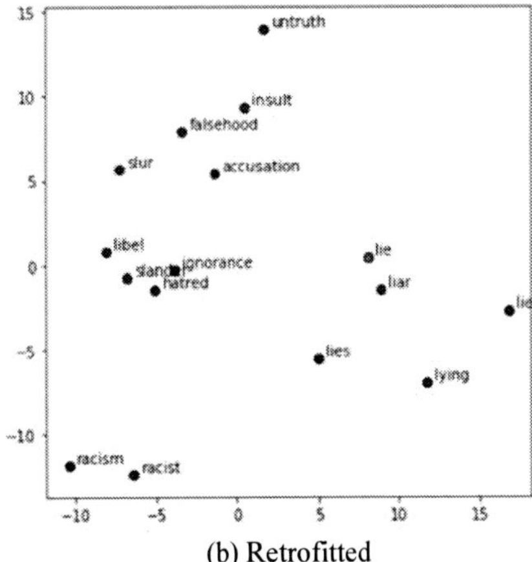

(a) Original   (b) Retrofitted

Figure 2. PCA projection of word embeddings (original vectors versus retrofitted vectors) for the fifteen closest words to the word 'lie' according to cosine similarity (300-d vectors)

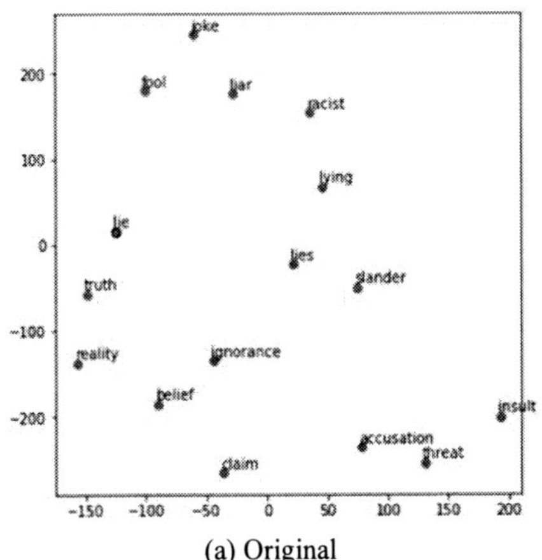
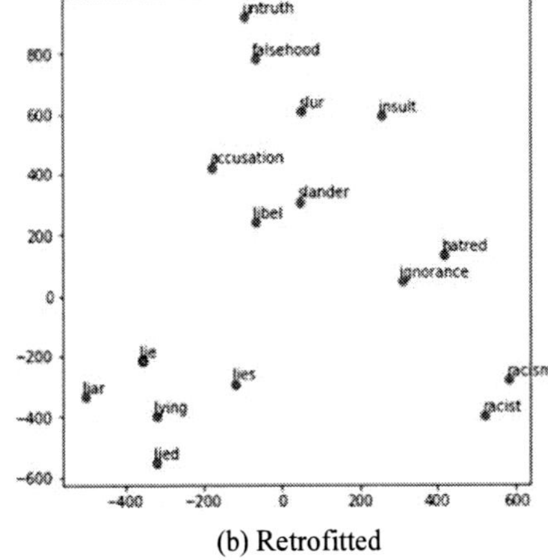

(a) Original   (b) Retrofitted

Figure 3. t-SNE projection of word embeddings (original vectors versus retrofitted vectors) for the fifteen closest words to the word 'lie' according to cosine similarity (300-d vectors, t-SNE perplexity=5, iterations=1500)

The word 'lie' has the word 'truth' as its closest word in the original embeddings (similarity = 0.54), and the word 'liar' in the Retrofitted embeddings (similarity = 0.75). Also, the word 'moron' has the word 'oxymoron' as its closest word in the original embeddings (similarity = 0.73), and the word 'retard' in the Retrofitted embeddings (similarity = 0.87). When we look at the twenty closest words of the word 'moron' using Retrofitted embeddings, the word 'oxymoron' is not in the list. When we pull the twenty closest words for the word 'bye', the results for the original embeddings include 'wanker', 'sup', 'dickface', and 'slut', while the results for the Retrofitted embeddings include no such words. Instead the Retrofitted results include 'farewell', 'goodbye', 'ciao' and 'adios', which are not in the original embedding results.

We additionally look at the same word-pairs with and without retrofitting. The similarity of 'happy' and 'delighted' is 0.54 in the original embeddings and 0.78 in the Retrofitted embeddings. The similarity of 'moron' and 'idiot' is 0.65 in the original embeddings and 0.84 in the Retrofitted embeddings.

At the same time, the similarity of 'user' and 'admin' is almost identical with and without Retrofitting (we checked and both words are in the semantic lexicon, PPDB-XL, used for the retrofitting). These results show that vectors for semantically related words do become more similar after retrofitting, while vectors for unrelated words stay unchanged.

Finally, we apply Principal Component Analysis (PCA) and t-Distributed Stochastic Neighbor Embedding (t-SNE) (van der Maaten and Hinton, 2008). Given the word 'lie' and its fifteen closest words (based on cosine similarity; fifteen was chosen for better visualization), Figure 2 shows a PCA projection and Figure 3 shows the t-SNE plot.

As shown in Figures 2 and 3, the fifteen closest words for the original embeddings contain close words such as 'accusation, 'insult, 'joke', 'claim'. At the same time, the closest words for the Retrofitted embeddings are more similar to the word 'lie'. In the t-SNE plot of the original embeddings (see Figure 3(a)), the work 'lie' is found close in the plot to 'truth', 'reality' or 'fool', while in the Retrofitted embeddings (see Figure 3(b)), it is close to 'liar', 'lies', and 'lying'.

6. Conclusion

In this paper, we explore the use of lexicons, semantic or sentiment, for embedding-based methods towards the detection of personal attacks in online conversations (Wulczyn et al., 2017). The two types of approaches we employ are quite different in the type of lexicons they employ (sentiment or sematic) as well as how they use the lexicons in the learning process.

The sentiment lexicon approaches use the lexicons to create additional sentiment lexicon embeddings that are then used alongside the word embeddings in different ways (concatenation, separate convolutions or using attention mechanisms). The semantic lexicon methods use the original word embeddings and "enhance" them to better represent semantic relationships in the vector space, using the relationships extracted from the semantic lexicon.

Our experiments provide evidence that enhancing word embeddings using semantic lexicons shows promise for the task of abusive language detection. Besides improving detection accuracy for our data (in the form of F1-macro), these methods are fast and flexible, for example, they do not alter or depend on the type of learning model.

We plan to extend the approaches in this paper to enhance embeddings using hate speech lexicons, such as the ones presented in (Bassignana et al., 2018) and (Wiegand et al., 2018). We also plan to explore BERT fine tuning as in (Bodapati et al., 2019) and to explore the applicability of these methods in different data and languages other than English.

7. Acknowledgements

We gratefully acknowledge the Google Cloud Platform (GCP) research credits program and the TensorFlow Research Cloud (TFRC) program.

8. References

Alawad, M., Hasan, S. S., Christian, J. B., and Tourassi, G. (2018). Retrofitting word embeddings with the UMLS Metathesaurus for clinical information extraction. *Proceedings of the IEEE International Conference on Big Data (Big Data).*

Basile, V., Bosco, C., Fersini, E., Nozza, D., Patti, V., Pardo, F., and Sanguinetti, M. (2019). Semeval-2019 task 5: Multilingual detection of hate speech against immigrants and women in twitter. *Proceedings of the 13th International Workshop on Semantic Evaluation SemEval-2019.*

Bassignana, E., Basile, V., and Patti, V. (2018). Hurtlex: A multilingual lexicon of words to hurt. *5th Italian Conference on Computational Linguistics, CLiC-it.*

Bodapati, S., Gella, S., Bhattacharjee, K., and Al-Onaizan, Y. (2019). Neural Word Decomposition Models for Abusive Language Detection. *Proceedings of the Third Workshop on Abusive Language Online, ALW3.*

Bojanowski, P., Grave, E., Joulin, A., and Mikolov, T. (2016). Enriching word vectors with subword information. *Transactions of the Association for Computational Linguistics*, 5(135–146).

Brassard-Gourdeau, E., and Khoury, R. (2019). Subversive Toxicity Detection using Sentiment Information. *Proceedings of the Third Workshop on Abusive Language Online, ALW3.*

Faruqui, M., Dodge, J., Jauhar, J., Dyer, C., Hovy, E., and Smith, N. (2015). Retrofitting word vectors to semantic lexicons. *Proceedings of the Annual Conference of the North American Chapter of the Association for Computational Linguistics NAACL.*

Gamback, B., and Sikdar, U. (2017). Using convolutional neural networks to classify hate-speech. *Proceedings of the First Workshop on Abusive Language Online, ALW1.*

Ganitkevitch, J., Van Durme, B., and Callison-Burch, C. (2013). PPDB: The paraphrase database. *Proceedings of the 2013 Conference of the North American Chapter of the Association for Computational Linguistics: Human Language Technologies.*

Glavaš, G., and Vulić, I. (2018). Explicit retrofitting of distributional word vectors. *Proceedings of the Annual Meeting of the Association for Computational Linguistics ACL.*

Gunasekara, I., and Nejadgholi, I. (2018). A Review of Standard Text Classification Practices for Multi-label Toxicity Identification of Online Content. *Proceedings of the 2nd Workshop on Abusive Language Online, ALW2.*

Hu, M., and Liu, B. (2004). Mining and summarizing customer reviews. *Proceedings of the tenth ACM SIGKDD international conference on Knowledge discovery and data mining.*

Kim, Y. (2014) Convolutional neural networks for sentence classification. *Proceedings of the Conference on Empirical Methods in Natural Language Processing, EMNLP.*

Koufakou, A., and Scott, J. (2019). Exploring the Use of Lexicons to aid Deep Learning towards the Detection of Abusive Language. *Proceedings of the 2019 Workshop on Widening NLP, ACL* (abstract).

Kumar, R., Ojha, A. K., Malmasi, S., and Zampieri, M. (2018). Benchmarking aggression identification in social media. *Proceedings of the First Workshop on Trolling, Aggression and Cyberbullying, TRAC-1.*

Mishra, P., Yannakoudakis, H., and Shutova, E. (2018). Neural Character-based Composition Models for Abuse Detection. *Proceedings of the Second Workshop on Abusive Language Online, ALW2.*

Mohammad, S., and Turney, P. (2013). Crowdsourcing a word–emotion association lexicon. *Computational Intelligence*, 29(3), 436-465.

Mohammad, S., Dunne, C., and Dorr, B. (2009). Generating high-coverage semantic orientation lexicons from overtly marked words and a thesaurus. *Proceedings of the Conference on Empirical Methods in Natural Language Processing, EMNLP.*

Mrkšić, N., Vulić, I., Séaghdha, D., Leviant, I., Reichart, R., Gašić, M., Korhonen, A., and Young, S. (2017). Semantic specialization of distributional word vector spaces using monolingual and cross-lingual constraints. *Transactions of the Association for Computational Linguistics*, 5, 309-324.

Nielsen, F. (2011). A New ANEW: Evaluation of a Word List for Sentiment Analysis in Microblogs. *Proceedings* of the ESWC2011 Workshop on "Making Sense of Microposts": Big Things Come in Small Packages.

Pavlopoulos, J., Malakasiotis, P., and Androutsopoulos. I. (2017). Deep learning for user comment moderation. *Proceedings of the First Workshop on Abusive Language Online.*

Saleem, H. M., Dillon, K. P., Benesch, S., and Ruths, D. (2017). A web of hate: Tackling hateful speech in online social spaces. *arXiv preprint arXiv:1709.10159*

Shin, B., Lee, T., and Choi, J. (2017). Lexicon Integrated CNN Models with Attention for Sentiment Analysis. *Proceedings of the EMNLP Workshop on Computational Approaches to Subjectivity, Sentiment and Social Media Analysis.*

van der Maaten, L.J.P., and Hinton, G.E. (2008). Visualizing High-Dimensional Data Using t-SNE. *Journal of Machine Learning Research.* 9: 2579-2605.

Vulić, I., Glavaš, G., Mrkšić, N., and Korhonen, A. (2018). Post-Specialisation: Retrofitting Vectors of Words Unseen in Lexical Resources. *Proceedings of the Conference of the North American Chapter of the Association for Computational Linguistics: Human Language Technologies.*

Waseem, Z., Davidson, T., Warmsley, D., and Weber, I. (2017). Understanding Abuse: A Typology of Abusive Language Detection Subtasks. *Proceedings of the First Workshop on Abusive Language Online ALW1.*

Wiegand, M., Ruppenhofer, J., Schmidt, A., and Greenberg, C. (2018). Inducing a lexicon of abusive words–a feature-based approach. *Proceedings of the Conference of the North American Chapter of the Association for Computational Linguistics: Human Language Technologies.*

Wulczyn, E., Thain, N., and Dixon, L. (2017). Ex-machina: Personal attacks seen at scale. *Proceedings of the 26th International Conference on World Wide Web WWW.*

Zhang, Z., Robinson, R., and Tepper, J. (2018). Detecting hate speech on twitter using a convolution-gru based deep neural network. *European Semantic Web Conference.*7

Proceedings of the Second Workshop on Trolling, Aggression and Cyberbullying, pages 158–168
Language Resources and Evaluation Conference (LREC 2020), Marseille, 11–16 May 2020
© European Language Resources Association (ELRA), licensed under CC-BY-NC

Developing a Multilingual Annotated Corpus of Misogyny and Aggression

**Shiladitya Bhattacharya[1], Siddharth Singh[2], Ritesh Kumar[2], Akanksha Bansal[3],
Akash Bhagat[2], Yogesh Dawer[2], Bornini Lahiri[4], Atul Kr. Ojha[3]**
[1]Jawaharlal Nehru University, New Delhi, [2]Dr. Bhimrao Ambedkar University,Agra
[3]Panlingua Language Processing LLP, New Delhi, [4]Indian Institute of Technology, Kharagpur
comma.kmi@gmail.com

Abstract

In this paper, we discuss the development of a multilingual annotated corpus of misogyny and aggression in Indian English, Hindi, and Indian Bangla as part of a project on studying and automatically identifying misogyny and communalism on social media (the ComMA Project). The dataset is collected from comments on YouTube videos and currently contains a total of over 20,000 comments. The comments are annotated at two levels - aggression (overtly aggressive, covertly aggressive, and non-aggressive) and misogyny (gendered and non-gendered). We describe the process of data collection, the tagset used for annotation, and issues and challenges faced during the process of annotation. Finally, we discuss the results of the baseline experiments conducted to develop a classifier for misogyny in the three languages.

Keywords: Misogyny, Aggression, ComMA Project, Hindi, Bangla

1. Introduction

The proliferation in Social Networking (platforms and users) has transformed our communities and the manner in which we communicate. One of the widespread impact can be seen through the hate that has been vocalised through platforms like Facebook, Twitter, and YouTube, where content sharing and communication are integrated together. The hatefulness itself is not a novel discovery but the intensity and hostility lying in the expression is a matter of grave concern. Articulation of hatefulness is often strong enough to break down or weaken the community ties. As the impact of such articulation travels from online to offline domain, resultant reactions frequently lead to incidents like organised riot-like situations and unfortunate casualties to ultimately broaden the scope of marginalisation of individuals as well as communities. Mr. Nilesh Christopher in his August, 2019 article published in the online news portal Wired has reported how one particular platform named TikTok came in handy to spread caste-based atrocities in Tamil Nadu, India. Banaji et al. (2019) in a research report on the assessment of WhatsApp abuses in India says in one of its key findings "... in the case of violence against a specific group (Muslims, Christians, Dalits, Adivasis, etc.) there exists widespread, simmering distrust, hatred, contempt and suspicion towards Pakistanis, Muslims, Dalits and critical or dissenting citizens.... WhatsApp users in these demographics are predisposed both to believe disinformation and to share misinformation about discriminated groups in face-to-face and WhatsApp networks." The report also observes that with the sweeping spread of WhatsApp, there has evolved newer forms of virtual violence against women as well ...."Forms of WhatsApp- and smart-phone enabled violence against women in India include unsolicited sexts, sex tapes, rape videos, surveillance, violation of privacy, bullying, forced confrontation with pornographic material, blackmail and humiliation."

Thus, it has become all the more important for scholars and researchers to take the initiative and find methods to identify and compile the source and articulation of aggression It is for this reason that we have initiated the building of a sizeable corpus comprising YouTube comments to understand misogyny and aggression in user-generated posts and automatically identify those. In recent times, there has been a large number of studies exploring different aspects of hateful and aggressive language and their computational modelling and automatic detection such as toxic comments[1] (Thain et al., 2017), trolling (Cambria et al., 2010; Kumar et al., 2014; Mojica de la Vega and Ng, 2018; Mihaylov et al., 2015), flaming / insults (Sax, 2016; Nitin et al., 2012), radicalization (Agarwal and Sureka, 2015; Agarwal and Sureka, 2017), racism (Greevy and Smeaton, 2004; Greevy, 2004; Waseem, 2016), online aggression (Kumar et al., 2018a), cyberbullying (Xu et al., 2012; Dadvar et al., 2013), hate speech (Kwok and Wang, 2013; Djuric et al., 2015; Burnap and Williams, 2015; Davidson et al., 2017; Malmasi and Zampieri, 2017; Malmasi and Zampieri, 2018; Waseem and Hovy, 2016), abusive language (Waseem et al., 2017; Nobata et al., 2016; Mubarak et al., 2017) and offensive language (Wiegand et al., 2018; Zampieri et al., 2019). Prior studies have explored the use of aggressive and hateful language on different platforms such as Twitter (Xu et al., 2012; Burnap and Williams, 2015; Davidson et al., 2017; Wiegand et al., 2018), Wikipedia comments[1], and Facebook posts (Kumar et al., 2018a).

Our present study is one of the first studies to make use of YouTube comments for computational modelling of aggression and misogyny (although there have

---

[1]http://bit.ly/2FhLMVz

been quite a few studies on pragmatic aspects of YouTube comments such as (Garcés-Conejos Blitvich, 2010; Garcés-Conejos Blitvich et al., 2013; Lorenzo-Dus et al., 2011; Bou-Franch et al., 2012)). Some of the earlier studies on computational modelling of misogyny have focussed almost exclusively on tweets ((Menczer et al., 2015; Frenda et al., 2019; Hewitt et al., 2016; Fersini et al., 2018b; Fersini et al., 2018a; Anzovino et al., 2018; Sharifirad and Matwin, 2019)). Also, all of these studies have focussed on either English or European languages like Italian and Spanish. And as such this is the first study on computational modelling of misogyny in two of India's largest languages - Hindi and Bangla.

In the following sections, we will discuss the corpus collection and annotation for this study and the development of a baseline misogyny classifier for the two languages.

2. Context of the Study: The ComMA Project

The use of a wide range of aggressive and hateful content on social media becomes interesting as well as challenging to study in context to India which is a secular nation with religious as well as linguistic and cultural heterogeneity. The present work is being carried out within the 'Communal and Misogynistic Aggression in Hindi-English-Bangla (ComMA) project'. The broader aim of this project is to understand how communal and sexually threatening misogynistic content is linguistically and structurally constructed by the aggressors and harassers and how it is evaluated by the other participants in the discourse. We will use the methods of micro-level discourse analysis, which will be a combination of conversation analysis and the interactional model used for (im)politeness studies, in order to understand the construction and evaluation of aggression on social media.

We will use the insights from this study to develop a system that could automatically identify if some textual content is sexually threatening or communal on social media. The system will use multiple supervised text classification models that would be trained using a dataset annotated at 2 levels with labels pertaining to sexual and communal aggression as well as its evaluation by the other participants. The dataset will contain data in two of the largest spoken Indian languages - Hindi and Bangla – as well as code-mixed content in three languages – Hindi, Bangla and English. It will be collected from both social media (like Facebook and Twitter) as well as comments on blogs and news/opinion websites.

The research presented in this paper focusses on one part of the project - automatic identification of misogyny.

3. Corpus Collection

3.1. Sources

For the purpose of the project, online sources laden with comments were carefully selected. In general, extensively used social media platforms were considered primary sources because of their massive footfall. Other than social media we also looked at some other popular streaming and sharing platforms. These were namely

- Facebook

- Twitter

- YouTube

The actual sources of information ranged from public posts, tweets, video blogs (vlogs), news coverage and so on. We have considered posts and discussion on current popular political issues related to feminine beauty and grooming related vlogs, discussions on the life-choices of female celluloid stars and national policy related debates pertaining to female empowerment. In the process of collection throughout, we have collected only the public posts and comments on them.

3.2. Sampling Criteria for Conversations

Given the desired output of the project and its requirements, conversations and opinions were selected on the basis of the points mentioned below

3.2.1. The Volume of Conversation

In order to prepare a considerable dataset for training and looking at the requirement, only those posts and/or conversations were selected which saw a large user engagement in terms of the comments received on them. On an average, we collected data from those posts/videos which had received a minimum of 100-150 comments. This not only ensured a higher volume of data but also more relevant kind of data since it was observed that there is a greater possibility of the presence of aggressive and misogynous comments in longer stretches of conversation.

3.2.2. The Relevance Criterion

As we mentioned earlier, the choice of source materials was not random. Rather, a selection criterion was followed. After copious deliberations with the members, it was determined that we can only entertain those sources where misogyny is more likely to be expressed. A list of domains of possible source materials was considered and to name a few of those included the following -

- women's fashion vlogs

- women's fitness tips videos

- news coverage of violent crime involving women

- celebrity news and gossip vlogs

- current socio-political commentaries and pertinent issues

- any other issue of immediate interest

3.2.3. Language

India is a multilingual nation, therefore, it was not surprising to find content from any one source expressed in multiple languages. As such during the initial process of data collection from designated sources we needed to carefully separate content in different languages. Therefore, a language identification task was taken up with the native speakers A separate task was also carried out to separate Bangladeshi and Indian varieties of Bangla since the two varieties differ substantially in the choice of lexicon as well as morpho-syntactic structures. At this point of time, we included only the Indian variety of Bangla in the dataset since we did not have sufficient instances of the Bangladeshi variety to be useful in the present task and mixing up the two varieties would have only made the dataset noisier. We are working to further expand the dataset and as we collect and annotate more instances of Bangladeshi variety of Bangla, we will include that in the future releases of the dataset.

The code-mixed English-Hindi and English-Bangla comments were separated out. The process of identification involved carefully analysed linguistically relevant information such as peculiar lexical choice, unique phonetic representation of chosen lexical items and regional colloquial usage.

This manual annotation of languages and varieties were used to develop an automatic language identification system for these languages. This system was developed using Support Vector Machines and uses word trigrams and character 5-grams for making the prediction about the language of the content. It achieved an F-score of 0.93 and has worked reasonably well for automatically classifying content into one of the languages before being sent to annotators or even misogyny and aggression classifiers.

4. The Aggression Tagset [2]

In this section, we present the detailed guidelines for annotating the text from social media with information about aggression and misogyny. It gives a description of these categories and the features and, how those were employed during the annotation process. All annotations have been carried out at the level where the annotation target was a complete post, a comment or any one unit of the discourse. We would like to mention here that all of the data are represented as they were from the actual posts/sources. The authors and the project members do not bear ill feeling to people/names mentioned in the examples. Also, we do not endorse such aggressive and misogynistic language as one may find in the examples.

---

[2]**Disclaimer:** We would like to mention here that all of the data / examples included in this section are represented as they were collected from the actual posts/sources. The authors of the paper do not bear ill feeling to people/ names mentioned in the examples. Also, we do not endorse such aggressive and misogynistic language as one may find in the examples and the research aims at only understanding and reducing such language usage.

The aggression annotation was carried out using the aggression tagset (discussed in (Kumar et al., 2018b)). The tagset is reproduced in Table 1.

TAG	AGGRESSION LEVEL
OAG	Overtly Aggressive
CAG	Covertly Aggressive
NAG	Non - Aggressive

Table 1: Aggression Annotation Tagset

5. The Misogyny Tagset

Misogyny identification is a binary classification task and the labels that we use for the task (Table 2) as well as the detailed guidelines (as developed and used by the annotators) are discussed below.

TAG	ATTRIBUTE
GEN	Gendered or Misogynous
NGEN	Non-gendered or Non-misogynous

Table 2: Misogyny Annotation Tagset

5.1. Gendered or Misogynous (GEN)

This refers to such cases where verbal aggression aimed towards

- the stereotypical gender roles of the victim as well as the aggressor

- aggressive reference to one's sexuality and sexual orientation

- attacks the victim because of/by referring to her/his gender (includes homophobic and transgender attacks)

- includes attack against the victim owing to not fulfilling gender roles assigned to them or fulfilling the roles assigned to another gender

Some of the examples of this class are given below.

- tere ma se puch sale tera bap kon h [Go and ask your mother who your father is.]

- Napushank tha Nehru... lesbo thi indira [Nehru was impotent, Indira was a lesbian]

- Is hijray Rajnath ko chori pahna do [Put bangles on this trans/third gender person Rajnath [3]]

5.2. Non-gendered or Non-Misogynous (NGEN)

The text which is not gendered will be marked not gendered.

---

[3]We are thankful to one of the reviewers for suggesting this translation.

5.3. Unclear (UNC)

This tag was employed in rare instances where it was not possible to decide whether the text is GEN or NGEN. It was not included in the final tagged document. It only served as an intermediary tag for flagging and resolving really ambiguous and unclear instances.[4] For the sake of clarity and removing ambiguities in the annotation guidelines, an additional set of guidelines were formulated (as a result of discussion with the annotators). They are reproduced in the following sections.

5.4. General Instructions

The task relates to figuring out the 'intentionality' of the speaker (as manifested in the language used by her/im). You need to figure out if, something that is being said,

- arises out of an inherent bias of the speaker or

- an acceptance of that bias or

- propagates the bias (knowingly or unknowingly) or

- endorses the bias (again intentionally or unintentionally; or covertly or overtly)

The task could be approached by looking at the text and trying to figure out if it

- attacks the victim because of/by referring to her/his gender (includes homophobic and transgender attacks) or

- includes attack against the victim owing to not fulfilling gender roles assigned to them or fulfilling the roles assigned to another gender

5.5. Attack against Women

Gendered does NOT mean any attack against women; it will be gendered only when the attack is BECAUSE of someone being a woman (or a man or a transgender or any of the countless gender identities). For example,

1. @KaDevender भडवा है साला खलिस्तानी और पाकिस्तानी एजेंट है और ये पाकिस्तानी स्लीपर सेल की मेंबर है यहाँ चुप के बैठी है किसी दिन बम बांध के कूद जाएगी और हजारो बेगुनाहो की जान ले लेगी ..निर्दोष हिन्दू के मारने पे ताली तो अभी बजाती है ..आप का चुसेन्द्र

---

[4] One of our reviewers suggested that it might be a useful tag to retain in the final dataset. We would like to clarify that we had a rather long discussion about the need for retaining this tag. It was decided that if a substantial number of instances were tagged by the annotators as 'UNC' then we may retain it. However, only 8 - 10 instances were annotated with this tag. Therefore, those cases were resolved via discussion among the annotators and the project staff instead of creating another tag, which has a negligible proportion in the dataset.

He is a bastard, a Khalistani and Pakistani agent and she is a member of the Pakistani sleeper cell. She is hiding here and will jump with bomb anyday and kill thousands of innocent people...she appreciates the killing of innocent Hindus .. your sucker

2. Meye r maa eki character er chi

daughter and mother are as same character, disgusting

In both (1) and (2), even though the attack is against a woman, the locus of attack may not be the gender. While in (2) the absence of a gender bias and misogyny is clear, in (1) it is little complicated because of the use of the last word and might be interpreted as gendered because of its use.

5.6. Jokes

One of the tests employed for resolving if a joke was gendered or not was to see if the gender of the target of the joke is changed, then the joke still works or not. If not, then it rests on some kind of gender bias. For example

1. Teacher : 'शीला कपडे पहन चुक' थी ' ईस वाक्य को अपनी भाषा में बोलो। Student -: भेनचोद लेट हो गए !!!!

Teacher: 'Sheela had already worn her clothes' say this sentence in your own language. Student -: Fuck, we are late!!!!

It is 'Gendered' since the joke will not work for other gender

5.7. Satire/ sarcasm

A lot of times, for the lack of complete context, it was not clear if a comment was satire / sarcasm or not. Such unclear instances were initially tagged 'Unclear' and later a decision was arrived at through discussion among the annotators and, if required, based on voting. For example,

1. "Jithna dethe hein is d Benchmark for Jithna lena hai... - A Father (of Daughters and a Son) #Dowry #Jehaz #Shukrana #Nazrana #weddingideas #weddingseason #wedding #weddingdress #weddinggift"""

The amount that we give is the benchmark

The idea expressed by the father in the above example is the dowry amount given by the bride's family works as the standard for accepting dowry when the son gets married. It could be a serious justification of dowry or a satirical take on those who accept dowries stating this reason. One of the ways of resolving such cases might be to look at hashtags and try to see the intention of the speaker. In this case, #Shukrana, #Nazrana etc seems to carry positive connotations. Also the tweet itself may look like a justification for dowry.

5.8. Poetry / shayari

If the intent was not clear in case of poetry then it was marked 'Unclear' and was later resolved using a majority voting. However, in other instances, it was marked as perceived by the annotators. For example,

1. सिमटकर चूड़ियों में छुपने लगा शायद मैंने जो चूम लिया उसको मुझको चुभने लगा शायद मैंने जब आगोश में भर लिया उसको मुझसे जलता है तेरा कंगन शायद... मैंने जो इश्क कर लिया है उसको #साहिब१ #चूड़ी #कंगन #हिंदी_शब्द #शब्दनिधि

   She hid herself in her bangles probably, when I kissed her, it started to prick me when I hugged her, your bangle is envious of me probably because I made love to you.

2. Ranuu goo Ranuu Lagboo tmr Karr Nunuu?? Himeshh Salmann nakii Sonuu??

   "oh Ranu! who's penis do you want? Himesh Salman or Sonnu??

In (1), the poetic verse is romantic in nature and talk about lovemaking. Such expressions can be gendered and express misogyny if they clearly represent lack of consent. Because the axis of consent is not clear here we do not mark it as Gendered. (2), however, is clearly gendered, despite being in verse (not really poetry, though) since the imagery of sex and sexual violence is unnecessarily invoked for attacking the victim.

5.9. Figuring out tacit intentions/underlying bias

In some cases, at the surface, speakers may seem to be speaking against a biased practice/behaviour but the arguments given by her/him may not actually be questioning those biases itself and might even be creating another kind of bias. Let us take a look at the following examples,

1. @ aajtak @ News18India @ sdtiwari Time has come that a debate on #Dowry should be organised on highest level. it is absolutely essential to abolish #Dowry from Hindu Society. A honest hard worker can't manage to satisfy Groom's demand, particularly when #Bride is highly educated.

2. Don't Support #Dowry at all.Thre is no point to strt a rltnshp on exchnge of Bt also nd to tch society ,all failed marriages r nt due to #Dowry.So stop nmng every broken marriage as #FakeCases_498A_DV_125_377_376 Real sufferers nvr gts justice,help them stop misuse of #laws

3. So according to you protesting against molestation is a crime ? Sir Don't you have any daughters or sister? #BHU_लाठीचार्ज #bhu_molestation

4. When a thousand years old #Hindu tradition is followed in #Kerela then Muslims came forward to say that it oppresses women's freedom, even Hindu Women" themselves says that they don't want to enter #Sabrimala & respect the traditions! #IslamExposed https:// twitter.com/theskindoctor1 3/status/1113435724269981696 ..."

5. भेनचोद ये गुलाबी पैंट कौन पहनता है बे

   Fuck man, who wears a pink trouser?

6. हम देश वासी जवानों के जित का #Abhinandan करते हैं. अब हम सबको मिलकार #SpecialStarus4Jawan सुनिश्चित करना होगा. जो अपने जान जोखिम में डालकर देश की रक्षा कर रहा, खुद को देश के लिए समर्पित कर दिया है, उसके लिए यह तो होना ही चाहिए. जवानों को #Dowry Act से बाहर करो @ ani @ dna @ aajtakpic.twitter.com/ezmfDEzxXQ

   We the people of this nation #Abhinandan (welcome) the victory of our soldiers. Now we all should ensure a#SpecialStarus4Jawan. The one who is protecting our country by endangering their lives, has donated his life for the cause of the nation, this should definitely be done for him. Exempt soldiers from #Dowry Act.

In tweet 1 and 2, the dissatisfaction is because of the inability to afford the demands (and not because the 'demand' itself is discriminatory and biased). Its a financial argument for an inherently 'gender' issue since only women are supposed to give dowry. It also creates a distinction between 'educated' and 'uneducated' girls, thereby, implying that it is okay for uneducated girls to pay dowry. This creates another bias (which clearly doesn't exist for the other gender). Thus, even though the comment seems to be opposing a gendered practice like dowry; it doesn't actually oppose the underlying bias in a practice like this. While (3) looks like a support for protest against molestation, it reinforces the stereotype of women as sisters and daughters. Also molestation is a crime and it doesn't have to do anything with whether there are other women in someone's life or not. On the face of it, (4) may look like a religious comment. However, an underlying attempt is made here to present a gender issue as a religious issue. The speaker supports a practice which is biased against a specific gender (and religion is used as a smokescreen for propagating that bias). (5) reinforces the stereotypical gender associated with the use of a particular colour by a particular gender. (6) Puts gender issues vis-a-vis army which is not at all relevant or comparable and favours a certain kind of preferential treatment based on job. It supports dowry in certain cases (since dowry is not considered a gendered act by the speaker).

5.10. Abuses

In general, abuses involving sex and sexual organs will be considered gendered since they emanate from an inherent gender bias. Let us take a look at the following examples -

1. @USER This game sucks donkey balls

2. bitch calm down you pussy when yo ppl ain't around

3. अबे ओ अपनी बहन से पैदा कीड़े । भड़ुआ बनना है तो पप्पू के लुंड पर बैठ।तेरी अम्मी का यार मत समझ मुझे झोपडी के। संघी आतंकवादी होते है क्या।अपनी बहन का हला ला करने कहीं और जा ।तेरे जैसे 10 रोज ठिकाने लगाता हूं। समझा नपुंसक

Hey you, a worm born out of your sister. If you wish to be a fucker then go sit on Pappu's penis. Do not think of me as your mother's boyfriend. Those who belong to the Sangh are not terrorists. Go somewhere else to perform your sister's halala. I deal with the likes of you everyday. Do you understand you impotent.

4. बॉसडीके, मधरचूत, तेरी माँ की, बहिन की छूट, रंडी का ौलत, खानदानी रंडी का ौलत, हीरामंडी का पिल्ला, भादवा लौड़ा लुंड कमीना, छूट के ढक्कन, छिपकली के गांड के पसीने

Motherfucker, your mother's your sister's pussy, son of a bitch, litter of heeramandi, pussy cap, sweat of the anus of a lizard.

5. চশমাপড়া মাসীমার গুদের নাম্বার টা কি জানতে পেরেছিলেন ?

Did you get the number of bespectacled aunty's vagina?

6. भेनचोद ये गुलाबी पैंट कौन पहनता है बे

Fuck man, who wears a pink trouser.

Even though there is no direct attack in (1), the abuse here arises out of an understanding about what is considered an homosexual act. The abuses used in (3) show the biased and misogynistic outlook of the speaker. Even though the attack is not because of the gender, it carries the connotations of attack against a specific gender as it reinforces the role of women as sexual objects. At the same time it propagates the stereotypical ideas of honor, masculinity, etc. Abuses like those in (4) and (5) evoke sexual imagery and are used for attacking someone, hence, gendered. In (6) the abuse is just an exclamation marker and therefore, not directed towards anyone. As such it is not gendered because of the use of this abuse (but see above for description of what makes it gendered).

5.11. Victim blaming

In a lot of cases of discussion around gender, it is the girls or the girls' side that are attacked - it is important to figure out the cases of blaming the victim for the problems they are facing (because of the patriarchal societal structure). For example,

1. #DAHEZ LDKIYO K MAA BAAP HI DETE HAI, JB KOI V CHEEZ AISE HI MIL JAAYE TO LOG Q NAA LE. AB MERE SAATH HI HAI MAI JISSE PYAR KRTA HU USKI SAADI 1 GOVT. JOB WAALE SE HO RHI H AND THEY ARE TAKING #DOWRY. BUT I AM AGAINST DOWRY, I JUST WANT HER ONLY. But govt. Job is in b/w

Dowry is gifted by the bride's parents only. When something is received without a price then why shouldn't one take it? Now look at my case. The one I love is getting married to a government employee and they are taking #DOWRY. BUT I AM AGAINST DOWRY, I JUST WANT HER ONLY. But govt. Job is in b/w

In this tweet, the speaker asserts that he is against dowry. However he still blames the parents of the girls for this kind of practice and at the same time also absolves the boys of any responsibility. Such cases of victim blaming is gendered.

5.12. Description of an event / fact

Describing a gendered act / incident / practice does not make the text gendered. In such cases, it will be gendered only if the speaker endorses the action or depicts an underlying bias. Let us take a look at the following examples -

1. IF YOU SAY ONLY #MOTHERINLAW #HUSBAND ARE ACCUSED. YOU ARE TOTALLY WRONG. BECAUSE IT'S HER OWN PARENT WHO MARRIED TO THAT GUY AND FORSURE EARLIER HER FATHER HAD GIVEN #DOWRY TO THEM. SO, HER PARENTS ARE ALSO INVOLVED. EVERY PARENTS WANT GOVT. JOB GUY AND PAY. AGAINST THIS SYSTEM.

2. Against the grain: In some parts of #Maharashtra, women get #dowry https://trib.al/gz1NTix

3. If the groom's family in China is unable to afford the bride prices, then he is not considered a good match. Learn more: https://buff.ly/2CUDzqv #China #marriage-market #matchmaking #dowry #brideprices #culturepic.twitter.com/v8MxjGsQz2

4. People were often coupled in European countries according to class and, thus, economic advantage. Learn more here: https://buff.ly/2umI6Nu #economicadvantage #dowry #Europe #culture #marriagepic.twitter.com/Pas1rKavLk

5. जब बर्तन मांज कर आयी वो तो गालों ने बताया..!! कि बर्तन काँच का कोई आज फिर से टूटा गया..!! @YadavsAniruddh @Anjupra7743 @KaranwalTanu @AmbedkarManorma follow @Rana11639322

When she came after cleaning dishes her cheeks revealed it all..!! that a glass dish has been broken again today..!!

(1) describes a biased situation. However there is no evidence to show that the speaker also endorses it. As

such even though the situation being described is gendered, the tweet itself is not. (2) doesn't question the gender bias in the dowry system and acts as an underlying support for dowry. Irrespective of who pays the dowry to whom – its always biased against a specific gender. Since the speaker seems to be endorsing this view, it is gendered. In (3) even though it may look like the description of a practice, the underlying intention of the speaker is to support and justify the practice of dowry by giving a parallel example from a different context. (4) is presented as a covert support for the dowry system, which puts one specific gender in a very disadvantageous position and as such the tweet itself is gendered as well. In (5) even though the incident being described is gendered, the tweet is not a support for that. Thus, it will not be gendered.

5.13. Mixed bias

In some cases, gender bias might be mixed with other kinds of biases (like religious or regional). These cases, are marked as gendered. For example,

1. Arnab @republic is visibly anti ChristoROPcommieFascists. But the #MeToo / Libtard women hv wrapped him in their fingers. So in their appeasement he took anti Hindu stand on #Sabrimala . Appeased LGBTQ during Section 377. Vilified the accused in #MeToo b4 Court Trial.

In this case, religion seems to be the locus of attack. However, it attacks a lot of other instances of support for non-male rights, hence, biased for a specific gender.

5.14. Other Ambiguities

Let us take a look at the following examples -

1. http://chng.it/DPFHRS9B4T.Please ... sign this petition. For men and their families falsely accused in #DomesticViolence, #dowry and #498a by leeching women, there are no laws to give them a fair trial and no laws to punish leeching women. #MenCommission and #GenderEquality in laws needed.

2. Next surgical strike she along with her entire terrorist clan shd be dropped in #Napakistan #Disgusting she is. She also orchestrated fake #Asifa narrative. Shameless ppl dance on dead bodies..

3. Should we go for GENDER INJUSTICE here? #sabrimala was the same But as I respect my religion and its beliefs i fully support this ritual and i am fully satisfied with whatever rule is imposed. Jay matadi

(1) is a call to punish those who misuse the law and so apparently promoting gender equality. However, when it is accompanied by a call to form a men commission, it seems to be ignoring and undermining the issues that a woman faces. There are several laws that are misused by several people - however this is the one law intended to protect the women that causes the maximum uproar. However, having said this, the intention of the speaker does not seem to be biased. In such cases, the annotators may annotate based on their intuition on case-by-case basis or mark it as 'unclear' so that annotations by multiple annotators may be taken. In such cases, they must also include a comment describing the ambiguity. In (2), the question to settle is this – is the criticism BECAUSE the person being criticised is a man / woman or the criticism is directed somewhere else? In this case, the criticism doesn't seem to be directed at gender. However bringing in #Asifa and calling it fake shows a gender bias. Such cases also have to be handled as mentioned above. In (3), the stand taken by the speaker is not clear here and as such may be marked unclear

6. Annotation of the Dataset

The annotation was carried out by a total of 4 annotators - two among these were speakers of all the three languages - Bangla, Hindi and English, while the other 2 did not speak Bangla. All the annotators were either pursuing or completed a higher degree in Linguistics and expected to have a centrist or left-leaning political orientation. Each of the instances in the dataset was annotated by 2 annotators and in case of disagreement, third annotation was taken/resolved through discussions and deliberations.

The issues that we face in annotation occur due to different level of understanding of the language in question or personal prejudices and bias over interpretation and so on. Basically, it involves the differing worldview of many individuals. The process of continuous discussions and sensitisation (especially towards gender issues) among the annotators helped us in taking care of different worldviews of the annotators and also ensuring that they share largely similar values while annotating. However, we also took care not to influence the annotations via each other's perspective as in tasks like these, it is necessary that annotators are not given strict guidelines for annotation and keep the option open for their own interpretation. Notwithstanding the personal interpretations, there were occasions where reaching a consensus was hard in this task. As the task involved more than one individuals, the inter-annotator agreement experiments and subsequent discussions helped the annotators in getting acquainted with each other's perspectives and worldviews and ensuring that a largely uniform annotation process of followed. Krippendorff's kappa coefficient is used to measure inter-annotator agreement which turns out to be 0.75. Although, in about 75 per cent or more cases the tags were unanimous, some data required special attention as different individuals tagged those cases differently. In such cases a three-way process was developed in the course of deliberations. This process is as follows,

1. Counterexample method is used to test the comment: The annotators were given counterexamples to argue against their stand on specific instances.

2. Annotators' vote are examined: All the collaborators joined in conference to deliberate over the data in question. Independent members were also consulted in the process to get a different view. Native speakers took part to disambiguate examples or provide explanations for parts not understood. Finally, a vote on the most relevant interpretation was carried on to reach a consensus.

3. UNC Tag: Instead of marking questionable data with GEN or NGEN, at times a less stringent approach was taken up. In this the annotators were asked to mark such data either as UNC or keep them untagged for a discussion later. This helped immensely in the smooth and timely flow of the annotation process, while a resolution was achieved later through discussion.

7. The Final Dataset

The final dataset contains a total of over 25,000 comments in the 3 languages - Hindi, Bangla and English. Figure 1 [5] shows the share of data in each language. Overall, almost 3,000 (over 11%) are gendered/misogynistic and more than 23,000 are non-gendered. The proportion of gendered comments in Hindi, Indian Bangla and Hindi-English code-mixed comments hovers around 10 - 15%, while in English it is just around 4%. A language-wise break-up and comparison is given in Figure 2.

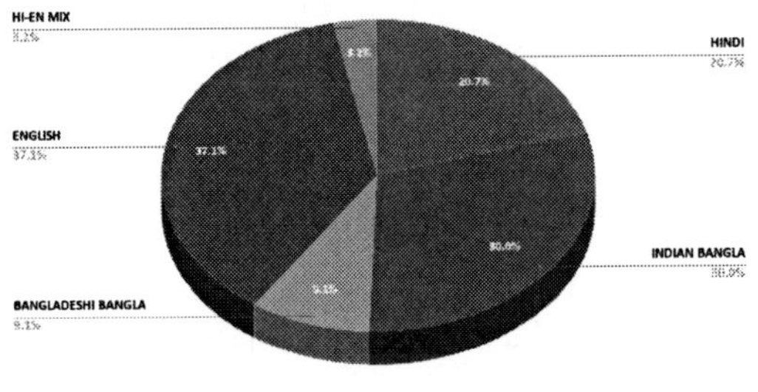

Figure 1: Languages in the Dataset

Almost half of these comments in Hindi, Indian Bangla and English are also annotated for 3 levels of aggres-

---

[5]One of our reviewers have pointed out that "They are easier to read, can be printed out, and do not cause issues for people with colour blindness". While we agree with the fact that it might be easier to print and 'read' the tables, we believe that figures serve an inherently different function in comparison to the tables. These are meant to be 'viewed' and not seen. The figures included in our paper intend to show the share of the different values and not necessarily to give a count of those numbers. In fact, we have included the tables to show the numbers. However, converting all the figures to tables will defeat the purpose of these figures: visualization. Hence, we have decided to retain the figures.

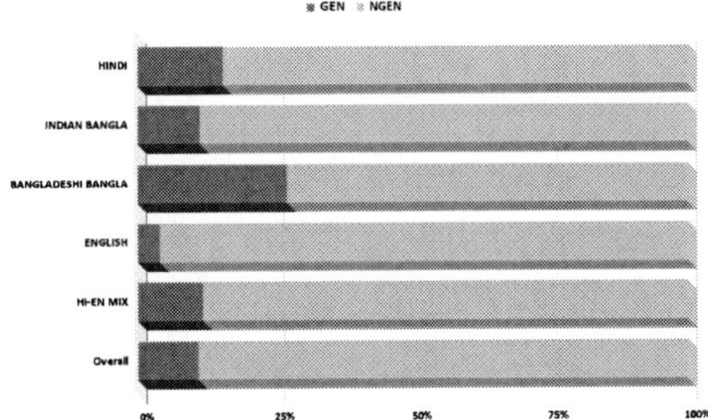

Figure 2: Misogyny in the Dataset

sion. A language-wise break-up and comparison of aggressive comments in the dataset is given in Figure 3

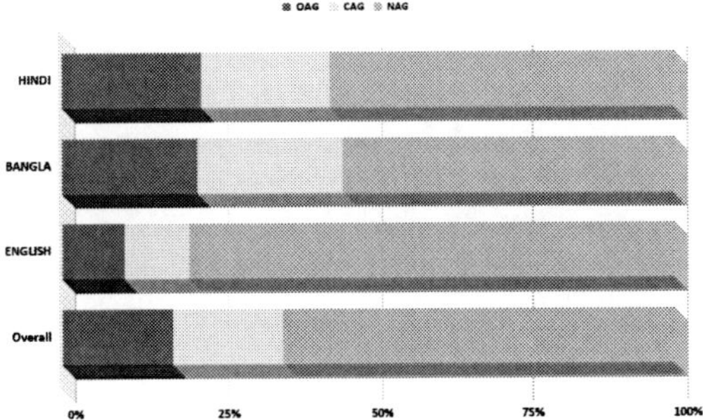

Figure 3: Aggression in the Dataset

The share of aggressive (taking together both overtly and covertly aggressive comments) comments in the dataset is around 45% of the total annotated dataset in Hindi and Indian Bangla, while it is around 20% in English. These are similar to what was reported in (Kumar et al., 2018b).

We also took a look at the co-occurrence of aggressive and gendered comments to see if most of the gendered/misogynous comments are also generally aggressive or not. Overall, it turns out that over 80% of the gendered comments are also aggressive; on the other hand, less than 30% of non-gendered comments are aggressive. These results shows that misogyny may be strongly correlated with aggression and even though a substantial proportion of non-gendered comments are also aggressive (in our dataset), a much larger proportion of gendered comments are aggressive. A language-wise break-up of proportion of aggression in gendered as well as non-gendered comments are given in Figure 4 and Figure 5.

8. Baseline Misogyny Classifier

Using a subset of the annotated dataset, we trained Support Vector Machine (SVM) for automatic identification of misogyny in Hindi, Bangla and English (in

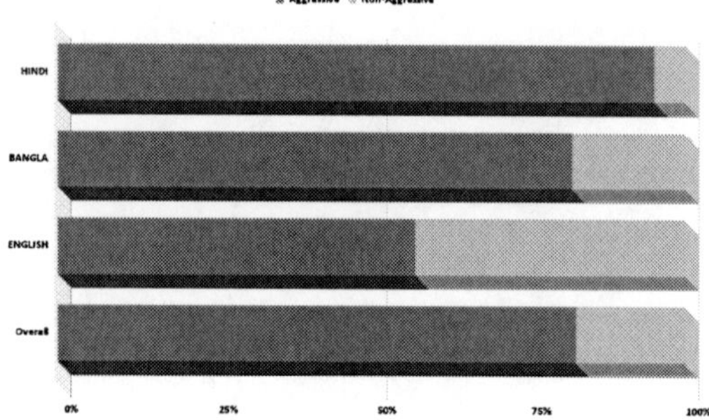

Figure 4: Co-occurrence of Misogyny and Aggression

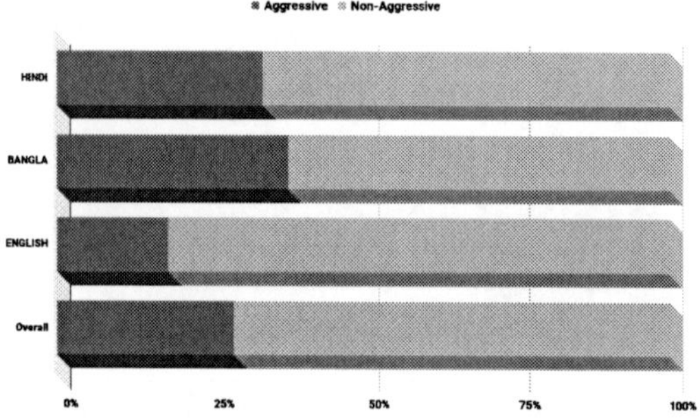

Figure 5: Co-occurrence of Non-gendered and Aggression

the Indian context). The statistics of dataset used for training and testing is given in Table 3. We experimented with different combinations of word (uni, bi and tri) and character (2 - 5) n-grams as features. We carried out a 10-fold cross validation and also experimented with the C-value of SVM ranging from 0.001 to 10. The best performing classifiers, along with their performance for each of the three languages is summarised in Table 4.

LANGUAGE	GEN	NGEN	TOTAL
Hindi	828	3,156	3,984
Bangla	871	2,955	3,826
English	393	3,870	4,263

Table 3: Training and Testing Dataset

Language	Character n-gram	Word n-gram	F-Score
Hindi	3	3	0.87
Bangla	5	NA	0.89
English	2	NA	0.93

Table 4: Baseline Classifier Result

As is evident from this, character and word n-grams prove to be quite a string baseline, which achieves an f-score close to 0.90 for Hindi and Bangla and for English it achieves an impressive score of 0.93.

9. Summing Up and the Way Ahead

In this paper, we have discussed the development of a multilingual corpora in Hindi, Bangla, and English, annotated with the information about it being gendered or not. The total corpus consists of more than 25,000 comments from different YouTube videos annotated with this information. The dataset has been made publicly available for research purposes [6]. We also trained a baseline classifier on this dataset which gives a high f-score of over 0.87 for Hindi, 0.89 for Bangla and 0.93 for English dataset.

We are currently working on expanding the dataset to include data from other platforms and domains and then test the classifier to see how well it performs across different kinds of dataset. Our goal is to have a dataset of at least 50,000 comments/units in each of the three languages and develop a multilingual classifier that can work reasonably well for different platforms/domains in automatically detecting misogyny over social media.

10. Acknowledgements

We would like to thank Facebook Research for an unrestricted research gift for carrying out this research. We would also like to thank our reviewers for their extensive reviews which have led to substantial improvements in the paper.

11. Bibliographical References

Agarwal, S. and Sureka, A. (2015). Using knn and svm based one-class classifier for detecting online radicalization on twitter. In *International Conference on Distributed Computing and Internet Technology*, pages 431 – 442. Springer.

Agarwal, S. and Sureka, A. (2017). Characterizing linguistic attributes for automatic classification of intent based racist/radicalized posts on tumblr micro-blogging website.

Anzovino, M., Fersini, E., and Rosso, P. (2018). Automatic identification and classification of misogynistic language on twitter. In Max Silberztein, et al., editors, *Natural Language Processing and Information Systems*, pages 57–64, Cham. Springer International Publishing.

Bou-Franch, P., Lorenzo-Dus, N., and Blitvich, P. G.-C. (2012). Social Interaction in YouTube Text-Based Polylogues: A Study of Coherence. *Journal of Computer-Mediated Communication*, 17(4):501–521, 07.

Burnap, P. and Williams, M. L. (2015). Cyber hate speech on twitter: An application of machine classification and statistical modeling for policy and decision making. *Policy & Internet*, 7(2):223–242.

---

[6]The dataset has been publicly released via a shared task on aggression and misogyny identification - `https://sites.google.com/view/trac2/shared-task`

Cambria, E., Chandra, P., Sharma, A., and Hussain, A. (2010). Do not feel the trolls. In *ISWC, Shanghai*.

Dadvar, M., Trieschnigg, D., Ordelman, R., and de Jong, F. (2013). Improving Cyberbullying Detection with User Context. In *Advances in Information Retrieval*, pages 693–696. Springer.

Davidson, T., Warmsley, D., Macy, M., and Weber, I. (2017). Automated Hate Speech Detection and the Problem of Offensive Language. In *Proceedings of ICWSM*.

Djuric, N., Zhou, J., Morris, R., Grbovic, M., Radosavljevic, V., and Bhamidipati, N. (2015). Hate Speech Detection with Comment Embeddings. In *Proceedings of WWW*.

Fersini, E., Nozza, D., and Rosso, P. (2018a). Overview of the evalita 2018 task on automatic misogyny identification (AMI). In Tommaso Caselli, et al., editors, *Proceedings of the Sixth Evaluation Campaign of Natural Language Processing and Speech Tools for Italian. Final Workshop (EVALITA 2018) co-located with the Fifth Italian Conference on Computational Linguistics (CLiC-it 2018), Turin, Italy, December 12-13, 2018*, volume 2263 of *CEUR Workshop Proceedings*. CEUR-WS.org.

Fersini, E., Rosso, P., and Anzovino, M. (2018b). Overview of the task on automatic misogyny identification at ibereval 2018. In Paolo Rosso, et al., editors, *Proceedings of the Third Workshop on Evaluation of Human Language Technologies for Iberian Languages (IberEval 2018) co-located with 34th Conference of the Spanish Society for Natural Language Processing (SEPLN 2018), Sevilla, Spain, September 18th, 2018*, volume 2150 of *CEUR Workshop Proceedings*, pages 214–228. CEUR-WS.org.

Frenda, S., Ghanem, B., Montes-y Gómez, M., and Rosso, P. (2019). Online hate speech against women: Automatic identification of misogyny and sexism on twitter. *Journal of Intelligent & Fuzzy Systems*, 36(5):4743–4752.

Garcés-Conejos Blitvich, P., Lorenzo-Dus, N., and Bou-Franch, P. (2013). Relational work in anonymous, asynchronous communication: A study of (dis)affiliation in youtube. In Istvan Kecskes et al., editors, *Research Trends in Intercultural Pragmatics*, pages 343–366. De Gruyter Mouton, Berlin.

Garcés-Conejos Blitvich, P. (2010). The youtubification of politics, impoliteness and polarization. In Rotimi Taiwo, editor, *Handbook of Research on Discourse Behavior and Digital Communication: Language Structures and Social Interaction*, pages 540 – 563. IGI Global, USA.

Greevy, E. and Smeaton, A. F. (2004). Classifying racist texts using a support vector machine. In *Proceedings of the 27th annual international ACM SIGIR conference on Research and development in information retrieval*, pages 468 – 469. ACM.

Greevy, E. (2004). *Automatic text categorisation of racist webpages*. Ph.D. thesis, Dublin City University.

Hewitt, S., Tiropanis, T., and Bokhove, C. (2016). The problem of identifying misogynist language on twitter (and other online social spaces). In *Proceedings of the 8th ACM Conference on Web Science*, WebSci '16, page 333–335, New York, NY, USA. Association for Computing Machinery.

Kumar, S., Spezzano, F., and Subrahmanian, V. (2014). Accurately detecting trolls in slashdot zoo via decluttering. In *Proceedings of IEEE/ACM International Conference on Advances in Social Networks Analysis and Mining (ASONAM)*, pages 188–195.

Kumar, R., Ojha, A. K., Malmasi, S., and Zampieri, M. (2018a). Benchmarking Aggression Identification in Social Media. In *Proceedings of TRAC*.

Kumar, R., Reganti, A. N., Bhatia, A., and Maheshwari, T. (2018b). Aggression-annotated corpus of hindi-english code-mixed data. In Nicoletta Calzolari (Conference chair), et al., editors, *Proceedings of the Eleventh International Conference on Language Resources and Evaluation (LREC 2018)*, Paris, France, may. European Language Resources Association (ELRA).

Kwok, I. and Wang, Y. (2013). Locate the Hate: Detecting Tweets Against Blacks. In *Proceedings of AAAI*.

Lorenzo-Dus, N., Blitvich, P. G.-C., and Bou-Franch, P. (2011). On-line polylogues and impoliteness: The case of postings sent in response to the obama reggaeton youtube video. *Journal of Pragmatics*, 43(10):2578 – 2593. Women, Power and the Media.

Malmasi, S. and Zampieri, M. (2017). Detecting Hate Speech in Social Media. In *Proceedings of the International Conference Recent Advances in Natural Language Processing (RANLP)*, pages 467–472.

Malmasi, S. and Zampieri, M. (2018). Challenges in discriminating profanity from hate speech. *Journal of Experimental & Theoretical Artificial Intelligence*, 30:1 – 16.

Menczer, F., Fulper, R., Ciampaglia, G. L., Ferrara, E., Ahn, Y., Flammini, A., Lewis, B., and Rowe, K. (2015). Misogynistic Language on Twitter and Sexual Violence. In *Proceedings of the ACM Web Science Workshop on Computational Approaches to Social Modeling (ChASM)*. Association of Computing Machinery, 1.

Mihaylov, T., Georgiev, G. D., Ontotext, A., and Nakov, P. (2015). Finding opinion manipulation trolls in news community forums. In *Proceedings of the Nineteenth Conference on Computational Natural Language Learning, CoNLL*, pages 310–314.

Mojica de la Vega, L. G. and Ng, V. (2018). Modeling trolling in social media conversations. In *Proceedings of the Eleventh International Conference on Language Resources and Evaluation (LREC 2018)*, Miyazaki, Japan, May. European Language Resources Association (ELRA).

Mubarak, H., Kareem, D., and Walid, M. (2017).

Abusive language detection on Arabic social media. In *Proceedings of ALW*.

Nitin, Bansal, A., Sharma, S. M., Kumar, K., Aggarwal, A., Goyal, S., Choudhary, K., Chawla, K., Jain, K., and Bhasinar, M. (2012). Classification of flames in computer mediated communications. *International Journal of Computer Applications*, 14(6).

Nobata, C., Tetreault, J., Thomas, A., Mehdad, Y., and Chang, Y. (2016). Abusive Language Detection in Online User Content. In *Proceedings of the 25th International Conference on World Wide Web*, pages 145–153. International World Wide Web Conferences Steering Committee.

Sax, S. (2016). Flame Wars: Automatic Insult Detection. Technical report, Stanford University.

Sharifirad, S. and Matwin, S. (2019). When a tweet is actually sexist. A more comprehensive classification of different online harassment categories and the challenges in NLP. *CoRR*, abs/1902.10584.

Thain, N., Dixon, L., and Wulczyn, E. (2017). Wikipedia Talk Labels: Toxicity. 2.

Waseem, Z. and Hovy, D. (2016). Hateful Symbols or Hateful People? Predictive Features for Hate Speech Detection on Twitter. In *Proceedings of the NAACL Student Research Workshop*, pages 88–93.

Waseem, Z., Davidson, T., Warmsley, D., and Weber, I. (2017). Understanding Abuse: A Typology of Abusive Language Detection Subtasks. *Proceedings of ALW*.

Waseem, Z. (2016). Are You a Racist or Am I Seeing Things? Annotator Influence on Hate Speech Detection on Twitter. In *Proceedings of the First Workshop on NLP and Computational Social Science*, pages 138–142, Austin, Texas. Association for Computational Linguistics.

Wiegand, M., Siegel, M., and Ruppenhofer, J. (2018). Overview of the GermEval 2018 Shared Task on the Identification of Offensive Language. In *Proceedings of GermEval*.

Xu, J.-M., Jun, K.-S., Zhu, X., and Bellmore, A. (2012). Learning from Bullying Traces in Social Media. In *Proceedings of NAACL*.

Zampieri, M., Malmasi, S., Nakov, P., Rosenthal, S., Farra, N., and Kumar, R. (2019). Predicting the type and target of offensive posts in social media. In *Proceedings of the Annual Conference of the North American Chapter of the Association for Computational Linguistics: Human Language Technology (NAACL-HLT)*.

Association for Computational Linguistics
209 N. Eighth Street
Stroudsburg, Pennsylvania 18360

ISBN 978-1-7138-1279-1